The IDG Books Advantage

We at IDG Books Worldwide created *Personal Computer Security* to meet your growing need for quick access to the most complete and accurate computer information available. Our books work the way you do: They focus on accomplishing specific tasks — not learning random functions. Our books are not long-winded manuals or dry reference tomes. In each book, expert authors tell you exactly what you can do with your computer and how to do it. Easy to follow, step-by-step sections; comprehensive coverage; and convenient access in language and design — it's all here.

The authors of IDG books are uniquely qualified to give you expert advice as well as to provide insightful tips and techniques not found anywhere else. Our authors maintain close contact with end users through feedback from articles, training sessions, e-mail exchanges, user group participation, and consulting work. Because our authors know the realities of daily computer use and are directly tied to the reader, our books have a strategic advantage.

Our authors have the experience to approach a topic in the most efficient manner, and we know that you, the reader, will benefit from a "one-on-one" relationship with the author. Our research shows that readers make computer book purchases because they want expert advice. Because readers want to benefit from the author's experience, the author's voice is always present in an IDG book.

You will find what you need in this book whether you read it from cover to cover, section by section, or simply one topic at a time. As a computer user, you deserve a comprehensive resource of answers. We at IDG Books Worldwide are proud to deliver that resource with *Personal Computer Security*.

Brenda McLaughlin
Vice President and Group Publisher
Internet: YouTellUs@idgbooks.com

PERSONAL COMPUTER SECURITY

PERSONAL COMPUTER SECURITY

Ed Tiley

IDG Books Worldwide, Inc.
An International Data Group Company

Foster City, CA ♦ Chicago, IL ♦ Indianapolis, IN ♦ Braintree, MA ♦ Southlake, TX

Personal Computer Security

Published by
IDG Books Worldwide, Inc.
An International Data Group Company
919 E. Hillsdale Blvd.
Suite 400
Foster City, CA 94404

Text and art copyright © 1996 by IDG Books Worldwide, Inc. All rights reserved. No part of this book, including interior design, cover design, and icons may be reproduced or transmitted in any form, by any means (electronic, photocopying, recording, or otherwise) without the prior written permission of the publisher.

Library of Congress Catalog Card No.: 96-75296

ISBN: 1-56884-814-5

Printed in the United States of America

10 9 8 7 6 5 4 3 2 1

1B/RU/QT/ZW/IN

Distributed in the United States by IDG Books Worldwide, Inc.

Distributed by Macmillan Canada for Canada; by Computer and Technical Books for the Caribbean Basin; by Contemporanea de Ediciones for Venezuela; by Distribuidora Cuspide for Argentina; by CITEC for Brazil; by Ediciones ZETA S.C.R. Ltda. for Peru; by Editorial Limusa SA for Mexico; by Transworld Publishers Limited in the United Kingdom and Europe; by Al-Maiman Publishers & Distributors for Saudi Arabia; by Simron Pty. Ltd. for South Africa; by IDG Communications (HK) Ltd. for Hong Kong; by Toppan Company Ltd. for Japan; by Addison Wesley Publishing Company for Korea; by Longman Singapore Publishers Ltd. for Singapore, Malaysia, Thailand, and Indonesia; by Unalis Corporation for Taiwan; by WS Computer Publishing Company, Inc. for the Philippines; by WoodsLane Pty. Ltd. for Australia; by WoodsLane Enterprises Ltd. for New Zealand.

For general information on IDG Books Worldwide's books in the U.S., please call our Consumer Customer Service department at 800-762-2974. For reseller information, including discounts and premium sales, please call our Reseller Customer Service department at 800-434-3422.

For information on where to purchase IDG Books Worldwide's books outside the U.S., contact IDG Books Worldwide at 415-655-3021 or fax 415-655-3295.

For information on translations, contact Marc Jeffrey Mikulich, Director, Foreign & Subsidiary Rights, at IDG Books Worldwide, 415-655-3018 or fax 415-655-3295.

For sales inquiries and special prices for bulk quantities, write to the address above or call IDG Books Worldwide at 415-655-3200.

For information on using IDG Books Worldwide's books in the classroom, or ordering examination copies, contact the Education Office at 800-434-2086 or fax 817-251-8174.

For authorization to photocopy items for corporate, personal, or educational use, please contact Copyright Clearance Center, 222 Rosewood Drive, Danvers, MA 01923, or fax 508-750-4470.

Limit of Liability/Disclaimer of Warranty: Author and Publisher have used their best efforts in preparing this book. IDG Books Worldwide, Inc., and Author make no representation or warranties with respect to the accuracy or completeness of the contents of this book and specifically disclaim any implied warranties of merchantability or fitness for any particular purpose and shall in no event be liable for any loss of profit or any other commercial damage, including but not limited to special, incidental, consequential, or other damages.

Trademarks: All brand names and product names used in this book are trademarks, registered trademarks, or trade names of their respective holders. IDG Books Worldwide is not associated with any product or vendor mentioned in this book.

 is a trademark under exclusive license to IDG Books Worldwide, Inc., from International Data Group, Inc.

About the Author

Ed Tiley is the author of more than a dozen computer books, including *Using Clipper, Special Edition,* the best-selling programmer's guide. He is also the co-author of *Using MS-DOS 6.2, Special Edition.* Other titles include *Tricks of the Windows Masters, PCs After Hours, Windows Stuff Microsoft Forgot,* and *Windows After Hours.* His most recent release is the best-selling *Windows 95 Unleashed.*

If you have any comments or suggestions concerning this book, send cheers and jeers to edtiley@supernet.net or to his CompuServe mailbox, 72007,3455.

Welcome to the world of IDG Books Worldwide.

IDG Books Worldwide, Inc., is a subsidiary of International Data Group, the world's largest publisher of computer-related information and the leading global provider of information services on information technology. IDG was founded more than 25 years ago and now employs more than 7,700 people worldwide. IDG publishes more than 250 computer publications in 67 countries (see listing below). More than 70 million people read one or more IDG publications each month.

Launched in 1990, IDG Books Worldwide is today the #1 publisher of best-selling computer books in the United States. We are proud to have received 8 awards from the Computer Press Association in recognition of editorial excellence and three from Computer Currents' First Annual Readers' Choice Awards, and our best-selling ...*For Dummies*® series has more than 19 million copies in print with translations in 28 languages. IDG Books Worldwide, through a joint venture with IDG's Hi-Tech Beijing, became the first U.S. publisher to publish a computer book in the People's Republic of China. In record time, IDG Books Worldwide has become the first choice for millions of readers around the world who want to learn how to better manage their businesses.

Our mission is simple: Every one of our books is designed to bring extra value and skill-building instructions to the reader. Our books are written by experts who understand and care about our readers. The knowledge base of our editorial staff comes from years of experience in publishing, education, and journalism — experience which we use to produce books for the '90s. In short, we care about books, so we attract the best people. We devote special attention to details such as audience, interior design, use of icons, and illustrations. And because we use an efficient process of authoring, editing, and desktop publishing our books electronically, we can spend more time ensuring superior content and spend less time on the technicalities of making books.

You can count on our commitment to deliver high-quality books at competitive prices on topics you want to read about. At IDG Books Worldwide, we continue in the IDG tradition of delivering quality for more than 25 years. You'll find no better book on a subject than one from IDG Books Worldwide.

John J. Kilcullen

John Kilcullen
President and CEO
IDG Books Worldwide, Inc.

IDG Books Worldwide, Inc., is a subsidiary of International Data Group, the world's largest publisher of computer-related information and the leading global provider of information services on information technology. International Data Group publishes over 250 computer publications in 67 countries. Seventy million people read one or more International Data Group publications each month. International Data Group's publications include: **ARGENTINA:** Computerworld Argentina, GamePro, Infoworld, PC World Argentina; **AUSTRALIA:** Australian Macworld, Client/Server Journal, Computer Living, Computerworld, Digital News, Network World, PC World, Publishing Essentials, Reseller; **AUSTRIA:** Computerwelt, PC TEST; **BELARUS:** PC World Belarus; **BELGIUM:** Data News; **BRAZIL:** Annuário de Informática, Computerworld Brazil, Connections, Super Game Power, Macworld, PC World Brazil, Publish Brazil, SUPERGAME; **BULGARIA:** Computerworld Bulgaria, Networkworld/Bulgaria, PC & MacWorld Bulgaria; **CANADA:** CIO Canada, ComputerWorld Canada, InfoCanada, Network World Canada, Reseller World; **CHILE:** Computerworld Chile, GamePro, PC World Chile; **COLUMBIA:** Computerworld Colombia, GamePro, PC World Colombia; **COSTA RICA:** PC World Costa Rica/Nicaragua; **THE CZECH AND SLOVAK REPUBLICS:** Computerworld Czechoslovakia, Elektronika Czechoslovakia, PC World Czechoslovakia; **DENMARK:** Communications World, Computerworld Danmark, Macworld Danmark, PC World Danmark, PC World Danmark Supplements, TECH World; **DOMINICAN REPUBLIC:** PC World Republica Dominicana; **ECUADOR:** PC World Ecuador, GamePro; **EGYPT:** Computerworld Middle East, PC World Middle East; **EL SALVADOR:** PC World Centro America; **FINLAND:** MikroPC, Tietoverkko, Tietoviikko; **FRANCE:** Distributique, Golden, Info PC, Le Guide du Monde Informatique, Le Monde Informatique, Reseaux & Telecoms; **GERMANY:** Computer Business, Computerwoche, Computerwoche Extra, Computerwoche Focus, Electronic Entertainment, GamePro, I/M Information Management, Macwelt, PC Welt; **GREECE:** GamePro, Macworld & Publish; **GUATEMALA:** PC World Centro America; **HONDURAS:** PC World Centro America; **HONG KONG:** Computerworld Hong Kong, PCWorld Hong Kong, Publish in Asia; **HUNGARY:** ABCD CD-ROM, Computerworld Szamitastechnika, PC & Mac World Hungary, PC-X Magazine; **INDIA:** Computerworld India, PC World India, Publish in Asia; **INDONESIA:** InfoKomputer PC World, Komputek Computerworld, Publish in Asia; **IRELAND:** ComputerScope, PC Live!; **ISRAEL:** PC World 32 BIT, People & Computers; **ITALY:** Computerworld Italia, Computerworld Italia Special Editions, Lotus Italia, Macworld Italia, Networking Italia, PC Shopping, PC World Italia, PC World/Walt Disney; **JAPAN:** Macworld Japan, Nikkei Personal Computing, SunWorld Japan, Windows World Japan; **KENYA:** East African Computer News; **KOREA:** Hi-Tech Information/Computerworld, Macworld Korea, PC World Korea; **MACEDONIA:** PC World Macedonia; **MALAYSIA:** Computerworld Malaysia, PC World Malaysia, Publish in Asia; **MEXICO:** Computerworld Mexico, GamePro, Macworld, PC World Mexico; **MYANMAR:** PC World Myanmar; **NETHERLANDS:** Computable, Computer! Totaal, LAN Magazine, Macworld, Net Magazine; **NEW ZEALAND:** Computer Buyer, Computerworld New Zealand, MTB, Network World, PC World New Zealand; **NICARAGUA:** PC World Costa Rica/Nicaragua; **NIGERIA:** PC World Africa; **NORWAY:** Computerworld Norge, Computerworld Privat, CW Rapport Klient/Tjener, CW Rapport Nettverk & Telecom, CW Rapport Offentlig Sektor, IDG's KURSGUIDE, Macworld Norge, Multimedia World, PC World Ekspress, PC World Nettverk, PC World Norge, PC World's Produktguide, Windows Spesial; **PAKISTAN:** Computerworld Pakistan; **PANAMA:** GamePro, PC World Panama; **PARAGUAY:** PC World Paraguay; **P. R. OF CHINA:** China Computerworld, China Infoworld, Computer & Communication, Electronic Product World, Electronics Today, Game Camp, PC World China, Popular Computer Week, Software World, Telecom Product World; **PERU:** Computerworld Peru, GamePro, PC World Profesional Peru, PC World Peru; **POLAND:** Computerworld Poland, Computerworld Special Report, Macworld, Networld, PC World Komputer; **PHILIPPINES:** Computerworld Philippines, PC Digest, Publish in Asia; **PORTUGAL:** Cerebro/PC World, Correio Informático/Computerworld, Mac•In/PC•In Portugal; **PUERTO RICO:** PC World Puerto Rico; **ROMANIA:** Computerworld Romania, PC World Romania, Telecom Romania; **RUSSIA:** Computerworld Rossiya, Network World Russia, PC World Russia; **SINGAPORE:** Computerworld Singapore, PC World Singapore, Publish in Asia; **SLOVENIA:** MONITOR; **SOUTH AFRICA:** Computing S.A., Network World S.A., Software World; **SPAIN:** Computerworld España, COMUNICACIONES WORLD, Dealer World, Macworld España, PC World España; **SWEDEN:** CAP&Design, Computer Sweden, Corporate Computing, MacWorld, Maxi Data, MikroDatorn, Nätverk & Kommunikation, PC/Aktiv, PC World, Windows World; **SWITZERLAND:** Computerworld Schweiz, Macworld Schweiz, PCtip; **TAIWAN:** Computerworld Taiwan, Macworld Taiwan, PC World Taiwan, Publish Taiwan, Windows World; **THAILAND:** Thai Computerworld, Publish in Asia; **TURKEY:** Computerworld Monitor, MACWORLD Turkiye, PC WORLD Turkiye; **UKRAINE:** Computerworld Kiev, Computers & Software Magazine, PC World Ukraine; **UNITED KINGDOM:** Acorn User, Amiga Action, Amiga Computing, Amiga, Appletalk, CD Powerplay, CD-ROM Now, Computing, Connexion, GamePro, Lotus Magazine, Macaction, Open Computing, Parents and Computers, PC Home, PC Works, The WEB; **UNITED STATES:** Cable in the Classroom, CD Review, CIO Magazine, Computerworld, Computerworld Client/Server Journal, Digital Video Magazine, DOS World, Electronic, InfoWorld, I-Way, Macworld, Maximize, MULTIMEDIA WORLD, Network World, PC World, PUBLISH, SWATPro Magazine, Video Event, WebMaster; **URUGUAY:** PC World Uruguay; **VENEZUELA:** Computerworld Venezuela, GamePro, PC World Venezuela; and **VIETNAM:** PC World Vietnam   10/17/95

Dedication

For Jill McClure, as good a friend as I'm ever likely to find in this world.

Credits

**Senior Vice President
and Group Publisher**
Brenda McLaughlin

Vice President and Publisher
Christopher J. Williams

Acquisitions Manager
Gregory Croy

Acquisitions Editor
Ellen L. Camm

Software Acquisitions Editor
Tracy Lehman Cramer

Marketing Manager
Melisa M. Duffy

Managing Editor
Andy Cummings

Editorial Assistant
Timothy J. Borek

Production Director
Beth Jenkins

Production Assistant
Jacalyn L. Pennywell

**Supervisor of
Project Coordination**
Cindy L. Phipps

Supervisor of Page Layout
Kathie S. Schnorr

Supervisor of Graphics and Design
Shelley Lea

Reprint/Blueline Coordination
Tony Augsburger
Patricia R. Reynolds
Todd Klemme
Theresa Sánchez-Baker

Media/Archive Coordination
Leslie Popplewell
Melissa Stauffer
Jason Marcuson

Development Editors
Nancy Stevenson
Jim Grey

Copy Editors
Nate Holdread
Kerrie Klein

Technical Reviewer
Mike Lerch

Project Coordinator
Sherry Gomoll

Project Coordination Assistant
Regina Snyder

Graphics Coordination
Gina Scott
Angela F. Hunckler

Production Page Layout
E. Shawn Aylsworth
Drew R. Moore

Proofreaders
Barb Potter
Gwenette Gaddis
Dwight Ramsey
Carl Saff

Indexer
Liz Cunningham

Cover Design
Stoller Design

Photography
R.J. Muna

Book Design
Drew R. Moore
Shelley Lea
Laura Puranen

Acknowledgments

Thanks to Theresa Pulido of Creative Labs for help with multimedia issues. Thanks also to Greg Croy, Jim Grey, Nancy Stevenson, Mike Lerch, and everyone else at IDG Books for putting up with me on this project.

Special thanks to Ron Harley, Richard Roccanti, Kim Roccanti, John Mueller, Rebecca Mueller, Allen Wyatt, Reggie and Wyntress Patterson, Jet Halligan, Jan Halligan, Buddy and Gina Gamble, Nino and Isolde Violante, George and Maria Sommer, and everyone else who lent moral support and encouragement.

(The Publisher would like to give special thanks to Patrick J. McGovern, without whom this book would not have been possible.)

Contents at a Glance

Introduction 1

Part I: Security and the Single Computer 7
Chapter 1: Threats to Data Security 9
Chapter 2: Hackers, Crackers, and Phreaks 37
Chapter 3: Sneak Attacks, Trojans, Viruses, and Other Vermin 53
Chapter 4: Password Protection 77
Chapter 5: Simple Security Measures 91

Part II: Security Online 113
Chapter 6: E-Mail Security 115
Chapter 7: The Risks of Online Transactions: Real & Imagined 135
Chapter 8: Internet Security 167
Chapter 9: Protecting Yourself from Unwanted Material 185

Part III: Security When Working with Others 213
Chapter 10: Enforcing Your Privacy 215
Chapter 11: Network Security and You 247
Chapter 12: Sharing Resources with Windows Networks 267

Index 301

Reader Response Card .... Back of Book

Table of Contents

Introduction 1
   Who Needs a Book on Computer Security? 1
   A Place for Your Stuff, and the Constitution, Too 2
   Protecting Yourself Isn't Difficult at All...Sort Of 3
   What's in This Book? 4
      Part I: Security and the Single Computer 4
      Part II: Security Online 5
      Part III: Security When Working with Others 5
   Conventions Used in This Book 6
   What Have You Got to Lose? 6

Part I: Security and the Single Computer 7

Chapter 1: Threats to Data Security 9
   Knowing Your Data's Monetary Value 10
   Understanding the Threats to Your Data 10
   Knowing the Ways Your Computer Can Fail 13
      Disks are mortal 13
      Software can fail you 13
      Natural disasters can destroy data 14
   Anticipating Disaster 15
   Creating a Disaster Recovery Plan 16
   Choosing Backup Tools 20
      Choosing a backup medium 20
      Choosing a tape backup device 20
         Tape capacity 21
         Internal vs. external tape drives 21
         The bottom line 23
   Creating a Good Backup Routine 23
      Zen and the art of backup 23
      Full vs. partial backup 24
      How often to back up your data 26
         Twice daily: partial at noon, full at end of day 26
         Once daily: full backup at end of day 26
         Three times weekly: full backup at end of day 26
         Twice weekly: full backup Tuesday, partial on Thursday 27
         Once a week: full backup 27
         Monthly: full backup 27

Other backup factors 27
    Your equipment's age 27
    The kind of data you keep 27
    The way you work 28
Making Sure Your Backup Works 28
    Cycling backup media 28
    Testing backups 29
    Storing backup tapes 29
Using Alternative Backup Strategies 30
A Sample Backup and Restore 31
Summary 36

Chapter 2: Hackers, Crackers, and Phreaks 37

Hacker Defined 38
    Hacker isn't a four-letter word 38
    Humor in uniform 40
Crackers 41
Phreaks 42
The World of the Computer Underground 44
    Government and commercial hackers 45
    Why worry about these folks? 47
Who Wants to See Your Stuff? 49
    Thieves 49
    Merely curious with low technical competence 49
    Curious with high technical competence 50
    The determined hacker with high technical competence 50
Summary 52

Chapter 3: Sneak Attacks, Trojans, Viruses,
and Other Vermin 53

Where Do Viruses Come From? 54
Major Sources of Virus and Trojan Programs 54
    Pirate software 54
    On disk 55
    Downloading files 57
Basic Truths and Myths 57
    Viruses only spread via COM and EXE files...NOT! 57
    You don't have to boot from a floppy to be infected 59
    Viruses are spread by downloading files 59
    Viruses can hide in data files and unused areas of disks 60
    An infected hard disk is a dead hard disk 60
A Veritable Menagerie of Vermin 61
What, Me Worry? 64
    Trojan horses 65
        PKZIP300B 65
        ChinaTalk 66

Cookies	66
FontFinder	66
NVP	66
Computer viruses	66
Virus classifications	67
Some major (virus) players	68
Safe Hex	71
How antivirus software works	71
Using antivirus software	71
Identifying virus infections	73
Summary	75

Chapter 4: Password Protection 77

The Mathematics of Passwords	78
The Effectiveness of Passwords	79
Rules of Thumb for Choosing Passwords	82
Password don'ts	82
Password do's	83
Choosing a password	83
Two word two-step	84
Derivative passwords	84
Make up words	85
Password Protection on Your Computer	85
BIOS boot passwords	85
Password protection of individual files	88
Spoofing	88
Summary	90

Chapter 5: Simple Security Measures 91

Stupid Computer Tricks	92
Hidden files	92
The old misdirection play	94
Deleted files	97
Simple and Cheap Security Measures	97
Shredding files	98
Nuke for DOS	98
Terminator 2.0 for Windows	101
Encrypting ZIP files	103
Encrypted PKZip files	104
Password protected ZIP files	105
Using WinZip to password protect files	105
DES encryption	107
The history of DES	107
DES for Windows	108
Summary	111

Part II: Security Online 113

Chapter 6: E-Mail Security 115

Types of E-Mail 115
The Security of E-Mail vs. Other Kinds of Mail 116
    E-mail and the law 118
    E-mail hackers and snoops 119
The Right to Privacy 122
    E-mail rights 122
    Privacy in the workplace 123
    What to include and what to exclude from e-mail 125
Fakemail and Anonymous Mail 125
    Fakemail 125
    Anonymous remailers 127
Making E-Mail Secure 128
    ROT-13 is not encryption 129
    Using encryption 130
        PGP encryption 130
        Using PGP with Eudora Lite 130
    PGP and other mail readers 133
Back at the Start 133
Summary 134

Chapter 7: The Risks of Online Transactions: Real & Imagined 135

How Financial Life Has Changed in the U.S. 136
    Early days 136
    Shop at home 137
    Media-based home shopping 138
    Reinventing the wheel with computers 138
        The Internet and the Web 139
        Who is on the Net? 140
The Greening of the Internet 142
    Electronic commerce 144
    Electronic checking 145
        The Electronic Check Project 145
        The FSTC Electronic Commerce Project 149
    Electronic cash 150
        Moving away from cash with smart cards 152
        So what is a smart card? 152
        What smart cards store 154
E-cash: The Details 154
    Electronic cash inside out 155
    Signature creation and transport 156
    Ensuring privacy with blinded signatures 157

Try E-cash for yourself 159
First Virtual 159
Secure Transactions on the Net 161
Netscape Communications Corporation 161
Netscape and commerce 162
Secure Sockets Layer Protocol 163
The nuts and bolts 163
Digital signatures 164
Summary 166

Chapter 8: Internet Security 167

Just What Is the Internet? 167
So who owns the Internet? 168
What's next? 169
Security and the Internet 170
One System Administrator's View 171
Summary 184

Chapter 9: Protecting Yourself from Unwanted Material 185

A Bad Rap 186
Freedom of Speech in Cyberspace 187
Cyberspace and the First Amendment 188
The impact of the Thomas Case on the Internet
and telecommunications 192
The bottom line 194
The Communications Decency Act of 1995 195
Analysis of the Communications Decency Act of 1995 200
Holding providers not liable 202
Self-Regulation of the Internet 205
Avoiding Offensive Web Content 205
Cyber Patrol 206
Other filtering sources 210
SafeSurf 210
Summary 211

Part III: Security When Working with Others 213

Chapter 10: Enforcing Your Privacy 215

The Art and Science of Encryption 215
Computers and cryptography 216
The alphabet soup of encryption 220
The U.S. Government vs. Communications Technology 223
Digital telephony 223
The NSA crypto monopoly jeopardized 226
Secret key encryption 227

A breakthrough 227
Cashing in on public key cryptography 228
Capstone, the Clipper Chip, and Key Escrow 231
Clipper 231
Clipper redux 234
Phil Zimmerman's PGP 234
Encryption politics 236
Using PGP 237
Installing PGP 237
Step One: generating keys 238
Step Two: certifying keys 241
Step Three: encrypting messages 243
Step Four: unencrypting messages 245
Step Five: signatures 245
More PGP 246
Summary 246

Chapter 11: Network Security and You 247

Who Can Access Data on a Network Server? 248
System administrator 250
Supervisor privileges 250
Managing Security on a Network 252
Just what is a security plan? 252
Why documenting security procedures is important 253
Novell Security 256
Keeping the sales department out of bookkeeping's files 256
Assigning security rights 260
Assigning rights to users 262
Assigning users to groups 265
Summary 266

Chapter 12: Sharing Resources with Windows Networks 267

The Windows Family 267
Windows for Workgroups 268
Windows 95 268
Windows NT Workstation 269
Windows NT Server 269
Network Terminology 269
Network Security Issues 270
Developing internal policies 270
Windows NT network policies 271
Account policies 271
User rights 274
Access logging 277
Windows 95 System Policy Editor 278

Server format	281
Security holes	282
Windows for Workgroups	282
Windows 95	282
Windows NT	283
Establishing Network Resources	284
Windows 95 specifics	285
Enabling sharing	285
Access control	286
Sharing directories	288
Windows 95	288
Windows NT	290
Sharing printers	292
Managing Users	296
Local groups	296
User accounts	298
Summary	300

Index 301

Reader Response Card .... Back of Book

Introduction

Most folks are in the habit of locking their front door when they leave the house, and most folks lock their car when they park. Few people would just give their credit card numbers to telephone solicitors making those annoying dinner-time calls. Yet when it comes to computers, most people are unaware of the security and privacy risks they can fall prey to.

Only a minority of computer users safeguard their data in any way, shape, or form. Only when every disk they own is infected with a virus or their hard disk crashes do they even think about backing up their data. Even worse, computer users habitually leave themselves open to snooping, theft, and vandalism of their data.

Who Needs a Book on Computer Security?

You do. If you share a computer with others in your family, if you use a computer at work, if you log on to the Internet or some other online service, if you exchange e-mail with other people, or if you work with any kind of sensitive data, you need to be, at the very least, familiar with the issues presented in this book.

Every time you use your computer you are creating or adding valuable and potentially sensitive data to your computer's hard disk. Your data is the most valuable component in your computer system. The costs of re-creating data or the costs of having sensitive data fall into the wrong hands can be much greater than the cost of the hardware used to store that data.

Computer users regularly leave such data as tax information, banking information, business-related letters, and spreadsheets totally unprotected. The problems are compounded greatly when you begin working and playing online. How secure is your e-mail? Are you putting personal information into the hands of people you'd rather not deal with?

Sad but true: Even if you have nothing to hide, there are people out there who simply want to trash your computer if they have the chance. These crackers and phreaks perform the digital equivalent of kicking over gravestones and spray-painting public buildings. Hundreds of different virus programs are in circulation, not to mention Trojan horses, worms, and other critters. Are you vulnerable? If you don't know how viruses and Trojans operate, or even what they are, you are vulnerable.

You also need to protect your computer data from mechanical failures and acts of God. It really doesn't matter if a virus wastes your disk drive or if a flood, hurricane, or lightning perform the same disservice.

A Place for Your Stuff, and the Constitution, Too

The comedian George Carlin recorded a routine about the tendency of humans to collect stuff. This comedy routine is funny because it is true. We do amass amazing amounts of stuff. In the case of computer users, some of this stuff is valuable and some of it would just be inconvenient to lose.

Whether your data is valuable or not, protecting it has been elevated to a question of U.S. Constitutional law. The Fourth Amendment contained in the Bill of Rights protects citizens from unreasonable search and seizure by government officials of their homes, possessions, and papers. Further, the Ninth Amendment states simply, "The enumeration in the Constitution, of certain rights, shall not be construed to deny or disparage others retained by the people." The U.S. Supreme Court has found in multiple rulings that the effect of these two amendments is to create an unenumerated right of privacy. Those rights are potentially threatened by recent actions within the U.S. government.

Your adult rights to view and read uncensored materials come into conflict with a parental right to shield children from such materials. Attempts to legislate online censorship seems, for the time being, to have been defused by a compromise agreement to develop rated lockouts, similar to movie ratings, that computer users can employ to protect their kids from stumbling across inappropriate materials.

The questions go even deeper than dirty pictures, however. What about your right to protect intellectual property, sensitive commercial information, financial data, and the right to communicate in private with other people? There is pressure to control or restrict your rights to use encryption as a means of preventing prying eyes from intercepting your confidential communications, viewing your sensitive financial data, and the like. The Clinton administration has endorsed the Clipper chip, an encryption tool that the government would have special keys to. Using this, officials could, with a warrant, decrypt messages, wiretap encrypted communications, and break personal encryption codes.

When do you give up your right to privacy? Does giving a store in an online shopping mall your name and address give it the right to sell that information to other people who might want to do business with you?

Who owns your e-mail messages? If you communicate with someone privately by using the Internet or an online service, your privacy rights may be very different from your privacy rights for communications routed through the e-mail server at your workplace. Who is allowed to read your e-mail?

Although this book can't tell you how these weighty social and ethical questions will ultimately be resolved, it does inform you of your rights and how to protect yourself. Protecting your computer system and the data it holds is a fundamental right, but it can become entangled with weighty issues.

Protecting Yourself Isn't Difficult at All...Sort Of

Locking your doors isn't terribly convenient, yet you wouldn't leave home without doing it. The same is true of keeping your computer system safe and secure. All it takes is a little common sense, the willingness to perform security monitoring, and just a little bit of technical knowledge.

No computer security system is foolproof. There's always going to be some fourteen-year-old kid out there who can figure out how to get into anything computer-ish and mess around with it. Fortunately, you don't run into that kid every day, but he's living proof that the only way to totally protect data from falling into the wrong hands is to destroy it.

Keeping people out of your computer stuff is a trade-off between the sensitivity of the data you are trying to protect and the inconvenience of taking protective measures. In this book you will learn valuable techniques for protecting your data as well as techniques for lessening the inconvenience of securing data.

An old saying states that "locks are made to keep honest people honest." If you've ever locked your keys in the car and experienced firsthand just how easily and quickly a locksmith can earn a fee, then you know that no lock is foolproof. Even were a lock to prove unpickable, a simple rock through the window would do the trick. I once got my family out of the rain and into our locked car by using a baseball freshly autographed by the famous San Diego Chicken.

But what if the lock had been unpickable and the windows unbreakable? I would have needed to use a torch to cut through the roof. The point is that each time you escalate security, it requires a higher-level act to get around the security. The most effective security tools are the ones that offer sufficient deterrence without being so inconvenient or difficult to implement that the security tasks don't get done.

Throughout the book you will learn how to balance security measures against what it takes to defeat those security measures so that you can perform your own risk analysis and decide what security measures are appropriate in any given case.

Risk analysis for personal computers can be divided into two types: a standalone computer system and a computer system that is connected to other computers either by modem or hard-wired into a network. This book is divided in this fashion as well.

The first part of the book deals with standalone computers both in the office and at home. In this part of the book you will be introduced to the basic concepts of computer security and the measures you can apply to keep your data secure.

The second part of this book tells you how to look out for yourself and your privacy when connected to online services and the Internet. There are a lot of technical developments in cyberspace that are only now being addressed as social and legal issues. In addition, security issues like e-mail and computer shopping are covered here.

In the third part of the book you will learn about privacy and working with others: how you can enforce the privacy of written communications and how you can control security on small networks.

What's in This Book?

This book is divided into three parts. Here is a quick rundown of the chapters you will find in each:

Part I: Security and the Single Computer

Chapter 1: Threats to Data Security — The monetary value of your data far outweighs the value of your hardware system, if you are like most people. So why then do people fail to protect that investment? Find out how hardware and software failure and the lack of good backup routines account for more lost data than any army of hackers.

Chapter 2: Hackers, Crackers, and Phreaks — Who wants to see your stuff? Depends on who you are and what kind of stuff you have. There is a whole counterculture out there called the Computer Underground. Find out why some of these folks do the things they do.

Chapter 3: Sneak Attacks, Trojans, Viruses, and Other Vermin — The people who create viruses and Trojan horse programs are the digital equivalent of people who kick over gravestones and set fire to churches. Your best defense for keeping them out of your computer is a good offense and knowledge.

Chapter 4: Password Protection — Most people consider their passwords to be secure. You might be surprised that more than 75 percent of all passwords can be cracked in a matter of minutes. Find out how and why you should create passwords that really protect your data.

Chapter 5: Simple Security Measures — There are a number of simple things anyone can do to keep the data on a system secure. Find out how you can take simple, inexpensive measures to keep your privacy.

Part II: Security Online

Chapter 6: E-Mail Security — Who has access to your e-mail? Actually, any number of people, from your system administrator to hackers trying to find out what you're up to. In this chapter, Richard Roccanti, an independent Internet service provider shows you where the vulnerabilities are and how you can protect yourself.

Chapter 7: The Risks of Online Transactions: Real & Imagined — The greening of the Internet has begun in earnest. The result is a whole new set of rules for conducting financial transactions. Find out how online commerce opens the door to a cashless society and what the privacy considerations are likely to be.

Chapter 8: Internet Security — In just four short years the Internet has become the hottest thing on the planet. Find out why it isn't just a passing fad and how it will affect your life for years to come.

Chapter 9: Protecting Yourself from Unwanted Material — To hear the media, the World Wide Web is little more than a red-light district. That isn't true, but there is some adult content. Despite the bluff and bluster of the media, it is clear that in most cases the government is actually powerless to regulate such content. Find out why the First Amendment applies in cyberspace and how you can filter out unwanted material.

Part III: Security When Working with Others

Chapter 10: Enforcing Your Privacy — Strong encryption is the single most effective tool for protecting your privacy. Find out why the U.S. government doesn't want you to have strong encryption, and then find out how to use one of the best encryption tools around — PGP (Pretty Good Privacy).

Chapter 11: Network Security and You — In this chapter, John Mueller explores the risks involved in running a network. Along the way you will find out how to begin administering a Novell NetWare-based network in a secure fashion.

Chapter 12: Sharing Resources with Windows 95 — Windows NT is the security workhorse operating system from Microsoft. In this chapter, Allen Wyatt shows you how to integrate NT with Windows 95 workstations to provide a secure network environment.

Conventions Used in This Book

Throughout this book you will find sections marked with special icons and graphics that let you know material that's worth noting.

Tip icons indicate that the material contains quick advice on security measures.

Notes provide more detailed information about certain topics of interest.

There are many Behind the Scenes sidebars that give you computer industry insider or historical information.

Horror Stories sidebars serve as an example of a security breach or mistake that acts as a warning to avoid having bad things happen to your own computer system or its data.

Techniques and Workarounds sidebars show you how to overcome hardware and software limitations.

What Have You Got to Lose?

As you can see, there are a number of issues that relate to computer security on a user level. These issues are real, not imaginary, meaning that what you have to lose is every single shred of data stored in your computer system and/or the monetary loss of having valuable data fall into the wrong hands.

On the other hand, you have nothing to lose, and perhaps much to gain, by familiarizing yourself with these issues. Take this book and curl up in a comfortable chair. At the very least you'll never look at your computer in quite the same way again.

Security and the Single Computer

PART

I

In This Part

Chapter 1
Threats to Data Security

Chapter 2
Hackers, Crackers, and Phreaks

Chapter 3
Sneak Attacks, Trojans, Viruses, and Other Vermin

Chapter 4
Password Protection

Chapter 5
Simple Security Measures

Threats to Data Security

CHAPTER 1

♦ ♦ ♦ ♦

In This Chapter

Knowing the value of the data on your computer

Understanding how your data can be threatened

Counting the ways your computer can fail you

Planning for, and recovering from, disaster

Creating a data backup routine

Verifying your backups

Planning alternative backup strategies

♦ ♦ ♦ ♦

Anything that can go wrong, will go wrong.
—Murphy's Law

In the natural world, death can come swiftly from accident, disease, and predators. Computer systems mimic the natural world to the extent that data can succumb to accident, hardware or software failure, and predators. Fortunately, however, data can be preserved to live another day with a minimum of foresight and effort.

This book deals with the predators that want to harm your data. This chapter deals with the issues of accident and disease. This chapter does not primarily deal with technological issues. The technology involved at this level of computer security is trivial compared to the concepts presented in this chapter — concepts you can apply to almost any computer system, large or small, Mac or PC.

It is ironic that the information in this short chapter, which is maybe 5 percent of this book, is sufficient to protect most computers and their users from well over 90 percent of threats to their data. The rest of this book is mightily important because it helps you to protect yourself from the mischief of other people who would like to see harm come to your computer's data or to restrict your rights and options.

Still the overwhelming majority of incidents where users lose data are self-inflicted or accidental. If you have a regular schedule of backups, and if you have properly physically secured your computer, you have done most of what you need to do to protect your data — your most valuable computer resource.

Knowing Your Data's Monetary Value

Whether you build monster spreadsheets for work or collect recipes for a cookbook you hope to write someday, at the end of the day all the work you have done is stored on disk. Your data's value depends on what your time is worth, how much data you've stored, and how long it would take to re-create your data. If you are working with cold, hard facts, such as spreadsheets and relational databases, and if you have excellent paper records, you can usually re-create your data exactly. But what if you're working on The Great American Novel? Or what if you've drawn cool illustrations for a children's book? Could Hemingway have re-created *The Old Man and the Sea* if the first half of his manuscript had been destroyed? Could Spielberg have re-created *Schindler's List* if the film were lost on the way to the editor? The answer is: Probably not. They might have come close in their re-creations, but creative talent is not easily repeated. A writer's inspiration varies from day to day, making it hard to reliably recapture emotions. For much the same reason, reshooting a film usually results in a much different movie.

If your computer is stolen or damaged by fire, the insurance company will buy you a new one. But no insurance company will reimburse you for your computer's most valuable component — its data.

The average computer system costs between $2,000 and $3,500, depending on the goodies the user feels constitute basic computing necessities. Still, the investment made in hardware and software is minimal when compared to the investment regularly made in accumulating data.

If, for example, you place the value of your time at $10 per hour, a nice round number, it takes only 250 hours — $6^1/_2$ 40-hour work weeks — for the value of the data you create to equal the cost of an entire computer system. Before your computer is two months old, you can easily invest as much in the contents of the hard disk as you did for all the hardware!

Understanding the Threats to Your Data

The two most common threats to the security of your data are

- ◆ Accidental erasure
- ◆ Hardware failure

Following closely behind are fire, flood, war, famine and pestilence, and your kids. The solution to all of these potential data killers is simple: back up, back up, back up. Oh, yes, and please learn at least the basics of computer operation. The most vicious hacker ever to prey on computer data can't hold a candle to the damage done regularly by people who know "just enough to be dangerous."

Some computer users are their own worst enemy. They regularly just plain do it to themselves. See if you recognize any of these people:

> Susan is an intelligent lawyer who can charm judges and juries with her brilliant organizational and argumentative skills. She lives in the Southeastern United States, where violent thunderstorms are as common as trucks on the interstate. There's no counting the number of times she has lost hours of work because the power flickered or went out during a storm. When you ask her why she just doesn't get into the habit of saving her work every 15 minutes or so, she just shrugs and says, "I can just never seem to remember to do it."

> Richard Roccanti, who wrote the chapter on e-mail security, and I do a Saturday morning computer call-in program on a radio station in Tallahassee. Walter (not his real name) is a regular caller. Walter usually begins by saying something like, "Well, I'm calling you guys, so it must mean I've messed up my computer again." Walter is a tinkerer. He likes to change around hardware, do backups, and restore one drive's contents onto his wife's machine regardless of whatever software drivers are, or are not, needed, or whatever stuff his wife has stored on the computer. (She has a secret stash of floppy disks where she keeps her important stuff out of harm's way.)

> Minerva is a strong, assertive woman who single-handedly raised three children in the turbulence of the 60s and 70s. Yet, she turns to putty when she sits down at a computer. Unfortunately, her job requires her to spend at least half of her day at the keyboard. During those hours Minerva is nearly a basket case, filled with dread and doubt. She uses a single application and wouldn't be able to use any other even if you stuck a gun to her head. She knows one way in and one way out. If anything even slightly unexpected happens, she wants someone at her side guiding her. It doesn't matter who it is, she'll take advice from anyone that happens to be near. She's lost lots of work over the years because someone told her to do the wrong thing. She once reformatted her hard disk because some stranger didn't know how to erase a whole directory full of unwanted files either.

> Lisa Marie works in the finance department of a multimillion-dollar company. She isn't afraid of computers — they just aren't important to her. She wouldn't willingly touch one outside the office. She runs two programs, and two programs only. Within those programs she is a queen. Outside of those programs, she is her own worst enemy. Although she's been working with the computer for four years, she can't be bothered to remember something so simple as the COPY command in DOS, preferring instead to pick up the phone and call the help desk to walk her through elemental tasks. Of course, she sometimes doesn't clearly explain what she's trying to do. Sometimes the help desk folks, who consider her a pest, don't give her their full time and attention. Armed with half an answer, she blithely copies a floppy disk to her hard disk. "Oops! I didn't mean to copy it to the C drive! Lessee, what did she say? **DEL *.*** ? Let's try it." No matter that her computer won't reboot anymore. Those little "vacations" give her time to slip outside to have a smoke or go to the snack bar to get a soda. Meanwhile some poor sap is rebuilding her machine for the umpteenth time. "Backup? What's a backup? I thought you guys did that by remote control from the server or something."

The classic case

There is a rich vein of computer users who dance the "I'm so stupid, I'll never figure it out, I'm not worthy" two-step. Every time they talk about computers or computing, they make some self-deprecating remark that says that they not only don't want to work with a computer, but that they are deathly afraid of them. Their fear of not having a job is only slightly stronger than their aversion to computers, so they submit to the intrusion of computers into their workplace. Some submit more willingly than others. These are the folks who made Dan Gookin's book, *DOS For Dummies,* the best selling computer book of all time.

These are the people who want to write down every step required to launch a program or perform some mundane task. No matter that the context may be different next week, they are going to use their script, sometimes with disastrous results.

If they ask a question (and they ask many), they never hear the answer because their brain is going a mile a minute worrying that they won't understand the answer, and they'll look stupid. If you put the page of the manual that answers their question in front of them, their eyes glaze over simply because it is a computer manual.

Away from the computer, the dummies are some of the brightest, most industrious people you'd ever want to meet, and a joy to work with. Put them in front of a computer, and you just want to slap them. They are so worried that they are going to do something wrong that it becomes a self-fulfilling prophecy, and they can be their own worst enemy in causing data loss and disaster.

A few of the Lisa Marie type actually abuse equipment out of frustration over lost data. Every computer technician and support person has heard the story about the secretary whose mouse broke every two or three weeks. The only logical reason for the failures was banging the mouse violently on the desktop out of frustration at losing a document; in effect, she had damaged her own unprotected computer data. Of course, the secretary denied anything out of the ordinary had happened to her mouse.

"Can't be," the company support person retorted, peering seriously into the hole in the bottom of the mouse. "The impact meter in this mouse shows a very definite jolt. You sure you didn't drop it on the floor or something?" Her next mouse was a keeper. It lasted a long time.

None of these folks are malicious vandals like the people you will meet in Chapter 2. They're just everyday people who have to coexist with their computers. Yet, this group unwittingly destroys more data in a year than the crackers, phreaks, and vandals have destroyed in all of the computer age.

Knowing the Ways Your Computer Can Fail

Two basic conditions can bring about the loss of data without an act of God and without the intervention of any of the folks described in the previous section: hardware failure and software failure.

Disks are mortal

Some floppy-disk manufacturers guarantee their products for a lifetime. Sure, why not — who's going to bother to return a single defective floppy to the manufacturer for replacement? All floppy disks fail sooner or later.

If you look at a hard disk drive's technical specifications, one measurement you might find is its *MTBF,* or Mean Time Between Failures. The MTBF is a semi-scientific guess at how many hours a hard disk will work before it fails. In other words, hard disks die, too. (And always, it seems, at the worst possible time.)

Sometimes, what appears to be disk failure actually isn't. The card in the computer's bus slot that controls the hard disk can suddenly go bad. When this happens, don't panic; you've probably not lost any data. Replace the controller card and reboot the machine, and your computer will behave as though nothing happened.

In rare cases, the controller card can develop problems that make it dangerous to write anything to disk. One such problem sends sections of your files into a bottomless pit somewhere. Another such problem corrupts your hard disk's *FAT* (File Allocation Table, which is like an index to your disk's contents) so badly that the cost of rescuing the data approaches the cost of the computer itself.

Software can fail you

One of the most notorious features of the C programming language is the freedom it gives the programmer to access any part of the computer at its lowest level. Among seasoned C programmers, this is known as "being able to shoot yourself in the foot." A misplaced character or a sloppy math routine can potentially cause a program to start writing data into the disk's boot sector or FAT. Such a renegade program can have the same destructive power as the nastiest virus you will ever find on the Internet or local bulletin board.

Of course, few computer users are C programmers, but that doesn't mean they are immune from the problems that a runaway program can cause. You always run the risk of falling victim to a bug in the software that you acquire.

In the best of families

Embarrassing disk-eating software doesn't just come from small programming shops. In the early 1990s, Microsoft — one of the best programming companies in the world — offered potential users of their then-new Word for Windows 2.0 a chance to buy a small demonstration version of the program for $9.95. The idea was to let users try the program's features to help them decide to buy the full-blown package. The demo came with a coupon offering a discount on the real thing.

Curious, I ordered the demo. As soon as it arrived, I eagerly slipped the install disk into my computer. About halfway through the setup routine, the system hung up tight and file copying halted. Giving the computer the three finger salute (Ctrl+Alt+Del) did nothing. The only way out was to shut off the computer. But the computer wouldn't reboot — the hard disk boot sector and the files in C:\ had been trashed.

To be fair to Microsoft, none of the files not residing on the C drive were damaged. You could still boot with a floppy and find all your files intact except those in the root directory of the hard disk.

After several hours of restoring the disk structure from tape, working with Microsoft tech support, and reproducing the problem three or four times, I discovered that the fly in the ointment was a memory-resident utility called SEARCH.COM. For some reason, this utility and the Word demo clashed, crashing my hard disk's boot sector and root directory.

An experienced user in this situation checks to see just what the damage is before taking steps to correct the problem. Imagine, however, a user who doesn't know how to boot to a floppy and survey the damage. That user might well reformat the disk — *unnecessarily* — before thinking of ways to discover the extent and nature of the damage.

(To this day, by the way, there is probably a routine buried deep within Word's Setup program that checks to see if SEARCH.COM is loaded, and, if so, takes evasive action.)

Natural disasters can destroy data

In the insurance business, such disasters as flood, lightning, hurricanes, and other natural phenomena are often called "acts of God." These "acts" are usually uninsured, unless specifically covered in the policy. Insurance companies are happy to sell you additional coverage against such calamities.

Fires are also often not covered, depending upon their origins. A standard homeowner's policy seldom covers fire caused by old, deteriorated, shorted-out wiring.

No matter what insurance coverage you have on your computer, *the data on the hard disk is never covered.* No matter what value the lost data has to you or your business, your homeowner's policy does not give you a dime for its disappearance. Business insurance policies may, if you pay through the nose, cover the data up to some theoretical amount — but you're going to have a devil of a time proving what the data is actually worth.

Anticipating Disaster

Actuaries are people who, based on history, statistical analysis, and educated guessing, try to predict just how often, statistically, something happens. Insurance companies employ actuaries by the carload to figure out how much to charge in premiums to be able to cover their losses and still profit. Actuarial tables predict our lifespans and predict how often flooding will occur in our neighborhoods. Never in the history of modern commerce has an actuary stated that there is zero chance of disaster. Disaster will strike at some point. The trick is to be ready. Preparing for computer disaster means having a good, clean backup of your data that you can access no matter what happens.

Disaster planning involves balancing the need to have backups of your data with the mechanics of backing up the data. The only time the disk in your computer ever agrees byte for byte with a backup is just after the backup is finished. Within minutes, if you keep working, the data on your system changes. What you have to do is balance the cost of rebuilding anything that has changed since the last backup against the time spent and the inconvenience of performing backup chores. The differential is your exposure. Only you can determine your comfort level for exposure.

Consider the act of writing a report using word-processing software. From the moment you open a blank document and begin typing until you save the document to disk, you are exposed to the possibility of losing what you have typed if the power goes out. Should you save the document after typing each letter? No, you'd never get the report finished. How about after each paragraph, each page, every five pages? Does the word processor have an autosave feature? All of the top-notch commercial word-processing software packages will save your document to a special backup file every five or ten minutes. So now how often should you save your work?

Disaster planning is based on the simple scenario outlined above. Just substitute any number of application programs for the word processor in the example, and backing up the disk for clicking the word processor's Save button. For example, how often you should save a spreadsheet and how often you back up are based on the same calculation of exposure.

The amount of exposure you are comfortable with determines your backup schedule. If you type only the occasional letter and use the computer for surfing the Internet most of the time, you can go longer between backups than a busy travel agency that stores all of their customer transactions on the network.

Tip

At the very least, you should do a backup after installing new applications, even if all you do is write the occasional letter and dabble with the Microsoft Paint applet that comes with Windows 95. That way, if you need to restore from tape, you won't have to re-install the newer software all over again. Of course, if you are stuck with doing backups to floppy disks, you may elect to backup only data files, since applications can always be reinstalled from their original floppy disks or CD-ROM disks.

If you have a home computer that is only occasionally used to bring home work, then you might need to back up only once a week or once a month. If you use the machine at work and you acquire large volumes of data daily, you might want to back up twice a day. In short, the way you use your computer should determine your disaster recovery plans.

Creating a Disaster Recovery Plan

Creating a disaster recovery plan is one of the first things major corporations and their Information Services (IS) managers do when they install new computer systems. They understand through experience just how much computer systems come to be relied upon and just how expensive it is to lose those resources.

Creating a disaster recovery plan for your home machine, or for the computers in a small office, doesn't have to involve a lot of work — just a lot of foresight and a little planning. The principles are the same, no matter what kind of computer you have: old Macintosh Plus or aging 386, or the hottest new P6 workstation.

In fact, creating a disaster recovery plan is as easy as answering five simple questions. If you know the answer to these questions, your disaster recovery plan is at least adequate.

1. **If everything in your office were to disappear tomorrow, how would you restore your computing capability?**

   OK, so that's a trick question — it's the only question you have to answer. It's tough to imagine how much of a hassle it would be to walk into your computer room and find it stripped to the bare walls. No disks, no monitor, no desk even; imagine that everything is gone. It makes no difference whether the reason is fire or theft. As Karl Malden used to say in those famous American Express commercials, "What would you do? What *would* you do?"

   A lightning strike may destroy your computer, yet amazingly leave your hard disk functional when placed into another machine. Your hard disk may malfunction, making it impossible to use an otherwise working machine.

   The questions that follow provide you with the individual pieces of the puzzle you need to combine in order to create the whole picture and answer the question above.

2. What would you replace the lost hardware with?

In the event your computer hardware becomes a total loss, you need to have a way in mind of replacing it quickly. A lot of people regularly pick up computer-related publications and drool over the new hardware ads. This is a good idea. Mentally building your dream machine isn't just idle fantasy. Few things change faster than computer technology. Computer manufacturers introduce new models monthly. It isn't anywhere near as orderly as, say, car manufacturers (which change models once a year). Chances are, the computer model you own isn't made anymore. It pays to keep up with hardware development so that you know what hardware is available at approximately what price.

If you haven't bought a computer in two or three years, you're either going to have to take some salesperson's word for things or do a real quick study. Of course, you know the difference between a car salesman and a computer salesman — the car salesman knows when he's lying to you.

You don't have to be a fanatic about it, but it's in your best interest to pick up *Computer Shopper* or some similar publication once in a while.

3. Is your computer hardware insured?

Some insurance companies include computer and other electronic equipment as part of the general coverage. If you're a small business owner, check with your insurance agent to see whether your computers are covered.

If your insurance covers hardware, you need to know the coverage's extent. Two factors tend to dilute any coverage you may have on computer equipment: the deductible and the method of arriving at a replacement value.

My friend George Sommer told me about a recent experience. Lightning followed the telephone wire into the computer in the family restaurant he helps manage. A few cards and the power supply were fried. The total damage sustained was only a few hundred dollars. He decided to pay for the repairs out of the restaurant's pocket. The deductible would cover only about half of the damage, and he was concerned that even a small claim could cause his insurer to raise its rates.

The way replacement values are calculated can also affect the extent to which your computers are insured. People are often surprised after having an automobile accident to find how little the insurance company values their car.

No matter that your 1985 Buick Park Avenue luxury sedan was in perfect condition with a new motor and a recently rebuilt transmission. Forget the $350 you spent on tires last week. Forget the fact that you can't replace a car like that today. The insurance company looks into its little book and picks up a number from a table. If the damage is less than that amount, it will tell you to get three estimates. If the damage exceeds that amount, that's the size of the check you get.

Over the years, used computers have become a hot commodity. The Boston Computer Exchange, among others, regularly publishes lists of prices similar to the car dealer's little blue book. In the event of a total loss of your computer, guess what most insurance companies look at to calculate the amount of your compensation. People are much more emotionally attached to their computers than they are to their cars. Try not to pitch a fit when the insurance company is finished adding.

4. How will you purchase a replacement computer?

This question is really a two-parter. In the first part, you figure out where you will come up with the money to make up the difference between what you get for your computer and what the new equipment is going to cost. In the second part, you decide where you buy the replacement.

Fortunately, the price of everything inside your computer system, except the memory chips, has dropped dramatically in the past few years. That 300MB hard disk you bought three years ago for $600 can be replaced with a 1.2GB drive for about $500. Still, there may be significant out-of-pocket expenses.

If you are one of those folks who has an over-contributed IRA, a 401K, and a safe-deposit box full of CDs (the paper kind you get at the bank, not the big silvery disks), then you probably already know how you're going to find the money you may need to take out of pocket.

If you own a small business and suffer a fire or flood, however, you may be in deep kimchi. Funding for new computer hardware needs to be part of the overall disaster recovery plan for the business. Check with your insurance agent to see if a rider can be added to your policy to provide extra funds in case of disaster. After all, computer replacement costs may be only a small item in the total costs associated with getting your business back in operation.

Paying extra insurance premiums to provide disaster coverage is a gamble. The insurance company is betting you don't have a big loss, and you are betting you do. Once again, those nasty old actuaries are setting the odds just like a Vegas bookie. Your banker may be able to help you to create your overall disaster plan by pre-approving a line of credit to be used only if disaster strikes. If you can get this arranged, then the gamble changes. You are betting that disaster will happen, but you don't have to pay up (in the form of interest charges) unless it does.

The question of where you buy your equipment isn't as simple as it may sound. You may have bought your lost equipment from a mail order company. If you have the luxury of waiting a few days for delivery, then you can do that again. If, on the other hand, you are in the middle of a project or have some other pressing need to be back up and running within hours, you're going to need a local supplier.

A business with more than one computer to replace, especially if the computers are networked, needs a local supplier willing to go the extra step of helping you get set back up quickly, a cost your insurance company isn't likely to reimburse you for.

Many computer users have come to the conclusion that price isn't always the best criterion for deciding where to buy something. Computer superstores have only two things going for them — stocking and price. Generally the folks who work in the computer department are low-wage employees who would have as much trouble replacing your network in 24 hours as you would have. If your area has a local, independent full-service computer store, it might pay off to develop a long-term relationship and pay the extra five or ten percent that kind of operation has to charge to stay in business.

5. Where will you get your data to restore onto the new system?

This question is the backbone of everything. You can find a suitable computer just about anywhere, unless you have special devices like bar code scanners or cash drawers. The biggest threat to your continued operation, even for a home computer, is the data that was on the lost computer. Your data is the one thing that is unique in all of computerdom. Without it, you have to start all over again.

Generally, you can pretty easily start over on a home computer system — assuming that you take copies of all the files you produce for work to the office on floppy disk as you create them.

For a small business, however, business records *must* be rebuilt — manually, if backups aren't available. You can't tell an IRS auditor that you can't give the IRS information because you had a fire. In such cases IRS agents probably have their own version of the little blue book, and you're going to get soaked when they estimate how much they think you owe in taxes.

So the $64,000 question is: How good is your backup? If you have a good backup, you will be back in business shortly. If you don't, the costs of re-creating your data may exceed the physical damage of fire, flood, or a plague of disk-eating locusts.

Replacing computer equipment, especially PCs, is usually trivial compared to replacing missing data. Having an effective backup routine in place day in and day out is essential to the health of your data and should be an integral part of your disaster recovery plan.

Choosing Backup Tools

The medium you use to back up your data is trivial compared to the effectiveness of your backup procedures. Early personal computers like the Commodore 64 and the Timex-Sinclair 1000 actually had no data storage capacity. The first data storage devices available for these machines was a simple cassette recorder. As personal computers have matured, so have data storage devices. Today it isn't uncommon for PCs to have hard disks that store more than *four billion bytes* of information.

Not too many years ago, you could use the DOS BACKUP command to copy the files from your computer's hard disk to floppy disks. Hard disks were small, and BACKUP was free. Now, however, hard disks are bigger than ever, programs are bigger than ever, and backing up onto floppy disks is all but impractical.

To back up 1GB of data onto floppy disks requires *700* high-density 1.44MB floppies. Every computer security task you will ever perform adds a degree of inconvenience simply because it is something you have to do over and above just using the computer. How often do you think you'd do a full disk backup if you had to stick 700 floppy disks into your machine? It would take two days to do a backup!

Choosing a backup medium

Clearly, the more painless and convenient you make backups, the more likely you are to back up regularly, and the more likely you are to have an adequate backup in case disaster strikes.

It is also clear that backing up onto floppy disks isn't an option unless you use an old 80286 machine with a hard disk of no more than 40MB. Most of you have bought bigger and better systems, so this book won't consider floppy-based backup routines as an option, except for rare special cases.

Tip

The most viable and affordable option open for backing up the massive amounts of data found on modern computer systems is to use a tape backup device. A little later I'll tell you about some alternative backup methods, but none offers the convenience and security of a good tape backup.

Choosing a tape backup device

Over the years, tape backup devices have changed only a little. The major changes have been to the controlling software, data compression algorithms, and tape formats. Most tape backup units use QIC (Quarter-inch Cartridge) tapes, but some of the newer high-end tape units use DAT (Digital Audio Tape) cartridges to record the data being transferred from your hard disk.

DAT backup units are, on average, a little faster, a little more reliable, and a little more expensive than the more common QIC-type units, but they provide much higher storage capacity. Whether you spring for the extra money depends on whether you're a Ford or a Cadillac kind of person (or company). Both get you where you need to be, but one does it with a little more comfort and style.

Whichever kind of tape unit you purchase, the two major decisions you need to make are tape capacity and whether the tape drive itself is internal to or external from your machine.

Tape capacity

The capacity of tape drive you should buy depends mostly on the size of your hard disk. Keep in mind, however, that a new hard disk is always in your life because the prices are falling so quickly and because software is growing in size so quickly. DOS 2.11 came on two uncompressed floppy disks. Windows 95 comes on 17 highly-compressed 2MB floppies. You may have a 300MB hard disk today, but your next hard disk will probably hold more than a gigabyte. It wouldn't be a crime to buy a tape drive that holds 800MB of compressed data on one cartridge. Large-capacity tape drives don't cost that much more than small-capacity tape drives.

If your tape drive holds less than your hard disk, when one tape gets full during backup, you have to put another tape into the drive — just like you had to swap floppies in the old DOS BACKUP days. And just like the old DOS way, flopping tapes in and out of the drive several times just to back up one hard disk is a pain in the neck. If you have to stand there and watch the backup, then you can't let it run unattended at night or while you're at lunch.

As you might expect, the rule of thumb for buying a tape drive is to buy the largest one you can afford. Say you have a 250MB hard disk. Furthermore, say that a 250MB tape drive is $200 and the 850MB drive is $350. It may be cheaper in the long run to buy the 850MB model. If you buy the smaller tape drive and then later buy a larger hard disk, you aren't going to be able to sell the tape drive for anything near what you paid for it, and so the final cost of the larger tape drive will be more than $500. If, however, you are in your mid-80s, and you're pretty sure this is the last computer you're ever going to buy, save some bucks and let the grandkids handle upgrading when the time comes.

Internal vs. external tape drives

An internal tape drive is physically installed inside the computer's case in a standard bay that can accommodate hard disks, floppy disk drives, CD-ROM drives, and so on. An external tape drive sits on the tabletop and connects to your computer by a cable and maybe a card. In some cases the choice between an external or an internal tape drive depends on whether you have an empty bay where the unit can be installed — no bay means external drive. But even if you have one of the new mega-tower units that has room for ten disk drives and a Jacuzzi, you may want to go external.

External tape drives are anywhere from $20 to $100 more expensive than a drive with the same capacity built for internal installation. The difference in price is the manufacturer's cost of building a case and a separate power supply into the unit. The advantage to having an external drive is the ability to use the same drive to back up more than one computer.

Some tape drives connect to your computer by using a special card that goes into one of the slots in the computer's bus. Other drives plug into a parallel port in the back of your computer. The newer IDE tape drives, meanwhile, plug into your hard disk controller or a special port on the motherboard. Obviously, just about every computer ever built has a parallel port, so you can easily move that kind of external tape unit from machine to machine without incurring any extra costs.

Most manufacturers of external tape drives will sell you extra bus slot cards at a reasonable price. Having cards installed in all of the computers in your office so everyone can share a single tape drive is an extra expense. It is primarily a convenience issue.

If a drive using a dedicated card is significantly faster than a comparable model that uses the parallel port, it may be worth the extra expense to buy extra cards for $50 a pop. After all, would you back up your computer every day if you had to open the case on another computer, take out the card for the tape unit, and then disassemble your system to install the card? The cost of the extra card is negligible when compared to the cost of the data stored on the system.

It is worth mentioning that many of the IDE tape drives that run off the floppy controller can be speed-enhanced by purchasing an accelerator card. Floppy drives normally transfer at 500K and the accelerators double the transfer rate to 1MB, literally doubling the backup speed. These aren't proprietary interface cards but generic floppy-controller accelerators that are compatible with most internal tape drives. In a workgroup installation, a card like this would only have to be put in the backup machine and the whole network would benefit from its enhanced speed.

The benefit of an internal tape drive is primarily convenience. Like a big friendly puppy, an internal drive is always there, just waiting for you to give it some attention. If you are one of those folks who leaves the computer on 24 hours a day, you can easily just slip in a tape, go home, and let the automatic scheduler start the backup at midnight. All you have to do in the morning is remove the tape and store it.

If you have a small network of computers using the Windows 95 client for Microsoft networking, you can actually use a single internal tape drive to automatically back up each of the systems in the workgroup and avoid the expense of duplicate hardware or having to buy interface cards for each computer.

The bottom line

The bottom line as far as what tape unit to use is simple. If the unit and the software that controls it are capable of putting a copy of your hard disk's contents onto tape quickly and easily, and most of all reliably, it will do.

If you are using Windows 95 or another advanced operating system that supports long filenames, you will want to make sure that the software used to perform the backup is compatible. A utility called MSBACKUP is supplied with Windows 95. If this utility is capable of controlling the tape drive, you can be assured long filenames will not be truncated.

This point about using appropriate software for your backup unit falls smack in the category of "what you don't know can hurt you." If you continue using the original backup software that came with your unit, you may not get a complete backup with Windows 95, OS/2, or Windows NT and will be looking at headaches down the road. In addition to truncating long filenames (which can render some apps useless upon restoration because they're hard-coded to look for the long filenames), older backup software doesn't back up the Windows 95 registry properly. Upon restoration, you've got a non-functioning copy of Windows 95 and are headed for a re-install. If you are upgrading to a newer operating system, check with the manufacturer of your tape unit. Chances are there is a free upgrade to the software, which you can download from the Internet or a commercial online service or a company-operated bulletin board system for free.

Of course, there are some newer tape drives that MSBACKUP cannot control. The capability of this utility to control the tape drive is not a litmus test, but it is a red flag warning. Check with the manufacturer of the tape drive to see whether a 32-bit Windows 95 version of its backup software is available, or look on the box for the logo that indicates a product is compatible with Windows 95.

If your tape drive and software are easy to use, reliable, and compatible with your operating environment, you have a tape drive that you can trust to archive your valuable data. Now all you have to do is set up a backup routine and stick to it.

Creating a Good Backup Routine

With backups, technology is secondary — lots of reliable tape backup units are on the market. Creating a good backup routine is a lot like exercising, dieting, or regularly adding to a savings account. Making the resolution to do it is easy. The hard part is designing a regimen so you will actually do it.

Zen and the art of backup

Devising a good backup routine for yourself requires self-knowledge. If you are a supervisor, you can usually get away with imposing your will on the peasants and chewing on their ears when they fail to deliver.

The whole trick to making sure your data *is* backed up is to make sure it *gets* backed up. Sure, you have to evaluate the amount of exposure to data loss that you can comfortably endure, and yes, you have to determine when the best times to perform backups occur. Beyond that, however, there are few subtleties to grasp.

When is it most convenient for you or your employees to perform backups? Certainly you don't want to schedule a backup that takes an hour to be done during the busiest parts of the day. If you schedule backups for 5:00 p.m. on Friday, will it get done? Not likely.

Everybody knows that backing up data has all the sex appeal of watching paint dry, but when you get into the habit, you'll begin to do it automatically, just as you would any other unpleasant task. The trick is to set a schedule and stick to it.

Full vs. partial backup

A full backup, as the name implies, saves every file on your hard disk to tape, a process that can take some time. Obviously, the bigger your hard disk, the longer it takes to do a full backup. The advantage of a full backup is its completeness. It is a snapshot of your hard disk's contents. A full backup is a frozen moment in time that you can return to, confident in the knowledge that everything is there.

A partial backup selectively targets files for backup. One style of partial backup focuses on all the files in a subdirectory or group of subdirectories. This kind of partial backup is useful when your work is concentrated in a specific area of the hard disk.

A good example of this kind of partial backup is a program I once wrote called the Golden Isle Vacation Property Management program. It takes reservations for condo rentals, beach cottage leasing, and so on, and it runs on a network. At any given time there may be eight to ten people taking reservations, posting payments, running reports, or logging housekeeping activity. All of these folks are using the computers on their desks, but all the data they generate is located in a single directory on the network server's hard disk.

The Golden Isle program is mission critical. Without access to the program and the data it contains, the users are dead in the water. All the letters to homeowners and customers, all the spreadsheets that show income from month to month are of secondary importance to Golden Isle. Backing that stuff up can wait.

By backing up just the Golden Isle directory on tape, the companies that use the Golden Isle program reduce their exposure to losing their most important computer resource. Backing up the one directory is quick and easy because it takes only a fraction of the time of a full backup.

> **Archive attributes**
>
> In DOS and Windows 95 (and every other major operating system), each file written to the hard disk has a set of attributes. All operating systems use "read only," "hidden," and "archive" attributes, but each operating system may have other specific attributes.
>
> The archive attribute is a toggle, meaning that it can be turned on and off easily. In DOS and Windows 95, when files are first created, their archive attributes are turned on to signify that they have not been backed up.
>
> When a backup program saves a file, the default behavior of the controlling software is to reset the archive attribute to off, signifying that the file is archived in the same condition as it is found on disk.
>
> Whenever a program opens and alters a file, the operating system turns the archive attribute back on to signify that it is now out of date with any previous archive tape or disk.

The other kind of partial backup, usually called an incremental backup, targets only those files that have changed since the last full backup. To do this, the backup software scans the attributes of files to see if the archive attribute is turned on. If so, the file is saved to tape, and the archive attribute is turned off.

By backing up only those files that have changed, the backup process can be shortened considerably because a large part of the data stored on any hard disk is application program and operating system code that never changes. Instead of backing up all your WordPerfect program files, only the documents you have recently worked on are backed up.

No matter which kind of partial backup you do, you will always need a recent full backup to use as a reference point. Partial backups can only partially restore the contents of a hard disk. If something happens to your hard disk and you need to restore from tape, you must first restore the most recent full backup tape to write the foundation files back to disk. When you have restored the foundation, you must then restore each partial backup in order.

For example, say you do a full backup to tape on Monday and do partials on Tuesday, Wednesday, and Thursday. Friday morning you come into the office and flip the switch to turn on the computer, but unfortunately a mouse has been chewing on power cords. What you actually get is a six-inch blue flame and a big crackling sound as your power supply surges and zaps the hard disk with way too many amperes of current.

The computer guy comes and performs the last rites on your power supply and your hard disk, both fried to a crisp. (Hey, it could happen.) Fortunately he's got a replacement power supply and hard disk in the trunk of his car, and you have your backup tapes.

> ### Backing up open, shared files
>
> One of the biggest impediments to backing up mission-critical data more than once a day has finally been removed. Backup software is beginning to appear that will back up open, shared files on Novell and other networks.
>
> In the past, everyone using the files to be backed up had to close the application. Even one user with a file open would cause most backup software to stop and issue an error message telling you that the open file could not be backed up.
>
> One such backup application is named NovaBack from North Star Systems. This program is compatible with most of the common tape drives in service today.
>
> By running part of the backup routine on Novell servers as an NLM (Netware Loadable Module), the program is able to copy the files even when they are open. For many companies, performing partial backups during their hours of operation is possible only with this type of software.

When the machine is fixed, you must first restore the full backup from Monday. Then you must restore the partial backups from Tuesday, Wednesday, and Thursday in order, because each builds upon the previous backup.

How often to back up your data

To make it easier to get an idea of how often backing up is appropriate for you, find yourself in the paragraphs that follow.

Twice daily: partial at noon, full at end of day

You should back up twice daily if you run a mission-critical application on a network shared by a number of people who are primarily engaged in entering lots of transactions. Schedule a partial backup for about midway through the workday. Schedule a full backup for the end of the business day.

Once daily: full backup at end of day

If you're part of a workgroup of five to ten users who share disk resources on a network and if your accounting data is updated daily, then do a full backup at the end of each day.

Three times weekly: full backup at end of day

Smaller businesses often have a part-time bookkeeper come in several times a week to tidy up accounts and pay suppliers. Typically, small businesses have five or fewer users who either are not networked or who are networked using Lantastic,

Windows for Workgroups, or Windows 95. Transaction volume is moderate. Do full backups three times during the week, such as at the close of business on Monday, Wednesday, and Friday.

Twice weekly: full backup Tuesday, partial on Thursday
The twice-weekly backup is usually sufficient for small service companies where two or three users share a single computer or where a small workgroup network is in place. Transactions are light, and the paper trail is adequate to rebuild the last two-and-a-half days' work with a minimum of disruption to the business.

Once a week: full backup
This level of backup is usually sufficient for someone who works at home, uses a reliable late-model computer, and generates a relatively small number of files and transactions.

Monthly: full backup
Most home computers are used for personal projects and homework. Between times, members of the family fight each other for time to play games and surf the World Wide Web. The monetary value of the data stored is minimal. Backing up a home machine serves as much or more to preserve the setup and optimization of the system than to archive precious data. Of course, if you make significant changes to the system by installing new applications or hardware, you should schedule a fresh backup.

Other backup factors

Now that you have a general idea where you fit along the scale, there are a few things you need to factor into your equation: age of your equipment, the kind of data you store, and the way you work.

Your equipment's age
Older equipment is more likely to break down as each of the components nears its own MTBF (Mean Time Between Failures) rating. Surprisingly, brand new equipment shouldn't be trusted as much as old equipment. Due to manufacturing flaws that can be hiding in chips, semiconductors, capacitors, and other electronic components, equipment that is just beginning its service life is more likely to break down in the first 90 days of service than it is in the second year. If a computer has operated flawlessly for three months, the likelihood is that it will continue to do so for several years.

The kind of data you keep
The kind of data you accumulate should also be factored into a decision on how often to back up. If you store a lot of mission-critical data that is unique to your business, you need to back up more often. If, on the other hand, you do research that primarily involves downloading information from online sources, you may be able to safely back up less often, assuming the material you download doesn't disappear from the source where you found it.

The way you work

If you do a lot of work on a home computer, but transfer that work to a machine at the office, you may safely assume that the data is archived elsewhere and do fewer backups on the home system. Again, it is a matter of assessing exposure.

Making Sure Your Backup Works

Nothing is more frustrating than finding out that your backup tape is damaged or blank. You're already stressed because something has happened to your system, and just when you need it the most, your backup fails to restore your hard disk to health. Bummer.

Fortunately, with a little thought and preplanning, you can avoid such situations.

Cycling backup media

Backup tapes can cost $30 or $40 apiece. While that may seem expensive, backup tapes are made to extremely high quality standards to reduce the likelihood of failure. Besides, $30 or $40 is a fraction of the value of the data they are designed to store.

Despite the best efforts of tape manufacturers to sell perfect products, occasionally a bad tape gets into the hands of a user. To minimize your exposure to a bad tape, it is a good idea to cycle several tapes through the backup schedule.

Tip

I recommend to my clients that they use at least five different tapes. I tell them to place different colored labels on each and use them in a set sequence like red, yellow, blue, green, black. If you don't have colored labels handy, just label them A, B, C, D, and E. By cycling through the tapes, you greatly reduce the possibility that you will have a bad tape completely ruin your disaster planning. If you cycle tapes, a bad tape will cost you only a day or two of work. You won't be left completely out in the cold.

Backups on backups

Don't use the same tape over and over — tapes do wear out. I once had a client who was justifiably proud of herself for instituting a rigid data backup program. The network drive was backed up every afternoon at 5:00. Problem was, unknown to me, the company was using the same tape every day. To this day I don't know whether that tape was ever good or whether it just wore out one day without letting anyone know. One afternoon, a new employee accidentally wiped out a whole directory full of correspondence files. That's when my client found out her one tape was bad. Fortunately, the whole hard disk didn't go down, or the company would have lost a lot more data than it did.

Testing backups

Once in a while, make sure that your tape unit is working properly. Mechanical failures can also cause you to have nothing on your backup tapes.

To test your backup unit, create a directory with several subdirectories on your hard disk and copy all kinds and sizes of files into those directories. Do your backup as you normally would, and then delete those directories from your hard disk. You should be able to restore the deleted files by using your backup tape.

One word of caution: Don't just decide, like a friend of mine once did, to *really* put his backup to the test. He simply reformatted his hard disk and then attempted to restore from disk. Needless to say, he had a lot of work to do in rebuilding his hard disk from scratch when he discovered the backup tape contained no useful files. For weeks afterward, his friends, myself included, began phone conversations with him by using the greeting, "Hey, stupid!"

Storing backup tapes

Another important consideration in safeguarding your tapes is how you store them. Just dropping them back into their protective case and tossing them into your desk drawer is a recipe for disaster. What would happen if the building burned to the ground one evening? A tape in a desk drawer is unlikely to survive in usable condition.

The two best places to store backup tapes are in a fireproof box and in another location. Fireproof boxes and safes come in a variety of sizes, shapes, and prices. Most good stationery or office supply stores have several to choose from. They can cost anywhere from $25 for a minimally acceptable box to several thousand dollars for a floor-mounted vault with a combination lock. This is your data we're talking about — buy the best lockbox or safe you can reasonably afford.

Tip

Another crucial element in disaster planning is to store your backups away from the office. My office is in a small bungalow behind my family's house. When I do a tape backup, I store the tapes in the closet of my bedroom. I also have a safe-deposit box at a bank in town where I occasionally put in a new tape and return the old tape to the cycle.

My office may burn down, my house may burn down, but I'm almost willing to bet that they don't both burn to the ground on the same day. Almost. I *am* willing to bet that my office, my home, and my bank don't all burn down on the same day.

Still, I live in hurricane country, and we have learned through experience that nothing should be taken for granted. Recently, as a particularly nasty storm approached, I bundled up the chapters I had written for a book and all the source code for programs I've written for clients over the years and placed these files into ZIP archive files. I then logged onto the Microsoft Network and e-mailed these files to myself just on the off chance that none of my other backup precautions were strong enough.

It is always a good idea to have your most recent backup away from the location where your computers are. Of course, the off-site location needs to be close enough so that you can lay your hands on the tape quickly.

A lot of folks simply get into the habit of taking the tape home with them. One note of caution needs to be mentioned about this practice, especially if the data on a tape is particularly sensitive or valuable. Your home may be more vulnerable to burglary than the office, and it is certainly less secure than a safe-deposit box.

Using Alternative Backup Strategies

Tape backup drives are not the only way you can safely store data. In addition to those good old floppy disks you've been using for years, newer technologies like floptical drives are becoming affordable. Floptical drives use a disk that is similar in appearance and storage capacity to a CD. Unlike compact disks, flopticals can be written to by the user.

There are also removable media drives like Iomega's Bernoulli or SyQuest drives that can be used for backup. Prices, especially on the Iomega's ZIP drives, are really tumbling. Backing up to them is as simple as typing **COPY *.*** or using a compression program like WinZip. They are more expensive than tape drives but far cheaper than flopticals. They also offer the added bonus of letting you work directly on them and then stashing them in a safe somewhere.

Prices on floptical drives are still too high for most people to afford, but just barely. A good floptical drive that writes your files onto a disk similar to a CD-ROM can run just $500 or less but are still much more expensive than a tape drive. For this reason, tape backup units are still the most commonly used archiving devices. Be ready for this to change in the next few years, though, as prices on floptical drives and other removable media come down in price.

Another often-overlooked adjunct to tape backup is the high-density floppy disk. While not a replacement for having a good backup-to-tape program in place, some data is especially suited to being archived separately on disk.

For example, at the end of each day I spend writing programs, I back up the source code files onto a floppy disk and store it in a box near my desk. When I deliver a new version of a program to a client, the source code goes onto a floppy and then is placed into a safe-deposit box. This backup to floppy is done in addition to my regular tape backup.

Floppies don't hold very much data, to be sure. Programs like LHA, PKZIP, WinZip, and TAR compress files to a fraction of their normal size and bind multiple files into a single archive file that can often be written onto a floppy disk. You can download these programs from most online services.

A Sample Backup and Restore

The mechanics of running the software for doing backup chores will differ depending on the operating system your computer uses. DOS and UNIX software will likely have a text–based menu system you can pick and choose options on. Windows and Mac users will find that the graphical interface of their systems makes backup nearly painless. The example shown in this section is the Windows 95 software that is included with the Colorado Trakker tape backup drive.

As you can see in Figure 1-1, when you first install Colorado Backup, there are two file sets automatically created for you. In Colorado's terminology, a file set is a list of the files that are to be backed up. You can create multiple special-use file sets that enable you to back up either the full disk or selected portions of the disk. For example, you could create a file set that backs up just your financial folders (directories) and another that just backs up the folders that contain source code for programs you have written. The automatic file sets Colorado creates do either a full backup or an incremental backup. The full backup (full system backup.fst) will archive your entire hard disk plus Windows 95 registry information. The incremental backup (modified backup.fst) will archive only those files that have been created or modified since the last full backup, using the Archive Attribute of the file as the guide.

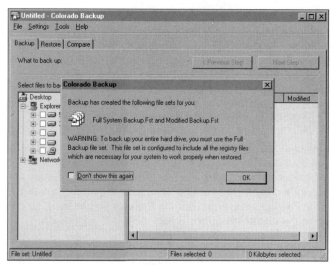

Figure 1-1: Colorado Backup comes configured to do full and incremental backups for you right out of the box.

If you open Colorado Backup, you get a window that has three tabs (Backup, Restore, and Compare). The format for the content of that window is similar to the Windows Explorer or the old Windows 3.x File Manager. The window is split into two panes, with the left-hand pane showing a hierarchical view of your disk resources. As you can see in Figure 1-2, the display is almost exactly that of Explorer, except that a checkbox has been added just to the left of folder names. To include a folder and all the files contained in the folder, all you have to do is check the box. In Figure 1-2 you can see that two folders have already been chosen, and a third is being added to the list.

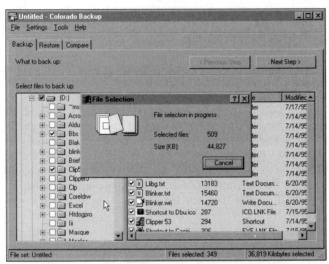

Figure 1-2: To include a folder and all the files it contains in a partial backup, just check the box to the left of the folder name.

Selected files and folders will appear in the right-hand pane of the window, allowing you to further refine your selections. Any file or folder that is checked will be included in the backup tape created by the current backup session.

If you have designed a set of files you want backed up as a group, you can save the selections to a file-set file by using the File⇨Save or File⇨Save As menu commands. Save lets you update your selections in an existing FST file, and Save As lets you create new FST files or save a modified duplicate version of an existing file set. Once you have saved the file set, the File⇨Open menu command allows you to pick the one you want to use for the current backup session (see Figure 1-3).

If you select Settings⇨File Filter (see Figure 1-4) from the Colorado Backup menu, you can specify whole groups of files to be excluded from the tape. Correct use of this feature enables you to make your backup tapes as small as possible while still backing up files needed to restore your system. For example, many megabytes of your hard disk's capacity is usually taken up with program code, device drivers, DLL files, and other file types that can easily be restored by re-installing the software that put those files on the disk in the first place. These files are always used in a read-only fashion, so they never change content.

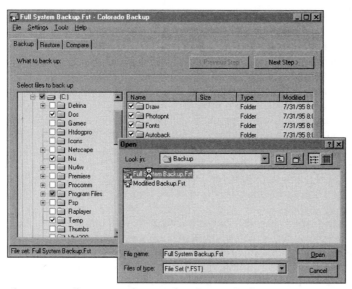

Figure 1-3: File sets can be saved and reused whenever you want to refresh the archive on tape.

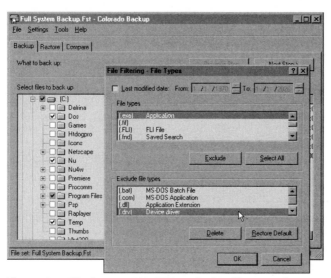

Figure 1-4: Filtering out DLL, EXE, and other file types that never change can save space on your tape for other files that change.

By filtering out those file types that are easily restored from other places, like factory install disks, you can reduce the space needed on tape to archive your system safely. The downside of filtering out files, of course, is that you may end up having to re-install many or all of your installed application programs in the event of a severe disk crash.

Once you have your file set created or you have selected one of the previously created file sets, you have only to click on the Next Step button to check the destination for your backup. By default, the tape drive will be selected, so all you have to do is click the Start Backup button to begin saving your files to the tape.

If you have previously used the tape, you will need to confirm that the tape should be overwritten. If your files taken together will not all fit on a single tape, you will be prompted to place a second tape into the drive at the appropriate time.

Restoring files from the tape is just as easy as backing up, with one possible exception. If you have suffered a severe disk crash, you will probably need to re-install the Colorado Backup software onto the new or repaired hard disk before you can proceed. Once you have Colorado Backup running, however, all you need to do is put a tape in the drive and click the Restore tab in the window. You can selectively restore just some of the files on the tape by unchecking those files and folders you don't want restored and by checking those files and folders you do want. Click the Next Step button, check that the tape drive is selected, and click the Start Restore button.

During installation, Colorado Backup copies a program to your system and places a shortcut in the Windows\Startup folder, which causes the Scheduler program to be loaded each time you start up Windows 95. As you can see in Figure 1-5, you are able to schedule backups to occur at a specified time every day by using the Automated Daily Backup. You can also click on the What's Scheduled tab to check on what events are scheduled to occur. As shown in Figure 1-6, you can set the schedule for running any backup set you may have.

One word of caution is in order if you intend to use an automatic scheduler, such as the one provided by Colorado: The placing of the proper tape into the drive is not automatic. You have to make sure that tapes get changed before the next scheduled backup occurs. It is all too easy just to leave the same tape in the drive and let the automated daily backup routine archive to the same tape every day. This is a bad idea. As mentioned earlier in this chapter, if you cycle a number of tapes, you have better protection against a bad tape.

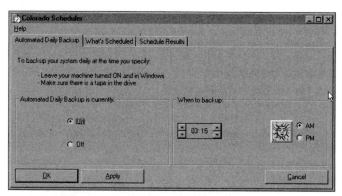

Figure 1-5: Automated Daily Backup lets you schedule a full backup to occur each day when the machine is on but unattended.

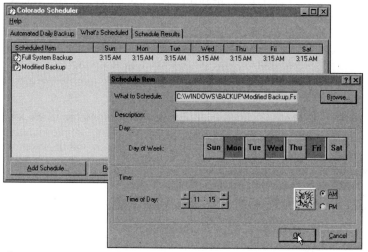

Figure 1-6: You can schedule any file set for backup by using the Scheduler.

Summary

This chapter told you about the most common ways the data on your computer is threatened and what you can do to protect yourself.

- Your data is valuable. It's not only hard but *expensive* to replace the stuff you've saved onto your hard disk.

- The two most common threats to your data are *accidental erasure* and *hardware failure*. If you better learn how to use your computer, you're less likely to make mistakes. And if you keep regular backups, you can recover from disaster with a minimum of inconvenience.

- Disaster *will* strike. You must prepare for it. The key is knowing the answer to the question, "If everything in your office were to disappear tomorrow, how would you restore your computing capability?"

- You *must* back up your hard disks to protect your data against disaster. Get a tape drive — preferably one that uses tapes that hold enough data to support the *next* (larger) hard disk you buy.

- There are three kinds of backups: the full backup, in which you back up your entire hard drive; the partial backup, in which you back up only selected directories; and incremental backups, in which you back up only the files that have been changed since the last backup.

- How and when you back up depends upon your situation. Home users who don't create much data can get away with full monthly backups. The more data you create and the more important that data is, the more often you must back up.

- Use a few different tapes for backups and cycle them. Test your backups from time to time to make sure that your tapes are still good.

- Store your backups where they're safe from natural disaster. Keep one copy in a fireproof box near your computer. Keep another copy in a different building.

- You can use floppy disks to create backups of single files or of a few important files. File-compression utilities are available to help you cram more data onto floppy disks.

The next chapter turns to another kind of data threat: hackers. While backups are a way to pick up the pieces after a hacker attack, the real key is prevention. The next chapter introduces you to the basic tenet of computer security and the kinds of threats you have to watch out for to head off hackers at the pass.

✦ ✦ ✦

Hackers, Crackers, and Phreaks

CHAPTER 2

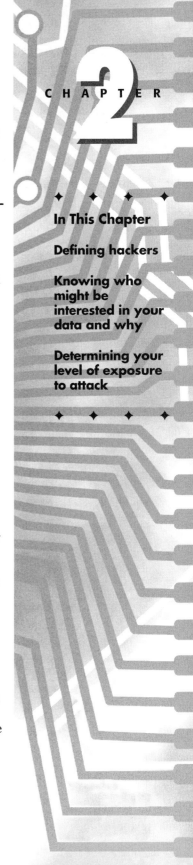

In This Chapter

Defining hackers

Knowing who might be interested in your data and why

Determining your level of exposure to attack

Children today are tyrants. They contradict their parents, gobble their food, and tyrannize their teachers.
—Socrates

You may give them your love but not your thoughts.
For they have their own thoughts.
You may house their bodies but not their souls,
For their souls dwell in the house of tomorrow, which you cannot visit, not even in your dreams.
—Kahil Gibran, The Prophet

In the 1950s, rebellious kids grew their hair, greased it back into a DA, wore leather jackets, and took full advantage of post-war automotive technology. In the 60s, kids grew their hair, wore denim jackets, smoked pot, and protested the war. The 70s in many ways was just a winding down from the fevered pace of the 60s right up until the first computer kit advertisements showed up in the back pages of *Popular Electronics*. From that time to the present, the computer underground has grown to become a haven for many of the more intelligent, disaffected youth. In short, the computer underground has become a significant counterculture all its own.

In his book *The Hacker Crackdown*, author Bruce Sterling advances the theory that the computer underground movement was born as a last gasp of the Yippies, as members and sympathizers of the Youth International Party were known.

According to Sterling, the late Abbie Hoffman and another person known simply as "Al Bell" began publication of the *Youth International Party Line* in June 1971. The *Party Line* was a newsletter dedicated to spreading the word that, in the American Land of Plenty, dissenting radical political enemies of the State could use the good old-fashioned rip-off as a political statement and an act of civil disobedience.

Stewart Bland, in his article *Blame It All on the Hippies,* which appeared in the Spring 1995 Special Issue of *Time* magazine, augments Sterling's arguments. It recounts the influence of the Hippie counterculture on the anarchistic model designed for the Internet, a loose confederation of computer networks. He points out that the hacker spirit helped to define life online as we are coming to know it.

Hacker Defined

The Jargon File is a public domain dictionary of hackspeak, edited by Hans de Wolf, and available for viewing at http://nws.cc.emory.edu/Jargon30/HOMEPAGE.HTML. *The Jargon File* defines the term *hacker* this way:

> **hacker** — [originally, someone who makes furniture with an ax] n. 1. A person who enjoys exploring the details of programmable systems and how to stretch their capabilities, as opposed to most users, who prefer to learn only the minimum necessary. 2. One who programs enthusiastically (even obsessively) or who enjoys programming rather than just theorizing about programming. 3. A person capable of appreciating hack value. 4. A person who is good at programming quickly. 5. An expert at a particular program, or one who frequently does work using it or on it; as in 'a UNIX hacker.' (Definitions 1 through 5 are correlated, and people who fit them congregate.) 6. An expert or enthusiast of any kind. One might be an astronomy hacker, for example. 7. One who enjoys the intellectual challenge of creatively overcoming or circumventing limitations. 8. [Deprecated] A malicious meddler who tries to discover sensitive information by poking around. Hence 'password hacker,' 'network hacker.' The correct term is *cracker*.

Hacker isn't a four-letter word

Because so few writers and journalists know much about the world of computers, the term *hacker* has all but lost its original meaning, except among professional computer programmers. Instead, it has become a catchall label applied to anyone who pulls off a computer-based prank or commits any of a growing number of computer crimes. To be a hacker is to be an explorer, a prober, a discoverer of previously unknown information about computers and the software that runs them. Among professional programmers, the term hacker is still recognized as an honorific — a recognition of technical prowess.

Because a fair number of people in the computer underground refer to themselves as hackers, the title has been given a sinister connotation. Hacker has come to be a four-letter word, rendering a stereotypical image of young cyberpunks bent on the destruction of anything in their path. In fact, self-proclaimed hackers vehemently deny that the true hacker would ever do anything destructive. They maintain the ultimate reward is in being able to access computers and computer resources, use them, copy information, and log off without leaving a trace of their activities behind to alert system managers to the fact that they have been hacked. In truth, hackers love nothing so much as a good practical joke, especially when it exposes the shortsightedness of large institutions, losers, and lamers.

A good analog (non-computer) example of the spirit and basic methodology of hacking occurred during the nationally televised Rose Bowl game in 1961 during a card stunt. Anyone who watches much college football has at one time or another seen a card stunt. Card stunts involve distributing large, colored cards to spectators along with instructions that will make pictures and messages appear to materialize from the stands. The giant billboard effect can be quite stunning. Since there were few available video special effects in the early days of broadcasting, card stunts were the darling of TV networks.

While the University of Washington Huskies beat Minnesota 17 to 7, the card stunt, which was part of the half-time entertainment, got hacked by a resourceful group of students from Caltech, the California Institute of Technology located in Pasadena, the home of the Rose Bowl. This band of students, dubbed the Fiendish Fourteen, hatched a plot to take over the Washington card stunt. A student, posing as a reporter, interviewed the coordinator of the half-time card stunt to learn how this particular stunt was done.

Armed with the knowledge gained from the fake interview, one of the students picked an office lock and swiped a blank direction sheet for the stunt. Several thousand copies of the blank direction sheet were printed up. The following day, the students again entered the office and stole the plans for the stunts. Using the large graph paper sheets as a guide for their own plans, they reprogrammed the stunt by creating new, and very different, instruction sheets. The third time they entered the office, the students returned the graph sheets and replaced the original instruction sheets with ones of their own making.

On game day, the pictures were quite different from those the University of Washington officials had in mind. When the word WASHINGTON was supposed to appear, the national TV audience instead read the word CALTECH; the word HUSKIES was displayed but spelled backwards, and instead of flashing a picture of the Washington mascot, viewers were treated to a picture of the Caltech Beaver mascot. The final score? Caltech 3, Washington 0.

It is true that this hack didn't involve computers, but all the classic elements are there. A surreptitious entry (usually illegal) gains knowledge, a program is altered, and another surreptitious entry puts the plan into motion, with the result that the hacker gets to sit back and watch the chaos he has created.

Humor in uniform

Sometimes hacker stories read like the humor sections of *Reader's Digest,* where they print cute stories under the headings of "Life in These United States" or "Humor in Uniform." For example, sometime back in the mid-1970s, some folks working at Motorola, who were users of the Xerox CP-V timesharing system, discovered a way to trick the system into letting a program run in supervisory status called *master mode.* Through this bit of chicanery, a program could do absolutely anything on the host computer — a dangerous prospect.

Going through the regular channels, Motorola's people informed Xerox engineers of the problem, and the bug in the system was duly logged. The log was distributed freely to users of the system, so in effect Xerox revealed publicly how to hack its system.

After several months and several muggings of the Xerox field support representatives, the bug was still not fixed. No patch to the code had been issued. That's when a couple of guys from Motorola, who originally reported the problem, decided to take the law into their own hands.

They created a pair of programs named Robin Hood and Friar Tuck. Both programs were created to act as *daemons* (**D**isk **a**nd **E**xecution **Mon**itor). A daemon is a UNIX term that means a program that isn't explicitly run by a user. Instead, it is loaded, usually during the boot process, into memory, where it lies dormant until a condition occurs. When the condition is satisfied, the daemon springs into action, performs a task, and then goes back to sleep. UNIX daemons are the ancestors of the DOS memory-resident, pop-up programs like Sidekick.

By running a program designed to exploit the security flaw in Xerox's computer system, Robin Hood and Friar Tuck were released into the CP-V system.

Soon after, the system operator of the main CP-V system in El Segundo, California, reported the following problems:

+ Tape drives would rewind and stop delivering data.
+ Tape drives would begin seeking data back and forth so violently that the drives themselves would walk and wobble across the floor.
+ Card punch machines would print out lace cards, a card with every hole punched, and would misdirect cards into the wrong output stackers, requiring operators to re-collate large stacks of punch cards manually.

When the Xerox folks tried to terminate the Robin Hood program, a dialog between the two programs would be displayed for the amusement of the computer's operators. Robin Hood would send a message for help to the Friar Tuck program which would immediately promise to "rout the Sheriff of Nottingham's men." The good Friar would then restart the Robin Hood program. Similarly, when Friar Tuck was terminated, Robin would come to the rescue.

The only way to stop the foolishness was to terminate both programs simultaneously, but that's tricky on a system whose transactions are measured in milliseconds. Finally the computer was crashed and rebooted, but Robin and the good Friar were soon playing havoc again. Only when the computer was brought down and restarted with an archive tape of the boot process were Robin and Tuck sent packing permanently. As you might imagine, a patch to plug the security problem was soon distributed to all users of CP-V.

The Xerox/Motorola story is also a classic because it shows the willingness of hackers to circumvent regular channels, as well as their ingenuity and determination to understand the environment they are working within.

While illegal and potentially illegal acts were committed by both the Fiendish Fourteen of Caltech and the folks from Motorola, these actions were basically benign practical jokes. In fact, in the case of the folks from Motorola, the intent was to improve the system.

Not all hackers are benign, however. Some are just common thieves, while others are malicious vandals. The politically correct term for these folks is *cracker*.

Crackers

The term *cracker* is preferred by many to the term *hacker,* especially when describing persons responsible for creating such potentially dangerous situations as crashing the phone system in a hospital or stealing credit card information. In the case of one group of German crackers, the KGB was involved.

In his book *The Cuckoo's Egg: Tracking a Spy Through the Maze of Computer Espionage,* author Clifford Stoll details how he became involved in one of the most interesting cracker cases yet revealed.

Stoll is by training an astrophysicist, but he found himself working in the late 1980s as a system administrator at the Lawrence Berkeley Labs in Berkeley, California. While tracking down a minor accounting error, Stoll stumbled upon evidence that the system he was administering had become the target of a series of unauthorized visitors. Despite an uninterested FBI, Stoll went in search of the persons who had hacked his computer system and left evidence that they were all too interested in connecting to military sites.

Stoll weaves an interesting tale that involves elaborate traps, including bicycling furiously to the office to answer intruder alerts in the dead of night. His story has a happy ending. Well, a happy ending for all but the young men arrested and charged with espionage once it was learned that this ring of German crackers was funded by the Russian KGB.

Few crackers are Cold Warriors. Most are looking to trash data, gain credit card information, or find some other method of causing mischief or getting something for nothing. Their methods are varied, but the main tools of the cracker are ignorance and complacence on the part of system administrators and users, and bugs in programs that produce loopholes in computer security. Their all-time favorite tool, the *crack program,* is shared by system administrators and crackers alike.

Crack programs have two basic components: code to dial up and access remote computers, and a dictionary of likely account names and passwords. The job of the crack program is to try to gain access to the remote computer by trying account names and passwords until, finally, a combination is found that will provide access to the system.

Once access is gained to the system, the experienced cracker knows how to increase his privilege level equal to that of a system administrator. With that level of privilege, you can be the proverbial 500-pound gorilla and do anything you want to do.

Phreaks

Wherever you go in the computer underground, you will find that the phone company is the most beloved target of all. Crackers who specialize in attacking phone systems are known as phone phreaks, or *phreaks* for short. Because telephones are such an integral part of everyday life, the phone system makes an inviting target. The fact that it is the largest computer network on the planet isn't lost on crackers and phreaks either.

The development of telephone technology, from Alexander Graham Bell's fledgling invention to the worldwide telephone network of today, is a fascinating story. Early telephone switchboards were entirely mechanical, requiring humans literally to connect one phone to another by using patch cords. As the volume of calls rose, however, mechanical switching systems were invented that used thousands of relay switches and complex mechanical parts. These switching systems were a marvel of technology but were constantly in need of repair and adjustment.

When the first computers were invented during World War II, the engineers and planners at Bell Labs immediately saw the value of developing computerized switching systems. Large amounts of money were spent on building the computerized tools that would eventually replace mechanical switches. In fact, it was the search for solid-state electronic switches that led to the second most famous invention to bear the Bell name, the transistor.

Before 1948, the most efficient method of building electronic circuits used vacuum tubes, a 1912 Bell Labs invention, to control the flow of electrons. Inside a sealed glass tube devoid of air, current applied to an electrode (positive) will only flow to the plate (negative) if a current is also applied to a small metal screen called a *grid*. The problem with tubes, however, is the energy they waste by generating heat, and lots of it.

The UNIX Operating System

An operating system is the lowest-level piece of software on any computer. The job of an operating system is to assume control of the hardware and provide a standardized environment where application programs can run. There are a large number of operating systems in common use throughout the world. Which operating system is used depends in large part on the hardware. Macintosh computers have their own operating system. DOS (Disk Operating System) is the most common operating system for text-based computing on Intel-compatible personal computers (PCs). In the burgeoning graphically-based computing community, Windows 95 is quickly inheriting the majority of DOS users.

In the 50s, 60s, and most of the 70s, however, Bell Telephone didn't own a single personal computer, mainly because personal computers hadn't yet been invented. Instead, Bell owned large numbers of mainframe computers. The UNIX operating system, and its symbiotic cousin the C programming language, was used extensively throughout the Bell System for administration, billing, and switching telephone calls.

Never a company to hide its light under a basket, AT&T made copies of the UNIX operating system available to colleges and universities, reasoning that they would, over the years, benefit from a steady stream of graduates already familiar with the technology found in the workplace. UNIX caught on, and soon there were several different variants on AT&T's original operating system created by colleges and universities.

Once freed from the trust restrictions that kept AT&T from marketing UNIX, the company found the computer business more than it wanted to handle. In the September 1995 announcement of the continuing breakup of AT&T into three separate companies, it was noted that most of the jobs lost in the restructuring are the result of closing down computer manufacturing operations. In a previous divestment, AT&T sold the rights to its UNIX operating system to Novell, the Utah-based company known for its networking software. After struggling with UNIX for two years, Novell recently announced that it had sold the rights to UNIX to SCO (the Santa Cruz Operation) for a 17-percent slice of SCO stock. Interestingly, powerhouse Microsoft owns a 14-percent piece of SCO, making rivals Novell and Microsoft partners in the development of new versions of UNIX.

The use of UNIX by institutions of higher learning and research proved to be a double-edged sword. Every year, the telephone system grew, and every year Bell Telephone hired college graduates who possessed the perfect training for the jobs the company was filling. Every year, a certain few of these students (or former students) would use their knowledge of UNIX to infiltrate telephone systems, to make free calls, to harass enemies, to create underground networks of like-minded individuals, and to potentially assume control over one of the country's most vital assets.

Since many of those involved in cracking and phreaking simply refer to themselves as hackers, I'm going to take the liberty of using that term for the remainder of the book, trusting in you, the reader, to remember that hacking still has a positive connotation in some circles.

The transistor opened up everything. Not only could circuits that used very little energy be built, but they were also smaller, more rugged, and, best of all, more reliable. The transistor was the beginning of semiconductor technology. The processor in your computer is the result of the early work on semiconductors at Bell Labs.

A byproduct of the development of computer technology at Bell Labs was the software needed to run those computers. Out of that work, the UNIX operating system was born. In the 1950s, Bell Telephone (AT&T) had a monopoly on long-distance telephone service in the United States. Bell Labs, the research and development arm of Bell Telephone, was just entering the computer age, and the world was changing rapidly.

The World of the Computer Underground

There are many subcurrents of culture running through modern society. As pervasive as computers have become, it is no surprise that a thriving culture has evolved around them. That culture is predominantly male and young. By the time they graduate from school and take on the responsibilities of adulthood, most hackers have long since left the underground behind. Twenty-five is old for a hacker.

If you go cruising the World Wide Web looking for information on hackers and hacking, you will undoubtedly find many learned white papers on the psychology of hackers. If you can understand academic double-talk, knock yourself out. I'll content myself with pointing out a few generalizations and stereotypes.

Some wag once said, "Not all men are created equal; that's why God created different caliber equalizers." A computer can also be a high-caliber weapon, given the proper set of fingers on the keyboard. Computing power isn't the most important element, since many hackers actually have fairly modest hardware setups.

The first requirement for a good hacker is intelligence. A dumb hacker is an unsuccessful hacker. The traditional image of a hacker is a social wallflower with a plastic pocket protector, who doesn't know his Nikes were designed for jogging and doesn't win Mr. (or Ms.) America contests. The revealing element of this stereotype may be that these folks feel more confident and powerful when they aren't dealing face to face with others and when intelligence is the key to popularity.

For many kids, hacking represents their first real achievement in life. The computer underground is the first place outside the safety of home where they feel accepted. Using the anonymity of the modem connection as a shield, hackers feel liberated to create their own world with its own pecking order, its own cultural values, and, of course, its own jargon. The *cognisanti* of the underground use terms that are half technical and half attitudinal. Average computer users are scorned as losers, or lamers.

In typical male fashion, young hackers tend to flock together. The computer bulletin board (BBS) has long been a favorite tool for connecting with other hackers. The undergrounders were also among the first to find and appreciate the Internet. To them the Internet is a digital playground.

Of course, once you have created your own virtual world on a bulletin board, what's to stop you from reinventing yourself? Nothing. Just like physical gangs of young men, much is done in terms of the way most hackers present themselves and in the jargon they speak to erect walls around their sacred ground.

Hackers regularly take up aliases to enhance their anonymity. Armed with names such as Ludichrist, Sicko, Packet Rat, Lex Luthor, Black Knight, PhiberOptic, and Sick Puppy, they congregate on local bulletin boards with similarly fantastical names and band themselves into high-tech street gangs with names such as Legion of Doom, Cult of the Dead Cow, and NuPrometheus League. (A hacker who uses his real name or whose real name is known is either a god who no longer needs anonymity, a loser, a lamer, or a dummy.)

In this world, tips and tricks are traded just like baseball cards. Stories of computer intrusion are told, exaggerated, and passed on to become mythic legend equal to or better than tall tales of sexual conquest. Anybody can find a girl, but how many people can bring down a PBX switchboard on a Monday morning?

Every culture has its subcurrents, and the computer underground is no exception. In the underground, you will find currents of anarchy, survivalism, racism, and all the other antisocial manifestations of the angry young man. Among hacker publications, you will find everything from how to make nitroglycerin to how to build a blue box for ripping off phone companies; you can read instructions for cloning cellular telephone codes and being a pain in the neck at your local McDonalds. You'll also find lists of phone numbers of university and commercial computer systems, identifications of the hardware those systems use, and common or default passwords. Sometimes you will even find lists of stolen credit card numbers or access codes for long-distance telephone calling cards.

Government and commercial hackers

Whether or not you even own a computer, a great deal of information about you is available through commercial sources. The magnitude of these issues would fill several other books so I'm not going to bore you with pages of information, only to scratch the surface and do a poor job of informing you. Suffice it to say that every time you go out into the world these days, you are likely to leave a computer record behind.

The Fourth Amendment to the Constitution of the United States reads: "The right of the people to be secure in their persons, houses, papers, and effects, against unreasonable searches and seizures, shall not be violated; and no warrants shall issue, but upon probable cause, supported by oath or affirmation, and particularly describing the place to be searched and the persons or things to be seized."

According to this magnificent document, U.S. citizens have the right to keep their stuff secret. You have a right to privacy. The first clause of the amendment doesn't pertain just to the government, while the second clause pertains only to the government. Under no circumstance does a private citizen have the right to inspect, seize, or view your property without your consent. Criminal and civil laws protect this right to privacy by outlawing burglary, unauthorized entry to a dwelling, trespassing, and other so-called crimes against property.

The second clause of the Fourth Amendment severely limits the ability of the government (local, state, and federal) to search you or your home. Only by swearing an oath that such an access is necessary, that there is a valid reason (probable cause) for the government to conduct a search, and that the items to be searched for are enumerated can the government obtain a judicial warrant allowing a search to be conducted.

Strangely, United States law and the Constitution are important in framing the discussions of computer privacy rights in other countries, since at present more than 80 percent of Internet users are from the United States. Still, groups dedicated to freedom and democracy are springing up all over the world, and the American example is used as a standard and as a litmus test.

Government and commercial interests have a wide latitude for collecting information about you and your affairs. Certain documents, such as real estate deeds, marriage licenses, and other records, are public documents. It is likely that your local newspaper published the price you paid for your home shortly after you bought it. They found out the price because the government published the information.

For example, you go to the grocery store and pick up a few items; you go to the checkout and watch carefully as the cashier scans each item into the register; then without giving it a thought, you whip out your credit card or write a check and lug your purchases to the car.

When your credit card or your check is placed into a reader, the purpose ostensibly is to validate that your card isn't over your credit limit, or that your check gets approved by one of scores of financial companies that, in effect, guarantee the merchant gets paid. But what other uses can that information be put to? Is it legal for the grocery or credit card company to analyze your purchases, to average them against the purchases of others in order to determine which items they should emphasize in order to increase sales? If you purchase potting soil and Gro-Lux bulbs, should those purchases be reported to the government so they can stop by your house some evening just to see if you are growing an illegal weed?

But this potential invasion of privacy isn't just happening at the local grocery store. Many large companies use hired guns to hack each other's computer systems. Fortunately, unless you are doing some powerful work at home, these guys just won't be interested in you. At the office, you should always be mindful that the competition may not be playing by the rules. No, the commercial guys are primarily interested in finding out all they can about you.

In some cases, the law is clear, and in other cases, the law hasn't visited the subject as yet, despite the fact that all but one or two of the states have enacted computer-specific statutes. Mostly, these statutes deal with property rights issues, making it illegal to hack and crack other people's computer systems.

Is it legal for the IRS to monitor your financial transactions in order to determine whether you should be audited for income tax purposes? Does the IRS have the right to let the credit bureau know the contents of your tax returns? Do you have the right to encrypt information to discourage its discovery? Does the FBI have the right, or even the duty, to monitor Internet communications to apprehend persons engaged in anarchist rhetoric or persons who post and download "dirty pictures?" What about erotic materials involving bestiality, scatology, or minors?

It is clear from crackdowns on AOL and other online services regarding kiddy porn, the furor raised by the bill submitted by Senator Exon to restrict indecent speech and other lewd materials on the Internet, and the Clinton administration's endorsement of the Clipper encryption chip that the government is indeed interested in monitoring and regulating your life in cyberspace.

Why worry about these folks?

As interesting as these stories and issues are, you may be questioning their relevance to you and your computer system. If the most inviting targets for hackers are large corporate and government mainframe systems, why should you have to worry about them? If you aren't visiting Usenet newsgroups on a nightly basis to advocate the violent overthrow of the U.S. government or trading nude pictures of twelve-year-olds, why should you worry about any of these folks? Good question.

The answer is simple, and just a touch philosophical. Each of us has a right to privacy, but that right must be balanced against the compelling interests of the community at large. In order to keep an orderly civilization free from the taint of anarchy and still provide the largest possible measures of individual freedoms, we must each voluntarily give up some freedoms to protect the rights of others. We restrict our rights of free speech so as not to promote slander and libel. We abdicate an absolute freedom to be secure in our papers, homes, and effects in order that the government might protect us from folks who want to bomb the World Trade Center or commercial airliners. We relax our demand to the right of absolute privacy by using more convenient financial instruments like credit cards and checks instead of carrying around large amounts of cash.

Still, we have the right, and sometimes even the duty, to protect the most private parts of our lives. In this regard, hiding an old boyfriend's love letters from your husband and keeping the details of your investment portfolio to yourself take an even footing with a Fortune 500 company's forthcoming marketing plans. Everyone has secrets, even the mildest and most blameless among us. Knowledge is power, and keeping knowledge to yourself is often necessary to restrain the power of others over you.

As a society, over the next 20 or 30 years, we will perhaps slowly come to grips with the nuances of the Information Age. In the meantime, love thy neighbor, but keep your doors locked. You may not be a Fortune 500 company, or even work for one, but the situations and security risks your computer poses are very similar to those of the "big boys," differing only in scale. The actual issues at stake are very much the same.

The fine line between security and paranoia

The whole idea of computer security is to create an environment that will keep people out of your stuff. Remembering that no security measure is foolproof, the goal isn't total protection. Rather, the goal is to make it sufficiently difficult for someone to gain unauthorized use of your data so that they will be discouraged from messing with your system. Motion detectors that turn on lights around your house, and sound alarms that wake the neighbors will usually cause house breakers to move on to an easier target. In the same way, the security measures you adopt should be just onerous enough to discourage intrusion, yet not be so much a pain in the neck that you fail to keep your guard up.

Building a fortress around your PC is probably paranoia unless you are storing a formula for making nuclear explosives from soap powder and bubble gum. Encrypting every scrap of text, no matter how trivial, goes too far. Running hard disk compression on your computer adds a slight amount of overhead processing that slows your computer down as you work. For most folks, the one or two percent of performance they lose is worth the extra storage capacity they get from compression. Encryption too creates overhead, but the performance hit is much more than that for disk compression.

What is needed is a balance between the costs of security and the threat to the privacy and safety of your data. In a world where PCs sit in spare bedrooms, are never connected to the outside world by modem, and are used only by trusted family members, you can afford to be a bit more lax about security. Isolated PCs, however, are becoming rare. Almost anyone you ask these days can give you an e-mail address. Computers are becoming connected to each other in rapidly increasing numbers as fast modems get cheaper and the lure of the World Wide Web beckons even inexperienced computer users.

If you have a home computer that never gets used for business, with only the kids' homework and some games stored on the hard disk, then go back and reread Chapter 1 on backup strategies. Once you've done that, pass this book on to someone else and grab that old Perry Mason story off the shelf and have a good life.

If, on the other hand, you use or are considering using computers in your work and in your play and you connect via modem to online services, bulletin board systems, corporate computer networks, or the Internet, stick around. There's information to follow that you can use.

Who Wants to See Your Stuff?

The people you need to guard your data and hardware from fall into four basic categories:

- Thieves
- The merely curious with low technical competence
- The curious with high technical competence
- The determined hacker with high technical competence

Each group represents a different type of threat, which in turn requires slightly different strategies to ensure computer security.

Thieves

Any consumer item that becomes popular soon becomes associated with a criminal element that would rather steal than buy. There are many different profiles. Some thieves are professional burglars. Some thieves are junkies looking to get their hands on something they can sell to buy whatever it is they are addicted to. You will immediately know when you've received a visit from one of these folks: Their calling card is devastation. Big, empty holes appear wherever expensive electronic equipment formerly resided. You come home from an evening on the town or a vacation to find everything of value missing.

The best defense against the common thief is physical security. Good locks, locks that get used, are the start. Alarm systems, neighborhood watch patrols, a big dog with a rough-sounding bark, a couch potato in the family who never leaves the house, and good relations with the community police force are all effective in establishing good physical security. In short, all the things that TV's McGruff the Crime Dog recommends for keeping your stereo and CD on their respective shelves are good measures to take when devising physical security plans.

Merely curious with low technical competence

Sad to say but this category of person who is a threat to your computer security is probably someone you know and love. It may be your spouse — you know, the one with the knack for erasing needed files, the one who always copies floppy disk-based files into the current directory and then can't figure out why they didn't go where they were supposed to. Your young children probably also fit this profile since they are prone to explore the computer but don't really know what they are doing.

Technologically unsophisticated curious users who aren't computer literate are the easiest to deal with since you can hem them in with menus that start their favorite programs, and you can do little low-tech things to thwart them from ruining your setup of important information. Examples of low-tech techniques would be turning on the hidden and/or read-only attributes of files and directories so they can't be erased easily. Note I said *easily,* for it seems anything can be erased by mindless users.

Keying your data security plans to this level of threat is adequate only for family computers that have little or no connection with online services, and only then when under your direct supervision. In short, assessing your enemies as posing only this low-level, non-malicious threat to your data security is safe only when dealing with children. A current backup is still your best weapon.

Curious with high technical competence

Older kids who have begun to learn the ins and outs of working with computers, co-workers in offices, and other more sophisticated users pose a different set of security issues. Outside of office politics, the curious but computer-literate people who may share your computer or who may try to access it in your absence involve a threat primarily to your privacy. Destruction of data is seldom on the mind of the curious person since it would cause their snooping to be discovered.

Also falling into this general category of computer risk are small networks, usually Novell or Windows for Workgroups, where users either share the resources of a file server or are linked in a peer-to-peer arrangement so they can share resources on any of the machines in the workgroup. Most small business networks fit into this mold since the average network is five to eight computers that lack a full-time connection to either a larger network or to the Internet.

This level of security risk usually involves safeguarding your data from people you know. Thwarting risks from people who have no malicious intention can usually be safely accomplished by putting important data on floppy disks stored in a lockbox or by placing data into password-protected ZIP files.

Tip

Curious users can present varied risks regardless of their technical competence. People who unwittingly infect computers with a virus by trading software game disks or downloading programs with a modem present a risk. Co-workers who damage data by experimenting with operations they are not qualified to perform present another kind of risk. Don't forget to take these risks into account when planning a security strategy. Always include a regularly scheduled virus check on your system as part of your security routine.

The determined hacker with high technical competence

The determined hacker is without a doubt the most dangerous animal in the computer jungle. If you are a target, chances are you will be a victim before you discover the method of your victimization. Determined hackers by definition are technically competent, perhaps even more so than yourself. You cannot underestimate the potential inconvenience and expense of cleaning up after you've been hacked.

To thwart the determined hacker, you have to be on your toes. Take, for example, a known bug in the design of the original IBM PC Monochrome Monitor that could be exploited by the Hercules graphic cards. The Hercules card was a wonder of its day, giving any user access to graphics. That may not seem so revolutionary today, but in the mid-1980s, it was the cat's whiskers.

The Hercules card could control the scan rates at which the monitor sweeps its electron gun across the phosphors of the screen to display an image. By instructing the card to set the horizontal sweep rate to zero, you can cause the coil at the back picture tube of the monitor to burn out by overloading the coil with current.

Armed with this knowledge, one or more hacker types wrote virus and Trojan horse programs (programs that do unexpected actions) purposely designed to damage the hardware. In at least one reported case, the monitor on the machine that was attacked caught fire.

As a user, you aren't likely to know about this kind of engineering flaw until you get to the repair shop. The only way to protect yourself is to consider that everything that goes onto your computer has made a visit to Phil Phreak's Hack City before it gets to you. Sooner or later, as a member of the cyber-citizenry, you are going to come into contact with a virus or a Trojan horse, or someone is going to try to dial into your network to snoop around.

Forewarned is forearmed, as the old saying goes. It is to this kind of threat that the remainder of this book is primarily dedicated. You can avoid the vast majority of the pitfalls you may encounter in cyberspace just by knowing what to look for.

Summary

In this chapter, you learned that *hacker,* in the original sense of the word, means someone who enjoys exploring computer systems and finding out how to totally control the environment. As originally used, the term was a compliment to programmers who really knew their stuff.

- You have also seen, however, that some hackers, often called crackers, are not interested in learning just the system; they instead are interested in vandalizing the systems of others — even complete strangers.
- Hackers come in all varieties of technical expertise, and there are some hackers who hack for a living.
- By now you should have a basic idea of how likely it is that someone might target you specifically for attack.

✦ ✦ ✦

Sneak Attacks, Trojans, Viruses, and Other Vermin

CHAPTER 3

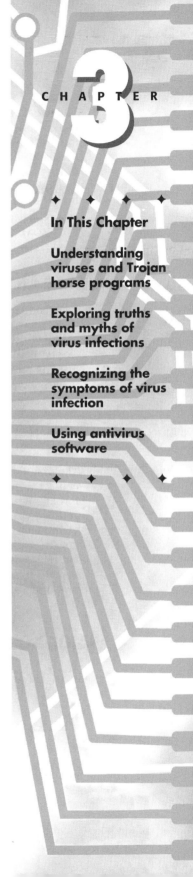

In This Chapter

Understanding viruses and Trojan horse programs

Exploring truths and myths of virus infections

Recognizing the symptoms of virus infection

Using antivirus software

Heaven knows, anything goes.
—Cole Porter

According to the 19th-century archaeologist Heinrich Schliemann, the legend of the original Trojan horse is based on actual events in the early 12th century B.C. Homer's *Iliad* and *Odyssey* tell the story of Helen, the wife of the king of Sparta, who was taken by Paris, son of the Trojan king, back to the walled city of Troy. Agamemnon, Helen's brother-in-law, was dispatched with troops from several Greek principalities to wage war on the upstarts. After a 10-year siege — which was largely unsuccessful — Odysseus (Ulysses) devised a battle plan that has become synonymous with deception.

One day the Greeks appeared to give up the fight. They packed up their fleet of boats and sailed away. As a gesture of "peace," they left behind a large wooden horse, the Trojan horse. That night, while the city slept, soldiers concealed inside the horse slipped out, ambushed the guards of the city, and opened the gates for the men of the Greek fleet, who had returned when the sun went down. The usual pillage, plunder, and mayhem ensued.

Perhaps the most dangerous group of all hackers is the modern day Trojans who write software to ambush personal computers anonymously. Instead of a single intruder attacking a single computer system, the folks who write Trojan horses, viruses, and other random sneak attack software can do damage to systems all over the world. Unless you practice good security measures, you are going to have an encounter with one of these computer terrorists.

The two major forms of sneak attack software are Trojans and viruses. There are some subtle distinctions between the two, although you could argue that viruses are a form of Trojan. In practical terms, however, a virus is a program that surreptitiously copies itself onto your system in such a way that it can spread outward, infecting other systems. The job of a virus is to live on your system for a time before delivering its *payload*, the term used to indicate the overt actions of a virus. A Trojan horse, on the other hand, uses trickery to get you to explicitly run the program. Usually this is accomplished by advertising the content of the program as something you would like. Instead, Trojans usually do things you won't like, such as reformatting your hard disk.

Where Do Viruses Come from?

People create them. While that statement may be obvious, the motivation for people to create viruses is nearly unfathomable to ordinary computer users. Some people create viruses to advertise their technical superiority over the losers and llamas of the world, the equivalent of the computer underground's rebels without a clue. Others just have a rage inside that requires them to destroy. Instead of kicking over gravestones and painting swastikas on synagogues, they create viruses that eat hard drives. Others, in fact, mean no harm. There are lots of benign viruses that let you know they are there, but do no harm. Whole other books have been written about the psychology of the hacker mindset and culture. It is enough to know that these folks exist and that their produce is circulating cyberspace.

The practical answer to where viruses come from is to state that they come from contact with other infected computers, much as we humans pick up colds, strep throat, AIDS, and other communicable diseases from each other. If you place a certified virus-free computer in a vault and never copy another file onto the hard disk, you will never find a virus or Trojan horse on that computer. Fortunately, few computers are so abused. It is the exchange of data and programs that makes life worth living for the average personal computer. Just as humans need physical contact with other humans to reach their full potential, computers require interaction with other computers in the form of files copied or transferred.

Major Sources of Virus and Trojan Programs

The major ways in which a computer virus can find its way to your computer is quite predictable, really. There are three main methods of transmission.

Pirate software

It is really hard for some people to grasp the concept of intellectual property. They hold a floppy disk in their hand and see only a dollar value. No matter that a single floppy disk is quite capable of holding the sum total output of a programmer's labors for a year or more. People who have no regard for the cost of producing software are quite likely to be willing to copy anything illegally. Why pay hundreds of dollars when you can copy five diskettes in just a few minutes for about $2.50?

Aside from the obvious moral teachings about copyright infringement, there are hackers out there ready and willing to exploit the greed of humans who think they are getting something for nothing. Bulletin boards and Web pages dedicated to the dissemination of free copies of commercial software spring up and die off like weeds. It is not uncommon for these copies of pirated software to be infected with a virus.

Some people collect pirated copies of software like other people collect coins. If they see it and it's free, they copy it and stick it into their collection. In a lot of cases, they don't have any possible use for the software they steal. They just want the complete collection. They install the software just to make sure of what they have and then put the disks aside. Sooner or later, of course, a virus ends up in the collection.

On disk

There have been a couple of rare instances where software companies have been victimized and actually sold software with viruses on the factory distribution disks. Much more common, however, is the passing of diskette from user to user.

Some boot sector viruses can infect a computer system only if the computer is booted from an infected floppy disk. Although, with the decline of DOS, they are becoming less common, many game programs work properly only if you boot the computer from the game's floppy disk. Multipartite (viruses that use a combination of attacking methods) and file infector viruses only require you to run a program that is infected.

Piracy as big business

If you have ever been to Hong Kong or mainland China, you know that pirated software is big business. Despite recent crackdowns by authorities, you can find just about any program you want in the marketplaces for less than $10 U.S. Legion are the unhappy tourists who found a bargain in the Golden Arcade of Hong Kong too hard to resist. When they installed their ten dollar copy of WordPerfect they got an extra free bonus program that hid out for a while, then ate their hard disk for breakfast.

Microsoft Corporation recently announced a joint venture with the Chinese government to develop and standardize a Chinese language version of Windows. Part of the negotiations in reaching that pact involved getting the Chinese government to begin taking intellectual property rights seriously. In mid-1995, American newscasts and newspapers all covered stories about Chinese government crackdowns of pirate operations. Ironically, many of the worst purveyors of pirated copies of programs in China have been government-owned or subsidized companies.

Shareware and freeware

Major commercial software programs number in the hundreds. Shareware and freeware titles number in the thousands, if not the tens of thousands. Shareware, for those readers who are unfamiliar with alternative software distribution, is a sales model for selling software that allows a prospective customer to have a look at and test software before buying it.

In the shareware model, a software author distributes copies of the product to bulletin boards and online services in the hope that a potential user will download the program, try it out, like it, then buy it. In some cases the distributed version is crippled by removing one or two key features. Other shareware authors prefer to place time bombs in the code so the program quits working after 30 days or so. When the user registers and pays his money, he gets the full-featured version.

Shareware titles run the entire gamut of computing and human nature. Some shareware programs are so dreadfully bad that you have to wonder why the author thought someone else would want to subject himself to them. Others are world class quality and fill a need not addressed by the big software companies. WinZip, a shareware program written by Nico Mak, puts a Windows face on working with ZIP files. JASC's Paint Shop Pro began life as an application to translate between graphic formats. It has grown into a graphic editor that has most of the popular features you'll find in Corel PhotoPaint or Adobe PhotoShop.

Because the shareware distribution model mostly bypasses the need for fancy packaging and advertising, most are modestly priced affairs that rely on online documentation instead of printed manuals. Often when you call for technical support for shareware programs, you will reach the authors themselves. Who could explain features better?

Freeware is similar to shareware, the single exception being that freeware authors don't ask you to pay them money for the program. One thing to note is that freeware does not mean public domain. Freeware authors generally tend to retain copyrights to their work, mostly as a protection against hackers who would turn their works into disguises for Trojan or virus programs.

Computer users commonly exchange data and programs with each other by using floppy disks. If you have a virus on your computer and you copy a program to disk and give it to friends or coworkers, they will infect their system the first time the program is run, unless they are following a rigid antivirus strategy and checking every file that comes onto their computer with an up-to-date antivirus program.

Downloading files

Ten years ago very few computers had modems or network connections. Today a fast fax modem is almost de rigueur. In an ever more connected computing environment, the door is open ever wider to the dissemination of viruses and Trojan programs. The convenience of ZIP files that compress and archive multiple files into a single file makes downloading programs and data to your hard disk simple, quick, and in some cases dangerous. The level of exposure you have in downloading files varies by source. Some system administrators are conscientious as can be, checking each file for viruses before making it available for downloading, while others will take just about anything that has been uploaded to them and make it available without testing.

Basic Truths and Myths

Sorting out fact from fiction when it comes to viruses and Trojan horse programs can be a daunting task. On one hand, some "computer experts" claim that the average person's chances of picking up a viral infection are less than being trampled by stampeding camels in New York City. On the other hand, other "computer experts" and the news media warn about just how commonplace these vermin are becoming. What's a computer user to do?

As the old saying goes, knowledge is power. If you are acquainted with the issues involved in virus transmission, you can better defend yourself against the nasty little beggars. Take a few minutes to go over the next few sections to acquaint yourself with the issues.

Viruses only spread via COM and EXE files...NOT!

Wrong! About 80 percent of all virus infections are of the boot sector type. Still, file infector viruses are not limited only to COM and EXE files. There are any number of other file types commonly found on DOS and Windows systems that can be targeted, as discussed later in this chapter.

It is common, and sometimes required, for special-purpose executable code to have file extensions other than COM and EXE. Two boot files that supply executable code to DOS computer systems are MSDOS.SYS and IO.SYS (IBMIO.SYS in PC-DOS variants). These files are loaded and run during boot up. Device drivers often have SYS extensions, and BIN extensions are also common. In order to get around the 640K barrier of DOS, applications often use OVL or OVR files to store overlay code that can be read into memory only when needed.

Windows makes heavy use of dynamic link libraries having the extension DLL. Most of Windows' internal functions are supplied as dynamic link libraries. DLL files are meant to be shared by more than one application, which makes them convenient targets.

> ## The Good Times virus hoax
>
> The Good Times virus hoax is a good example of how some computer users can be stirred up out of all proportion to the actual dangers involved. Somewhere around the end of 1994, messages began appearing on the Internet and on commercial online services about the Good Times virus. The gist of these messages was a warning to people that a new and ultra-vicious virus had been released into the wild that made Michelangelo and Natas seem tame.
>
> The strangest part of the claim was that you could infect your system simply by reading e-mail messages infected with the virus. When I first saw the message, I personally got a short laugh out of the idea and moved on, never realizing that thousands of uneducated computer users would take this idea seriously.
>
> Most e-mail is delivered from system to system as plain old DOS text (ASCII). To infect anything, a virus has to be capable of executing program code. Try as you will, you cannot get DOS text to execute anything. It can only be displayed or printed.
>
> Thousands of unsophisticated computer users automatically deleted, without reading, any e-mail message that had Good Times in the title of the message for fear that they would be the next target. Of course, in erasing these messages, they never got to read the replies from experienced computer users who did their best to debunk the Good Times virus as a hoax. All of this would be laughable if it didn't point out so graphically the vulnerability of many computer users with low technical expertise, who end up at the mercy of anyone who seems to know what he is talking about.
>
> Of course, the story doesn't end there because just a few months later a real file infector virus named Good Times was released (probably from Australia) into the wild. To make matters worse, the real virus helps to perpetuate the hoax because the program code contains comments that say in effect that loading a message with the title Good Times executes the virus which infects the system, so the reader of the code should call all his friends and warn them against the Good Times virus.

Recently a new type of virus was discovered that uses macro code to infect systems. Commercial software applications like Microsoft Word often have built in programming languages called macros that are used to automate tasks. Recently the Word Prank virus, which is written in Word Basic (the Microsoft Word macro language), was discovered. Loading a Word file that contains the Prank macro infects your NORMAL.DOT file, which in turn infects any other documents you open. Prank is benign, but it is a pain in the neck because normal antivirus software doesn't check for it. For more information on the Prank Macro virus, check the Microsoft sections on the commercial online services, or visit http://www.microsoft.com/.

Any file capable of loading and executing program code is potentially a target to become a host for a virus.

You don't have to boot from a floppy to be infected

You don't actually have to boot from a floppy for it to deliver a virus to your hard disk. The reason is that even non-bootable floppy disks have a program written on their boot sector.

When you format floppy disks with the /S parameter to make them system (bootable) disks, a program is written on the boot sector that causes the system files written on the disk to be loaded so that DOS can be booted. Early versions of DOS actually reserved space on the disk for the system files so that even if you erased the boot files, the available disk space remained the same.

If you leave a non-system disk in the A: drive when you power up the computer, DOS will by default attempt to boot up from that floppy. When this happens, the small program DOS places in the boot sector executes and presents you with the "Non-system disk or disk error" message. If that program is infected, you will pass the infection along to your hard disk.

According to some experts, this is the most common way viruses are spread. The solution is simple: never power up your computer without checking the floppy drive and removing any disk that may be in the drive.

Viruses are spread by downloading files

True, several classes of file infector viruses can be brought into your system by downloading software from bulletin boards, network servers, and commercial online services. The operative word is can. In fact, the most common viruses, such as Michelangelo and Stoned, can be spread to your system only by booting from an infected floppy disk.

Many games designed to run on DOS-compatible PCs don't, in fact, use DOS. Instead, they boot up from a floppy disk into customized environments. The reason for this aversion to DOS is simple: DOS is relatively slow in such critical areas as displaying graphics and accessing disks. Game programmers long ago discovered that the best way to get maximum performance is to take over the hardware completely, bypassing DOS altogether.

A cleverly-written virus needs only to be booted from floppy disk in any environment to write stuff to the hard disk. After all, the hardware doesn't change, and you still have to talk to the processor in its own language. You can avoid the vast majority of viruses simply by never using a floppy disk you didn't create yourself or purchase from a reputable store to boot your computer.

Viruses can hide in data files and unused areas of disks

A commonly held myth is that viruses can hide in unused portions of the hard disk. To fully appreciate how someone, even experienced users, might buy into this old wives' tale, you need to grasp a single technical concept.

Your computer's hard disk is divided into tracks and sectors where data can be written. Each sector is of equal storage capacity, the size of which depends on the physical configuration of the hard disk. The minimum number of bytes that can be reserved to store a new file is called the allocation unit. On a typical floppy disk, files are written in 4K chunks because the allocation unit of a floppy is 4K. If the file is only 500 bytes in length, 3.5K is wasted

As the size of a disk increases, so does the allocation unit. Many 1+GB hard disks have an allocation unit of 16 or 32K. Thus a 1K file resides in a sector of the hard disk that is perhaps 32K in length, wasting 31K. The reason allocation unit sizes are so large on big hard disks is that most files are going to be larger than just one or 2K, and chopping up a hard disk into 4K allocation units would make the size of the directory table unmanageable.

Several factors make using this wasted space on hard disks impractical as a method for hiding virus code. First, you still need executable code to infect the system, and code written in these areas would never be run. Also, this wasted space is actually reserved for the expansion of the file written in that sector. If your file increases from 3K to 20K, it will still fit into the single sector where it was originally written. File systems don't check to see if anything is written in the dead space; they simply overwrite anything previously written there. Hiding virus code in such a dead space would make it extremely vulnerable to being overwritten.

Defragmenting a hard disk rearranges the sectors where files are written. Anything written in the dead spaces would be routinely overwritten. Finally, using a disk compression utility like Stacker or DriveSpace eliminates this dead space because your files are compressed and written as one single file. Thus, the dead spaces between files that would otherwise exist are no longer available.

An infected hard disk is a dead hard disk

This one is only half a myth. One of the most important features of a virus, from the virus author's point of view, is that it remain undetected long enough to spread to other computers. For this reason, most viruses have a fairly long incubation time before they deliver their payload. During this time you have ample opportunity to use an antivirus program to discover and eradicate the virus.

If you wait long enough (and virus authors know that most users don't regularly scan their computers), the virus will react to its environment and deliver its payload. If the virus isn't benign, that's when you end up with a dead hard disk.

Dead is perhaps too strong a term, since viruses don't actually destroy the disk itself. They are limited to destroying the data the hard disk contains. Whether you lose your data entirely depends on your backup habits.

Tip

Computer geeks like me are always harping about having a good backup, but ironically any recent backups you may have probably contain the virus infection as well. It isn't enough to simply reformat the disk drive and restore your backup from tape. You will also need to spend some time with a good antivirus program to disinfect the newly restored hard disk in order to assure that you won't be going through the same routine in just a few days.

A Veritable Menagerie of Vermin

We humans are biological creatures, and the computer systems we have designed often fit nicely into biological metaphors. Programmers often speak of their creations as though they have a life of their own. The metaphor also extends to the jargon used to describe computer situations. In no other subset of computer jargon does the biology metaphor apply more than it does when describing software designed to attack computers and their data randomly. Words like *infect, virus, hygiene,* and *inoculate* have become part of the lexicon.

There are a goodly number of terms used to describe destructive software. Most of them have links to the animal kingdom. In the spirit of "know thy enemy," here are a few of the most common terms and their meanings:

> **Bacterium.** A program that propagates itself by creating copies of itself that get passed along to other users and computers. Bacterium are close relatives of the virus.
>
> **Bug.** A bug is a defect in a program that causes it to do something unexpected. While seldom malicious, bugs can often be destructive. Programs written in low level languages like C or assembly language are especially prone to destructive bugs because errors in addressing memory can result in overwriting data stored in areas usually reserved by the operating system. Understand that C and ASM are not bad tools, it is the mistakes of programmers that can make these things happen in a sloppily written program.
>
> **Mockingbird.** A program designed to intercept communications, usually login transactions, which looks and behaves just like the program the user thinks is running. All the while, each transaction is stored for later pickup. Stealing IDs and passwords in this manner has lately become known as spoofing. A mockingbird is related to a Trojan horse in that the user never suspects the program is not what it appears to be. A mockingbird differs from a Trojan in that no destructive behavior is programmed into the mockingbird in order that it remain undetected.

A bug by any other name

Commander Grace Hopper headed some of the U.S. Navy's initial research into using computers. Legend has it that one day, while testing an early computer made up of vacuum tubes and miles of wire, the computer malfunctioned. Hopper dispatched one of her technicians to find the problem. A few minutes later he returned to report that a big waterbug had tried to crawl between two contacts, with the result that the computer had malfunctioned, and the bug was now in a far, far better place. A log entry was made to reflect that there was a bug in the computer, and the name stuck as a catchall term for computer malfunctions, especially those due to programming errors.

Rabbit. A program designed specifically to waste the resources of the victim computer. Similar in construction to bacterium, rabbits replicate themselves in order to use up all available CPU time, disk space, or some other resource in an effort to degrade performance or render the computer inoperative. Rabbits are usually found only in mainframe environments, but PCs are not immune to such attacks and you should at least be aware that PC rabbits are possible.

Trojan Horse. A term first used by an MIT hacker named Dan Edwards (later turned National Security Agency official). A Trojan horse is a program that appears to be doing one thing while doing something else entirely. Examples would include programs that claim to sort files, optimize the computer's environment, or play a game, that when run erase files, reformat hard disks, destroy hard disk partition tables, and so on. One extreme case was a program for Macintosh users that claimed to be an antivirus program, and a dummied-up "version" of PKZip.

Virus. The term virus, as applied to computers, was coined by Fred Cohen at the University of Southern California. The word *virus* comes from Latin and means poison. A computer virus is a program that attempts to write itself onto computer disks without being detected. It is therefore secretly loaded each time the computer is started from an infected disk. There are literally thousands of viruses in circulation, although many are copies or slight alterations of others. While many viruses are benign, in the sense that they are non-destructive, others are extremely hazardous to the contents of infected disks and sometimes even to the hardware itself.

Worm. The term *worm* is derived from a science fiction novel, *The Shockwave Riders,* by John Brunner, which describes programs that migrate from one system to another as tapeworms. Worms were originally designed to find other computers on a network with spare resources to enable distributed computing, or to perform cataloging and research. Some worms, however, are designed to clandestinely crack sensitive information like password lists and report back to its originator. Worm technology can be quite helpful when used properly. For example, the World Wide Web Worm builds a searchable index of Web sites using a variant on the worm technology.

The Internet Worm

The Internet Worm is probably the most famous computer security incident of all time. For millions it was the first mention they ever heard of a mysterious thing called the Internet.

Around 7:30 on the evening of Wednesday, November 2, 1988, a twenty-three year-old graduate student at Cornell University released an experimental worm program onto the Internet. As an exercise in computer science, its results were a mixed bag. The program worked all too well as it replicated itself around the country in a matter of hours. Since it affected only Sun 3 and Vax systems running versions of UNIX descended from the Berkeley flavor of the operating system, many computers on the Internet remained immune. Those that were affected showed strange entries in message log files, and files were written to directories on some machines. Not only were university computers affected, but similar machines on a low-level military network connected to the Internet were also infected.

While the worm program appeared not to be designed to do harm, a flaw in its programming caused it to reproduce wildly. So wildly in fact that the worm's major consequence was the spawning of many copies of itself. These multiple copies used so many resources that infected computers became overloaded and crashed. In all, some 6,000 computer systems were impacted.

By Thursday morning a group of techies at the Computer Systems Research Group at Berkeley had figured out a way of neutralizing the worm. Shortly thereafter another group of folks at Purdue University discovered an even easier method of disarming the worm. Unfortunately, many system administrators failed to get the message because they had disconnected themselves from the Internet to prevent further infection.

The worm, as you might expect, shook the Internet community to its roots as the press had a field day reporting the story all out of proportion to its actual significance. Within a few days the worm was completely eradicated. The major security flaws that the worm program exploited were patched up and the Internet returned to near normalcy, with a lot of system administrators the wiser for the experience.

Shortly after Robert Tappan Morris, Jr. was discovered as the author of the worm, he was investigated by Cornell University. On May 16, 1989, he was suspended for the remainder of the school year for violating the university's Code of Academic Integrity. On July 27, 1989, the *Boston Herald* reported that the United States Department of Justice gave Morris the ignominious honor of being the first person charged with violating the Computer Fraud and Abuse Act of 1986. This law prohibits breaking into a federal computer network and preventing authorized use of the system.

(continued)

(continued)

In a twist worthy of a television soap opera, it was revealed that Morris' father was none other than Robert Tappan Morris Sr., Chief Scientist at the National Computer Security Center, a division of the National Security Agency. A heck of a hacker in his own days at Bell Labs in the 1950s, Morris Sr. has been reported to be one of the inventors of a computer game that used self-replicating programs considered to be the prototypes for today's worms and viruses. Named Darwin, the game's foundations evolved into Core War, a mildly popular diversion for modern hackers. Dad had testified to Congress only a few years earlier of the need to deglamorize hackers, likening hacking to stealing a car and joyriding.

During the trial, held before Federal District Judge Howard G. Munson, Morris Jr. took the stand and testified that a bug in his programming code caused the worm to run out of control, crippling the Internet computers. Morris's lawyer, Thomas Guidoboni, argued that Morris never intended to prevent authorized use of any computer, although Morris' actual intent in releasing the worm was never disclosed. The prosecution introduced evidence that the worm used several methods for gaining user passwords on infected systems in order to further propagate, and that Morris' code contained attempts at camouflage to make the worm difficult to detect. Evidence also showed that Morris launched the program from a computer at MIT, making it appear that the program had originated at U.C. Berkeley. Several earlier versions of the worm code were found in Morris' Cornell computer accounts, and comments embedded within that code used words like *break-in* and *steal*.

It took the jury all of six hours deliberation to find Morris guilty on a single felony count. On May 4, 1990, Judge Munson, declaring that federal sentencing guidelines did not apply to this case since fraud wasn't involved, sentenced Morris to three years probation, 400 hours of community service, a $10,000 fine and administrative costs.

In March of 1991 a three-judge panel of the U.S. Court of Appeals for the 2nd Circuit in New York upheld Morris' conviction. Despite arguments that because Morris had legitimate accounts at Cornell, he had authorization to transfer documents and programs within the network, the panel denied the appeal, stating simply that Morris had exceeded his authorization.

What, Me Worry?

So there you are going through your buddy's floppy disk collection looking for interesting utilities. You might be browsing through the files in the download section of your local bulletin board, or even cruising the Web. You see a file description of a program that looks like it will do something that you'd really like to have done on your system. Watch out because you just entered the danger zone.

If you are one of those people who believes that locking a car only invites thieves, pass on to the next chapter. Everyone else should pay close attention. One of these days you are going to meet up with a program similar to some of the nasties I want to tell you about. The Trojans and viruses listed in the following pages are by no means a complete list of the vermin you may encounter in your digital travels. Rather, the programs listed are meant as a representative cross section of what you'll find in the wild. To give you a complete list would be impossible, since new viruses are being released by the dozens each month. That is why you should update your virus software on a regular basis.

Trojan horses

The Trojan horse is a program that promises to do something useful for you, but when run does something else entirely. Usually Trojans are crude affairs. It takes much less technical skill to hack together a program that actually runs FORMAT than it does to create an arguably elegant polymorphic stealth virus. To create a Trojan program, all you need is a rudimentary knowledge of the DOS DEBUG command or Microsoft Access, and that special savoir faire it takes to savage another human being's property.

One of the most insidious aspects of a Trojan horse program is the misdirection and sleight of hand used to suck users into running the code. Heck, the Trojan may even do what it promises to do. One Trojan, which I have not personally seen, reportedly plays you a video of Madonna while it is busy underneath trashing your hard disk.

When dealing with the possibility of Trojan horse programs, the watchwords are definitely *caveat emptor* ("buyer beware"), despite the fact that most Trojans purport to be freeware, which you don't have to buy. Once caught, you will know it immediately, since your computer system will be rendered helpless with no warning.

Let me introduce you to a few of the more common Trojans.

PKZIP300B

PKZip, distributed by PKWare, is the most widely-used compression and archiving program in the world. The PK stands for Phil Katz, a dark haired, mild mannered middle aged gentleman who ranks among the pioneers of the shareware industry. His products over the years have become widely respected as world-class software. He wouldn't intentionally harm someone's data if you put a gun to his head.

So why would someone choose to put a file into general circulation that purports to be a new version of the old classic? Only because lots of people will download and install it without blinking an eye. For the second time in the last five years, some lowlife has done Phil a dirty. A file has recently been making the Internet and bulletin board circuit claiming to be version 3.00 of PKZip. The file is being circulated in both EXE and ZIP formats. Try running it, and you will have your PC's hard drive trashed in about ten seconds. Now you know why I came on so strong about having a good backup.

ChinaTalk

ChinaTalk is a program that claims to be a female-voiced MacinTalk sound driver that will give your speech synthesizer a gender change. In actuality, ChinaTalk is a system-level Trojan that erases directories from the hard disk.

Cookies

Next to Famous Amos and the Pillsbury Doughboy, perhaps the most famous purveyor of cookies is Mrs. Fields. The Cookies program promises to tell you the secret to making cookies as good as Mrs. Fields. However, the only thing about to get baked is the file allocation tables of your PC's hard disk.

FontFinder

FontFinder is another Macintosh-based Trojan that proves that the greatest amount of imagination that usually goes into a Trojan horse program is the pitch the author thinks up to get you to try it. Instead of giving you a list of the fonts used in a word processor document, FontFinder predictably erases directories on your hard disk.

NVP

At least the author of this Macintosh Trojan had a semi-original idea. When run, the program modifies the System file to omit vowels as you type. Clever, no?

The NVP Trojan is sometimes disguised as a program entitled New Look, a legitimate program that enables users to customize their screen display. In System 7, the Mac equivalent of DOS, the system file is modified so that when the system is restarted, you cannot type vowels. Fortunately, this Trojan doesn't trash your hard disk.

Computer viruses

The real glamour-pusses of the hacker underground are computer viruses. They have a certain appeal to vandals. Unlike a Trojan horse program, a virus attempts to lay dormant in your system undetected. Like some grotesque product of evolution, the virus' dormancy is a survival mechanism. It uses that time to reproduce and pass the infection along to other computers through your unwitting cooperation.

The way most viruses operate is to modify your computer's system files so that the virus gets loaded every time your computer is booted. Some viruses target your system's boot files, while others specialize in infecting EXE, COM, and other program files on your system. Whenever you copy files to floppy disk, or send infected files across a modem, a copy of the virus is transferred to a new disk where the virus will attempt to install itself.

The actions a virus is programmed to perform are collectively called the payload. A virus is usually designed to deliver its payload when some triggering event occurs. Whether that trigger is Michelangelo's birthday, Friday the 13th, or some other date, or some internal condition of the computer, such as the disk becoming 90 percent full, is left to the imagination of the virus author.

> **Beware the Jabberwocky**
>
> The unveiling of the Microsoft Network in August of 1995 presents an interesting new avenue for the delivery of Trojan programs to unsuspecting computer users. Messages delivered via MSN are written in Rich Text Format (RTF), which is a standard that includes text formatting commands, and also allows for attaching separate documents (pictures, ZIP files, and so on) that show up in the message as icons.
>
> Because Windows is a disk-intensive environment to begin with, most Windows users are tolerant of their system's churning the hard disk for a few seconds before anything visual appears onscreen. This short few seconds is all it takes for a Trojan to make hash out of your hard disk.
>
> It is a simple matter to send an MSN user a message with a Trojan file attached. The minute the user double-clicks on that cute icon, bang! If you are a Microsoft Network subscriber, you need to learn now what experienced Internet users, who have had the ability to attach files to messages for a long time, already know. If someone you don't know sends you a message with an attachment, be suspicious.
>
> In a related vein, Microsoft's Internet Explorer also allows shortcuts to files on the Internet. These files can be launched as soon as they are downloaded. Users should avoid doing so, however, as you should always check a file with an antivirus program before running it.

A great deal of technical innovation has gone into the development of modern computer viruses. Still, most viruses are imitations and knockoffs of other viruses. There are enough places on the Internet and on bulletin boards around the world where programming source code for creating virus programs can be found that even inexperienced programmers/hackers can find the recipe and cook up a variant new virus.

Virus classifications

Viruses can be classified by their behavior into distinct species. The following list documents the most common virus types:

- **Boot Sector.** A boot sector virus attempts to replace or infect the portion of a floppy or hard disk normally reserved only for the operating system to store its startup files. Keep in mind that even DOS disks formatted as non-system disks still contain a boot sector that runs a small program to announce to the user that the disk is not bootable. Boot sector viruses are particularly insidious because they are loaded into memory every time the computer is started up, giving them the best opportunity to monitor every process the computer performs. They are the most efficient propagators, able to spread themselves to new disks at will.

(2) **File Infectors.** In an effort to remain undetected, many viruses will attempt to infect executable files. Normally their preferred targets are EXE and COM files, the files used to deliver program code to your system. With the increased popularity of Windows, however, some virus authors are also attacking dynamic link library (DLL) files, which are commonly used to share program code between two or more Windows programs. File infector viruses tend to propagate more slowly than boot sector viruses because the infected file must be run in order for the virus to propagate.

One requirement for propagation is that the program files that viruses infect must be executed in order for the virus to be loaded into memory, where it can go to work. That's why, among early DOS PC file infectors, the COMMAND.COM file was the most common target. Since COMMAND.COM is always loaded at boot-up on a DOS system, a successful virus will also be loaded every time.

(3) **Multipartite Viruses.** Some viruses use both the boot sector and file infection methods to infect a computer system. While this gives a virus detection program a double shot at identifying a virus, the strategy is often effective in propagating the virus very quickly.

(4) **Polymorphic Viruses.** Now that the Iron Curtain has fallen, Bulgaria has become one of the virus capitals of the world. I suppose it's better than shooting at the Pope, but it's not a reputation that is likely to endear you to the computing community. Reportedly, virus construction is taught in several Bulgarian universities as part of the computer science curriculum. Out of this cauldron of activity comes the Bulgarian Dark Avenger's mutating engine, which has been published in various locations. The result is a new breed of virus that mimics biological retroviruses, like HIV or Hong Kong B, by mutating each time it replicates in an effort to stay one step ahead of antivirus software.

(5) **Stealth Virus.** One of the ways antivirus software identifies the presence of a virus is with a checksum, short for summation check. Originally used in communications, a checksum is the result of a mathematical algorithm used to ensure that the length of a file received agrees with the length of the original copy. A number of antivirus programs create lists of checksums based on the files on your disk. Stealth viruses employ a number of techniques to mask their presence by falsifying their actual checksum value in an attempt to evade detection.

(6) **Systemic Viruses.** In an attempt to avoid detection, systemic viruses target parts of the operating system other than the boot sector of disks. Common targets include DOS's file allocation table (the table of contents for your disk), partition tables, device drivers, and system files like IO.SYS and COMMAND.COM.

Some major (virus) players

As you can see, there are a number of methods used by virus authors to infect computer disks and avoid detection. Unlike the comparatively crude Trojan horse category of vermin software, viruses can be quite masterful in their use of technology.

Some computer viruses are arguable works of software art that rank with VisiCalc and Windows NT in their quality of innovation. You may have no respect for the purpose of a virus program, yet still feel compelled to tip your hat to the knowledge and expertise it takes to create such a program. With that thought in mind, let me introduce you to a few of the neighbors.

Stoned. The Stoned virus, also known as the New Zealand virus, is one of the most common infectors found in the wild (a term used by virus experts to mean general unfettered circulation). Stoned has many variants. Computers infected with Stoned will sometimes pause during the boot process to announce that "your computer is stoned." Contrary to popular legend, this virus does not display the message "legalize marijuana," although that phrase can be found as a character string within the source code.

The original Stoned virus was apparently designed to be harmless, but due to a design flaw, 1.2MB floppy disks with more than 96 files in the root directory are likely to be damaged. Stoned is a systemic virus that resides in the partition boot record instead of the more commonly used boot sector.

Flame. The Flame virus is a cousin to the Stoned virus. Flame is a typical boot sector virus that attempts to replace the master boot record of your system. It documents the current month when it infects your system, and when the virus detects that the month has changed on your PC's internal clock, it displays multicolored flames on screen while overwriting your master boot record. The Angelina variant contains stealth algorithms to make it harder to detect and contains the message "Greetings for Angelina!!! /by Garfield/ Zielona Gora." Zielona Gora is a town in Poland, where, assumedly, Garfield pines away for his Angelina. Love makes people do strange things, doesn't it?

Jerusalem. Also known as the Israeli virus because of its geographical point of origin, Jerusalem is one of the most common and oldest viruses in circulation, with a large number of variant mutations. Jerusalem is a file infector that targets EXE and COM files. Earlier versions of Jerusalem contained a bug in the code that caused EXE files to be infected multiple times, bloating the size of the target file and making detection fairly easy. On every Friday the 13th, Jerusalem activates and deletes any program files run that day. Another portion of the Jerusalem payload sets a timer that causes the system to slow down a half hour after an infected program is run.

Some versions of Jerusalem also cause the bottom of the screen to scroll up two lines, but this is a surefire tip-off of infection, and this behavior has been deleted from later Jerusalem versions. Jerusalem is probably itself a variant of the Suriv virus that produced the slowdown effect only 30 seconds after an infected program was run, making detection much easier. Another variant of Jerusalem is called the Sunday virus because it activates if the current date is a Sunday and demands to know why you are working so hard.

Breasts. Also known as Shehas and Titz, Breasts is a shoddy bit of workmanship that is so buggy that it seems unable to deliver its payload. Designed — if that's the right word — to be a standard boot sector virus, it contains the character string "Virginia/Shirley — She has breasts, yes she has!!!" Neither the message nor the execution is very mature, yet it is still in circulation.

CODE-1. CODE-1 is a Macintosh virus that is designed to activate if your computer is booted on October 31 (Halloween). It seems that the virus was intended to be non-destructive, since its payload is designed only to rename your hard disk to Trent Saburo. Because it is a combination file infector and systemic virus, and the interaction between the two parts is symbiotic, infected systems may become erratic and crash.

The CODE-1 virus infects both the System file and any executable files that have their first jump table entry in CODE 0 pointing to CODE 1, thus the name. If an application is run on a Mac with an infected System file, the executable file will be infected, while running an infected program file will attack and infect the System file.

Michelangelo. Currently the most notorious virus in circulation, thanks to the extreme press coverage it received in 1995, the Michelangelo virus activates on March 6th to celebrate the birthday of its namesake. Its payload overwrites the first 17 sectors of the first 256 tracks of the boot disk. Since the boot disk is usually a hard disk, the result is catastrophic for any data stored on the disk because the file allocation table and directory structures are erased.

Due to the publicity surrounding the Michelangelo virus, many computer users actually made a point of not turning their systems on last March 6th for fear of losing their data. Add the total dollars of revenue missed by people who got no work done that day to the normal costs associated with viral clean-up, and you can see that Michelangelo is an expensive infection.

Natas. Natas is Satan spelled backwards, and it is a real devil of a virus because it is a boot sector, file infector, and a stealth virus all rolled into one. Most common in the United States and Mexico, the Natas virus has a 1 in 512 chance of activating whenever an infected program is run. As a special gift to programmers, Natas will also activate if it detects the presence of a debugger, a software tool used to find flaws in programs under development.

nVir. According to Symantec, makers of antivirus software, nVir is probably the most contagious of all Macintosh viruses. There are two major strains of nVir, A and B, as well as nine known variants. First detected in Europe almost a decade ago, nVir infects both the System file and any applications it can find.

nVir delivers its payload after every 8 to 16 reboots, or after 4 to 8 infected applications are run. Thankfully, about all nVir does to the system is to make the speaker beep. One variant of nVir, however, can launch MacinTalk to say "Don't panic" instead of a simple beep.

Safe Hex

The biological metaphor for viruses goes well beyond mere names. The metaphor can be extended as a parallel of the AIDS epidemic, which is why one anonymous wag coined the term *safe hex* to describe computer prophylactics. Just as a condom provides a physical barrier that is highly effective in preventing the transmission of HIV in humans, good antivirus software is also highly effective in preventing the infection of your system by computer viruses. Kindly note that "highly effective" does not mean immune. Nothing in this life is 100 percent, with the single exception of death. Everything else, it seems, is variable.

How antivirus software works

The best way to protect yourself from viruses is to regularly run an antivirus program. Antivirus programs are designed to check out the memory and files in your system and look for viral signatures. A viral signature is some unique characteristic of a virus program that betrays its presence on a computer system. Antivirus programs typically have a database of virus signatures that gets updated on a periodic basis. When the antivirus program is run, it inspects your computer system and compares what it finds against the database of signatures. Most good antivirus software uses other techniques in addition to finding a match to a signature in its database. Such software will attempt to detect viruses that may use methods similar to a known virus, even when the new virus has not yet been specifically identified. Still, most viruses are detected by finding a specific match in the database. If it finds a match, the antivirus program will attempt to clean out the virus it has found.

It is important to keep your signature database up to date. Most vendors of antivirus software make update files available to users on company sponsored bulletin boards, online services, and via home pages on the World Wide Web on the Internet.

There are lots of companies that make antivirus software for both PCs and the Macs. To get more information on specific antivirus products, check out your local bulletin board, the Internet, or online services such as CompuServe, AOL, Prodigy, and MSN.

Using antivirus software

There are three main ways in which antivirus applications are run. Many virus scanners can perform all three methods. The first method is to perform a scan for viruses at boot up by placing a command to launch the antivirus application in AUTOEXEC.BAT. While this method is effective, it increases the length of time it takes to boot up the computer, and impatient users are likely to remove the command. The advantage to boot up scanning is that it is always done automatically.

The second method is to perform a system scan for viruses whenever the user launches the antivirus program manually. This method can be just as effective as scanning every time the computer starts up, provided scans are done with the same religious fervor with which backups are performed. The disadvantage to this method is that it may be weeks or months between scans if the user is lax. If you have Microsoft Plus!, the companion package to Windows 95, installed, you can use the System Agent utility to run periodic virus scans automatically.

Figure 3-1 shows a virus scan under Windows 95 being performed by McAfee's VirusScan software. As you can see in the figure, the McAfee utility has the same general appearance as the Windows 95 Find utility. If viruses are found, corrective action is taken to rid the system of whatever virus has been found.

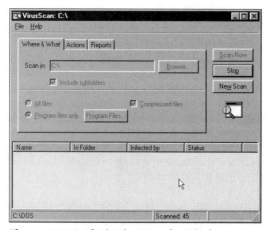

Figure 3-1: McAfee's VirusScan for Windows 95 looks and acts a lot like the Windows Find utility.

The third method of scanning for virus infection is to scan each file you download individually. If you get into the habit of scanning each program you download before using it, you will not need to manually scan your entire system as often as you might otherwise do to keep infections out. Figure 3-2 shows how WinZip, a great shareware program for managing ZIP, ARC, LHZ, and other archive formats, can be used to scan newly downloaded files.

With McAfee VirusScan you can also right-click any file or folder in Explorer. Choose Scan for Virus from the context menu that appears to start VirusScan working. WinZip will automatically create a command line to start VirusScan so that only the archive you are working with is scanned, instead of a whole drive or folder.

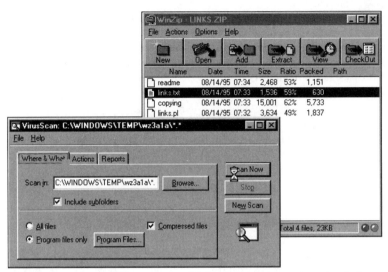

Figure 3-2: Using WinZip to scan a ZIP file that has been downloaded.

Identifying virus infections

The best way to identify virus infections on your hard disk is to use one of the popular antivirus programs. There are, however, sometimes indications that you may have a virus infection just waiting to deliver its payload on your system.

Keep in mind that viruses need an incubation time to spread out to other disks and systems before they deliver their payload. Otherwise they would quickly die off. Here are a few things to watch for:

Changes in file sizes. File infector viruses will almost invariably change the file size of infected files. In order to remain undetected, the virus cannot change the function of the infected file in a noticeable way. That means none of the original code can be removed. If code were removed, the target program file either wouldn't operate properly, or some obscure feature wouldn't work because needed working code was replaced by viral code. If you notice that a particular file, especially COM and EXE files, has grown by a few kilobytes, you should immediately scan your disks with antivirus software.

Changes in interrupt vector mapping. Don't feel badly if you just said, "What?" Most readers will, too. This is a symptom that only power users and programmers will be immediately familiar with. DOS stores program code in memory that can be utilized by programs whenever they need some basic operating system service. These functions are called *interrupts* because they stop all other processing while they do their job, displaying a graphic screen, writing to the disk, or performing some other chore. The term *vector* means that there is a value that can be used to trigger the interrupt. One of the features of DOS is that memory-resident *Terminate and Stay Resident* (TSR) software can monitor interrupts and change the way DOS reacts to calls for system services. It is not uncommon for viruses to *hook* (monitor) interrupts to keep an eye on requests for services, and when a service is called on, to take over the machine and deliver the payload. If you detect new or unusual mapping of interrupts with tools like Spy or other memory scanning programs, scan the system for viruses.

Unexplained changes in available RAM. To be effective in spreading its infection, a virus has to be in memory, which will inevitably reduce the amount of RAM available for running programs. Most users will optimize their use of memory once with a utility like Member or QEMM and stay with those settings. If you haven't done anything that would change the amount of available memory yet you detect a drop in the amount of RAM available for running programs, it is time to scan for viruses.

Unusual behaviors. You simply cannot load a new program, virus or otherwise, into a computer system without in some way changing the behavior of the system. It might suddenly take an extra five or ten seconds to reboot, the hard disk may seem to be doing more than it did before during bootup, or you may see unusual messages flash across the screen briefly. All of these symptoms, if noted, should send you scurrying for your antivirus software.

If, after noticing any of the behaviors listed above, you run an antivirus program that fails to detect a virus infection, you should be on the lookout for imminent hardware problems or bugs in the software you use. It pays to keep an eye on what your computer is doing, but do try to avoid becoming paranoid and blaming a virus infection every time the CPU burps.

Create a virus recovery disk

One of the conditions that makes disinfecting your system in case of virus infection easier is a clean boot to DOS (or whatever operating system you are using). Booting from an uninfected floppy disk will keep virus code from loading into memory.

Create a virus recovery disk by formatting a floppy disk as a system (bootable) disk. Copy your antivirus program onto the floppy along with any other utilities you may think necessary. Candidates include FDISK, FORMAT, ATTRIB, SYS, and snacks to keep your energy up while you wrestle with the problem. Don't forget to transfer and modify your current AUTOEXEC.BAT and CONFIG.SYS files along with any drivers you need to make sure that your CD, SCSI interfaces, and disk compression software will operate properly. You may need to put everything you need onto multiple floppies. Also it is a good idea to write protect the disk by sliding the plastic tab on the back of a 3.5-inch floppy or putting a write protect tab onto a 5.25-inch disk.

Once created, be sure to write protect your recovery disk(s) and store them away in a safe place where you can get to them when needed. If your system becomes infected, use the recovery disk to reboot and then run the antivirus utility.

Summary

This chapter introduced you to Trojan horse and virus programs. You learned where these programs come from and what you can do to lessen the chances you will lose data to one of them.

- ✦ Trojan horse software often pretends to be a utility that performs a useful function. In reality, however, the Trojan program is busily reformatting your hard disk or scrambling your file allocation table.
- ✦ Viruses need an incubation period so that they can lay undetected, waiting for an opportunity to infect other disks. During this incubation period, the job of the virus is to infect other disks.
- ✦ Symptoms of virus infection include changes in sizes of like target files, reduced available RAM, and strange behavior of the computer system.
- ✦ Most viruses are boot sector viruses that copy themselves to the root directory of floppy and hard disks where they hide and attempt to replicate.
- ✦ Viruses infect other systems by transferring themselves onto any floppy disks they may come into contact with or by stowing away inside program files you may transfer to other computers via network connections.
- ✦ Antivirus software relies on a database of virus signatures to compare against the contents of memory and of the disk.

✦ ✦ ✦

Password Protection

CHAPTER 4

In This Chapter

The basics of password protection

Do's and Don'ts of choosing passwords

Using passwords to protect sensitive data

Protecting your system with boot time passwords

Using password protected archive files to store documents

Say the secret word and the duck will drop down and give you a hundred dollars.
— *Groucho Marx*

Open sez me!
— *Popeye the Sailor*

Passwords are everywhere. If you are connected to a network, you have an account name and a password that you must type into the system before you can log in. Your phone cards and credit cards have Personal Identification Numbers (PINs) that you enter to validate yourself to the telephone network or the ATM machine at the grocery store. Your Internet account requires a password so you can log on, as does CompuServe, America Online, Prodigy, and so on.

Passwords are a fact of life. Passwords are a royal pain in the...well, let's just say they are sometimes inconvenient.

And that's just the point. They are inconvenient for you, and they should be doubly inconvenient for anyone who wants to gain unauthorized access to your stuff. The idea behind passwords is to make it so someone trying to access your data or hardware is thwarted by inconvenience. The harder you make it to guess or hack your passwords, the more secure your data is.

The Mathematics of Passwords

The length of a password has a great deal of influence on security. For instance the PIN you use at the ATM machine to empty out your bank account each weekend is generally four digits long. You enter your credit card or ATM card number plus a four-digit identifier. Your card may fall into someone else's hands, but without the PIN they cannot withdraw money.

PINs are an interesting example because they are probably the least secure passwords commonly used today. Because ATM machines and telephones (phone cards also use a four-digit PIN) don't have full keyboards, PINs are restricted to using only the digits 0 through 9. Four digits, ten characters to choose from, equals 10,000 possible combinations. That's a lot of combinations if you are talking about a human being standing at an ATM machine trying different PINs at random, but if you are talking about a computer using a *brute force* method, it isn't a lot of combinations at all.

A brute force attack involves trying every possible combination of passwords until one works. As the length of the password, or key, increases, the difficulty in launching a brute force attack is complicated greatly because it takes time to try all the possible passwords. Thus a password that has several billion possible combinations will be tougher to crack than a password that is limited to only four characters.

Of course, banks use other techniques like video cameras and card eating ATMs to augment PIN numbers, but the security measures often vary from bank to bank. Most banks also have a little feature where you can call the bank and enter the card number and the PIN to find your current balance. In this scenario, your PIN is vulnerable because someone can sit at a telephone and just keep trying.

Your phone card has the same problem, because long distance phone networks like AT&T, MCI, Sprint, and so on also use four-digit PINs to authenticate the placement of calls. Suppose you lose your wallet. Your first reaction is to mourn for whatever cash it contained, as well as your driver's license and other personal effects. Your second reaction probably is to call your credit card companies and let them know the wallet is lost so they can cancel your cards. Most people, however, forget that phone calling cards are also credit cards. So how hard is it for some kid with a computer to hack that PIN? Not very.

All they have to do is write a little computer program to dial the phone and try PIN numbers in sequence until it works. I'm assuming you aren't a programmer, so I'll keep things simple. Here's a little bit of pseudo-program code that will do the trick:

```
FOR i = 0000 TO 9999
   DialAccess(i)
NEXT
```

The FOR command means to run the code that follows 9,999 times, adding 1 to the value of i each time. The NEXT command evaluates the value of i and loops the program back up to the FOR if i is less than 9999. The DialAccess( ) function would be another little snippet of code that would dial up the access line of the phone company and enter the card number using the value of i as the PIN. This is a classic example of the brute force method.

Eventually, the program will try the right PIN number, and whoever has your card can spend the weekend talking to his friends in Trinidad, Ghana, and American Samoa. By then he will have shared your number with several of his closest friends. By the time you realize that you forgot to tell the phone company your card is lost, you find a bill in your mailbox for a few thousand dollars. And since you didn't report the lost card, don't expect the phone company to be very understanding.

So a four-digit password — your PIN — has 9,999 possible combinations. Most computer passwords, however, are longer and can contain letters in addition to the numbers 1–9. A four-digit password that can use numbers and letters is much harder to break, because it can contain 1,679,616 unique combinations.

Here's the formula for calculating the total possible number and letter combinations:

```
C = x ^ y
```

In this equation C is the number of possible combinations, x is the number of characters you have to choose from, and y is the number of characters in the password. Using the PIN as an example, $C = 10^4$. For a password that uses only numeric digits, the number of possible combinations equals 10,000. There are 10 unique digits and 26 letters in the alphabet, making a total of 36 possible characters. So a 4-digit password that accepts letters has 36^4, or 1,679,616, unique combinations.

Expand the password to 5 characters in length and the number of unique combinations increases exponentially to 60,466,176. Each time you increase the length of your password by a single character, you square the number of possible combinations, making it harder to guess or to crack by brute force. By increasing the number of characters to 6 in a password that accepts letters and numbers, you get 36,561,584,400,630,000 possible combinations.

Keep in mind that most systems are case sensitive and accept punctuation marks, so the number of possible combinations is staggering.

The Effectiveness of Passwords

Since most passwords have billions upon billions of possible combinations, you might think that password protection is an extremely secure way of guarding your system from unauthorized access. You would, unfortunately, be wrong. On a typical UNIX system where users are allowed to create their own passwords, experience shows that better than half the passwords chosen can be easily guessed or cracked.

In 1978 Robert Morris (father of the soon to be famous Robert T. Morris who unleashed the fabled Internet Worm) and Ken Thompson published a paper entitled *Password Security: A Case History* in the Communications of the ACM, reprinted in the Berkeley Software UNIX System Manager's Manual in 1986. In that paper they detailed the vulnerability of computer systems that relied on password protection. Although the research is now dated, it is still quite valid, because computer users still do the same dumb things when selecting passwords. If you want to read the whole paper for yourself, you will need to configure a helper app that can read PostScript documents. You can find the paper at http://hightop.nrl.navy.mil/passwords.html.

In their paper, Morris and Thompson came to some startling conclusions about how typical users choose passwords. They sampled 3,289 passwords of typical users and found that 15 users had single character passwords, 72 used two characters, and 464 used three characters. Fully 492 passwords were words that could be found in a dictionary or by comparing the passwords to a mailing list of names. In all, 2,831 (86 percent) of the passwords gathered by the authors were classified as insecure.

Like crackers, Morris and Thompson attacked the list of passwords by using a dictionary search, a technique utilized five years later by the younger Morris in the code for his infamous Internet Worm. The dictionary search, which only took five minutes to run, revealed about 33 percent of the passwords tested.

The relevance of this information to you as an owner of a modern PC is a bit different than it was to the UNIX system administrators the Morris-Thompson paper was written for. In UNIX, user passwords are often kept in simple lists that contain encrypted versions of account passwords. These encrypted strings are kept in the same record with the user's other account information. Since that time, more secure password techniques have been employed by using *shadow files* (an encrypted list of passwords, hidden from view) and other methods.

On a normal PC you don't have centralized lists of passwords, except on PCs used as network servers. For example, the optional password login routine used by Windows 95 stores the password in the configuration database called the Registry. Other passwords may be stored either in the Registry or in a file associated with a specific program or function. For example, in Windows 95 the password for Dial-Up Networking is stored in the Windows folder in a file named for the user, with the extension PWL.

Although PC passwords are less centralized than they would be on certain types of network schemes, they are still vulnerable. On a typical 386/486/Pentium computer running Windows for Workgroups or Windows 95, you can require a logon password just to start up the system. Additionally, as you will see later in this chapter, you have the ability to use passwords to protect individual files on an application level or to create password protected ZIP files where you can archive sensitive data.

Potential security flaw in Windows 95 Dial-Up Networking

Microsoft Plus!, the add-on enhancement package for Windows 95, has a feature to enhance Dial-Up Networking that allows your system to function as a dial-up server. This feature allows another computer to dial up your computer and log on to your system. While connected, the two computers can share system resources like disk space, printers, and so on. This can be really handy when you want to be able to call into the system from a remote location or when you share data with one or two other users.

When you or another caller dials into your system by using Dial-Up Networking, any resources you have marked as *shared* become available just as if you shared the disk via a network server or workgroup. The caller can be required to enter a password in order to gain access.

The access password for Dial-Up Networking is stored in a file having the extension PWL and is located in your Windows folder. If you have set Windows up so that Dial-Up networking remembers passwords for Internet accounts, they are stored in this file as well.

You won't find this tip in the Microsoft documentation, but if you forget the password, all you have to do is delete the PWL file. Then you simply go to the Dial-Up Networking folder, click on Connections in the menu, click on Dial-Up Server, and click on the Allow Caller Access radio button. To create a new password, click on Change Password and enter a new one, leaving empty the text box for the old password.

If you are lax about security, leaving the computer accessible in your absence, someone who knows Dial-Up Networking can easily delete the PWL file, create a new password, mark sensitive resources as shared, and then wait for an opportune time to call in. If you don't use Dial-Up Networking very often, the door could be left open for people to access anything on your system at their leisure for days or weeks at a time.

The only real solution to this problem, other than deleting the Dial-Up Server portion of Plus! every time you finish using it, is vigilance. Make sure you are using a logon password so that someone can't just turn on your system and do what he wants with it.

Change your Dial-Up Server password frequently. If you don't use Dial-Up Networking very often, find the PWL file on your system and make a note of the date and time stamp. Make sure, every once in a while, that the time stamp has not changed. Or dial up yourself and make sure the password you created is still in effect.

Anyone who has access to your computer and some time to mess around has the potential to crack open anything you have protected by a password. Again, your situation is different than a UNIX system administrator's because you may not even be connected to another machine by network or even a modem. This eliminates the possibility of someone using a crack program to repeatedly try passwords until they find the one that works. But if you have chosen weak passwords, the odds are that an experienced cracker can gain access to your system by using that experience, plus guile and intuition. The trick is to choose passwords that are difficult, if not impossible, to guess. By following a few simple rules when choosing passwords, you can dramatically increase the security of your system.

Rules of Thumb for Choosing Passwords

It makes no difference whether you are choosing a password for an account on the network in your workplace or locking up those racy pictures of Cindy Crawford you don't want the kids to see: the rules for creating passwords are the same. There are a few do's and don'ts you should go by.

Password don'ts

- **Forget Names.** Don't use your name or the names of anyone else as a password. Someone who knows your spouse's name or the names of your children, dogs, cats, or hamster is going to try those first.

- **Don't Be Cute.** Spelling names backwards is also not a good idea. Too many other folks have come up with that idea. Doubling, like using *RayRay*, or *JanJan*, is also too cute for a hacker not to try. Oh, and *biLL* isn't about to fool anybody either.

- **Don't Use Personal Information.** Besides names, people also like to use other personal information because they can remember it easily. Such things as social security numbers, house numbers, phone numbers, license plate numbers, street names, subdivision names, and so on are simply not original ideas. Someone dedicated to hacking your system will eventually tumble onto these, as well.

- **Don't Use Occupational Jargon.** Every line of work seems to have its own jargon. Undertakers shouldn't use words like *embalm* for a password, and cowboys shouldn't use *rodeo*. The added danger of using jargon terms is that people tend to use one term for this account and another jargon term for another. That all but removes the guesswork for someone trying to hack multiple passwords.

- **Don't Repeat.** Passwords that use repeating digits like 99999 or BBBBBBB are all but useless, especially if the password can be tried via another computer. These kinds of passwords are as easy as taking candy from a baby.

- **Don't Use Real Words.** This tip is especially important if you are connected via a network or phone link where repeated tries can be made by computer. The average word list for a word processor's spell checker is about 250,000 words. There are password cracking programs out there that can test that many passwords in less than two minutes.

The lone exception to the rule against using real words is when you are choosing a password for a home or business machine that isn't connected to other computers so that using a crack program is impractical. In this limited case, a word from the dictionary chosen at random by blindly pointing at a word on a randomly chosen page can be a good way to choose a password. If the word has no pertinence in your life and is at least six characters in length, use it. While it may not take a computer program more than a minute or so to try 250,000 words, a human being who has just broken into your house trying one word after another is unlikely to discover a word truly chosen at random.

Password do's

+ **Do Choose Longer Passwords.** By choosing only passwords that have at least six or seven characters, you increase astronomically the number of combinations that have to be tried. For example, a password that can contain letters, digits, and punctuation marks and is case sensitive allows the user to choose from about 56 different characters. A 6-character password in this context would have 30,840,979,456 different combinations. That's more than 30 B (as in billion) different combinations. Increasing the minimum password length to 7 characters renders 1,727,094,849,536 possibilities. That's T, as in trillion. It would take considerable time to test that many combinations with a supercomputer. Do you have any data so important that someone would use a supercomputer to hack your passwords?

+ **Do Mix Case and Use Punctuation.** Having a password that uses only lowercase letters reduces the number of possible combinations drastically. A 6-character password that uses only lowercase letters has 308,915,776 possible combinations, far fewer than the 30 billion possibilities using mixed-case letters, numbers, and punctuation marks.

+ **Do Choose an Easily Remembered Password.** Whatever the password you choose, it should be easy enough to remember. What good does it do to password protect an application if all the hacker has to do is open the drawer to find the note where you've written down the passwords? None.

+ **Do Choose a Password You Can Type Easily.** There is a term used by hackers called *shoulder surfing,* which is especially effective if the person whose shoulder you are looking over is a slow typist. You want to create a secure password yet be able to type it quickly and easily.

Choosing a password

The do's and don'ts may make it seem like no password is an acceptable choice. If it is short and easy to type, it's insecure. On the other hand, long passwords are hard to type, easy to forget, and easy to shoulder surf. There are, however, several schemes you can use that fulfill all the requirements for security and convenience.

Two word two-step

The first method is one I like to call the two word two-step. All you have to do is to create a two word password and separate the words with a punctuation character. For example *Your+lamB* combines two unrelated words with a plus sign. *Shift=meLon* again uses unrelated words joined with an equal sign.

There are four features that make the preceding examples decent choices for a password:

- ✦ The mixture of uppercase and lowercase letters makes the password harder to crack by brute force, and the unusual capitalization of the letter B in the first example makes guessing less likely.
- ✦ The length of the password reduces the chance it will be cracked by brute force or guessed.
- ✦ Both of the words you combine will probably be in a dictionary, but the combination of two words and a punctuation mark make a dictionary-based crack unlikely.
- ✦ The combination of two simple words is easy to remember, even though they are unrelated. There will be less temptation to write the password down and hide it where it might be discovered.

The use of unrelated words is an important deterrent to password guessing. A password like *My:friend* would be a poor choice because the words are combined in a commonly used phrase.

Derivative passwords

The second commonly used method for creating effective, yet easily remembered passwords is to create a derivative of a longer phrase. For example, you could take the phrase "happy birthday to my darling wife" and turn it into something like *HB2-mdw* or whatever mind association works for you.

WYSIWYG would be a poor choice because it is a common acronym for "what you see is what you get." Other poor choices would be phrases that you use every day that people associate with you. For example, if you often joke around, give the Vulcan hand signal, and say "live long and prosper," or if you quote Shakespeare's "To be or not to be, that is the question," on a regular basis, don't use those phrases or anything related to create a derivative password.

When creating derivative passwords, make sure you use mixed case and at least one punctuation mark. Even if someone guesses your phrase, the case sensitivity of most password systems will make it difficult for someone to easily hack out the proper combination and placement of capitals and punctuation.

Make up words

The third method you can employ for choosing passwords is to make up words. You can easily manufacture made-up words by alternating consonants and vowels. Another technique borrowed from Hip Hop is the substitution of numbers for word fragments. The result is always gibberish, but often the words are so absurd that they are memorable, even funny. For example *Plamiten2* means nothing and would be hard to remember without a good mind association, but you can, in an imaginative frenzy, just picture some guy on TV saying, "Heartburn? Try Plamiten2." Absurd, but such a mind association makes it easy to remember weird phrases.

Made-up words have almost no chance of being in a dictionary, but if you have any question at all that a made-up word sounds too real, you should look it up in a big, thick dictionary just to be on the safe side. Made-up words are not as easy to remember as two words separated by a punctuation mark, but they often have a whimsy about them that makes them catchy and memorable.

Tip

Using the same password for weeks, months, or years on end is probably a waste of time. If someone has figured it out, he will be able to gain access to your data and sensitive documents at will. Part of the deterrence of password protection is changing your password every once in a while so that a compromised password doesn't remain an ineffective barrier.

Password Protection on Your Computer

In addition to passwords you use to access network accounts, Internet connections, and so on, there are a number of password protection features generally available to computer users. These include BIOS-based password protection that requires a password to boot the computer, application-specific password features that lock individual files, and password protected ZIP files.

BIOS boot passwords

When your computer starts up, a program written on the chips inside your machine comes to life. Known as the POST (power on self-test), this program is usually discernible only to users when it tests RAM chips and displays the amount of available memory that has been tested. The invisible part of the program reads your CMOS (complimentary metal oxide semiconductor) chip to load the information stored there. This information includes the date and time, as well as hard drive specifications and a table of installed floppy drives.

Manufacturers of computers seldom make their own chips, preferring instead to buy ready-made ones. Phoenix Technologies and AMD are two manufacturers of BIOS that are widely used. For this reason, many different brands of computers have the same BIOS (Basic Input/Output System) chip set.

Many of the modern BIOS chip sets contain an optional program that enables users to password protect the operation of the computer by providing a password that must be entered before the computer will boot up to the operating system. Because the program is self-contained and because it runs before the operating system is loaded, this feature is independent of any operating system you may choose to run — it doesn't matter if you are running UNIX, DOS, or Windows. The password stored in CMOS must be matched by user entry, or the machine refuses to cooperate.

To enable password protection you must typically enter the CMOS setup utility by pressing an unusual keystroke combination like Ctrl+Alt+Esc. The actual combination depends on your computer's BIOS. Check your user manual or call your computer dealer for details on your system.

Inside the setup program, if your BIOS supports password protection, there is usually an entry box or a prompt telling you what keystroke to enter. In all cases, you will have to type the password exactly the same way *twice* for the password to take hold. From that point on, you will have to enter the password at boot time.

There are both advantages and disadvantages to using this feature. The advantages are that the machine is fully protected. Nothing about the system works unless a password is given. The disadvantage is that nothing about the system works unless a password is given. Let me run that down for you.

Using BIOS level password protection disables the entire machine if the password isn't given. While this may be desirable in most cases, there are some specific scenarios where this doesn't work out so well. For example, some people leave their computer on so they can dial up and collect e-mail, check for faxes, or simply download files if the need arises.

What happens if the power goes out and the computer system goes down? As soon as power is restored, the machine will attempt to reboot since the switches are all still in the ON position. Unless someone is there to physically enter the boot password, the machine will simply stop and wait for the password to be entered. If you are on the road, you will have to call up a trusted friend or family member, give him the password, and rely on him to stay out of your stuff. Unless you write a program specifically for the job, it isn't possible for you to change the password from a remote location because you can't run the CMOS setup.

Another similar situation involves systems that provide shared resources within a workgroup. Until you enter the password and boot the system, none of the shared files, printers, or modems is available to other members of your workgroup.

If you can't use boot time password protection

In those situations that prohibit the use of boot time password protection, you may use a workaround. Many computer systems come with a set of keys that enable you to lock the keyboard circuitry so that no keyboard entry can take place. This effectively prevents normal use of the computer so that you can allow it to boot up and act as a server of shared resources or enable the system to accept dial-up access.

Some keyed lockouts, however, are less than secure because the mouse is often left operational. This means that someone can use your system as long as they don't need to keyboard anything. If the mouse is unaffected by the key lock on a graphical operating system like Windows, an intruder can easily open files and even print them without ever typing a keystroke.

One other problem with key lockouts is that there are lots of keys floating around and not a lot of different key patterns. Most professional technicians have a set of keys that will unlock most machines.

The effectiveness of boot time password protection is dependent, in part, on the physical accessibility of your system. If an intruder has the time to take the system apart and fiddle about with the hardware, boot time password protection can often be defeated quite easily. By removing the wires that plug the battery power source into the CMOS chip's power supply, he can effectively erase the password and render the machine unprotected.

Some systems, however, require that a pair of specific pins be shorted together to erase the current password. Your motherboard's documentation may not give you the pin locations. If you forget the password, expect to pay a service technician to call the manufacturer and learn what has to be done. On the other hand, an unauthorized person is going to have just as much trouble bypassing the CMOS password as you.

The most lasting effect of pulling the plug on your CMOS can be the loss of information, especially hard disk drive type specifications, that occurs when the CMOS loses electrical power from its battery. If you are not intimately familiar with hardware maintenance issues you may need professional help getting your system running again because you will lose hard drive specifications for cylinder, heads, and sectors per track. An experienced repair technician shouldn't have too much trouble restoring the information, however.

Password protection of individual files

Many of the top-of-the-line word processors, spreadsheets, and data management applications available today allow users to save individual files in password-protected form. The password you enter is used to seed an encryption function that scrambles the contents of the file. Only by entering the same password can the unencrypt function restore the original form of the data.

In general, the password protection features of these applications is seldom, if ever, used by the vast majority of users. There is a very simple reason. It is nearly impossible for all but elite, top-crust MENSA members to remember more than a few passwords at a time.

The temptation is to settle on a single password to encrypt all protected documents, but this is a bad idea. If the password is compromised, every file is open to the would-be snoop. Some users keep a list of passwords and the files they pertain to tucked away somewhere in their office. This, too, is a bad idea because anyone finding the list can open any file.

Still, the ability to password protect individual files has some handy applications. If you have just a few files of a sensitive nature, or if you need to send sensitive data on a floppy disk to another person, protecting files with a password can prevent prying eyes from seeing your data.

Figure 4-1 illustrates how documents can be password protected by using Microsoft Word for Windows 6.0. Open the File menu and then select Save As. In the dialog box that appears, click on the Options button. You will be presented with a dialog box that lets you enter a password that restricts the opening of the document. You can alternately enter a password that must be entered before the contents of the document can be changed.

Tip

The biggest potential danger of password protecting data files individually is the possibility that you will forget one or more passwords, rendering the file useless. It is a really good idea to store an unprotected copy of sensitive material on a floppy disk (or backup tape if the file is large) and place the floppy into secure storage like a safe deposit box. That way if you ever forget the password to a file, a backup copy is available that you can read.

Unfortunately, password protection is application specific. Placing password protection on a file will not prevent deliberate or accidental deletion of protected files. This is one more good reason to have a rigid backup routine.

Spoofing

Although much less of a problem these days, you need to be aware of a particularly insidious type of password attack called *spoofing* that originated in the heyday of UNIX. Spoofing is the installation on a computer system of a program that appears to

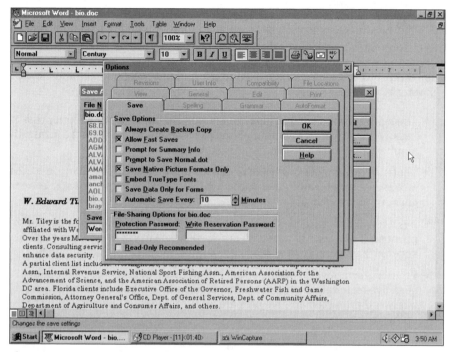

Figure 4-1: Many applications let you password protect individual files.

be a normal logon script, but in actuality records the keystrokes of users who try to log on. In this way the budding young hacker doesn't have to go through the trouble of cracking passwords. He simply collects the entries of those users who try to log on.

Typically, the spoof script maintains its appearance of legitimacy by giving the user some plausible reason why he cannot log on at that workstation. The user usually walks away without ever suspecting that his account is now vulnerable to attack.

With greater use of Windows 95's ability to let users log on to their own desktop from any machine on the network, spoofing is liable to come back into fashion in the PC world. If you ever attempt to log in to your account and get a strange message telling you that you can't do so, and you are certain you have made the correct entries, contact your system administrator immediately. It is also a good idea to immediately change the password on your account.

Another defense against being spoofed is never to trust a computer that appears to be just sitting idle, waiting for your login. If you always assume that the login display is part of a spoof and reboot the computer, you will usually manage to avoid being spoofed.

Summary

This chapter introduced you to the basics of password protection. Network accounts and Internet access accounts are just two of the many examples of places where password protection schemes are used to prevent unauthorized use and viewing of computer resources.

- ✦ The length of password strings is an important factor in the security that passwords provide. Each time you add a character to a password string, the number of possible combinations is squared.

- ✦ There are several good ways of creating secure passwords. All involve the use of mixed-case letters and punctuation marks to make it harder for someone to guess or crack your passwords.

- ✦ It is a terrible idea to use the same password for more than one account or purpose. If someone manages to crack your password, everything you have secured is vulnerable to attack.

- ✦ PC users have several options available to them for password protecting sensitive materials. BIOS boot passwords, individual file passwords, and password-protected archive files are all available tools for keeping prying eyes out of your stuff.

✦ ✦ ✦

Simple Security Measures

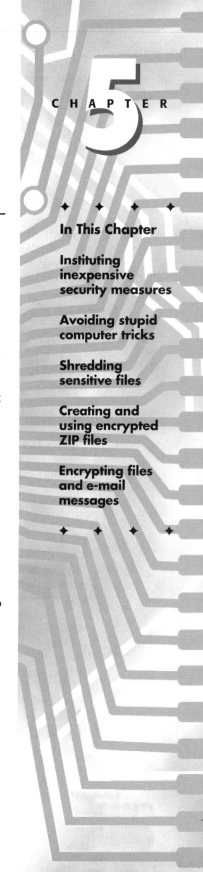

CHAPTER 5

In This Chapter

Instituting inexpensive security measures

Avoiding stupid computer tricks

Shredding sensitive files

Creating and using encrypted ZIP files

Encrypting files and e-mail messages

Don't overestimate the decency of the human race.
—H. L. Mencken

No security scheme is absolutely foolproof. The only reason Fort Knox hasn't been robbed yet is because nobody has figured out how to rob it and get away with it. Up to this point the security at Fort Knox has been adequate. Give someone bent on robbing Fort Knox enough time, information, and resources, and it could probably be done. From a thief's point of view, however, robbing Fort Knox is just too worrisome a task and would take too many resources.

That's the whole point behind computer security: make it just difficult enough that a potential intruder gets discouraged and moves on to another target. Just as lights and alarm systems make buildings less tempting targets for burglars, taking a few simple security measures will usually deter people from hacking your system.

No matter how cunningly you hide or protect sensitive data, it is still vulnerable to an expert hacker who is determined to get into it, if he or she has the knowledge and opportunity to do so. In assessing your exposure to risk, you need to take into account who is likely to try and get into your stuff.

If your computer system is at home and physically isolated (not connected to a network), then your biggest risk is probably the chance that you, or one of your household, will pick up a virus or Trojan horse program. The second largest risk is that the entire computer will be stolen in a burglary along with all your other electronic gear. Because the typical computer user isn't working with highly sensitive documents on a home system, you can usually get away with only a minimal security regime, such as encrypting files.

A computer system in an office is another matter entirely. Most offices are open and have lots of contact between co-workers. A common practice in many workplaces is to leave office doors open, even while workers are in meetings or out to lunch. Under these conditions, sensitive documents require an extra measure of security.

In designing your personal computer security strategy, you have to make the critical decision about how much security to apply. You also have to balance the need to protect sensitive data against the worth of the data and against the hardships that security imposes on using that data when you want it. It is worth repeating that any security system that places too many demands on users and makes following the regime inconvenient will soon fall into disuse. Only you can decide where the balance point is.

Stupid Computer Tricks

On David Letterman's late night TV program, people who have strange and demented talents line up for their 15 minutes of fame. During this segment, dubbed "Stupid Human Tricks," Dave and the audience make great sport of people who make milk squirt out of their eyes or people who juggle ping pong balls by spitting them into the air. There are some security measures that fall into the same type of classification, called *stupid computer tricks*.

Before we cover some real computer security measures, there are some old-time techniques that need to be debunked for the false security they provide. All rely on some little known, but hardly undocumented, feature of the operating system that can be easily circumvented by anyone who is at least as clever as the person trying to protect his or her stuff.

Hidden files

In the early days of DOS, hidden files were a fairly secure way of keeping folks from messing with things they shouldn't get into. Of course, those were the days of Conestoga wagons, when versions of DOS still numbered in the 2s.

Version 2.0 of DOS borrowed heavily from the UNIX model of disk storage and incorporated directories and file attributes into the PC environment, including hidden files. *File attributes* determine how a file is handled by the operating system. The DOS file attributes are as follows:

- **Archive.** The archive attribute is turned on whenever a file is altered. This allows backup software to record only those files that have changed since the last backup. Backup software usually resets the archive bit to off.
- **System.** The system attribute is given to files that are required for proper running of the system and that should never be altered by end users. System files are hidden from the directory command and are protected against erasure.

- **Hidden.** The hidden attribute is similar to the system attribute in the way that files are hidden from view of the DIR command. Hidden files, however, have no special status when it comes to deletion.
- **Read Only.** Files that have the read only attribute set to on can be displayed and copied, but they cannot be saved back to disk in an altered form. Configuration files and other files that shouldn't be changed by users are often assigned read only status.

Windows has inherited these same file attributes from its text-based DOS ancestor. It is still possible today to assign hidden and read only attributes to files. The amount of protection they give you is considerably less than it used to be. In the heyday of DOS, relatively few computer users were familiar with the ATTRIB command, which is the DOS tool for changing attribute settings, but ATTRIB is commonly known these days.

Consider the following screen output from a DOS session:

```
D:\BBS>dir *.zip

Directory of D:\BBS

WBLOCK10 ZIP        503,521  11-01-95 10:44p wblock10.zip
CMED104  ZIP        354,180  11-02-95 11:58p cmed104.zip
GUESTB1  ZIP         13,362  09-14-95 12:17a guestbook2_1.zip
        3 file(s)         871,063 bytes
        0 dir(s)      113,836,032 bytes free

D:\BBS>attrib c*.zip +h
D:\BBS>dir *.zip

Directory of D:\BBS

WBLOCK10 ZIP        503,521  11-01-95 10:44p wblock10.zip
GUESTB1  ZIP         13,362  09-14-95 12:17a guestbook2_1.zip
        2 file(s)         516,883 bytes
        0 dir(s)      113,836,032 bytes free
```

Say, that looks like it works pretty well. You enter a single ATTRIB command that turns on the hidden attribute for all ZIP files whose names begin with C, and poof, CMED104.ZIP disappears. The problem is that Microsoft has added and documented a switch to the DIR command that displays even hidden files:

```
D:\BBS>dir *.zip /A

Directory of D:\BBS

WBLOCK10 ZIP        503,521  11-01-95 10:44p wblock10.zip
CMED104  ZIP        354,180  11-02-95 11:58p cmed104.zip
GUESTB1  ZIP         13,362  09-14-95 12:17a guestbook2_1.zip
        3 file(s)         871,063 bytes
        0 dir(s)      113,836,032 bytes free
```

Oops! Any number of third-party replacements for the DIR command from DD.EXE to Xtree Gold show hidden files in their display as a matter of course. They may even be highlighted and displayed in a different color, making them stick out like a sore thumb.

Windows 3.*x* has a File Manager setting that displays hidden files, as does Windows 95. If you set Windows to show all files, the hidden attribute is absolutely worthless. This is one stupid computer trick that perhaps had some value a few years ago, but is completely bogus in this day and time.

The old misdirection play

One of the earliest stories I ever heard about computer deception was about a programmer who had written a little DOS utility that barely made the floppy disk chirp when copying it to a hard disk or when loading. Fearing that his customers would resent paying exorbitant amounts of money for a really small program, he used the COPY command's capability to concatenate (or link) files to create a fraudulent file. He did something like

```
COPY UTIL.EXE + FILLER.TXT BIGUTIL.EXE /B
```

The result was that he padded his small executable file with a bunch of junk at the end to create a file that was considerably larger than it needed to be. The computer would dutifully churn the disk drive an appropriately long time and load the entire file into memory before running it, even though most of the "code" was nothing more than a discarded text file. The results of the program were not compromised because the program never tried to access any of the extra memory allocated for the bogus program code, so the program ran just fine.

There are some computer users who, not knowing any better, use similar techniques to hide data on their systems. The most common of these techniques is renaming a document so that it doesn't appear to be a document at first glance.

This falls into the stupid computer trick category on two counts. First, changing the size of an EXE file with a virus scanner in place will surely set off alarms, because that is one of the things virus scanners are programmed to watch for. Second, this trick won't fool any but the most computer illiterate users.

For example, many Windows shareware applications install Dynamic Link Libraries (DLL) files in their directories or in the WINDOWS\SYSTEM directory. You could rename SENSTIVE.DOC to RL43VMA.DLL and hide it in a directory occupied by some little known shareware application. Few people, including experienced computer professionals, would think twice about checking out some obscure DLL file. Problem is, this little bit of deception can be discovered quite easily. An inexperienced user may even stumble across this trick by accident.

Assume for a moment that you are working on a white paper for your company that documents some time-sensitive material. Early disclosure of the information could have a detrimental effect on the company's stock price. You take the word processing document you are working on, rename it as a DLL, and tuck it away in an obscure directory.

Take a look at Figure 5-1, specifically the next to last entry. Using the Advanced text search feature of Windows 95's Find utility to search for the string "white paper" took less than five minutes to spot the ringer among thousands of files. Why would the words "white paper" be stuck inside a DLL? Very strange because the only text most DLLs contain are error messages and user notifications.

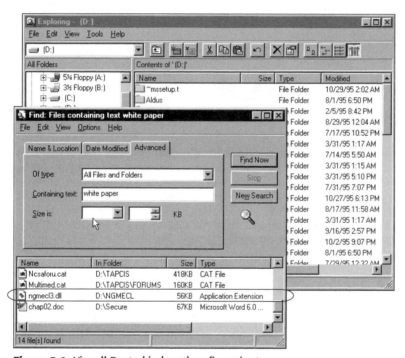

Figure 5-1: Yipes!! Busted in less than five minutes.

Even worse, once identified as a suspect file, all someone has to do to reveal the contents of the file in Windows 95 is to right-click the file and choose Quick View from the context menu. Figure 5-2 shows the exposed file.

The file shown in Figure 5-2 is like no real DLL file in existence. All it takes to defeat this method of hiding data is a simple tool like the Find utility (supplied with every copy of Windows 95) or a utility like the DOS version of Norton Utilities TS.EXE (text search), which would find the bogus DLL file trick just as easily.

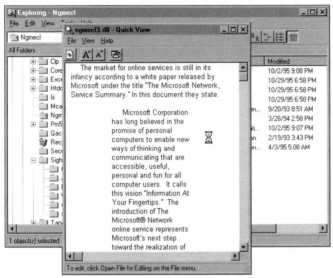

Figure 5-2: A Quick View of the suspect files reveals its text-based nature.

As you can see in the preceding examples, misdirection is useful only if you are sure that only dumb-as-a-rock computer users are going to have access to your machine. You might use this technique for fooling a six-year-old, but I wouldn't try it on a bright seven-year-old.

File formats

Most commercial programs, like word processors and spreadsheets, use proprietary file formats that are easily identifiable. Most file formats consist of a header section followed by the actual data. Headers are used to place custom information about the data, or the tools used to create the data, into the file. They almost always have an entry in the header that identifies the type of file.

For example, every .DOC file created by Word carries a text tag in the header of the file that identifies the version of the software. Each of the files that contain the chapters of this book has the words "Microsoft Word 6.0 Document" in the header as unencrypted text. JPG format picture files all have the string JFIF starting seven bytes into the file header, and they also have a space where comments about the image can be embedded as well. Just about every file format, except TXT format, has some identifiable combinations of characters in the header that positively identifies the file type. These telltale markers nullify any attempt at using misdirection schemes for security.

Deleted files

Accessing disk storage is without doubt the slowest function your computer performs. In order to speed up user-perceived performance, files are not really deleted when you use the DOS DEL command. Instead, the entries in the File Allocation Table for deleted files are simply marked as erased. The mark signals to the operating system that the area is now available for another use. Not until another file is written into the same area is the old file actually written over, and that isn't guaranteed. When a new file is written, performance is optimized by first using *empty* sectors closest to the drive's heads, so all or part of the old file may remain on the disk for quite some time until those sectors are reused.

When you delete files in Windows 95, by default, they are moved to the Recycle Bin just in case you decide you want them back. When you empty the Recycle Bin, the data remains on the disk until you create another file that is written to the formerly reserved sectors.

An old DOS trick involved deleting files to hide them and then using an undelete program to recover them when the "danger of discovery" passed. There are two major problems with this method, besides the fact that it provides lousy security. First, if anything is written to the disk while the sensitive files are temporarily deleted, they may be written over and become unrecoverable. Second, undelete utilities are no longer rare. The popularity of such programs for stupidity recovery convinced Microsoft to include the feature, beginning with DOS 5.0.

Windows 95 uses the Recycle Bin to cache deleted files, so deleting them simply places them in another place. The percentage of disk space allocated to the Recycle Bin is limited to 10 percent by default, which means that 100 megs of deleted files can be cached on a 1.2GB hard disk before the first file is actually deleted to make more room in the Recycle Bin for newly deleted files. When that data actually becomes overwritten is anybody's guess. Although the Recycle Bin can be disabled, most users don't, so sensitive data can remain on the hard disk long after it has been "erased."

Simple and Cheap Security Measures

Security is a trade-off. You trade convenience for security. If, in your own assessment of your risk situation, you determine that consumer-strength security tools will suffice, the tools and tips covered in the pages that follow will protect you from the prying eyes of 98 percent of the human race.

If you need industrial-strength tools that provide a strong degree of protection, you may want to skim this chapter before checking out the encryption tools presented in Chapter 10.

Shredding files

The potential security problems presented by the fact that files aren't actually erased when you issue the delete command has long been an issue among the computer literate, but the average computer user is often oblivious to the potential problems. Businesses have long understood the value of shredding paper documents, but the realization that similar computer tools are also necessary has come late. In this section, I'm going to show you two shareware products that completely erase files by obliterating the disk sectors where the file is written so that the file cannot be recovered.

There are two major issues to watch out for when shredding files. The first is that files become truly unrecoverable once they are shredded. No unerase utility can bring them back. This is a double-edged sword because they are safely out of the hands of anyone who wants to snoop around in your stuff, but they are also beyond repair if you do something stupid like shred the wrong set of files. You have to be careful when shredding.

The second issue involves the use of scratch files, used for temporary storage by many applications. If your word processor has an autosave feature that backs up your work every *x* minutes, or if it uses a scratch file for editing before writing to the *real* file, it is possible your system has deleted copies of these scratch files that an intruder can recover. You must manually cleanse the disk by writing a file into the areas where scratch files have been saved and shredding the temporary files.

Nuke for DOS

Nuke has been around since the days when DOS 3.3 ruled the Earth. It still works today just as well as it did the last time it was updated in 1989. Nuke is a shareware program that can be downloaded from the Internet by using FTP at ftp://ftp.u.washington.edu/pub/user-supported/dosutil/. The file to download is NUKE111.ZIP. The author is Charles M. Hannum II.

Nuke is a really simple command replacement for the DOS ERASE or DEL commands. All you do is unzip the contents of NUKE111.ZIP into a directory that is included in your PATH statement. To see the command-line switches available in Nuke, just type the word NUKE and press Enter. Figure 5-3 shows you the response that will print out on your screen.

The two most important of the available switches are /Cn and /G. The /C switch determines how many times the disk area where the old file was stored is overwritten, where *n* is the number of times to overwrite. The /G switch uses the government standard of three overwrites. Overwriting the file several times prevents someone from using fancy equipment to interpret and record the faint echoes of the characters that have been overwritten.

```
C:\>nuke
NUKE(TM), version 1.11, (C) 1988 by Charles Martin Hannum II

Usage: NUKE [d:][path]filename.ext ... [/GLNPTV!/Cn]

Switches
    /Cn     Specify number of cycles for nuking
    /G      Use government specs; 3 cycles
    /L      Log mode (for future use)
    /N      Non-nuke; just erase
    /P      Pause when screen full
    /T      Terse; display totals only
    /V      Verify; confirm each file

Hidden, system, and read-only files are confirmed in all modes

C:\>
```

Figure 5-3: Nuke command-line switches.

Dig deeper

For many readers, it will come as a revelation that you can actually recover the records of files that have been written over. Here's how it can be done.

Hard disks use magnetized surfaces to record the ones and zeros used to write files. When a file is deleted, then overwritten, there is no erase head that degausses the surface of the disk like there is in a tape recorder. When a character is written to disk, an electrical pulse from the disk drive's head causes the magnetic material's molecules to align in a certain pattern for a 1 and another pattern for a 0. Because the molecules aren't randomized by an erase head, faint traces of previous characters remain behind.

If you don't get the concept, try a little trick right out of eighth grade science class. Take a square pan of iron filings and use a magnet to arrange them in a square, without actually touching the filings with the magnet. Then, without shaking the pan, use the magnet to arrange the filings into a circle, again without letting the magnet come into contact with the filings. Even though you arrange most of the iron filings into a circle, there will often be telltale signs that the shape used to be a rectangle.

These faint remainders on your disk can be distinguished by extremely sensitive equipment. In fact, the intelligence community has equipment that can read as many as three previous levels. Fortunately, your average hacker, who doesn't carry a badge and gun, doesn't have access to this type of equipment.

The concept behind Nuke and other file shredders is to overwrite both the directory entry in the File Allocation Table and the disk sectors that the file to be shredded occupies. Take a look at Figure 5-4, and you can see the information revealed by the Norton Utilities about the file DETLOG.OLD. Note the sector number, and the inset at the bottom of the figure that shows the contents of the file, hex values on the left, and the ASCII on the right.

If you issue the command

```
NUKE C:\DETLOG.OLD /G
```

the program will confirm that you want the file shredded and then tell you it was found and nuked if the program is successful. Figure 5-5 shows you the contents of the disk beginning at the starting sector where DETLOG.OLD was written. As you can see, it has been overwritten with the F6 character, which is the same character that the DOS FORMAT command uses to fill newly formatted disks.

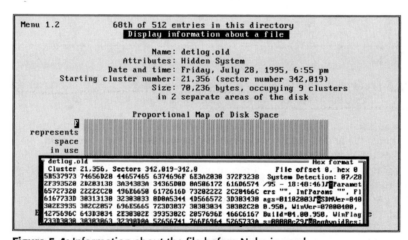

Figure 5-4: Information about the file before Nuke is used.

If you work in DOS all day long and have a need to eliminate sensitive files, Nuke should be on your shortlist of programs to acquire. It is simple to use, allows wildcards for the shredding of multiple files, and is reliable.

One word of caution. You should never use DOS utilities, including Nuke, to perform file maintenance chores on a Windows for Workgroups 3.11, Windows 95, or Windows NT system. Although the new Windows 32-bit file systems are backwardly compatible with DOS, they offer features such as long filenames that DOS applications developers never contemplated. You can severely damage your disk structure by using old DOS apps to delete and rearrange files, with the result that you will need to reformat the disk to straighten out the mess. Nuke is safe to use with any version of Windows that requires DOS to be loaded first and doesn't have Workgroups installed.

[Figure 5-5 screenshot of hex dump showing repeated F6F6F6F6 values]

Figure 5-5: After Nuke, the sector is effectively reformatted.

Terminator 2.0 for Windows

Although Windows 3.1 has no problem with file management utilities because it runs on top of DOS, shredder applications for Windows 95 present a potential problem because the 32-bit extensions to the file system weren't released when most shredder applications were written. Fortunately, several shredders written for Windows 3.x will work nicely until Windows 95 versions come along.

One of the most interesting shred programs is called Terminator. Written by R. J. Hill, Terminator is simple to use. Terminator also has a View feature that lets you double-check the contents of a file before it is shredded because, as the startup window of the program says, "Your files won't be back." You can download Terminator 2.0 from the Internet at http://www.csusm.edu/cwis/winworld/filemgr.html. Just click on the file TERM20.zip.

As you can see in Figure 5-6, the user interface for Terminator is simple and clean. Locate files in the file list and then drag and drop them on either the viewer or the shredder, represented by the Arnold Schwarzenegger look-alike. Figure 5-7 shows the viewer in action. The viewer lets you take one last look at a file before deciding whether it should be shredded.

There are two levels of shredding available in Terminator, listed as Quick Termination and DOD Termination under the File menu. You can select either the semi-secure, one-pass, quick method, or the Department of Defense-compliant method, which uses seven passes. During each pass, the sectors where the file is written are overwritten entirely.

As you can see in Figure 5-8, all terminations are confirmed, just in case you drag the wrong file onto the shredder. In the progress bar, you are notified which level of shredding is chosen. Unfortunately, Quick Termination is the default method; you have to remember to turn on the seven-pass mode each time you launch Terminator 2.0.

Figure 5-6: Terminator 2.0 gives you a drag-and-drop interface for shredding files.

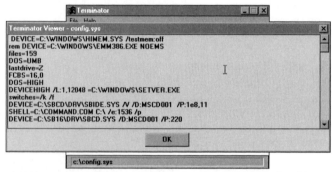

Figure 5-7: You can drop a file on the viewer before shredding it to confirm the contents.

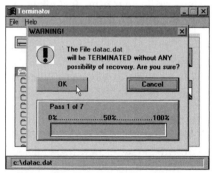

Figure 5-8: All file shreddings are confirmed, and the number of overwrite passes to be performed is shown.

Figure 5-9 shows the output of the Norton Utilities (run under DOS) to reveal that the sectors where the file once resided have all been overwritten to the value of 02h, which is the smiley face character.

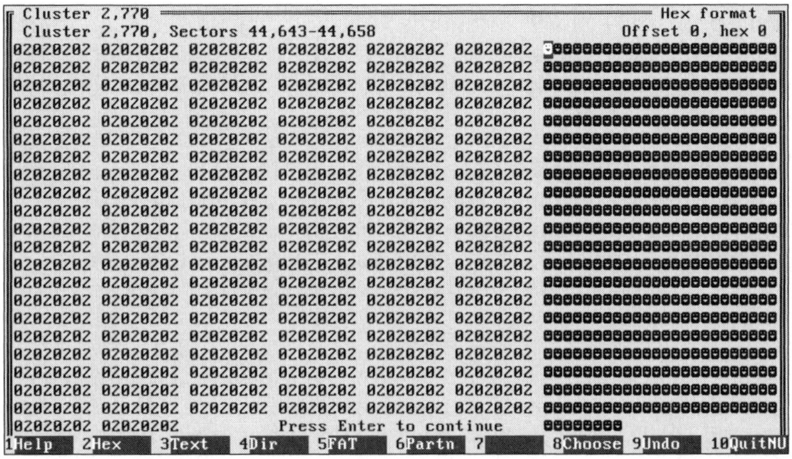

Figure 5-9: Norton Utilities confirms that the sectors once occupied by the file are indeed shredded.

There are a surprising number of applications out there that purport to provide security by locking down Windows Program Manager groups so that they can be opened only with a password or cannot be altered. Although these programs do a fine job of keeping users from altering or using desktop groups, they do nothing to restrict access to the underlying files. This means that lock programs can be circumvented by the simple act of launching File Manager.

If you are trying to restrict access to sensitive material, be aware that these types of programs are effective only in discouraging the rank beginner computer user and small children.

Encrypting ZIP files

Encryption is a controversial topic, as you will see in Chapter 10, which deals with encryption in depth. The controversy is twofold. Government is concerned that strong encryption methods make it possible for criminal activities to go undetected, and users want strong measures to keep extremely sensitive data secure. The issue in encryption is the relative security of various encryption methods.

In the pages that follow, I cover two simple encryption methods. One is vulnerable but is convenient, whereas the other is reasonably secure as well as convenient.

Encrypted PKZip files

One of the features of PKZip, the compression and archiving utility from PKWare, is the capability to encrypt the contents of the archive. A few years ago, PKWare offered a thousand dollar prize to anyone who could break open a ZIP file PKWare distributed.

Of course, the prize was claimed within the year by a man named Paul C. Kocher. He co-authored with Eli Biham a paper, entitled *A Known Plaintext Attack on the PKZip Stream Cipher,* which was presented in December 1994 at a security conference in Belgium.

To greatly simplify a very complex topic, one of the problems in hacking an encrypted document is knowing when to stop. You can try every combination of possible passwords, but if you don't know that your result has been achieved, the program will just blithely continue trying passwords needlessly. Thus, a short dictionary is used to provide some text samples to test whether they are present in the unencrypted stream of characters.

Kocher's attack on the PKZip encryption involves using plain text known to be part of the encrypted data stream. Because you can see the names of files that are contained in the encrypted ZIP file, you can often make an educated guess as to some character strings that might be contained within. For example, a cracker familiar with C programming may see STDIO.H as a filename in a ZIP file and immediately recognize that it is the standard C header file. It just so happens that a copy of that file is already sitting on the cracker's hard disk so he or she doesn't have to go looking for plain text to use in the attack.

Since the first break of the ZIP file encryption, a number of versions of cracking programs have been devised. Any self-respecting hacker has a copy of ZIPCRACK.EXE laid away somewhere on his or her hard disk, yet. . . .

People still use ZIP encryption, and PKWare hasn't updated its version since 1993. What gives? The same mindset that enables you to lock your car doors and consider the box on the back seat relatively safe. Remember, someone has to want your stuff, know how to crack it, and have the opportunity to do so in order for your security to be breached.

Cracking a ZIP file can take hours and hours of trying. If the cracker has to use your machine, he or she may be foiled simply by lack of access. Crack programs are often left running overnight and are thus discoverable. Of course, if an archive fits on a floppy disk, the would-be cracker can just make a copy and take it somewhere else to crack. You can up the discouragement level a bit if your archive is too big to fit on a single floppy. In that case, assuming that you aren't connected to a network or online service, the would-be cracker must break the file into parts that can be reassembled later in order to steal your data.

Tip

If you have a document that you want to put into a ZIP file for encryption, you can up the discouragement ante if you are willing to burn some disk space. Take a really big file of ten or more megabytes and put it into the archive along with the data you really want encrypted. One of the music video AVI files that comes on the Windows 95 CD is ideal if you can spare 30 megs. Because the AVI file is already compressed, it won't shrink much when zipped. A file that size is a pain to break into floppies and is too long to communicate surreptitiously by mode. A stupid computer trick to be sure, but sometimes stupid computer tricks work.

The bottom line is that putting payroll information files into a ZIP file certainly won't protect them from the Legion of Doom or Club 2000, but it will keep most people out. You are at least using a mild deterrent to snooping when you create an encrypted ZIP file. You don't want to entrust your most sensitive data to an encrypted ZIP, but it's better than nothing. It may be suitable for hiding financial information from the kids, but don't bet the company's future on the security of a ZIP file.

Now that you know the risks of using encrypted ZIP files, here's how you use them.

Password protected ZIP files

Many users of PKWare's excellent shareware PKZip utility are unaware that you can password protect ZIP files. If you type PKZIP at a DOS prompt without any command-line arguments and then press 2 to see more options, you will see the help display. The entry -s [pwd] that appears about two thirds of the way down the list shows you how you can scramble (encrypt) the resulting ZIP archive file, providing a password that must be entered to unarchive the contents.

For example, entering the following command at the DOS prompt

    PKZIP -sRock+Dime PROTECT *.DOC

will create an archive file named PROTECT.ZIP that requires you to enter the command

    PKUNZIP -sRock+Dime PROTECT

to unarchive and unscramble the contents of PROTECT.ZIP.

Using WinZip to password protect files

There are about five shareware programs that I consider indispensable and that I use everyday. One of these is WinZip, Nico Mak's shareware archive manager. Both 16-bit and 32-bit versions of WinZip are available, so you can use WinZip on any Windows machine, whether it is running Windows 3.x, Windows 95, or Windows NT.

WinZip is compatible with a variety of archive file formats, including ZIP, LZH, ARC, and TAR. During the setup of WinZip, you tell the program where the software for each of the supported archive formats can be found. You can also specify a virus scanner. In some cases, WinZip acts as a launcher and shell manager for underlying archive software. As the name implies, WinZip really shines when it comes to handling

ZIP files. Most of the functionality of PKZip is built in, so you seldom need an underlying copy of PKWare's products.

What makes WinZip so handy is its capability to open an archive and show you the contents. The file list acts a little like Windows 3.*x*'s File Manager or Windows 95's Explorer. Double-clicking on a registered file type launches the associated application with the file open for editing. You can use WinZip to manage a single archive of sensitive files, protected by a single password.

As you work with documents, you simply make your edits and save them in the application as usual. When you close the application, and the file has changed, WinZip detects that the two versions are different and will automatically offer to update the archived version of the file.

What this means is that you can now have a convenient way of managing sensitive documents by placing them into encrypted ZIP (or other format) archive files and never working with them outside the archive. You can enter the password one time by selecting the Options menu, then Password, and work with any or all of the files in the archive without having to extract them to disk. Rearchive them when you are done.

Figure 5-10 shows WinZip in action. You can download an evaluation copy of WinZip at http://www.winzip.com from any of the commercial online services and from most bulletin boards of any size.

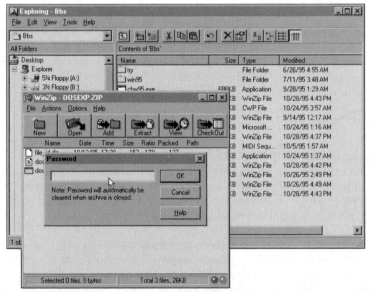

Figure 5-10: WinZip makes it convenient to place sensitive files into password-protected archive files.

Two notes of caution are necessary if you use WinZip to store sensitive documents. First, the password entry dialog box displays the password you type instead of displaying asterisks, as most programs do. You need to be on guard against shoulder surfers while entering the password for an archive.

The second thing to watch out for is that WinZip extracts documents to a temporary directory. Although WinZip is very good about erasing scratch files, experienced computer users know that files are never actually erased until the disk sectors they occupy are overwritten by another file. This is an operating system thing, and no fault of WinZip.

A knowledgeable snoop could use low-level disk editing tools to recover the *erased*, unscrambled version of the file from the temporary directory that was used by the application during editing. If the data you are working with is truly sensitive, you can find utilities like Norton's WipeFile utility that will overwrite areas of the hard disk so that old files are fully erased. The Speed Disk utility that comes with Norton Utilities for Windows 95 has an option to wipe the disk clean as it defragments.

DES encryption

DES stands for Data Encryption Standard and is the same algorithm used in the ANSI standard DEA (Data Encryption Algorithm). DES was designed by IBM in response to a call by the National Security Agency for computer cipher software. After a period of development, DES was given the blessings of the U.S. government in 1977.

The history of DES

Cryptography is an arcane and highly complex art full of concepts that require an advanced degree in mathematics to comprehend. Even among persons at that level of understanding, there is always plenty of room for debate. Despite the fact that no incidence of cracking DES has ever been reported, there has been speculation for the last 20 years that the government has a method of cracking DES-encrypted documents via a back door intentionally left open at the government's request during the adoption process almost 20 years ago.

Despite the paranoia of some folks that the NSA intentionally weakened the standard and the fact that exporting DES encryption is illegal, DES is probably the most widely-used encryption method in the world. Originally designed as a hardware-based encryption system, the advent of powerful personal computers has made it practical to translate the DES algorithm to software-only encryption products.

DES is a single key cryptosystem, which means that the same key (password) used to encrypt the data is needed to unencrypt the data. That means both the sender and the recipient need to have the same key, or the data cannot be extracted properly.

Theoretically, DES encryption is vulnerable to brute force cracking methods, but with trillions of possible key combinations, only corporations and governments with millions of dollars to spend can put together the resources to crack it. If this has been done, it has never been reported. The Federal Reserve uses it in certain financial transactions, so it can't be too shabby.

In short, DES encryption is secure enough that the U.S. government continues to use it as a standard for all but the most highly classified data. It will probably withstand anything that someone going after your data can throw at it.

DES for Windows

DES for Windows, written by Jeff Saltzman, is a shareware encryption utility that can be downloaded from ftp://winftp.cica.indiana.edu/pub/pc/win3/programr/. DES for Windows enables you to create encrypted forms of your data quickly and easily and will run on both Windows 3.1 and Windows 95.

Figure 5-11 shows DES for Windows in action. As you can see, there are several choices that enable you to determine how to handle the data to be encrypted or decrypted. DES will even let you use the Windows Clipboard as the vehicle for input and output. When you encrypt a file into a different file, DES has an option that enables you to shred the original document once you have determined that the encrypted version of the file is OK.

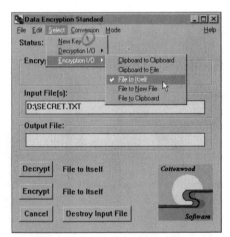

Figure 5-11: DES for Windows lets you encrypt and decrypt using both files and the Windows Clipboard.

To encrypt a file, follow these steps:

1. Choose New Key from the Select menu and enter a password key of up to 19 characters.

   You can also choose Encryption I/O and Decryption I/O from the Select menu to choose the data path for encrypting and decrypting your material.

wwwaccess = http://www.winsite.com/pub/pc/win3

Once you have made a selection, it is displayed next to the Encrypt and Decrypt buttons so you know whether your input is coming from a file or the Clipboard, and what form it will be written to.

2. Use the File menu options to specify filenames for encryption and decryption.

You can select multiple files from the Open dialog box by using Ctrl and Shift as you select the files you want to encrypt or decrypt.

Figure 5-12 shows a before and after view of the encryption process. In the top left of the figure, you can see the unencrypted text. The lower right shows the same file after encryption using the file-to-itself data path. The encrypted version can be returned to its original form only by decrypting the file using the same password.

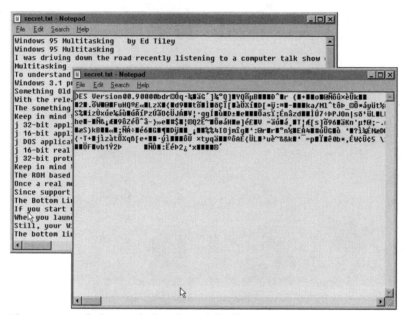

Figure 5-12: A before-and-after view of the file SECRET.TXT.

Once a file is encrypted, you can handle it just like any other file you work with. The only difference is that you can't read it anymore.

DES for Windows supports both single DES and triple DES encryption. Triple DES encryption is reputed to be among the toughest to crack. When you select Triple DES from the Mode menu, you are prompted for two password keys instead of just one when you choose New Key in the Select menu. According to Mr. Saltzman's documentation, Triple DES provides encryption that is "probably as good, or better, than military grade codes." Keep in mind, though, that using Triple DES is much slower than the Single DES mode.

the ultimate

ftp://ftp.winsite.com/pub/pc/win3/programs/
des3.zip = file

By default, DES for Windows operates in the Binary mode, meaning that the output of the DES algorithm can be any ASCII character. Because many e-mail systems cannot handle non-printable characters in message text, DES for Windows has an ASCII mode that can be selected from the Conversion menu. Text encrypted in ASCII mode is converted into straight printable text characters in a process similar to Uuencode.

In Figure 5-13, you see the result of encrypting a reply to an e-mail message by using Clipboard-to-Clipboard as the data path. The message was received and a reply made, but before the return message was sent, the text of the message was cut to the Clipboard, encrypted, and then pasted back into the message.

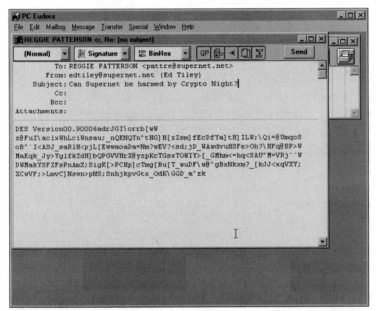

Figure 5-13: Encrypting e-mail is a snap when you use the Clipboard-to-Clipboard data path.

Because DES is a single-key encryption system, you have one small problem to overcome before you can share encrypted data with someone else. You have to make sure that they use the same password key to decrypt as you used to encrypt. This can present a problem because the key must somehow be disclosed to the recipient secretly. If you even thought about e-mailing the key in a separate message, you need to move to the rear of the line!

Of course, you could be Cold War about it and make an understanding with your correspondent that each day's key will be some randomly chosen public text. One person I know had an agreement with a friend that he would encrypt financial e-mail messages using the first 12 characters of the second bit of dialog in their favorite newspaper cartoon strip. This pact worked fine until one day when the cartoon was a total sight gag with no dialog! Whatever system you work out, make sure that it is at least as secure as your encryption software.

Summary

This chapter showed you how you can begin protecting your sensitive data even if you are a relatively new computer user. You learned how DOS and its ancestor operating systems manage files, leaving an opportunity for someone to recover deleted files.

- There are some stupid computer tricks that users have used for years to gain a measure of security for sensitive data. The problem is that all of these schemes can be easily defeated by a knowledgeable user.

- DOS and its ancestor operating systems save time by not actually erasing files when you delete them. Instead, the file allocation table is simply edited to mark the file's name entry as invalid and return the sectors where the file is written to available status. This means that files you erase can be recovered by using a variety of widely available tools.

- Shredder programs completely obliterate a file by overwriting all the information in the FAT about the file and by overwriting the sectors where the file is written.

- Although the PKZip password protection feature has been shown to be vulnerable to attack, it is still a popular way of encrypting ZIP archives. You should never trust high-level secure data to this method because there are several programs on the Internet that will enable the password to be cracked by using a plain text attack.

- It can be simple to apply strong encryption to individual files and to e-mail messages by using government standard DES encryption.

✦ ✦ ✦

Security Online

PART II

In This Part

Chapter 6
E-Mail Security

Chapter 7
The Risks of Online Transactions: Real & Imagined

Chapter 8
Internet Security

Chapter 9
Protecting Yourself from Unwanted Material

E-Mail Security

CHAPTER 6

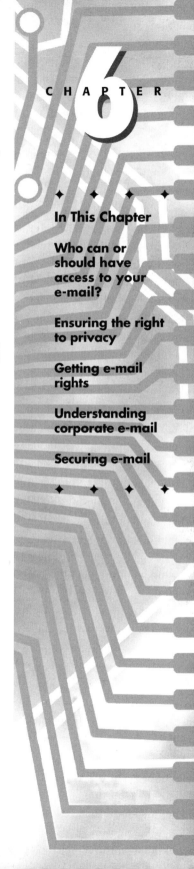

In This Chapter

Who can or should have access to your e-mail?

Ensuring the right to privacy

Getting e-mail rights

Understanding corporate e-mail

Securing e-mail

by Richard Roccanti

They that can give up essential liberty to obtain a little temporary safety deserve neither liberty nor safety.
— Benjamin Franklin

One hundred years ago, if you wanted to get a message to a friend in another city or town, you may have done several things. Your first option was to write it down and have the Pony Express deliver it. You may have given a verbal message to a friend going in that direction. Or you may have sent a telegram.

When you sent that telegram, you knew that the person working in the telegraph office (on both ends) would have to read your note to send or receive it across the wire. Security was not an available option. We may have come a long way, but today's electronic mail (e-mail) has some of the very same pitfalls.

Today we can send very elaborate messages with text, sound, pictures, and motion around the world. Although the content may be radically different, the same age-old concern still exists. Who can intercept and view the contents of your messages?

Types of E-Mail

The term *e-mail* is a loosely fitting, one-size-fits-all way of describing any kind of communication using computers and modems. If you send messages to another person by using a local bulletin board, a commercial online service, a company network mail system, or the Internet, you are sending e-mail.

In the case of a local bulletin board, your message may be publicly readable, or it may be stored as a private message until the person you sent it to picks it up. Some bulletin boards are part of informal networks like FidoNet. These networks convey messages posted to the board to other computer systems in a relay hand-off situation where computer A calls computer B to deliver all its new messages. Computer B is, in turn, called by another, and so on down the line. In this way, people who subscribe to different local bulletin boards are able to send messages back and forth, even though no permanent link between their BBS systems exists.

All of the major commercial online services like CompuServe, AOL, and Prodigy offer e-mail services. Via these services, you can address messages to other commercial services like MCI Mail, or any Internet address in the world. Most large companies have internal e-mail systems that can connect to the outside world. For example, billg@microsoft.com will drop a note in Bill Gate's inbox. Each employee at Microsoft has an Internet account that serves as his or her company inbox as well. Other companies have ways of routing messages to places outside their internal networks.

Just as every telephone in the world has a unique number that identifies that single phone line, every e-mail address is different and serves to specify a single, particular inbox.

The Security of E-Mail vs. Other Kinds of Mail

Whether you're on a local area network (LAN) or a wide area network (WAN) like the Internet, everyone who has the supervisor's password or login has the capability to access everything on the network, or at least the traffic that passes through the system.

When you send a *snail mail* letter to another person by using the Postal Service, there are known risks. First, you put that letter in your mailbox in the morning before you leave to go to work. You pull up the little metal flag that tells the letter carrier you have outgoing mail. That little flag also tells everyone else there is a letter waiting, too. Your letter may sit in the mailbox, vulnerable, for several hours before it is picked up.

At the post office, your letter is handled by many different people and put in many different mail vehicles until it is placed in the recipient's mailbox, where it lies unguarded until your uncle or sister or friend from college checks his or her mail.

There are numerous examples of ways that physical letters can be lost or tampered with. The letter might be stolen by someone looking for money; it might be misplaced by the post office; the stamp might fall off and the letter then come back to you. Someone looking for information about you may even try to steam the letter open and read it.

Is Internet e-mail any more or less secure than a letter? Probably not. Although there are numerous possible pitfalls to a letter arriving at its destination intact and unread, the vast majority of letters are delivered by the Postal Service without incident, millions of times a day.

The same is true of Internet e-mail: millions of messages arrive safely at their destination address intact and unread every day. The sheer volume of messages dictates that it is impossible to try and intercept all but a few.

E-mail, whether sent across a company network or the Internet, differs radically from a letter in several respects. Although some mail routing programs like cc:mail and Microsoft Mail have the capability to encrypt messages as they are passed from one "post office" to another, most e-mail currently travels from origination to destination as plain text. Most Internet Service Providers use POP (Post Office Protocol) or SMTP (Simple Mail Transfer Protocol) to send messages from sender to recipient. By default, both of these protocols use plain text.

E-mail has been likened to sending postcards rather than letters. Tucked away safely inside an envelope, most letters are safe from prying eyes. An envelope that has been opened almost always shows evidence of tampering, whereas an e-mail message can be copied undetectably. Just as you can make a Xerox copy of a piece of paper or copy a file on your hard disk without altering the original in any way, an e-mail message can be duplicated before it is sent on, and the receiver will never know it.

One thing a letter and an electronic message have in common is that people handle them: e-mail resides on computer systems that must be maintained by people. Just like your average postal worker, system administrators usually have much too much work to do to be worried about reading your mail, but it is possible for an unscrupulous administrator to monitor your mail.

However, there is a major difference between paper and electronic mail. One of the tasks of a scrupulous operator may be to make archive copies of all e-mail that passes in to and out of the system, so that the system can be restored in the event of a crash. That way you won't miss an important message just because the system went down. This person may also read undelivered messages, which have no envelope to keep out prying eyes, in an attempt to reroute them to the proper person.

By law, most federal agencies of the U.S. government must comply with the Federal Records Act, which was upheld in the *Armstrong v. Executive Office of the President* case, which states, in part:

"All . . . machine-readable materials, or other documentary materials, regardless of physical form or characteristics, made or received by an agency of the United States under Federal law or in connection with the transaction of public business and preserved or appropriated for preservation by that agency . . . as evidence of the organization, functions, policies, decisions, procedures, operations, or other activities of the Government or because of the informational value of the data in them [be preserved]."

The court in the Armstrong decision required the actual computer records to be archived instead of stored as paper printouts because the paper records lacked information about the sender, time stamps, the receiver, and so on.

E-mail and the law

The controversial Supreme Court decision in *Roe v. Wade* did more than legalize abortion on demand. In the decision, the majority noted that other rights enumerated in the Bill of Rights created a penumbra, a shadow, that embodied a right to privacy. In *Roe,* the court addressed reproductive freedom specifically, but as a result of that decision, a generally recognized right to privacy was affirmed. Until the Electronic Communications Privacy Act of 1986 was passed, however, certain types of communication did not enjoy the same protections as telephone communications. A series of Supreme Court decisions ruled that computer communications could be intercepted without obtaining a warrant because they were not oral communications as specified in then existing wiretap law.

The Electronic Communications Privacy Act of 1986 codified communications privacy to provide equal protection to computer originated communications. Language in the law states that anyone who " intentionally intercepts, endeavors to intercept, or procures any other person to intercept or endeavor to intercept any wire, oral, or electronic communication" is guilty of a felony. The Act also makes criminal the "intentional disclosure or use of the contents of any wire, oral, or electronic communication that is known or could reasonably be known to have been intercepted."

A separate section of the Electronic Communications Privacy Act of 1986 provides an out for service providers, including Internet Service Providers. It says, "It shall not be unlawful under this chapter for an operator of a switchboard, or an officer, employee, or agent of a provider of wire or electronic communication service, whose facilities are used in the transmission of a wire communication, to intercept, disclose, or use that communication in the normal course of his employment while engaged in any activity which is a necessary incident to the rendition of his service or to the protection of rights or property of the provider of that service, except that a provider of wire communication service to the public shall not utilize service observing or random monitoring except for mechanical or service quality control checks."

In other words, service providers can, if their duties dictate, check communications to make sure that the service is working properly. It does not, however, allow a system administrator to snoop around the messages stored on the service provider's system just to kill time or to dig up the dirt on account holders.

Section 2518 of the Act requires law enforcement agencies to obtain search warrants before they can intercept the contents of electronic communications, although it does not prohibit devices that record the flow of communications. Thus the law gives e-mail the same status as a phone call. Just as law enforcement officials can use *pen registers* (devices that record what numbers are called or call a particular phone line) to monitor phone calling patterns, they can also use trap and trace devices to check out who is sending you mail and whom you send mail to without a warrant.

E-mail hackers and snoops

So who is interested in reading your e-mail? Two basic categories come to mind immediately: hackers and snoops. It's hard to say which is the more dangerous.

According to the *American Heritage Dictionary,* the term *hacker* has two definitions: "One who is proficient at using or programming a computer; a computer buff; one who illegally gains access to or enters another's electronic system to obtain secret information or steal money." The first definition is closest to the original meaning of the word.

The second definition of a malicious break-in artist who is trying to steal information or money is the type of person with whom we are most concerned. As you may remember from reading Chapter 2, hackers aren't necessarily just kids out looking for something to tear up. Many corporations use hackers to spy on competitors.

The two most dangerous places for e-mail are your outbox and the recipient's inbox. Almost every e-mail software package enables you to archive your incoming and outgoing messages. Some, like Netscape's mail reader, have an option that lets you send a copy of every outgoing message to the address of your choice. This option lets you use a second account as a repository of your outgoing correspondence. The danger lies in the fact that a stack of e-mail messages stored on the server system is easy prey to inquisitive eyes.

Similarly, the length of time an e-mail message sits on the recipient's server waiting to be downloaded to the recipient's computer represents a point of exposure. It is a simple matter in some cases to gain access to these messages.

The point is that a message sitting still in one place is a much more likely target for hackers because of the trouble and expense of setting up a *sniffer*. A sniffer is traditionally a system administrator's tool that enables him or her to monitor traffic patterns so that network connections can be inspected. It is possible to use a sniffer to intercept all traffic and to generate reports on the messages that fit some criterion, such as specific words or phrases used, or messages to and from a specific address or group of addresses. Setting up a sniffer is expensive, takes a fairly high degree of proficiency, and is easy to detect because it has to be plugged into the circuit. For someone to go to all that trouble, he or she almost certainly has to have a specific target account in mind, or else he or she is looking just for specific types of information, such as unencrypted credit card numbers.

On the other hand, for an experienced hacker, logging into some systems and gaining root (supervisor) privilege is a piece of cake, especially on those systems that are not rigorously managed by security-conscious administrators. Once a hacker gains root status, he or she can look at anything on the system, including e-mail stored or waiting to be delivered.

Remove already read mail from server

Most e-mail reader software gives you the capability to check a selection that is marked something like "remove read mail from server." This option may prove to be misleading to some users.

Some users prefer not to delete messages until they are sure that they are no longer needed, so they would choose to store old incoming messages in their inboxes. The inbox simply stores the messages in a file in a directory of the server's hard disk, which is dedicated to servicing your account. In effect, selecting to remove the mail from the server deletes it from your mailbox. That doesn't necessarily mean that it will remove it from the server entirely. Some service providers mirror all incoming traffic to a separate hard disk or a second server so that, in the event of a system crash, users' mailboxes can be brought back up to date.

A hacker who gains supervisor status on such a system can read several days worth of messages at will, even though the user thinks that they have been deleted. Other systems may make tape backups that are stored for weeks or months until the tape comes up in rotation to be reused. You may remember a certain Lt. Col. Ollie North, whose links to Iran-Contra were confirmed by backup tapes, even though he thought his e-mail messages were erased.

Unless you are at risk as a target of industrial espionage, your biggest risk is probably from a plain simple snoop. Snoops come in all shapes, sizes, and flavors, and each has his or her own reason for being interested in reading other people's mail. Snoops range from unscrupulous system administrators to curious kids who find your e-mail and decide to read your messages.

In general, system administrators are pretty good about not reading people's e-mail, but there are always exceptions. For example, many universities use student workers to install software on various local area networks around the campus. To install the network components, you need to have supervisor status. How many of these students keep track of various passwords and then use those passwords to snoop around in files?

Other snoops have hacker abilities. Andre Bacard, the author of *The Computer Privacy Handbook,* reports in an FAQ about e-mail that he once asked the head of a Silicon Valley company if he used e-mail. The executive's reply was, "Hell no, Andre. Half the nerds in my company can hack e-mail. E-mail is a party line!"

Another weak link in the e-mail security chain is the fact that your message may pass through umpteen computers on its way to its destination. Remember, the design of the Internet, and most other modern large networks, is supposed to let messages route themselves in order to bypass bottlenecks or down computers without causing errors. You might send five messages to your friend at greg@some.isp.com and no two of them will take the same path.

E-mail propagates

When you send a message to a friend, you may consider that the message exists in only one or two places: your computer (if you keep copies of outgoing mail) and the recipient's computer. That may not be the case. Consider the following scenario.

First, you type the mail and save it in your outbox on your hard drive (copy #1). If you are diligent about your backups, you will likely make a copy of the message on a tape (copy #2). You mail the message to your friend through your provider where it may get onto the service provider's daily backup (copy #3). Along the way, the message passes through any number of relays who theoretically shouldn't make copies, until it arrives at your friend's service provider where it is placed in your friend's inbox (copy #4 at least). His service provider may backup its system onto tape (copy #5). When your friend retrieves the message to his hard disk, it is written to his hard disk (copy #6). If your friend archives his mail and does backups, the message will eventually make it onto one or more of his tapes (copy #7). That is a lot of copies, but think of all the trees saved transmitting paperless messages. Still, with all those possible copies floating around out there, it is more likely that the security of such a document might be compromised.

Many of the computer systems that relay traffic between origin and destination are operated by university and government facilities. Each of these facilities has a strong policy regarding the monitoring of messages. The Electronic Privacy Act allows service providers to read messages only when necessary to perform their job. Does that mean that some student working the midnight shift in the computer room hasn't scanned passing e-mail messages? Does the Electronic Privacy Act prevent government employees from reading passing messages? No, it only provides the penalties for those who get caught.

Snooping is very easy to get away with because the original message doesn't get altered in any way. There is no envelope to show that the message has been opened and read. The message simply shows up at its destination. Like banks who cover the indiscretions of tellers in the belief that you would lose trust in the bank if you knew of them, service providers likewise have a motivation to handle breaches of security behind closed doors. A snooper who gets caught may get a slap on the wrist, or even fired, but seldom is he or she prosecuted. That would cause customers to lose trust in the telephone company or online service provider.

Snoopers are always a problem no matter what data is stored and no matter how the data is stored. Locked file cabinets or computer files are no match for a curious human mind bent on obtaining information. Information is power. Snoopers are looking for power, even if that power is as simple as knowing something they aren't supposed to know.

The Right to Privacy

Do you care that there are people out there who may be reading your e-mail? If your answer is "I have nothing to hide," you might as well stop sealing your envelopes when you send a written letter. Would you be comfortable sending all your personal and business correspondence on postcards via the U.S. Postal Service? Not many people would be.

The United States Constitution does guarantee the "right to privacy," so most of us claim that right and seal our envelopes, with the expectation that no one will violate that seal. Most computer users would like that right to privacy to include our electronic mail, too. As you will see, the how, when, where, and why behind your e-mail largely determines your privacy rights.

E-mail rights

Who has the right to read your e-mail? Obviously the intended addressed recipient, but what is intended by the e-mail sender is not always reality in cyberspace. For example, the *sysops* (systems operators, those hardworking geeks and nerds who keep your service operating smoothly most of the time) of your online service are governed by the Electronic Privacy Act. Under this law, they can read your mail only when it is necessary as part of performing their duties. Unfortunately, the language in the law is a bit vague about which duties require reading mail. The intent of the law, it seems, is to protect system administrators from liability if they have to read a misdirected message in order to figure out where it should be sent, or if they need to make sure that the system is delivering messages to the proper mailboxes, or other similar situations.

Some system administrators have taken the vague language in the Electronic Privacy Act to mean that they should scan messages to protect their Internet service or bulletin board service because they could be closed by law enforcement officials if illegal activity by users is occurring on their service.

Speaking of law enforcement, do police officials have a right to read your e-mail? To wiretap any communication, law enforcement officers must get a court order to approve their request after supplying enough evidence to show probable cause for a warrant. Could that change in the future? Keep in mind that the FBI, in pursuance of its authority under the Digital Telephony Act, which requires communications providers to make wiretaps easily available for law enforcement, has asked for the technical capability to tap up to one percent of all domestic phone calls. The FBI's position is that it would never tap that many phone calls, but the need to be able to tap quickly and easily requires that level of penetration. Just because the Digital Telephony Act exempted online service providers of computer network services doesn't mean that similar mandates won't be passed to cover cyberspace.

As you will see in Chapter 10, the NSA, FBI, and other federal agencies have been pushing for new encryption standards that would have the effect of outlawing private encryption software that the government can't crack. The floating of the Clipper chip idea was met with so much resistance that the government has now backed down on its position. It is now offering the computer industry the capability to export strong encryption software if the keys to break the encryption are escrowed between agencies so that even encrypted messages can be read by law enforcement officials with a warrant.

Privacy in the workplace

With few exceptions, legal custom and tradition in the United States are inherited from English common law. Under the common law, property rights often take precedence over other rights. Thus, there are no laws effectively prohibiting employers from conducting workplace surveillance. Hidden cameras are allowed to be trained on cashiers, telephone calls can be monitored, and so on. Privacy rights, according to multiple court rulings, take a back seat to the property rights of business owners. There are, of course, some limits placed on such surveillance, but about the only place you can't be monitored in the workplace, in some fashion, is the bathroom.

Does e-mail belong to you or your company? The answer is fairly simple. If you are provided an e-mail account by your employer, your mail messages can be monitored for nearly any reason. A survey by *Macworld* magazine found that about 25 percent of the businesses it surveyed routinely monitored employee computer files, e-mail, and voice mail messages. Legislation to curb monitoring of employees and to require notification to employees that they are being monitored has died without getting out of Congress.

That isn't to say that many, if not most, companies offer a measure of privacy to their employees. Most large companies have a policy statement available to all employees that informs them of monitoring procedures performed by the company. If, in the publication of monitoring policies, a company, university, or other organization makes promises of confidentiality, it is bound to those promises. A breach of those promises is actionable in civil courts.

It should be the responsibility of each employer to inform the employees or users of the policies of the company network e-mail system, and whether the employees' e-mail can be or is being monitored or read. Because, in many companies, procedures and guidelines are just now being written, it is advisable that you make it your duty to ask your employer what the current company policy on e-mail monitoring is. In a lot of workplaces, these issues are only now being addressed. A lot of owners and managers are only now tumbling to the idea that the system administrators of networks hold all the keys to the entire company information repository, including the chairman of the board's e-mail messages. Some of them aren't any more comfortable about privacy matters than you are. There may be an opportunity for you to help shape your employer's policies by taking an active and advisory role.

NII?

On September 15, 1993, President Bill Clinton signed Executive Order 12864, which established the Advisory Council on the National Information Infrastructure, or NII, for short.

The Executive Order established the Advisory Council NII to advise the Secretary of Commerce in developing a national strategy for promoting the development of the National Information Infrastructure. This infrastructure is supposed to make it easy and affordable to connect people with each other and with a vast array of services and information resources.

Members of the Advisory Council include representatives from broadcast networks, computer companies, consumer groups, the Electronic Frontier Foundation, newspapers, banks, and other interested parties. The organizations represented on the Advisory Council read like a Who's Who of American Business. The Coucil's first report, published in March of 1995, is entitled *Common Ground: Fundamental Principles for the National Information Infrastructure*. In this document, the group outlined a basic view of privacy rights as related to electronic communications. The report, which overall affirmed positive directions in privacy rights, largely ignored the issue of workplace privacy. The report reads in part, "Privacy is a cherished American value. In designing the technological infrastructure and the policy environment for the NII, the United States is establishing the framework for individual, social, economic, and political life in the 21st Century. It is important that fundamental American values — including protection of privacy, freedom of speech and association, freedom from discrimination and protection of property rights — be comprehensively and consistently considered in the NII. These values are not absolute, and need to be addressed in the context of the public interest. The application of privacy principles may differ according to the type of information being considered and the nature of the relationship between providers and users."

In short, even the Advisory Council on the National Information Infrastructure (the much vaunted Information Superhighway that most people take to be the Internet) still believes that if you own the ball, you can make the rules. Workplace privacy simply isn't given the same weight as other privacy rights.

You should keep in mind, however, that it is impossible for any employer to control every action of every employee. Even though your company may have a policy of respecting privacy in the workplace, there will be users on the network system who will not always share that respect. Human nature being what it is, there will always be system administrators and managers whose heads swell at the mere smell of info-power and who will try to establish their own fiefdoms with themselves among the gods. You should always be wary of such persons.

What to include and what to exclude from e-mail

My father always told me, "Plain and simple, Richard, if you want to keep a secret, never write it down." Even though you may take measures to make your e-mail more secure, my father's advice is still true. If it isn't written down, the only source of disclosure is your own mouth.

As you will learn later in this chapter, and in Chapter 10, the safest way to make your communications secure is to use encryption. Still, every cipher known to man can be broken, given enough time and computer resources. Therefore, you must decide for yourself what communications are to be trusted to the public transport and in what form.

Your e-mail message is only one of millions that travel the Internet every day. The actual chance of someone having a look at your message is relatively small, assuming that you are not specifically targeted for attack. If you are John Doe and sending e-mail to your sister Jane about your family visit to Boston next month, it isn't very likely that information is of interest to anyone outside your immediate circle of friends and family. If, on the other hand, you are the CEO of a company that is currently trying to get a new product out ahead of the competition, you are more at risk.

Even if you decide that some of your correspondence needs extra protection, you will probably not want to encrypt every piece of e-mail you send or receive. As with all security measures, there is a penalty to be paid in terms of convenience. Protecting yourself is always more inconvenient than working out in the open. Later in this chapter, I will show you some of the less intrusive ways of protecting your messages from prying eyes.

Fakemail and Anonymous Mail

There are two aspects of e-mail technology that every user of the Internet or online service needs to know about: *fakemail* and *anonymous remailers*. Using either technique, an attempt is made to hide the identity of the sender. The difference between the two techniques is simple: in fakemail, you are trying to hide your identity completely; you use an anonymous remailer if you want to attempt to hide your identity from all but the recipient.

Fakemail

Fakemail is the capability to send e-mail over the Internet by using an altered return mail address. It is surprisingly easy to send out such a message as a practical joke. Can you imagine sending a friend a message like

```
Return-Path: billg@microsoft.com
Date: Sun, 21 Jan 1996 18:47:31 -0600
From: Bill Gates  <billg@microsoft.com>
To: My Buddy <edtiley@supernet.net>
Subject: Programming

It has come to my attention that you are doing Internet program-
      ming projects. We at Microsoft are in dire need of your
      talents. We are prepared to pay you $1,000,000 to come to
      Redmond and help us out. Can you come?

Bill Gates
```

No doubt your friend would flip out. How about a message from GOD@heaven.org? It really isn't hard at all to send such a message. All you have to do is telnet into port 25 of a UNIX-based computer network that is part of the Internet and enter a few commands like this:

```
HELO somesystem.com
MAIL FROM: nobody@somesystem.com
RCPT TO:president@whitehouse.gov
DATA

This is my message to you. Check out the cool return address.
 QUIT
```

All you have to do is put the return address you want to appear in the MAIL FROM line. In the vernacular of the computer underground, this is called *spoofing*. If you telnet into a system that has RFC 931 loaded into the system, a patch that prevents spoofing mail origination, your real mail address will be sent instead of the fake you enter. Test for ROC 931 by sending mail to yourself first. It shouldn't be a surprise, I suppose, but it is interesting that not all server systems have this patch loaded.

The main reason spoofing the return address works is found in the implementation of e-mail transport protocols. E-mail protocols in current usage use a metaphor of an envelope and letter. Each message is surrounded by a digital envelope in the form of a header and a termination. The header is separate and distinct from the message itself and contains several pieces of information, including the return address for the message. All you need to do is change the header before sending the message, and pouf! Instant fakemail.

For a time, a guy by the name of Ryan Scott operated a Web page that allowed visitors to send fakemail messages at http://www.netcreations.com/fakemail/. You can go to his page and get the story of how he created one of the most controversial sites on the Web by inviting people to send fakemail. Unfortunately, a project that was taken up with a sense of humor and rebelliousness fell prey to some folks who abused the service to send messages a lot nastier than a practical joke.

Strangely, though, as Ryan points out in a sample fakemail generated by his page, the actual origin of the message was buried in the preface material to the message. In other words, if the recipient looked carefully at the header information printed in the message, it was obvious that the messages were faked. Thus, the numbskulls who used the service to send threats and other nasty e-mails to public officials were easily identified. Still, the service caused more problems for Ryan than it was worth. All that remains is a testimonial to what was once a fun Web site.

The lesson to be learned in all of this is simple: "Things are not always what they seem." Ed is a decent programmer, but Bill Gates isn't going to be sending him any million dollar offers any time soon. If you get an e-mail that just doesn't quite ring true, check it out very closely.

Anonymous remailers

An anonymous remailer is a mail server that is designed to take a message sent to it, strip off all the identifying information in the header and replace it with anonymous information, and then pass it along the way to the destination. When the e-mail message arrives at the recipient's inbox, he or she has no way of telling the actual origin of the message. The truly cautious, some would say paranoid, even use multiple remailers, sending their messages through five or more remailers before the message is sent to its destination. There are any number of reasons, legitimate and not so legitimate, for wanting to remain anonymous. These range from secret business negotiations and intimately personal communications to covering up illegal activities. Often, anonymous remailers are used as a way of participating in controversial Usenet groups without revealing your identity.

Usenet, for those readers unfamiliar with it, is a part of the Internet landscape. It is a loose amalgamation of more than 10,000 special interest groups similar to bulletin boards. No matter what interests you may have, it seems there is a Usenet group that specializes in that topic. A large number of these groups deal in controversial political, social, and sexual topics. It is not uncommon for people to participate in these groups by using an anonymous remailer hiding their identity. It was the use of an anonymous remailer in the alt.religion.scientology group that sparked one of the biggest news stories to date concerning anonymous remailer usage, described in the accompanying sidebar.

For more information on anonymous remailers, check out http://www.skypoint.com/members/gimonca/anonmail.html, which presents a document called *Keeping Your Opinions Anonymous*. This page discusses both the need for and the use of anonymous remailers. It is written by Charles A. Gimon, who teaches at the English Learning Center in South Minneapolis, MN.

HORROR STORIES

anon.penet.fi

Perhaps the best known and most used of the available anonymous remailers is anon.penet.fi, located in Finland and run by a computer scientist named Johan Helsingius.

According to a *Time* magazine article dated March 6, 1995, Helsingius reported in a Usenet group that Finnish police, accompanied by agents from Interpol (the international European law enforcement agency) raided the headquarters of anon.penet.fi on February 18th, 1995. Acting on a request from American law enforcement, the Finns demanded to know the identity of a person who had allegedly posted copyrighted and secret Church of Scientology documents onto the Internet in a Usenet group.

The way anon.penet.fi works is that a user sends an e-mail message to the penet server, where the sender is given an ID, and all identifying marks on the message are stripped off and replaced with penet identifications. In effect, Helsingius' system keeps a monster database of everyone who has ever used the system so that reply messages sent to a penet ID can be routed back to the originator of the communications.

The police at Helsingius' door demanded to be told who the originator of the message was. Faced with confiscation by warrant of his entire database, Helsingius decided that discretion was the better part of valor and gave the police the information.

According to the *Time* article, "Helsingius has become the keeper of the Who's Who of the computer underground. Stored in his 200-megabyte database is a master list of the names and e-mail addresses of everybody who has ever sought the shelter of his service: pornographers and political exiles; software pirates and corporate whistle blowers; the sexually abused and their abusers."

Making E-Mail Secure

Internet security is best described as an oxymoron. There is nothing secure about the Internet. All transmissions go through countless other machines until they finally end up at the right destination. The only thing you have working for your privacy is the relative insignificance of your letter, compared to the relative significance of someone else's e-mail. Bill Gates' e-mail has a higher probability of being intercepted than Bill Smith's e-mail. Still, almost any transmission has the potential to be intercepted. How does one stop it? Just as electric barbed wire fencing, attacking guard dogs, steel bars, and an alarm system will help discourage burglars, the idea behind e-mail security is to make it so hard to get to that the hacker or snoop will not bother with it.

ROT-13 is not encryption

Many new users are confused by the security features offered in Netscape 2.0. They hear about SSL (Secure Sockets Layer) and other features of the Netscape browser, and assume that they are getting a level of protection that simply doesn't exist. In order for most of the security features in Netscape to kick in, you have to link to Web pages mounted on a secure server. If the little key icon in the lower left corner of the screen has a break in it, then nothing you are doing is secure.

In particular, one of the most common mistakes people make is confusing the Unscramble ROT-13 feature of Netscape with encryption. It isn't. ROT-13 is actually a simple Cesarean substitution cipher designed for discretion, not for encryption (see Figure 6-1). ROT-13, which actually stands for ROTATE 13, simply substitutes letters in a message by rotating them 13 places. Thus, A, the first letter, becomes M, the 13th letter, and so on.

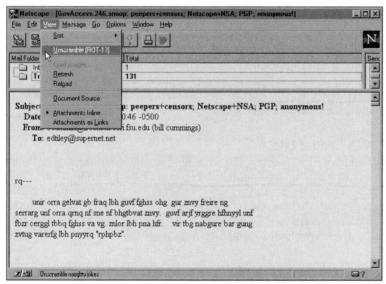

Figure 6-1: ROT-13 is a simple character transposition designed for discretion on Usenet.

The reason for having ROT-13 in the first place is simply to screen potentially offensive messages from the view of casual browsers of Usenet messages. For example, if you were to post a message full of expletives, four-letter words, and other foul language (you wouldn't actually do that, now would you?), you could scramble it using ROT-13. In that way, those words don't just POP off the page at a casual passerby who may not be used to the fact that in some Usenet groups such language is acceptable, if not required, to fit in with the group. To read such a message, you simply use ROT-13 to unscramble it.

Using encryption

In Chapter 10, you will get a working knowledge of encryption techniques and the climate in which encryption is used today. The U.S. government, it seems, is not thrilled that people have strong encryption software available to them. Several of the law enforcement agencies, chiefly the FBI and NSA, are worried that strong military encryption will facilitate criminal and terrorist activities. The executive branch of the government has made several proposals that will have the effect of regulating or even banning the use of strong encryption software by average citizens.

Despite these worries on the part of the government, the concerns of individuals and businesses about the security of their online communications demand the availability of encryption. Phil Zimmerman's PGP (Pretty Good Privacy) has emerged as a practical standard for encrypting e-mail and other documents.

PGP encryption

In Chapter 10, you will be introduced to many of the concepts involved in cryptography. Without going into detail at this point, all you really need to know is that PGP uses public key technology to perform its encryption. In public key cryptography, there are two keys needed for the encryption process: a public key that can be freely distributed and a private key that you must protect from anyone else. Anything encrypted with your public key can be decrypted only with your private key. You can also use your private key to sign documents digitally, and people can use your public key to prove the authenticity of your signature.

Using PGP with Eudora Lite

If you want to get started with encrypting your most sensitive messages, there is a fairly new product available on the Internet that integrates PGP with Eudora Lite, the free version of Qualicomm's excellent mail reader. Called PGP-Eudora, this utility is available for downloading from Hans Bausewein's Comerwell Software in the Netherlands at http://www.xs4all.nl/~comerwel/. Eudora Lite is a free version of Eudora Pro for 32-bit Windows, and can be downloaded from http://www.qualcomm.com/ProdTech/quest/.

In an effort to be as up-to-date as possible, the coverage of PGP-Eudora uses a beta version. At the time this chapter was written, the product was not widely released. By the time you read this, the name will probably be changed, and the functionality will have improved. As with all beta software, some bugs are bound to exist in the product. That's what testing a new product is all about. Publisher schedules did not permit waiting until the product was finished and released before I included it in this chapter.

If you are not familiar with public key encryption, and PGP in particular, you may want to read Chapter 10 before continuing.

PGP is a DOS program that uses a command line. The function of PGP-Eudora is twofold. First, it adds an item to Eudora's message menu, and second, it sends commands to PGP.

If you weren't using PGP-Eudora or a similar program, you would have to create a text file containing your message, run PGP from a DOS prompt, and then cut and paste the resulting encrypted text into your mail reader software. When you install PGP-Eudora, it puts an executable file on your disk that calls up Eudora Lite and runs it after inserting the Run PGP item to the Message menu. Figure 6-2 shows the screen you see when you ask PGP-Eudora to encrypt a message by choosing Message⇨Run PGP. As you can see, it picks up what you have typed and offers to send it to PGP for you.

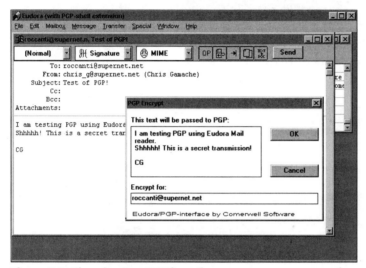

Figure 6-2: Choosing Run PGP from the message menu causes the typed text to be extracted for encryption.

The Encrypt For box will usually have the name of the recipient already filled in. If, however, your recipient did not embed his name and mail address when he generated his public key, you may have to fill in this box manually.

Figure 6-3 shows how PGP-Eudora shows you the result of the PGP DOS command, and Figure 6-4 shows you the resulting ASCII-based encrypted message.

Once you have encrypted the message, all you have to do is send the message as you normally would. The person on the other end will decrypt the message using his private key. Using PGP in this way provides you with several security benefits. First, your mail is unreadable to anyone who doesn't have the receiver's private key. (Guard your private key with vigor to keep it from falling into the wrong hands.) Second, you know whom you are talking to because it is possible to use PGP to embed digital signatures that verify the source. Third, you are helping to legitimize strong encryption at the user level, which makes it more difficult for the government to outlaw strong encryption.

Figure 6-3: The DOS command and its result are displayed for you in a window.

Figure 6-4: The resulting encrypted message is placed into the message space of Eudora.

> **Export law!**
>
> Because of U.S. government export regulations, PGP and other strong encryption tools are classified as munitions of war. Under these regulations, PGP is treated just the same as an F-14 fighter jet. You need a license to export both, and you aren't going to get the PGP license. Exporting PGP outside the United States and Canada could get you several years in jail. It is not a good idea to add links to direct downloads of PGP to your Web page or to put copies of PGP on your bulletin board for others to download. Phil Zimmerman, the author of PGP, was under federal grand jury investigation for over a year because he was suspected of exporting PGP.

PGP and other mail readers

Eudora is not the only mail reader you can link PGP into. There are plug-ins for just about every popular mail reader, including Elm and Pine on the UNIX platform. When you search your favorite online service or the Internet with one of the popular search engines by using the keyword PGP, you are likely to find several plug-ins to try out for adding PGP security to your e-mail reader.

Back at the Start

At the beginning of this chapter, I told you what my father said about not writing down anything you want to keep secret. He was right. For example, I often do work for federal corrections facilities repairing their computers, installing networks, and so on. There are a number of items that you are not allowed to carry into a federal prison. Weapons and drugs are obvious items, but so are beepers, cellular phones, and a whole list of other things that would take the rest of this book to list.

Ten years ago I was a fresh face, and every time I went to a prison to work, I was scrutinized carefully. After ten years you get to know people, and they get to know you, and the tendency is for security to ease up a little. One afternoon, I forgot that my cellular phone was in my toolkit, and I didn't leave it at the main gate for safekeeping. It raised quite a ruckus when the guards heard it begin to ring as I was walking through a maximum security cellblock.

The point is, no security system is 100 percent effective. If you have become lax and somehow let your private key get into someone else's hands, you aren't encrypting anymore, just delaying the reading of your mail by a few seconds. You, and you alone, are responsible for safeguarding your secrets. If you really want to keep it a secret, don't write it down, and never speak it aloud.

Summary

The vast majority of e-mail is sent across the Internet and other online services as plain text, which can be read by anyone. The Electronic Privacy Act raises the level of Constitutional protection of your e-mail to the same status as a telephone call.

- You should always be aware that trusted personnel who act as system administrators of networks have all the tools needed to read the e-mail stored on their system. There are even times when it is necessary for them to look at e-mail to make sure the system is running smoothly.
- Hackers and snoops differ in the way they gain access to your mail, but both categories of individuals can still read your mail, unless it is encrypted.
- If you have sensitive information that you must protect, use PGP (Pretty Good Privacy) to encrypt it before you send it.
- Chapter 10 contains more details about the use of encryption products and about PGP in particular.

✦ ✦ ✦

CHAPTER 7

The Risks of Online Transactions: Real & Imagined

In This Chapter

Viewing the Internet as a global marketplace

Understanding the foundations and risks of electronic commerce

Paying with digital cash, a new kind of currency

Protecting privacy in electronic financial transactions

Securing credit card purchases with Netscape 2.0

A feast is made for laughter, and wine maketh merry: but money answereth all things.
—*Ecclesiastes 10:19*

A U.S. dollar bill is one of the most exquisite works of art on this planet. Each dollar bill is an *engravure,* a 19th century process in which ink is transferred to specially designed paper by using hand engraved plates. Only the serial numbers and Federal Reserve shields are printed by using conventional methods. However, the dollar bill is an anachronism destined for the endangered species list, figuratively and literally.

Since the introduction of the first credit cards in the 1950s, people have predicted that money, as we know it, will become obsolete. They were right. Electronic funds transfers have all but eliminated the transference of large amounts of cash among business trading partners. Vaults which once were used to transfer large amounts of currency and gold among nations grow dusty with disuse.

The emergence of the Internet as a commercial vehicle is destined to once again change commerce itself. Entirely new financial instruments are being developed that will fundamentally change the way the world looks at money. The greening of the Net has begun in earnest.

How Financial Life Has Changed in the U.S.

The current trends of moving financial transactions through the Internet are causing profound changes in the way business is done and the way money is handled. These trends are raising fundamental questions about the security of buying and selling. To understand what is coming, it might be helpful to take a moment and look at where we have been.

Early days

The history of retail trade in America is one of dynamic change, spurred on by advances in technology and transportation, and having roots in the European traditions of guilds and market commerce. Trade in the New World and in the Old World have followed remarkably similar paths.

In Colonial America, few people ever traveled more than 100 miles from their birthplace. What few manufactured goods were available were imported from England and were expensive. As the road network improved, more and more commerce between the newly joined states began to take place. The Constitutional Convention of 1787 was called to create a document to replace the original Articles of Confederation. That document formed the basis of the government of the United States, as the former colonies called themselves. One of the most divisive issues dealt with by the convention delegates was the issuance of money.

The convention nearly foundered over the issue of paper money and over the rights of states to issue currencies of their own. In the end, the new Federal government was given total dominion over the issuance of money, with the result that all the states shared a single currency, the dollar.

The invention of steam engines for boats and locomotives and the transport industry they spawned opened new avenues of commerce for the growing land. Because of improvements in transportation, whole industries were able to concentrate in areas where conditions were favorable for business, even though the raw materials were not close at hand. A good example of this phenomenon is the growth of the textile industry in New England, where streams and canals provided not only a means for transporting raw materials and finished goods, but also supplied the power for the machines needed to spin and finish fibers into cloth. Southern cotton was shipped to New England, and finished goods were distributed from there to every part of the country. Commerce on this scale required the creation of whole new financial arrangements. Bonds were needed to raise capital to buy materials and equipment. Bank checques and notes were needed to insure payment of suppliers. Special contracting considerations had to be arranged and tested in the courts.

The advent of the automobile brought improvements in the road network, allowing trucks to deliver goods from ports to outlying towns. This increased mobility made it possible for people to live farther from the center of large cities, which in turn spawned suburban development, department stores, strip shopping centers, and finally the malls of today.

While this view of American retail is simplified, failing to take into account other social and technological events, the lesson is clear. Merchants are, as a class, willing to reinvent themselves as circumstances — and profit — warrant.

Shop at home

It is interesting to note that Americans, a nostalgic people to be sure, all but ignored the passing of a great American institution when Sears closed its catalog division. In a previous era, Sears and Roebuck revolutionized the way business was done by making it possible for great numbers of isolated, mostly agrarian, Americans to purchase top quality merchandise by mail. From farm tools and kitchenware to lingerie and shotguns, anything the sons of the pioneers really needed could be found within the pages of "the wish book."

Long evenings were spent pouring over each page in the glow of burning kerosene. People marked down necessities and circled desires. The number of brides who walked down the aisle in a mail order gown is impossible to imagine. The number of nickels and dimes collected in jars to save for some special item is uncountable. And, as a result of this mail order existence, and because sending cash through the mail is a risky business, banks began issuing money orders.

Throughout the years the Sears Catalog reigned supreme with an untarnished image of quality, rebuffing every competitor. Lifetime guarantees on tools and tremendous customer service were the hallmarks of the second most important book (behind the Bible) in America. Rising printing costs, a proliferation of convenient shopping malls, and the emergence of television marketing companies like the Home Shopping Network and QVC finally took their toll, however, and the catalog's final printing came in 1994.

Even with the demise of the Sears Catalog, the United States is catalog heaven. There are thousands and thousands of different catalogs printed every year. The trend in recent years has been toward specialization and tightly targeted markets. If you listen to National Public Radio, collect sports trading cards, wear clothes, read, climb mountains, eat, sleep, own a dog, or have a sense of humor, there is a catalog out there just for you. There are even catalogs of catalogs that let you order the catalogs you'd like to see. Americans are not slavishly bound to spending cash at the retail store as their only source for purchasing goods. Mail order, or more accurately direct marketing, is a multibillion dollar business. In the 20 years between 1974 and 1994, sales increased nearly tenfold, going from $15 billion to $133 billion annually.

Americans are perfectly willing to send off a check or a credit card number to a merchant in another city or state. However, it is only a matter of time until the U.S. Postal Service and toll-free phone lines are discarded as a means of ordering, and the computer takes over.

Media-based home shopping

In the late 1960s and early 1970s AM radio fell on hard times, pressured mostly by AM radio's crude fidelity and susceptibility to static from atmospheric interference. As rock music became more and more sophisticated, a generation of audiophiles began flocking to the FM band in large numbers so they could hear their favorite songs in high-fidelity stereo without the static and fading signals.

In the late 1970s Lowell W. "Bud" Paxson was struggling to keep his AM radio station in Saint Petersburg, Florida, solvent. Legend has it that Paxson, while out personally collecting on overdue advertising invoices, paid a call on an advertiser with no cash. However, this advertiser did offer 112 brand new, still-in-the-box electric can openers. Paxson, sensing that it was better to get something of value in hand rather than risk getting nothing, accepted delivery of the appliances. In retrospect, that decision was the catalyst for a multibillion dollar industry that would soon make itself felt in the highest circles of the media business.

Paxson returned to the station with a carload of can openers, each with a retail value of about $20, and began announcing that anyone showing up at the station could take home an electric can opener for just $9.95. He sold all 112 can openers that day, spawning a regular radio bargain-hunting program that was later to move to television as the Home Shopping Network. By 1990, HSN was grossing better than a billion dollars a year in revenue — and Paxson retired, taking $70 million in profits by selling his stock.

In the meantime, the rival QVC Network, headed by Barry Diller and partly owned by cable giants TCI and Comcast (both of whom are also part owners of HSN), began gaining ground and making noise as a player on Wall Street in the merger and acquisitions game. During his tenure Diller, who was one of the architects of the Fox Network, attempted, and nearly succeeded, in gaining control over media powerhouses CBS and Paramount.

Between them, HSN and QVC currently have gross annual sales of just over $2 billion, about one percent of the total retail sales in the U.S. While this figure represents a miniscule portion of overall retail sales, HSN and QVC have proven that U.S., British, Mexican, and Canadian shoppers are willing to spend their money outside of traditional retail channels. Mail order shopping has gone high tech. Transactions are processed by using automated systems controlling thousands of telephone lines, and viewers make payment by credit card.

Reinventing the wheel with computers

Advances in technology have played no small part in the dynamism of U.S. retailing. Just as the telephone and telegraph improved communications in an earlier era, the adoption of computers in the 1950s and 1960s improved the ability of retailers to more efficiently manufacture, import, and sell their wares.

The American broadcasting industry was greatly influenced by the early adoption of commercial messages, which provided the profits on which our current system is based. From the earliest days of radio in the 1930s, advances in broadcasting were fueled by the dollars of advertisers. When television first appeared after World War II, the radio companies simply shifted gears, using the new medium like radio with pictures. Many popular radio programs became early television hits simply by adding scenery and a camera. Television quickly became the dominant advertising medium, taking revenue away from radio, magazines, and newspapers.

As reliable phone hookups became feasible in the 1970s and 1980s, more and more companies and individuals began linking their new personal computers with other computers. Ward Christensen's CBBS, the first bulletin board software for CP/M computers, created a revolution all its own. Computer users began going online, first into local bulletin board services and then into online services like BIX, MCI Mail, GEnie, CompuServe, and others, primarily for processing electronic mail communications. Whole communities of people, who know each other only as electronic pen pals, sprang up overnight. Hackers, gardeners, soap opera fans, chess players — you name it — all began flocking together.

Of the commercial online services, the Source (later acquired and merged into what is now CompuServe) offered a unique service. It created online forums — miniature bulletin boards with global reach — that provide computer users with areas where they could explore favorite topics, get software and hardware support, and generally interact with thousands of other members of the service. In addition, CompuServe pioneered online commerce, offering a wide variety of products and services for home and business. By connecting with CompuServe, you can register shareware, buy airline tickets, purchase merchandise, and have the charges for some items put on your CompuServe bill, which is generally paid by weekly invoices placed against your credit card.

By the mid 1990s, CompuServe, America Online, and Prodigy, the three largest online subscription companies, had garnered more than 5 million subscribers, a number which represents only 4 percent of American households. Clearly, something is lacking the commercial appeal that will draw huge numbers of subscribers. As a means of comparison, keep in mind that the ranks of Internet users swells by 5 million every few months.

The Internet and the Web

In the 1960s, at the height of the Cold War, the U.S. Government funded a computer network designed to enable reliable military communications even in the aftermath of the unthinkable, nuclear attack. Linking military installations and major university research centers, the Internet remained the private playground of the Pentagon and the intelligentsia for nearly 30 years. Commercial activities were all but banned from the Internet until the explosion called the World Wide Web.

The World Wide Web grew out of research by Tim Berners-Lee at CERN, the European Particle Physics Laboratory nestled against the mountains in Geneva, Switzerland. Beginning in 1989, Berners-Lee began creating a method of publishing formatted documents quickly and easily to any computer connected to the Internet via a new kind of software called a Web server. All a Web server does is assemble requested documents and associated attachment files and send them to the requesting computer. The received documents are assembled into a viewable format by a companion piece of software called a Web browser. At the beginning of 1993, around 50 Web servers were in existence. Users with browser software numbered in the thousands.

By the end of 1995, there were more than 200,000 Web servers in existence and users numbered in the tens of millions. The major online services all offer subscribers an onramp to the Internet, and Internet Service Providers (ISPs), offering local Internet access to computer users who own modems, are springing up like weeds.

The growth of the World Wide Web has been phenomenal. In less than six years the Web has gone from a concept to the single hottest new technology on the planet. How hot? Consider that major corporations have begun establishing a Web presence that is astounding given the short time the Web has been in existence. You can't sit in front of your television for an hour without seeing Internet addresses plastered at the bottom of the screen during commercials.

The beauty of the Web is that you don't have to be a computer geek to use it. If you see something that interests you, all you have to do is click on it to connect. It makes no difference if the document is on a Web server in your city or in a city clear across the world. The existence of the Web has become the catalyst for millions of people all over the world to connect to the Internet. The Internet has become the newest form of mass media, the next television. Major players in the advertising business are looking at the Web as an extension of the print and broadcast media. Every month, the number of sponsored Web pages increases.

Companies like HSN and QVC have focused operations on the Net. Nearly every commercial ISP has links to online shopping. Internet shopping malls are springing up all over the globe. Most are in their infancy. Operations like HSN and QVC decline to publish accountings of their Web revenues, presumably because so far they are nothing to write home about.

You see, there is one major problem with electronic commerce via the Internet yet to be solved. Because the Internet is, for the most part, open, unsecured, and unencrypted, paying for items purchased via Internet vendors with a credit card can be a risky business, or at least it is perceived as risky.

Who is on the Net?
To fully understand the financial climate online, you first have to understand who is online. According to statistics presented by CBS News Overnight, about one in every four American households has a home computer. The numbers are higher, 32 percent,

for white households than for minority households, 18 percent. Of these households, however, only 4 percent subscribe to one of the commercial online services, according to a 1994 Microsoft white paper.

Demographic information about the users of the Internet is hard to come by because of the nature of the Net itself. There is no central registration point. CommerceNet, a nonprofit organization that promotes business use of the Net, and the A. C. Nielsen Company (the folks who do the TV ratings) have joined together in an effort to measure Internet use. Here are some of the highlights of their survey:

- 17 percent of all persons aged 16 and over in the United States and Canada (37 million) have access to the Internet.
- 11 percent of all persons aged 16 and over in the U.S. and Canada (24 million) have connected to the Internet in the last three months.
- Of those 24 million, 18 million used the World Wide Web resources of the Internet in the last three months.
- Internet users, on average, log almost five-and-a-half hours a week plugged into the Net, a time factor equal to the playing time of all the video tapes rented in the United States and Canada per week.
- 25 percent of Internet users have annual incomes over $80,000, 50 percent classify themselves as professionals or managers, and 64 percent have college degrees.
- 64 percent of users have access from home, 54 percent have a connection at work, and 30 percent connect from school. More than half of all users have more than one connection point, which is why the numbers add up to more than 100 percent.
- The Internet population is predominantly male, 66 percent, and males account for 77 percent of all usage.
- Only 14 percent (about 2.5 million) of Web users have purchased products or services via the Internet.

Slightly different numbers are estimated by Matrix Information and Directory Services (MIDS). Their projections are based on a survey of Internet users from the end of 1994 and concluded there were 13.5 million Internet users. The study also claims about 27.5 million users are peripherally connected to the Internet via e-mail connections. Projecting those results into July of 1995 gives you 22.6 million Internet users and 35 million e-mail connections. Those numbers overlap, by the way, because the 22.6 million would also be included in the 35 million, since presumably they would have e-mail access. The disparity of the MIDS numbers results from counting people whose e-mail providers (generally employers) do not allow unfettered Internet access.

According to the MIDS figures, taking into account two previous similar surveys, the number of Internet users is doubling every year. Here is a capsulation of its findings, some of which are quite different from the CommerceNet/Nielsen numbers:

- MIDS finds a larger gender gap, as it reports that only 15 percent of Internet users are female, with 82 percent male usership.
- Connections to the Internet come from three main sources: ISPs (27.9 percent), commercial online services (27.5 percent), and educational providers (26.5 percent).
- Of those users who use a commercial online service as their onramp, Prodigy leads the pack at 37 percent, followed by America Online (30 percent), and CompuServe (21.9 percent).
- Despite the fact that 26.5 percent of all connections are made through an educational service, the average age of Internet users is a surprising 35 years old.
- Internet users have a median income between $50,000 and $60,000. Computer (31.4 percent) and educational (23.7 percent) professionals make up the majority of Internet users. MIDS identifies the remainder of users as professionals (21.9 percent), managers (12.2 percent), and all others (10.8 percent).
- 50 percent of Internet users are married, 40 percent are single, with just 5.7 percent reporting that they are divorced.
- Users are concentrated within the United States, with 80.6 percent of users; 9.8 percent are European, and 5.8 percent are from Canada and Mexico. All other regions of the world make up the rest.
- Just over one-fifth (22.6 percent) of persons responding to the survey were adamantly opposed to paying fees to access material on the Web.
- Surprisingly, perhaps, 85.7 percent of respondents said their computers were shared with other users.

Despite the differences in the numbers between the CommerceNet/Nielsen survey and the MIDS survey, one thing is clear: these are the kinds of numbers that make Madison Avenue types and marketing directors salivate profusely. No wonder Internet addresses are showing up in all kinds of advertising.

The Greening of the Internet

 In the next chapter you will be introduced to the technical underpinnings of the Internet. For the purposes of this section of the book, all you have to know is that the day will soon come when a single cable coming into your office or home will become a central point in your universe. This single cable will, in all likelihood, provide you with cable television and radio programming, digital telephone service, and digital telecommunications at speeds much faster than your current modem can ever hope to deliver.

There are risks in this technology, some of them as yet unknown. In order to protect yourself, you need to talk intelligently with your banker and your Internet Service Providers about what they are doing to make electronic commerce safe.

There is no technological reason why your telephone and cable service are at present wholly separate physical networks. The breakup of AT&T into regional phone companies included a prohibition against those companies competing in other aspects of telecommunications. Ten years later the gloves are off, Congress is changing the face of communications regulation, and your world is about to change. The only hurdles to overcome are the security issues.

At present, the majority of online transactions are processed by debiting the purchaser's credit card. And if you are thinking of online transactions as people shopping via their personal computer, think again. It wasn't so long ago that a clerk accepting your credit card in payment was required to call a toll-free number, give an operator your transaction information, and receive (hopefully) an authorization number that guaranteed the merchant he would be paid. Nowadays phone authorizations are largely reserved for problem transactions. More likely the clerk or cashier will simply swipe your card through a magnetic card reader to take your card information, the cash register will connect with a bank computer, get an authorization code, and even print a transaction ticket for you to sign. Big stores have leased lines that enable connections to the bank computers without having to wait while a phone connection is dialed up. Small stores use dial-up phone connections because leased lines are too expensive for occasional use.

It is axiomatic that credit cards, in their present form, are targets for fraud and abuse. In the heyday of voice phone authorizations, anyone able to tap the telephone network could sit and listen and copy down credit card numbers at will. This is a similar situation to the current technological state of e-mail transactions on the Internet, where dishonest system administrators or hackers can intercept a copy of any e-mail message that passes through their system. More than one credit card number has been snagged and used for fraudulent purchases, which is why sending credit card information across unsecured e-mail links has such a bad reputation. No matter that much more credit card abuse results from lost or stolen cards and from shoulder surfing. (Shoulder surfing is the practice of simply looking over someone's shoulder to read and remember the card information of the person in line in front of you.)

By moving to automatic card readers, banks were able to institute an additional layer of security into credit card processing. Snoopers at least needed better and more expensive equipment. In stark contrast to the hurly-burly of the Internet, bank computers have long been seen as a bastion of security. Some of that security has been an illusion, however. Despite the availability of encryption schemes for the last decade, many financial transactions are sent in the clear. Billions upon billions of dollars flow through financial networks on a daily basis, mostly without a hitch, and mostly because hackers have steered clear, believing that messing with banks is a good way to earn a prison sentence if discovered. The vast majority of bank computer fraud, however, is done from the inside.

> ### Electronic fraud
>
> Banks and financial institutions are, by nature, secretive organizations. Few of them will admit it, but losses due to theft and fraud are, to some extent, considered just a cost of doing business. Dishonest tellers are seldom prosecuted for petty thefts, for to do so would expose the bank to unfavorable publicity that would possibly cause the public to lose confidence in bank safeguards. Instead, dishonest tellers are most often just quietly sacked. Banks who call to ask for employment references are never told the details of the former employee's transgressions for fear of defamation suits from the thieves. It is not uncommon for someone to string together three or four bank jobs before he is prosecuted.
>
> Computer fraud is an even touchier subject for banks. Millions of dollars each year are lost to bank fraud without much in the way of publicity. The news story of how a Russian graduate student by the name of Vladimir Leven used a PC and a modem in St. Petersburg, Russia, to fraudulently remove as much as 10 million dollars from CitiBank accounts in New York is the exception, rather than the rule. Leven was arrested in England when the plan, which involved an accomplice in San Francisco, went awry. At last account he was in custody in England, fighting extradition to the United States.

Electronic commerce

Financial institutions are coming to grips with the new realities. Some of the heavyweights of the industry have banded together to develop and implement a variety of interesting solutions to providing consumers convenient and safe ways of making payments for goods and services by using public networks. One such organization is called the Financial Services Technology Consortium (FSTC). Made up of banks, university research organizations, government agencies and others, FSTC's membership rolls read like the Who's Who of money.

Normally, companies like Bank One, Bank of America, CitiBank, Wells Fargo, American Express, Chemical Bank, NationsBank, Bank of Montreal, and Barnett Bank are busy competing with one another. By funding the FSTC, they are working together with other organizations like Deluxe, Equifax, and newcomer First Virtual. Their goal is to create electronic versions of current financial instruments, as well as new financial instruments, designed to be used in a secure fashion over public networks like the Internet. If you would like to review the documents cited in the next few pages, link to the Lawrence Livermore Labs at http://www.llnl.gov/fstc/.

Electronic checking

According to the FSTC, the three most common forms of payment for consumer transactions are cash, check, and credit. The FSTC documents don't say so, but of these three, cash is probably the least secure, and the least flexible. Cash, if lost or stolen, is hard to trace, and almost impossible to track back to its owner, unless bill serial numbers are recorded. Cash is inflexible because it must be transferred from payer to payee physically. In most cases, however, cash is, the most anonymous payment method available.

Credit cards are more secure, in that there is at least some recourse if the card is lost or stolen, and payments of credit card transactions can be verified. Credit card usage on public networks like the Internet can be risky because card numbers, if sent in an unsecured fashion, are easily readable by anyone with a little knowledge and high level access (authorized or not) to a network router. Credit card transactions are not anonymous at all. In fact, as was pointed out in an earlier chapter, merchants can gain a profile of your buying habits by matching purchases against the credit cards you use to make those purchases.

Checks are a convenient substitute for carrying large amounts of cash. A check represents, in financial terms, a promise from the payer to the payee. It is a promise that the bank the check is drawn against is holding funds which will be transferred to the payee when the check is physically presented for payment. For most large purchases, checks are preferred because they are more secure than using cash. When you have checks, you don't become a target of muggers and thieves because you are carrying large amounts of cash. A single document replaces a wad of bills, there is no need for the payee to make change, and so on. Checks are less secure, from a privacy standpoint, than cash or a credit card. If you are like most people, your name, address, phone number, and bank account number are all printed on the face of the check. Optional items like social security numbers and driver's license numbers also are often printed on the check right where anyone handling the check can read them.

To be sure, there is plenty of check fraud going on, but it is less of a problem than credit card abuse. That's because it is easier to trace a physical document through the maze of banks and clearinghouses that it must pass on the way to the paying bank. Also, most payees who accept checks perform at least a pro forma identity check by requiring a photo ID card.

The Electronic Check Project

People like the convenience and relative safety of using checks for making payments. It is a comfortable and familiar metaphor for money. That's why the FSTC is in the process of developing a computer-based equivalent through their Electronic Check Project. As envisioned, electronic checks would be paperless transactions that could be created by the customer using computers, ATM machines, cash registers, or any other similar point of sale device. Using object-oriented programming techniques, the Electronic Check Project creates a model for creating a software entity known as a *check object* that models, in computer memory, a real paper check.

Can bad checks be good for business?

Strangely enough, there are some places, like Florida, where the "passing bad check laws" are so rigorously enforced that many businesses will accept your check without requesting identification. The grocery store where I normally shop is one such place. If you are a bit older (my town, Tallahassee, is a college town) and have a preprinted check with a sufficiently high check number (indicating the account is long established), the clerk simply says thank you, pops the check in the cash drawer, and hands you the receipt.

Throughout the book you have been told and shown how security is a trade off between convenience and security. My grocery store's check acceptance policy is just one more example, albeit with a twist. Look at it from the store's point of view. Unintentionally bounced checks are far and away the largest proportion of problem checks it gets. More than 99 percent of such checks have the correct contact information on them. Finding the payer and assessing a $20 penalty for the bounced check is no problem (especially when you consider the State Attorney is only too happy to do the collecting if there is a problem).

Of course, the State Attorney charges the store's *customer* a fee, so the check writer normally pays the 20 bucks gladly to avoid paying a $200 fine to the state. Bounced check fees probably cover the store's lost income from truly worthless checks, plus a small profit. Customers like the practice because it makes them feel more welcome in the store. As a result, they shop there more often, thereby increasing the store's sales and overall profits.

Now if you wanted to cheat the store (stay with me on this; it gets complicated), you could go open a fraudulent bank account and order checks that start with check number 8501. Two weeks later, after the checks arrive, for several day's running, you could buy all kinds of stuff by using worthless checks at the grocery store and any other store that doesn't require ID. Of course, you would have to know the town because you would have to know the places that don't ask for ID. Asking a clerk if ID is required is a sure way to make sure it is required, at least for you. After you had racked up a few hundred dollars in purchases, you would have to skip town forever. Would you go through all that trouble for a couple of hundred bucks in groceries? Me neither.

The store is counting on circumstances to help keep check fraud down. In the current social climate, it's just too much hassle and trouble for too little money for someone to go through the fraud I've just described. If I could do it for a million or more, I'd be a lot more tempted, and so would a lot of other people. But because it just isn't worth it, the losses the grocery store incurs are just a cost of doing business, and a very small percent of the cost at that.

Electronic commerce on the Internet is only slightly more risky for the banks than it is for stores that take checks. These same banks are willing to put up with a small percentage of fraud, simply as a cost of doing business. You need to remain vigilant when providing financial information online anywhere, not just the Internet; otherwise, you may end up paying part of the bank's cost of doing business.

From the viewpoint of the banks, an electronic check has several benefits. Since electronic checks aren't paper documents, the costs of employing people and equipment to sort and process paper documents is all but eliminated. All electronic handling means is that settlement, the process of transferring funds from the payer's account to the payee's account, is faster, cleaner, and less prone to human error. Such a system could easily be grafted onto the clearinghouse and settlement systems already in place. Since this kind of system would be much less costly to the banks, you can imagine that they are all for it.

One of the predominant computer programming concepts of the last five years has been object-oriented programming (OOP). Almost all major languages and programming tools currently in use by professional programmers support object-oriented programming. In object-oriented programming, an object is a software entity that contains both data and, optionally, the programming code necessary to operate on the contained data. This is what the FSTC document talks about when it describes a *check object*. An object isn't a computer program because it cannot be run independently, like a word processor. An object lacks the programming to provide the overall framework for processing data. However, an object can include the code for specific routines to handle the data it contains, and these routines can be executed by a piece of software designed to work with that type of object.

Electronic checks are created in the image and likeness of paper checks in order to increase customer acceptance. The major differences between electronic checks and paper checks are stunning, however. Electronic checks are signed and endorsed digitally using *public key encryption*.

As you will learn in Chapter 10, public key encryption schemes let someone give out a public encryption key that anyone can use as the basis for encryption. A corresponding private key is needed to unencrypt anything encrypted with the public key. In this case, the public key wouldn't actually be made public. Instead, secure bank computers would keep encryption keys on file and answer only queries about the validity of an encrypted signature. The same key would be stored on your computer as part of your electronic checkbook software. Encryption of the check itself isn't necessary for the prevention of fraud, but it remains an option for privacy concerns.

Public key encryption of signatures and endorsements provides a measure of security superior to handwritten signatures, which can be forged. Because the payer's bank can be queried about the validity of a signature, authentication can take place quickly. In the case of a paper check, the check has to be physically presented to the branch where signature cards are stored and compared manually by a bank employee. Similarly, encryption of digital endorsements can also let the paying bank verify that the proper payee is receiving the funds.

Electronic checks can be used in much the same way as paper checks. They can be issued person to person, customer to business, business to customer, or business to business. Unlike paper checks, however, issuers of electronic checks can, with the click of a mouse or a touch of a key, turn an ordinary electronic check into a certified check, travelers check, money order, or credit card slip. The goal of the FSTC is to design a financial instrument that can be used in any instance where a paper check might be used today, but also extends the ability of consumers to send payments over public and private networks.

Electronic checks can be issued in a number of interesting ways. You could pay your dry cleaner with an electronic check by connecting your portable computer to its cash register or by presenting the store with a *smart card,* a credit card-sized device that contains memory to store information. Later you would tie into your main computer, access your electronic checkbook and download the records of checks you have issued, and possibly transfer funds to your smart card.

I'm only speculating here, but it would also be quite simple for the bank to make your statement of accounts available to you online, as many already do, so you can keep your electronic checkbook straight without the bother of downloading transactions or the risk of forgetting to do so.

Electronic checks would be routed by direct transmission over proprietary networks and through electronic mail systems via public networks like the Internet. Existing banking channels would then be used to provide settlement activities. Freed from the constraints of handling paper checks, banks could accelerate the settlement process to take a matter of hours or minutes to clear a check, versus the days it takes to physically transport paper checks from bank to bank, to clearinghouse, and back to a bank.

Consumers will find in the electronic check a financial instrument that is at the same time familiar and secure, as well as convenient. Banks are hustling to find the right mix of hardware and software to accomplish electronic checking because they perceive some powerful benefits of the electronic check. Here are a few of the benefits cited by the FSTC:

- ✦ Electronic checking enables consumers to use public networks to present payments to creditors in a secure and familiar way, even when transactions are conducted using public networks.

- ✦ Electronic checking enables account holders, consumer and businesses alike, to gather deposits electronically and present them to the bank without physically visiting a branch bank. The fewer branches needed to handle financial transactions, the less cost of doing business the bank has.

- ✦ Electronic checking, as currently contemplated, will be rapidly adopted by the market because the basic paradigm of the familiar paper check is retained. Even with enhanced features, electronic checking can be easily understood by anyone who understands how a paper check works.

- ✦ Electronic checks, because they are digitally signed and endorsed, reduce the possibility for forgery, alteration, or other fraud. Payers can also issue guaranteed instruments easily by issuing them as travelers checks, money orders, or certified checks, making it much less risky for businesses to accept checks, especially checks not drawn on local banks.

- Electronic checks have other features that enable more convenient payment models, including future dating checks, placing limits on the value of checks to be honored, and writing checks in foreign currencies or in multiple currencies.

- Electronic checks can easily be integrated into payment systems and accounting programs, lessening the amount of keyboarding necessary to match payments to invoices, track the posting of payments, and so on.

- Electronic checks can be made much more fraud-resistant than paper checks, even when using public networks to interface with banking computer systems. Settlement and payment can be accelerated. Electronic checks can be used to enhance privacy because they can be encrypted. Because they are digitally signed by using encryption verification, consumers may be able to limit information given to businesses, eliminating items like account numbers, addressees, and phone numbers from the check.

- From the point of view of the bank, electronic checks carry less risk of fraud than electronic cash because most people would be reluctant to commit fraud using their own account.

- Currently the biggest causes of losses incurred by banks are forgery, alteration, duplication, and fraudulent deposits of paper checks. The digital signature on an electronic check will be created by using secure hardware (either a smart card or a board plugged into your computer). Alteration is prevented by a secure hashing technique that records and encrypts the original state of the check at issuance so that it can be compared to the information in the check object at settlement. Duplication can be prevented by encrypted serial numbers that cannot easily be broken or hacked. Because endorsements are electronically verified, fraudulent deposits will be much less of a problem.

The FSTC Electronic Commerce Project

A parallel project to the Electronic Check Project called the Electronic Commerce Project is also being undertaken. Focusing on the *behind the scenes* functionality, the Electronic Commerce Project is engaged in adapting current banking communications and clearinghouse activities to unsecured public networks (like the Internet) as a way to facilitate consumer services like electronic checking.

Three basic types of transactions must be handled:

- **Push Payments.** The originator of the transaction is the payer who wants to pay a bill or transfer funds from one account to another — his own or someone else's.

- **Pull Payments.** The originator is the payee, transferring funds from another's account by using a direct debit agreement. Examples include automatic billing for utilities or online services where the payer has agreed to allow the transfer, according to a schedule.

- **Credit Payments.** The originator of this type of transaction is the payee, usually a merchant, who must acquire an authorization from the payer's bank.

Although there are currently systems in place like FedWire, a Federal Reserve Bank system for electronic funds transfers, these systems need to be adapted to life on a public network like the Internet. The development of a network payment protocol that will allow banks to communicate with each other, regardless of hardware or software differences, is needed to facilitate transactions among bank systems. Provisions must also be made for reverting to manual procedures when one of the banks involved in the transaction isn't wired for electronic commerce transactions.

It is likely that a two-tiered approach that recognizes the difference in the need for timeliness and security will be taken for transactions. One side of the system used for transfer of low-value amounts under $1,000 would warrant settlement within one working day. A more secure side for larger payments might even make settlement within minutes or seconds of the origination of payment.

It is envisioned that more secure versions of encryption than would be used for electronic checking would be used in bank-to-bank transactions to safeguard against fraud. In addition, safeguards must be developed to prevent accidental or fraudulent deletion of payments, misdirection of deposits, and so on. Some of the techniques similar to encrypted signatures and verification codes will be used for authenticating transfers.

Electronic cash

In the movie *Star Trek IV: The Voyage Home,* Captain Kirk and the Enterprise crew slingshot themselves around the sun in a stolen Klingon ship to return to the Twentieth Century to save the whales and civilization as they know it. In one of the film's lighter moments, Kirk sells his antique glasses in a dusty little shop because, of course, they have no money since money has become obsolete in their time. Science fiction has always had the knack of predicting things that will someday become true, even if they are technologically impossible at the time the story is written.

Electronic checks don't float

One side effect of moving to an all electronic payments system is that the float (the time it takes a payment to be paid by the payer's bank) will decrease significantly. Because paper checks must be physically transported from merchant to bank to clearinghouse to bank before payment is deposited into the payee's account, it can take several days for a check to clear, making it possible to spend money before you even have it in your account. If you mail a check to an out-of-town creditor, you can add several days to the float because of the time it takes the post office to deliver the envelope.

Using electronic checks has the potential to eliminate float altogether, either by verifying and holding funds at the time the electronic check is accepted, or by processing and settling the check within seconds. Either way, a merchant can be assured the payment is guaranteed before you walk out of the store.

Science fiction writers and futurists have long agreed that one day money — as we know it — will be obsolete. In these last days of the century, a lot of brilliant people are on the brink of making secure cashless transactions an everyday occurrence. If you are less than 70 years old, you stand a good chance of living to see this age-old dream become a reality.

When Diners Club issued the first credit cards in the 1950s, few people outside the banking industry could foresee the enormous industry that would grow up out of these little plastic cards that represented little more than a customer's promise to pay the bank. They were, in retrospect, the first step toward the mythical, cashless society.

In order to generate merchant acceptance, banks guaranteed payment to the payee, taking on the risks of collection for themselves. In return, of course, the banks charged a small handling fee, effectively making the bank a partner in every credit card purchase. Given the fact that most card issuers charge double-digit interest rates and an annual fee to their customers, and take an average cut of four percent off the top of every sale, you can see that issuing credit cards is a very lucrative business.

Banks have long used private computer networks to facilitate the daily flow of billions of dollars between accounts. It is a fairly straightforward operation to initiate a secure connection between two known points, apply encryption, and constantly monitor the circuit for minute changes in electrical characteristics that might indicate the circuit is being monitored by someone else. It is quite another to operate securely on a public network like the Internet.

The addition of magnetic stripes that can hold small amounts of information increased the utility and security of credit card transactions, as well as opening doors for alternative uses like telephone prepayment cards, medical information cards, and the like. Magnetic cards, however, are insecure because they can easily be damaged, erased, or altered.

Debit cards are a variation on the credit card. When using a debit card, the customer is effectively writing an electronic check (far less sophisticated than the ones discussed earlier in this chapter) because the transaction is approved only if the customer has funds on hand in an account with the bank. Still, the merchant must contact the bank to verify the transaction.

The introduction of the automatic teller machine, or ATM, represents another step down the path to a cashless society, despite the fact that most people use their ATM cards to get their hands on cash when the bank is closed. Connected to the bank via a proprietary network, ATMs use many of the techniques for electronic checks outlined earlier in this chapter to communicate with the bank's computers. Because proprietary, secure networks are fairly expensive to build and maintain, banks are just itching to find the right set of tools that will let them set up shop on the Internet, where they will be able to operate at much higher profit margins. The role of ATM machines is likely to expand, too, as new features like paying bills and transferring money from one account to another are added to online ATMs.

Moving away from cash with smart cards

The French telephone system, France Telecom, was for many years a shining example of government bureaucracy at its worst. Service was poor, cost was high, and it took forever to get a phone line installed. Today the French telephone system is a shining example of modern communications. The national network that is integrated into the phone system is efficient. In fact, it was credited with being a tool of democracy when it was used by university students several years ago to help coordinate an uprising against government education policies and tuition hikes.

In 1994, France Telecom had a terrible problem with pay telephones. Approximately 40,000 incidents of vandalism or break-ins to pay telephones were reported each year. In an effort to remove incentive for thieves, France began replacing coin-operated telephones with smart card-operated telephones in 1985. By 1989 reported incidents had declined to fewer than a thousand a year, and by 1994 almost no vandalism or break-ins were occurring at all. From a 10 percent increase in telephone fraud each year, the introduction of smart card-operated phones has brought fraud statistics down to under one-half of one percent. Users of the phone system provided an extra benefit: they talked longer. In most of Europe, pay calls are measured in chargeable units, unlike most North American pay phones, which let you make local calls of any duration for your coin. Because the French no longer have to fish about for coins, the average call has increased in length by about 50 percent. In short, the adoption of smart cards was a smashing success.

So what is a smart card?

A smart card is a credit card-sized device that, unlike cards with magnetic stripes, contains information stored on integrated circuit chips. There are four basic types of smart card:

- **Memory Cards.** A memory card contains no internal processing capability, only a small amount of non-volatile memory. In a typical application, the customer buys the card for a fixed value, which is then divided up into units. A good example is a phone card where each unit corresponds to a usage billing unit. As each unit is used it is erased from the card. When the card is depleted, it is simply thrown away. Memory cards are cheap, disposable, and not very secure, lending themselves only to low risk applications where relatively little value is at stake.

There is more than one way to skin a cat, as the old saying goes. Our technical editor, Mike, recently got a Sprint "Spree" card in a box of cereal! The way it worked was that the card was valued at five minutes of long distance. To use it, Mike called a Sprint number and entered the card code. A computer voice told him how many minutes were left on the card and then allowed him to call the number he wanted. In this case it wasn't the card itself that carried the memory (there was no magnetic strip, for instance), but a central computer whose memory treated card numbers like passwords. Future systems may combine the memory of a smart card with the processing power of the remote computer.

2. **Shared Key Cards.** A shared key card is similar to a memory card, but there is more memory available. A processor called a microcontroller is able to so some simple processing of encryption keys used to authenticate the card as genuine when it is inserted into a reader that is also programmed with the same encrypted key. The biggest problem with a shared key card is that each point of sale must have a secure hardware or software module that contains the same key as the card.

3. **Signature Transport Cards.** A signature transport card uses the same hardware as a shared key card, only the software burned into the card is different. When used, a digital signature is created that can be verified. Signature transport cards have two major enhancements over shared key cards. First, each transaction uses a different encrypted signature, which avoids the problem of a single breach of security compromising an entire group of shared key cards and eliminates the need for secure hardware modules at the point of sale. Second, because the signature is blinded, nobody, not even the issuer of the card, can trace a payment back to a particular card, providing the privacy of cash.

4. **Signature Creating Cards.** The most sophisticated of the card types, a signature creating card, contains an onboard processor that can create digital signatures instead of using signatures already embedded on the card. This sophistication comes at the price of slower performance, which renders signature creating cards unsuitable for most applications. The framework of this technology can, however, be applied in some interesting ways if a more powerful processor is available to create the electronic wallet, which you will learn about shortly.

Digital signatures

The idea behind a signature is to authenticate data. By signing a check, you authenticate the fact that you and you alone created the check. A digital signature acts in much the same way. First proposed in 1976 by Whitfield Diffie of Stanford University, a digital signature can be used to authenticate the originator of encrypted data, in this case monetary value. A digital signature goes one step beyond a traditional written signature, however, because it also verifies that the data has not been altered since its creation. It can do this because the data itself is used as a portion of the encryption key.

It is supposed that digital signatures may one day be used to execute contracts and validate other legal documents online. Blind digital signatures, however, are digital signatures that have been encrypted by the originator so that only the originator can actually determine if the signature is his. Blind digital signatures enable transactions to have the same privacy as cash, yet you always can retain a *receipt* in the form of a blind signature so you can later prove you made the payment.

What smart cards store

Smart cards get their name because they have the capability to securely store all kinds of different information in addition to storing cash value. There are two types of access to the data stored on a smart card:

- **Who.** By using encryption techniques, access to any or all of the data stored on a smart card can be left open to anyone holding the card, restricted to anyone except the card's owner, or restricted to anyone who lacks the proper authentication code.

- **How.** A second level of security can be imposed on a smart card that restricts how the data can be accessed. Reading, altering, or erasing the data stored on the card is controlled by passwords. Thus, only a doctor could read or edit medical information on a card, but the doctor could not access or tamper with financial information.

By subdividing functions of the card and granting access only when appropriate, sophisticated smart cards could provide the basis for a one-size-fits-all approach that enables a single card to store medical information, to provide access security to work sites, to be used as a credit card, and to issue electronic checks and other financial documents.

In the end, however, smart cards are only a vehicle. The underlying concept of electronically stored value is what's important. Just as money orders, checks, and other financial documents are a metaphor for cash, so, too, is electronic storage.

E-cash: The Details

Dr. David Chaum may someday come to be regarded as the father of electronic money. He is the founder and managing director of DigiCash, a Netherlands-based company founded in 1989. A recognized expert in cryptographic technology, Chaum holds a Ph.D. in computer science from the University of California at Berkeley, and is the founder of the International Association for Cryptologic Research. His articles on cryptography have been widely published.

Beginning with a road toll collections system developed for the Dutch government that enables tolls to be collected without requiring drivers to stop and pay in cash, DigiCash has since expanded into providing open, secure systems of payment that provide safety, security, and privacy.

MasterCard International has licensed DigiCash's patented cryptographic technology to create smart card programming to conform with the EMV (Europay, MasterCard, VISA) standard for electronic payments. Among them, Europay, MasterCard, and VISA currently manage more than 800 million conventional credit card accounts.

The European Commission and DigiCash, along with about a dozen other participants, are currently developing and implementing the CAFE (Conditional Access for Europe) project. Using advanced smart card technology, CAFE's goal is the creation of electronic wallets that can be used to make payments securely, both at point of sale and across public networks like the Internet.

The proposed electronic wallet also has some other features that will keep civil libertarians awake at night. Under the proposed specifications, the electronic wallet can also be used to regulate access to information services, serve as an identification card, and can also be extended to carry medical information, serve as a driver's license, and even work as a house key. In short, smart card technology and electronic wallets could eventually evolve into a person's electronic shadow.

Electronic cash inside out

The E-cash™ system, developed by DigiCash, is a three-stage process. You first withdraw funds from your bank account and place them into the E-cash mint; the E-cash mint then turns those funds into digital coins which are downloaded onto your hard disk. Once they are on your hard disk, or in future versions on your smart card, you then can spend them with anyone who can accept E-cash just as you would real cash. If you would like more detailed information on electronic cash, link to the DigiCash Home Pages at http://www.digicash.com.

The inner workings of E-cash are based on RSA public key cryptography. RSA stands for Rivest-Shamir-Adleman, the men who developed public key ciphers at (where else?) MIT. As you will see in Chapter 10, a public key cryptosystem enables a person or company to publish a long character string that can be used as the *password* for creating an encrypted version of a document, or in the case of E-cash, a serial number. When you withdraw funds from the bank and pass them through the E-cash mint, the funds you withdraw are converted into encrypted *coins*. Each coin bears the bank's digital signature.

In order to prevent counterfeiting, there has to be a way for the issuer of electronic funds to prove or disprove that it actually issued the funds in question. Authentication works only when the originator of data, in this case electronic coins, is the only party that can decrypt the information. Public key cryptography eliminates the need to develop a new key each time something needs to be encrypted. In public key cryptography there are two keys, public and private. The private key is used to encrypt a message that only the public key can decrypt correctly. Thus, a bank can publish its public key so users can decode the signature on an electronic coin. If the result of the decryption returns a meaningful message, the user can then trust the fact that the bank encrypted the data and that it is genuine.

Traditional secret key cryptography, where the same key or password is used at both ends of the process, is unsuitable for electronic payment systems because the merchant would have to have a copy of the secret key in order to verify that the payment being made is genuine. Imagine the security risks if even a single merchant terminal fell into the wrong hands. The entire cryptosystem would be compromised, and each merchant in the system would have to be given a new decoder before transactions could continue. VISA alone processes more than 600 billion dollars in transactions yearly. Losing a secret key would endanger every one of those dollars.

By using public key cryptosystems, each party in a transaction can put its own signature on a transaction to verify that it is genuine. The bank's digital signature authenticates the value and origination point of the funds. The payer's digital signature authenticates that the payment indeed comes from the payer, and the payee's digital signature authenticates that he (the payee) is the proper person to be presenting the electronic coins for deposit.

Signature creation and transport

Using public key cryptography to create a signature at the time a transaction is authorized is called signature creating, and this method of creating signatures presents a couple of problems. First, the secret half of the key, used to encrypt and decrypt data, has to be stored in the originating device (computer, smart card, and so on). If the security of this device is breached, the private key can be used to forge electronic coins. Second, creating signatures requires more processing power than the typical smart card has available. Requiring smart cards to create signatures would make the cost of smart cards prohibitive.

In the signature transport method, the resource-intensive creation process is done before the electronic coins are delivered to the user. This is the function of the E-cash mint. In the signature transport method, the entire signature isn't created. Instead a *pre-signature* is generated and applied to the electronic coins. The pre-signature is then downloaded into a smart card or computer under the control of the user and stored until needed.

When you withdraw $20 and pass it through the E-cash mint, the product you download to your computer or smart card is an envelope containing a bunch of pre-signatures and a cash value. There are enough signatures (coins) in the envelope to cover any payment pattern you choose, even if you disburse the $20 one cent at a time. When the value is depleted, the remaining coins are worthless.

By downloading an envelope of electronic coins, the processing power needed to initiate a transaction is reduced significantly to a point where a personal computer, electronic wallet, or smart card needs to have only minimal processing power to complete the signature. The payer's system doesn't contain the bank's secret key, so there is no way for a thief to crack the bank's secret key, even if he manages to crack a smart card or the payer's information. Thus, the only amount of money at risk is the value that is stored in the smart card or on the payer's system. Any amount of money you are holding in a card or on your hard drive should be regarded as if it were cash in your pocket.

Ensuring privacy with blinded signatures

In an article that appeared in *Scientific American* magazine in 1992, Dr. Chaum describes his invention, the *blinded digital signature*. In that article he points out that each time someone makes a purchase with a credit card, subscribes to a magazine, pays taxes, and so on, an entry is made in a database somewhere. By connecting all these seemingly insignificant fragments of data, it is possible to discover a great deal of information about individual citizens. It is almost impossible, Chaum notes, to find out who knows what about your life, to control the accuracy, or even to regulate who can gain this information. He notes that the government isn't above a bit of snooping either, pointing out that the U.S. Internal Revenue Service has attempted to identify targets for tax audits based on estimates of income gleaned from publicly-traded mailing lists.

In an effort to provide a mechanism that makes E-cash as anonymous as the dollar bill, Chaum, in cooperation with other scientists at the Center for Mathematics and Computer Science in Amsterdam, developed a twist on digital signatures called blinded digital signatures.

When you authorize your bank to withdraw funds for your account and place them in the E-cash mint, the software you use creates a random number containing a large number of digits, and the random number is encrypted using your private key. This is your digital signature. The bank then authenticates your signature by using your public key, which it keeps on file, and returns an envelope containing electronic coins.

If you then want to pay for a purchase, either via the Internet or in person, you connect your computer or smart card with the merchant's point of sale system. The merchant's system authenticates the bank's signature and, if it is genuine, accepts the electronic coin as payment. When the merchant deposits the coin into his account, the receiving bank verifies the issuing bank's digital signature, the merchant's signature, and if the receiving bank has access to your public key (and it probably will), it can verify and identify you.

These signatures warrant the integrity of the payment. You can't forge the bank or the merchant's signature, and they can't forge yours. Even two of the three parties acting together cannot cheat the third party. The digital signatures also guarantee that you cannot spend the same coin twice, the merchant cannot fraudulently copy your coins, and the bank cannot deny that it issued the coins.

A right to privacy

In the debate over ratification of the U.S. Constitution, opponents successfully argued that the rights of citizens needed to be enumerated in order to guarantee liberty. Consequently, the first ten amendments, commonly known as the Bill of Rights, were added to the document drafted by the Constitutional Convention to ensure ratification. The Fourth Amendment guarantees the "right of the people to be secure in their persons, houses, papers, and effects, against unreasonable searches and seizures," and the Fifth Amendment states that no person "shall be compelled, in any criminal case, to be a witness against himself." In addition the Ninth Amendment states that the "enumeration in the Constitution, of certain rights, shall not be construed to deny or disparage others retained by the people."

The Supreme Court has held that these three amendments, when considered together, create a penumbra — a shadow, that is, in effect, a right to privacy. This right to privacy was the basis for the Court's decision in *Roe v. Wade*, the case in which it was decided that a woman has a right to have an abortion. Regardless of your stance on abortion, the recognition of a privacy right is an important safeguard to liberty, especially in an era when technological advances make it possible to monitor virtually every financial transaction.

As the world stands on the brink of widespread electronic commerce, it will be necessary for everyone to defend his or her right of privacy. One of the major advantages to cash transactions is that they provide a modicum of anonymity. Consumer acceptance of electronic cash systems will depend, in large part, on the ability to retain the same privacy rights when paying electronically as when paying with cash. You don't have to be a criminal to appreciate financial privacy. It is simply nobody's business what movies you go to, what magazines you read, what brand of condoms you buy, or whom you call from a pay phone.

Individual vigilance in protecting privacy rights must be maintained. For example, the legislation that created the Social Security Administration specifically forbids the use of social security numbers as identification. Over the intervening years however, the SSN has become increasingly ubiquitous as an identifier. It is used in the processing of tax returns and as an identification code for bank accounts; and many states use social security numbers as driver's license numbers. These days, if you want to know about someone, all you have to know is his social security number, because the SSN is increasingly used as a unique identifier in computer databases.

The problem is the customer has no privacy. If the bank records the numbers used to generate the E-cash coins, it can read the signatures of coins it accepts for deposit and can link individual purchases to the purchaser. Even if you pay a private debt to a friend using E-cash, the bank, and presumably regulatory agencies, would be able to trace the transaction.

If your software or smart card generates random numbers for making a withdrawal and the number is multiplied by another random number, the bank cannot decipher what it is signing. All the bank knows is that it carries your digital signature. The bank adds its digital signature and returns to you an envelope full of coins. At that point, your software divides out the second random number. In effect, the bank has issued coins with an anonymous serial number. The bank can verify that it issued the E-cash coin, but it cannot identify the person to whom the coins were issued. You can then spend those coins in complete privacy.

Later, if a question arises about the transaction, you can make the blinding factor known as a way of proving you made the payment or as a way of stopping payment on a particular coin. Of course, in a real time system you would have only a matter of seconds to stop payment.

Try E-cash for yourself

DigiCash's E-cash system isn't some pie-in-the-sky, Buck Rogers prediction of the future. As the late George Allen, former coach of the Washington Redskins, used to say, "The future is now." On October 23, 1995, Mark Twain Bank of Saint Louis, Missouri, and DigiCash released a joint announcement inaugurating a pilot project of the E-cash system, limited to 10,000 accounts.

After testing the DigiCash system for a year, using the Internet and people's computer systems as the test bed, Cyberbucks (essentially play money), DigiCash, and Mark Twain Bank have come together to issue real E-cash. This E-cash is denominated in U.S. dollars or any one of 25 other currencies. There is a small service charge assessed each month. The amount of the fee depends on your usage of the system. To test the E-cash system for yourself on your own computer, contact Mark Twain Bank at http://www.marktwain.com.

Sweden Post, which owns the bank that is used to process more than half of all value transfers in Sweden, has also announced that it will be conducting a test of the E-cash system. Launch dates have not yet been announced.

First Virtual

Another company offering secure payment options is First Virtual Holdings, Inc. Although the name would lead you to believe First Virtual is a bank, *American Banker* noted in its October 20, 1994 issue that the First Virtual payment scheme almost totally bypasses traditional banking companies.

As was noted earlier in this chapter, CompuServe members can already make secure transactions because CompuServe has their credit card information on file; thus credit card numbers do not have to be transmitted over unsecured networks. The First Virtual concept (FV) is similar. To make purchases from Internet-based merchants, you first contact First Virtual and give it your credit card information. You are then assigned a FirstVirtualPIN, a unique account number that identifies you. When you find a merchant who has something you want to buy, you simply give the merchant your FV account number. The seller notifies First Virtual of the sale by posting the transaction to its FV merchant account. First Virtual then contacts you by e-mail, asking whether you authorized the purchase.

You have three options in responding to First Virtual: you can answer yes, no, or fraud. If you answer yes, your credit card is charged the amount of purchase. If you answer no, the seller is notified that payment has been refused, and the product will not be shipped. If you answer fraud, the seller is notified that payment is refused, and the FirstVirtualPIN is canceled immediately.

When you authorize payment, the transaction is performed off the Net. Electronic Data Systems, Inc., the computer services company founded by billionaire H. Ross Perot and acquired by General Motors, handles the transaction. EDS secures proprietary networks that are not connected to the Internet by processing the transaction with First USA, the Dallas-based credit card company.

In effect, the First Virtual system adds a second layer to the transaction process by acting as middleman and settlement clearinghouse. After First Virtual receives the funds, Internet merchants who accept First Virtual payment are charged $0.29 plus 2 percent of the purchase price, so they bear the brunt of the costs associated with the system, just as in traditional credit card transactions. There is also a small charge each time a deposit is made to a merchant's bank account.

According to FirstVirtual's president, Lee Stein (already famous as a lawyer and accountant to the stars), one of the biggest impediments to average folks setting up shop on the Internet is the difficulty of opening credit card merchant accounts. By providing First Virtual with bank account information for depositing funds, and paying a $10 service fee, just about anyone can hang out his wares on the Web.

There are two possible routes for abuse in the First Virtual system, both negligible. The first possible abuse is the possibility that someone will learn your First Virtual account number and attempt to use it. To be successful, however, he must also have access to your e-mail account, since no transaction is ever completed without confirmation from you.

The second opening for abuse is an unscrupulous buyer who purchases information services. For example, a vendor may be offering tutorials or white papers dealing with subjects of interest for downloading. As each document is downloaded, the vendor keeps a running tab and then forwards a charge for that amount to First Virtual. If the buyer refuses payment, the vendor is the one who takes the loss because it has already *delivered* the product.

In the case of hard goods, the vendor can hold off shipment until the confirmation of the buyer's acceptance is received. Buyers who abuse the system by downloading products and then refusing payment are dealt with by First Virtual, who reserves the right to cancel an account at any time. Likewise, unsuitable vendors can also be weeded out of the system. For more information on obtaining a First Virtual account, link to http://www.fv.com.

Secure Transactions on the Net

Although electronic commerce on the Internet is in its infancy, the trend toward providing a secure environment where consumers can safely supply vendors with credit card information at the time of purchase is seen by many as the preferable way to do business on the Internet. This way of effecting payments is closer to the traditional credit card purchase where the consumer presents the seller with the card, or just the number when doing business over the phone. As the customer, you are not limited to using only a specific card that you have pre-registered, and the vendor has the opportunity to process the transaction with the bank at the time of purchase, just as merchants do now when they swipe the card in a reader connected to the cash register.

In fact, a whole system of financial procedures that depend on encrypted signatures, secure message transmission, and wide acceptance of secure protocols is fairly far along in the development process. Assuming the fact that most people will interact with the Internet primarily through browser software, the contents of the pages that follow focus on that aspect of secure electronic commerce. Currently Netscape's Navigator and Commerce Server software offerings enjoy the lion's share of this market.

Netscape Communications Corporation

Netscape, like a number of other companies, was born out of university research projects. The company was founded in April of 1994 by Dr. James H. Clark and Marc Andreessen. Jim Clark helped pioneer computer graphics when he left Stanford University in 1982 to found Silicon Graphics to exploit technology that he and his students developed. Silicon went on to become a Fortune 500 company with revenues of $1.5 billion in 1994. Netscape's president is Jim Barksdale, who previously headed McCaw Cellular and the postmerger AT&T Wireless Services and who rose from chief information officer to become the chief operating officer of Federal Express. In short, Netscape's roots are firmly embedded in America's business bedrock.

Netscape's products are the creation of Marc Andreessen and his development team. As an undergraduate at the University of Illinois in the early 1990s, where he worked at the university's National Center for Supercomputing Applications, Andreessen learned of the CERN project and began development of the original NCSA Mosaic browser that literally shaped the face of the Internet as we know it today. Released in 1993, Mosaic quickly caught on, garnering more than 2 million users within a year.

Netscape's development team includes five of the six other original Mosaic developers, as well as other heavyweight codesmiths, and they have picked up where they left off before. Netscape's Navigator browser now accounts for approximately 75 percent of all the traffic on the World Wide Web, the Internet's user interface. It is safe to say that the vast majority of the estimated 25 million Web surfers use Netscape as their primary interface.

In the early days of the Web, there was no thought given to securing communications for financial transactions. Early users of the Web were largely university students and staff exploiting the Internet as a play toy and for pure research. If they wanted to communicate securely, they would simply encrypt their messages using PGP or some similar program. The explosion of the World Wide Web as the vehicle for getting onto the much vaunted Information Superhighway has changed every notion of what Web browser software should do. At this point Netscape seems to be setting the pace in the race to become your interface to the Internet for surfing, sending and receiving e-mail, reading newsgroups, and conducting electronic commerce.

Netscape and commerce

By the time this book is in your hands, version 2.0 of the Netscape Navigator, the browser software that most folks refer to simply as Netscape, will be generally available. With encryption routines licensed from RSA and support for a number of protocols old and new, Netscape 2.0 provides a model for secure communications and commerce on the Internet.

In addition to its browser software, Netscape also offers server software, the programs that Internet service providers use to distribute the contents of the World Wide Web. In addition to its Communications Server, Netscape offers a product known as the Commerce Server that adds security features such as server authentication, data encryption, and user authentication.

Just where Netscape fits into the greening of the Internet is a bit woolly to understand for those folks not intimately familiar with how the Internet works. Keep in mind that communications over the Internet are based on a series of open standards like the HyperText Transfer Protocol (HTTP), the method of transporting documents over the Internet developed by Berners-Lee and the folks at CERN who created the World Wide Web in the first place. In addition to the basic communications protocols, there is a standard for every different type of task that users want their software to perform. There are standards committees made up of the big players in Internet technology that formulate and publish specifications for sending e-mail messages, newsgroup messages, file transfers, and the like. These protocols are discussed in detail in Chapter 8.

By supporting standard protocols and making it easy for users, Netscape has gained its preeminent position in the Web software market. The fact that Netscape has gained a 75 percent market share makes it the proverbial 800-pound gorilla, enabling it to become a de facto standard itself, and enabling it to promote standards like the Secure Sockets Layer protocol. Anyone who wishes to compete with Netscape for a piece of the market either has to do everything Netscape does and more, or face oblivion. In short, there are other Web browsers that users can work with, but their impact on the direction of the development of the World Wide Web is negligible at the beginning of 1996.

Secure Sockets Layer protocol

The major contribution of Netscape to electronic commerce is the Secure Sockets Layer protocol (SSL), which has been endorsed by a list of companies as long as your arm, including Bank of America, Wells Fargo, First Data Corporation, IBM, MasterCard International, MCI, Microsoft, and VISA International. Based on encryption technology developed by RSA, SSL enables secure point-to-point communication over the Internet. If Netscape is successful in gaining widespread acceptance of the SSL protocol by users, Web software developers, vendors, and financial institutions, the company will perhaps be able to overcome the mistrust people have of conducting financial transactions over the Internet.

The nuts and bolts

The whole problem with passing payment information across the Internet is the openness of the Internet itself. The protocols that specify how e-mail and documents are transported from one computer to another across the Internet are based on plain text. The SSL protocol enables several security mechanisms to be imposed as part of a security layer without interfering with the normal operations of other communications protocols, which are used normally for transactions that don't need security (such as surfing Web pages for research or entertainment). SSL is a layer that sits between the basic TCP/IP connection and any application-specific protocols like HTTP, FTP, and so on.

Whom do you trust?

USA Today reported in its Sept. 20, 1995, issue the results of a survey of computer users conducted by Intelliquest. The subject of the survey was the level of trust computer users have in various financial dealings. It found

- 77 percent trust bank automatic teller machines (ATMs).
- 62 percent trust conducting banking transactions by phone.
- 57 percent feel comfortable banking by computer.
- 57 percent trust using a credit card or phone calling card at pay phones.
- Only 43 percent are comfortable with writing credit card information on mail order catalog forms.
- Only 5 percent of computer users surveyed trust the security of sending credit card information over the Internet.

When a user connects to a secure server that has electronic commerce as its main purpose, the browser — in this case Netscape — and the server perform a handshaking routine that authenticates the identity of the server by its digital signature. They then secretly agree on the level of security needed for the transaction and a set of public encryption keys to be used. After the connection is established, the data stream between the user and the merchant is encrypted by using technology licensed from RSA.

Not only is credit card information encrypted, but the entire transaction is scrambled as well. The benefit to privacy and security of this arrangement is that snoopers are prevented from discovering anything about the transaction, including what items are ordered, quantities, and so on. The transaction is completely private on both ends.

In addition, there is a provision in Netscape 2.0 for users to obtain their own digital signatures so that merchants can authenticate the source of orders. User authentication is the equivalent of a customer providing identification in a normal transaction by presenting a driver's license or some other picture ID card.

In the secure environment provided by SSL and in complimentary protocols like secure MIME and secure HTTP, customers can provide payment information without fear that their credit card information will end up in the wrong hands. Server authentication assures that the customer is connected to the proper server, eliminating the chance that someone is intercepting communications intended for other destinations by spoofing. Spoofing is the practice, thankfully fairly rare, of presenting an impostor server that appears to be one the user wants to connect to in order to discover credit card information, passwords, or other sensitive data.

Digital signatures

Authentication services for Netscape's security implementation is being provided by a trusted third party arrangement with VeriSign, a spin-off company from RSA Data Security. Shareholders in VeriSign include Ameritech, Bessemer Venture Partners, Fischer International, Mitsubishi Corporation, VISA International, RSA Data Security, Security Dynamics, and an as yet unidentified Fortune 50 technology company. The chairman of the board of VeriSign is RSA's president Jim Bidzos.

In keeping with their advertising slogan, VISA, the world's largest issuer of credit cards, is aggressively supporting the search for viable payment methods via public networks like the Internet. To that end, VISA is fully or partially funding a number of experimental projects ranging from issuance of smart cards, to VeriSign, to developing standards in partnership with Microsoft, in order to facilitate the use of the millions of credit cards already in circulation for electronic commerce.

Under this arrangement, companies setting up a Netscape Commerce Server are able to register with VeriSign for a small fee to receive a Digital ID that can be used by browser software to authenticate that the server reached is indeed the target server. In addition, users can establish their own digital signatures so they can identify themselves to merchants.

The digital signature, or Digital ID as VeriSign calls them, consists of a public encryption key and the user's name as well as an expiration date and the digital signature of the certifying authority issuing the Digital ID. Thus a merchant's system can identify the user and authenticate that the user's digital signature is genuine by using the issuer's digital signature.

By combining encryption of the transaction with authentication procedures, the Internet becomes a viable vehicle for electronic commerce. Users are protected from their credit card information falling into the hands of hackers and crackers, and merchants are able to handle purchases in real time, including the authentication of customer information and the processing of credit card authorizations. If the system performs as designed, it won't take long before the 95 percent of computer users who don't trust sending credit card information via the Internet will change their minds. When that happens, electronic commerce will blossom as rapidly as the World Wide Web.

Summary

In this chapter, you have seen how the Internet's World Wide Web has the potential to become the logical extension of the traditional mail order business. You have also seen how the entire shop-at-home industry is trying to turn the Internet into a virtual bazaar where all kinds of products and services are bought and sold.

- In this chapter, you learned how traditional mail order businesses are morphing into electronic commerce and how new forms of media like the World Wide Web are ripe for commercial exploitation.

- You also learned how new technologies like smart cards and public key encryption are being used to explore new ways of conducting financial transactions.

- You have also seen how the long-predicted cashless society may come into being based on the work of Dr. David Chaum and DigiCash.

- Companies like First Virtual are positioning themselves to reduce the risk of credit card fraud by acting as an intermediary between customer and merchant so that consumers don't have to pass credit card information across the Internet in an unsecured fashion.

- In this chapter you also learned how Netscape Navigator, the dominant software program for accessing the World Wide Web, is using Netscape Communication Corporation's Secure Socket Layer specifications as the basis for safely allowing users to send credit card payment information across the Internet.

✦ ✦ ✦

Internet Security

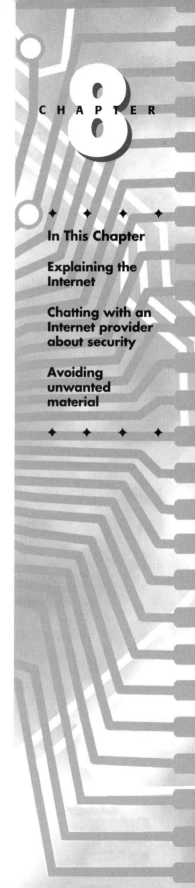

CHAPTER 8

In This Chapter

Explaining the Internet

Chatting with an Internet provider about security

Avoiding unwanted material

Out the 10BaseT, through the router, down the T1, over the leased line, off the bridge, past the firewall...nothing but Net.
—*Anonymous*

Although the Internet has existed for a long time, it has recently become the hottest thing on the planet. To millions of users, the unfathomable Information Superhighway is a lot of fun to mess with, yet still remains a mystery. In this chapter, you will learn just a little bit about what the internet is and isn't. Along the way we will talk to the chief administrator for an Internet service provider about security on the Internet, and we'll look at some of the things you can do to protect your children (including co-workers) from coming into contact with materials on the Net that you don't want them to access.

Of course, there are whole books dedicated to the subject of the Internet and its inner workings, so our coverage will be brief. If you want more information about how the Internet works, check out IDG's book, *Internet SECRETS*.

Just What Is the Internet?

The Internet, as we know it today, is an artifact of the Cold War. It began life as an experiment in building communications networks that would reliably continue to function even though parts of the network could be destroyed by nuclear attack. In the early 1970s, the U.S. Department of Defense established the ARPAnet as a packet-switched network model that automatically routed messages to other computers on the network. These messages bypassed non-functioning portions of the network and allowed computer hardware to talk to dissimilar hardware in a peer-to-peer arrangement.

Using TCP/IP (Transmission Control Protocol/Internet Protocol) as the basis for this new inter-networking model enabled the original ARPAnet to blossom, and soon universities that were engaged in defense research began connecting to the backbone (the main communications links between distant networks).

With the rise of local area networking in the 1980s, the Internet, as the groups of connected networks became known, began to grow rapidly. It grew because it became easy to connect all of the users on your local network to Internet access. As new networks were designed and implemented, the success of Berkeley UNIX networking and the IP model of ARPAnet was emulated over and over.

Perhaps the most important of these was a network of five supercomputers constructed by the National Science Foundation called NSFNET. NSFNET was intended to make it possible for university folks doing research to get computer resources, but because of the expense of the early supercomputers, it often had to share resources. At first the connections between machines was scheduled to be on the ARPAnet, but staffing problems and turf wars torpedoed the plan. The alternative plan was put into effect, and the five centers were connected with 56,000-bit-per-second lines (56 Kilobaud). The main problem with that solution was the expense of leasing lines. Instead of connecting each university with a supercomputer center individually (a very expensive proposition), the universities instead connected with one another in regional networks, forming a relay chain. Any university could communicate with any other university or supercomputer center by sending traffic down the backbone. Each network in the chain cooperatively passed traffic addressed for another network along the lines to its destination. These were the good ol' days of what was to become the Internet as we know it today.

For many years the military, government, and academic users of the Internet consisted of an elite club of text-based users who had to know a little something about UNIX. Each of these users could e-mail any other user. The early Internet was also a great place to do academic research, for you could browse through publicly-available libraries of documents on computer systems thousands of miles away as easily as you could browse your own network.

So who owns the Internet?

Nobody and everybody owns the Internet. To be sure, AT&T and MCI are big players in the Internet because they are the actual owners of many of the lines used to carry Internet traffic. Over the years, they have provided increasingly sophisticated and speedy network hookups. As common carriers, however, they have done little more than provide the technical and hardware support, and they have been prohibited by law from becoming involved with selling services other than leased lines. Recent legislation in the U.S. Congress, along with rulings by the FCC and by U.S. federal courts, all point to a big change in that relationship, however. (More on that shortly.)

There is no Internet Corporation, and that is really hard for some folks to grasp. Instead, the Internet is "governed" by a committee that promulgates and adopts standards and has some power (mostly peer pressure) to keep connected networks in line. The way the Internet functions is not dissimilar to the world of ham radio operators. The radio frequencies they use to broadcast to each other are owned by the people of the country in which the ham operators live. All the details of which country gets what frequencies and call signs, and so on, is negotiated by treaty. Ham operators need a license to fire up their transmitters and begin communicating. Each ham operator owns his or her own equipment, but that equipment is legally useless without the license. Ham operators routinely take messages from another operator and relay them to other operators when the target destination for the message is out of range of the originating station's transmitter. If Charlie is off the air, Wanda will kick in and offer to relay the message.

Occasionally you will find a renegade ham operator who will violate the rules, scream obscenities into the microphone, and so forth. The first thing that will happen is other operators will simply refuse to answer anything the renegade does or says. Usually that is enough to make the renegade ham operator lose interest and go away. After all, such behavior is done to attract attention, and the best way of defeating such behavior is to ignore it. In the rare few cases where the problem doesn't go away by itself, the miscreant can expect a certified letter from the FCC, then a visit, handcuffs, and criminal charges. How far it goes is usually dependent on how hardheaded the offender is.

The Internet operates on a model similar to that of ham radio operators. In place of the FCC, only with much less authority, is the Internet Society, an organization made up of volunteers who act as a governing board through various subcommittees like the Internet Architecture Board or the Standards Committee.

Funding for the Internet is a nebulous thing. Remember that there is no Internet Incorporated to collect fees and sell hookups. Instead, each network connected to the Internet pays for its own little piece and just enough extra to be able to honor its commitments to other members as far as forwarding traffic goes.

What's next?

Two factors have made the Internet the juggernaut that it has become. First, large corporations, many of whom have had research departments connected to the Net for a long time, have begun to realize the impact that universal computer suffrage can have on economic activity. For years, they have had to rely on mass advertising to blanket the population with sales messages. To that end, they have been wildly successful. More people can identify the Pillsbury Doughboy, Orville Redenbacker, and Ronald McDonald than can identify the President of France, the Pope, or the Dali Llama. Still, this advertising has been expensive. A single minute of broadcast time can cost hundreds of thousands of dollars and as much as a million and a half dollars for special high-ratings events like the Super Bowl. For that kind of money you could staff an Internet presence for years.

The second breakthrough came when Tim Berners-Lee and the folks at CERN (Switzerland's advanced physics laboratory) unveiled their concept of a World Wide Web. This Web was an interlocking network of server machines that would share information with each other and allowed text in documents to provide a link to another document stored elsewhere — even on a computer halfway around the world.

Another breakthrough occurred when Marc Andreessen and friends responded with NCSA Mosaic, a graphical Web browser that is the ancestor of Netscape Navigator (also written by Andreessen and friends). Suddenly the Internet didn't have to have a UNIX face. Text-only browsers like Lynx were largely abandoned in favor of Mosaic and Netscape. Users didn't have to learn an operating system that was even more complex than the DOS they were already struggling with. Instead, users of Windows, X-Windows, and Macintosh systems could hook up to the Net and point and click their way around the world.

What's next in the development of the Internet is more of the same, but even more so. In recent years, the number of users on the Internet has exploded as commercial ventures that sell individual access to the Net have begun to come online. Online services like CompuServe, Prodigy, and America Online have also contributed millions of users through their Internet gateways.

The breakup of AT&T in the mid 1980s had a profound effect on the future of the Net. Prohibited from venturing into information services, the Baby Bell companies and their competitors have laid back, biding their time, all the while covering the United States with fiber-optic cable. Recently, many restrictions were lifted, and it looks as though Congress will pass the Telecommunications Act sometime in 1996.

The result of the Telecommunications Act will be to legitimize a trend that has been building for quite some time. By the end of this century, a scant five years away, it is likely that your telephone, computer, and cable-TV providers will have all climbed inside a single fiber-optic or twisted-pair cable drop to your home. Want to watch a movie? Just go to the HBO home page and click an icon to download it. Want to share a file with your brother or a co-worker? Just dial him up and use FTP. Want to sell widgets? Call the phone company, order a high-speed line, and set up a Web server in your garage. The possibilities are limitless, but there are a few risks that go along with any new technology.

Security and the Internet

Assuming that you took the lessons of Chapter 1 to heart and you are now religiously backing up your data, the biggest threat you face in using the Internet is loss of privacy. There are a few incidental risks as well, but as an average user, your risks are negligible when compared to the potential benefits. If you need stronger security measures than the average user, Chapter 10 gives you specific ideas about how to protect your privacy more forcefully.

For most folks, a romp through the World Wide Web presents minimal risks for security. It stands to reason actually. Consider that no major technology has much chance of being accepted by the masses if the risks of using the technology outweigh the benefits. If early telephones had electrocuted people or if computers had exploded, wiping out whole city blocks, we would still be sending telegrams and using manual Rand adding machines.

Because it is new, the Internet sometimes draws more than its fair share of criticism. To hear the news media talk, there is nothing but sedition, satanic cults, and dirty pictures on the World Wide Web. For every story you hear about computers being hacked and cracked, there are millions more productive Internet sessions that go unreported simply because folks had a nice, uneventful time checking out some neat stuff.

Recently I sat down with an administrator of an independent Internet service provider in a medium-sized city to talk about user security on the Internet. I was surprised when he asked me — and this was after he agreed to the interview, mind you — why I wanted to raise the general background level of paranoia. I was taken aback by the question because I thought he knew me well enough to know I wasn't out for sensationalism.

Now this is a guy in the trenches, who works on the Net full time, so I offered to let him tell it to you directly instead of filtering his thoughts. His only hesitation was the kind of unwelcome attention his system might receive as a result of his statements in a book about security. I've agreed to call him Jim instead of his real name and to use xyz.com as an alias for his real network.

One System Administrator's View

Q: *Jim, let's start out simple. What are the security risks to Jane and Joe Average when they decide to start jumping into the Internet community?*

A: Realistically, the average person on the Internet isn't going to have security problems. What I do think is that there is a lot of paranoia. The reality is that most individuals have a better chance of winning the lottery than they have of somebody's trying to hack their computer.

Now that is not necessarily true for people who are putting up servers. Servers become focal points, and they are subject to more problems. But individuals who are out there surfing the Web or individuals that are out there trying to send e-mail back and forth to other people really have very little need to be concerned about hackers; it just isn't happening. Anything is possible, I suppose, but people are being scared by stories of what is possible and are ignoring what is practical.

Q: *OK, given the disparity between possible and practical, let's explore possible, and you can point out what's practical along the way. What is the single biggest security problem people face when they open an Internet account?*

A: From my view as a system administrator, it is weak passwords. Most providers [organizations which give users access to the Internet] initialize accounts by making your password the same as your account name. It is up to the user to immediately change the password to something that isn't easily guessed or cracked.

Passwords are key. Change them regularly and also be observant of little details. If you go into your account and there is new mail and it doesn't tell you there is new mail, you may have a problem. Somebody may have already read your mail. If you see files in your account drive space that you didn't put there, be suspicious. Anytime you are suspicious, the first thing to do is change your password and second notify your provider. They may be able to find out who is breaking into your account.

If someone has your password, they have access to absolutely everything you do. They can read and erase your e-mail; they can change your home page, send messages in your name — anything you can do they can do better, or at least more maliciously.

More importantly, on my side of the fence, is that anybody you let on the system with a weak password has jumped the first hurdle, and it's now up to me to keep them out of the rest of the system.

Q: *All right, what's next on the list of risks?*

A: Well, I guess the next risk is loss of privacy, but that's just common sense. It's not that you may have anything to hide particularly, but you don't want to put out too much personal information like home addresses, phone numbers, and that kind of thing. You definitely want to teach your children never to give out personal information or to ever try to meet someone they may have met in a chat in person without your knowledge.

Q: *What about risks that may occur to the user if someone hacks your provider's server?*

A: There isn't, relatively speaking, much of that type activity going on, thankfully. It is possible that somebody can hack a server, any server, and make changes, delete or copy files, and so on. The likelihood of it happening is pretty small, but there is always a possibility.

On any network, you are at the mercy of the system provider's security measures. That's true always. There is no such thing as a system that cannot be broken. So no matter who your provider is, there is always the potential that there is somebody knowledgeable enough who wants to break in and mess with the system.

There are some providers better than others in terms of vigilance. Many providers do not pay any attention to what is going on. They don't watch their logs and they do not manage the security risks or update programs when they find that there are holes in them. This is one of the reasons that hackers are able to succeed because the system administrators do a poor job of maintaining security. There are others who are very vigilant, who will continually make changes to add more security, who will update the programs at any time holes are discovered, will implement security measures, and analyze logs. So there are definitely providers who will do a better job of security than others.

Q: How do you tell a good provider from a bad provider?

A: I don't have a good answer as to how you can tell what kind of provider you have. When you are talking to a provider about coming to him, he is going to tell you what he thinks you want to hear because he is trying to sell you a service. So if you ask him if he does security, if he watches lists, you can't depend on his answers unless you are otherwise convinced the person you are dealing with is honest.

Q: Is a big provider that has thousands of accounts better than a smaller one with just a few hundred?

A: On a security level, I don't think size is the issue. Some of the large companies will actually have a manager or security staff who is assigned that function and therefore spends time on it and will do a good job. Others, even though they may have the same large staff, do not put the same priority on security. Contrast that with the small guy, one of those one-man shows. They may put more time and energy on vigilance and security than the folks with the big staff. I do think, though, that there may be a correlation between size and your ability to work with your provider.

If you are dealing with a small local or regional provider and you know the person you are talking to when you call up to ask a question, there is some value in that. In working with a local provider, you can build a relationship and know if you can trust this guy or not. Some of the big national firms, well, you might call every day and never get hold of the same person twice. I guess I'm letting my prejudices show.

Q: OK, some hacker might want to mess with the system as a whole, but outside of playing a game of "Who Do You Trust" with service provider security, what might make an individual user a target?

A: Well, the likelihood of anything happening to an individual user goes up as you become known, or worse, infamous on the Net. If you are known on the Net for making trouble or being a nuisance in a newsgroup, for spams, for an unpopular movie or unpopular book, or anything else that might tick somebody off, the potential goes up for somebody to seek retaliation against you.

[Ed. Note: *Spamming* is putting unsolicited advertising on the Net, either by e-mailing a big mailing list, or posting ads in Usenet newsgroups where those sorts of messages have been prohibited, usually by the consensus of participants of the newsgroup. The word *spam* comes from the Hormel meat product Spam, which is often a favorite of institutional kitchens, like those of college dining halls, where it is not always a favorite with diners. Stung by this pejorative use of its trademark, Hormel has recently become aggressive in defending its name, going so far as to sue venerable Jim Henson Productions because a Muppet-like character had the name Spam.]

As a minor example, there was a recent movie, *Hackers*, and the movie studio put up a Web site to promote this movie. Certain hackers did not like the movie, didn't like the way it was promoted, didn't like the way hackers were represented, or whatever. To show their disapproval, they broke into this Web server and they modified the Web pages — effectively, they painted graffiti all over it to show their disapproval. Is your average user capable of doing that? No, not by a long shot. Are there people out there who can? Yes. Are they coming after you? Probably not.

If you have a strong password and don't store much on the server, except maybe the files for a Web page, and you empty your mailbox often, your exposure is really limited to someone messing up your Web page. You ought to have copies of those files backed up on your own system, so that kind of stuff is just more of an aggravation than anything else. If a hacker can't break into your account, about the only exposure you have is perhaps a denial of service attack.

Q: *Could you explain that?*

A: The Internet is self-policing to a large degree. If you are doing things to upset people — spamming, for instance — you better be on the alert because you will be attacked. You will be the recipient of mail bombs, and be the target of denial of service attacks. A mail bomb very simply is a large quantity of mail all directed at you. There are several ways that can be done. Someone can set up a little script that would send you a large file over and over. Send someone 10,000 copies of a binary file, and you would overwhelm the mail system and eat up all available disk space on some systems. You either slow the system to a crawl or make it crash altogether, hence the name mail bomb.

Q: *But that would also affect other users of the system.*

A: Sure, that's part of the rationale for a mail bomb because my only recourse as a system administrator is to cancel the account to stop the attack. Otherwise, the whole system and all the other users suffer, and that's just what the attacker wants to happen to punish the offender. By filling up the offender's mailbox or having their account canceled, the attacker prevents the spammer from receiving mail from potential buyers.

Q: *So what should non-hackers do to react to unwanted advertising messages? I guess if everybody who got a spam message returned it unanswered 25 times it might have an effect.*

A: Maybe, but not likely. Often spam messages have a fake address that bombs when you try to respond to it. You have to respond to an address in the message or something. Instead of that, however, the best thing you can do is look at the header of the message and try to determine where the message came from. For example if the first domain name listed is XYZ.COM, then try sending a message to webmaster@xyz.com. Messages like that usually get taken care of pretty quickly. At the very least, they are read and noted. System administrators hate getting that kind of webmaster mail because it makes their service look bad. They may have a mall they are trying to get off the ground or something, and the last thing they need is a spammer making life hard for them.

Q: *Let's switch gears here for a minute and talk about system administrators as the bad guys. One of the recurring concerns I hear from users is their fear that they are leaving a trail on the Internet that can be used to gather information about them. Apparently, there is a fair amount of information that gets passed by your provider when you go surfing the Net.*

A: Oh, whatever system you are linking to will know a few things about you. Nothing sensitive really. Any time you access a Web page, that Web provider gets certain information about you. You don't have a whole lot of control over that.

They can tell what IP address you are using, and what the domain name is, if you've got a domain name assigned to that address. They can tell what browser, and which version, you are using. In addition to that, there is typically some other information that is passed that you may have some control over. For instance, during the configuration of most Web browsers, there are places where they ask for your e-mail address, your real name, things of this nature. The reason that [the provider] asks for [your address] is convenience for you so it can use it in the appropriate places; however, be aware that some of that information is also potentially passed and logged by Web providers. They are not trying to build a profile of your personal tastes; instead, the purpose of logging Web service is usually to identify domains that have linked into your system, and where your traffic is mainly coming from.

Can you imagine the amount of reportage that would be generated if a system administrator tried to log everything that happened on their system? They'd never be able to get any work done because users would be banging on the door wondering why the system is bogging down. That takes a lot of overhead.

Q: *OK, so what you are saying is that for most Internet providers, with the volume of traffic that they are handling, if they tried to log everything you did, keep track of every file that you downloaded, they'd basically implode because they'd use so much of their computer resources.*

A: Absolutely, it is just impracticality. I didn't say impossibility, I said impracticality.

Q: What logging do Internet providers typically do?

A: They log things such as when your account is accessed, when you log in, when you log out. The main reason they log that information is most of them are using it in some form or fashion to bill you or to track usage so they can maintain suitable resources. They also tend to log system activity that doesn't necessarily have anything to do with you. Many log FTP activity to some degree. That doesn't necessarily mean they are logging filenames that are being copied in and out; it just means that they are logging that somebody has connected to their server as FTP and that they disconnected. Some of them bill for that.

Q: So they may log FTP service on their own server, but they are not logging that you got up on the Microsoft FTP server?

A: Oh, no. They typically log Web activity on their Web server. They want to know how many people are accessing their Web server and those types of things. You'll hear people talk about how many hits they got. They are usually getting that information from the log that tells how many people have accessed that page. They do not tend to log other pages that you may go surfing. In fact, they usually have no idea what pages you are out there looking at.

Q: What about Usenet newsgroups? Typically, where is the file that documents what groups a user may subscribe to?

A: It is located on the user's machine. The location is determined by the news reader software the user has. If you are using a shell account and using a shell newsreader like TRN or NN, then the file is located in your home directory in your account area.

Q: So if you are subscribing to alt.commie.pinko.graffitist or some other group you wouldn't want to be public knowledge, then you should be using a newsreader installed on your own system?

A: If you are subscribing to something, and you don't want people to know, using a reader like Agent or Netscape 2.0 doesn't present a privacy problem with your provider's server, but again we get into the possible versus the practical.

When you access a news server, which may or may not belong to your provider, that server has the ability to log activity. Now, they can only know you by your IP address. If you have your own IP address, a permanently assigned IP address for a full time wired connection, then obviously that points right back at you. Most people have accounts where the provider assigns them an IP address, and they use that address during their session only. Lots of people may potentially use that same address in the course of a day, so there is nothing there that identifies you specifically as the person who accessed the news server.

Now, is it possible that two system administrators working together can document your access and prove that you are spamming or looking at specific material?

Yes. Are they likely to? Not unless requested to do so by law enforcement authorities, and then only under a court order to do so. By the time John Law gets that interested in you, you are probably already in deep trouble.

Q: *So if you are accessing alt.sedition.kill.the.queen, having a permanent IP address might provide a circumstance where you generate some form of incriminating evidence for her Majesty's secret service.*

A: Correct. But understand, that would be one in a few hundred million. Typically, newservers log information for statistical purposes only. They want to know which newsgroups are the ones most often accessed. They want to know which newsgroups are never accessed. They want to know what amount of material is coming in and what amount of material is going out. That helps them to size the machine properly and size the bandwidth properly. They are logging information, not to track information on you, but to assist them in administering their newsserver. Again it's a matter of what's practical. Most system administrators are just too busy to care who is downloading dirty pictures and who is entertaining radical political thoughts in some newsgroup.

Q: *When you log onto the Internet, what status does that give your system? A lot of folks are worried about other people being able to access their computer when they are connected to the Internet.*

A: That can be a very real problem, but one that is usually pretty easy to prevent. When you log onto the Net, you are in essence a peer. You are just another node on the network, equal to any other machine anywhere in the world. You have the same potential capabilities, or lack thereof, that any other machine has, with some exceptions. Routers, the systems that tie the network together, can filter out certain types of traffic. This is called a firewall, and it blocks certain types of traffic, so machines inside the firewall are not vulnerable to snooping. Firewalls are found mostly on corporate systems. Few small networks or standalone computers have firewalls.

Q: *OK, I don't have a firewall, and I'm logged onto the Net as a peer. What exposure does that present for somebody to look at my machine's file system?*

A: As a peer, you have the same potential to receive requests for information as any other machine. Usually you have to be running some kind of server software, but under the right set of circumstances, your machine is vulnerable.

Q: *What are those circumstances?*

A: The way in which connections are made on the Internet is through standard protocols. HTTP, FTP, and so on are examples of protocols. Now a part of these protocols is the determination of which port the protocol will use. Ports are addresses that are intended to be the place that services are requested and routed through. A protocol is like a language that two computers can speak even if they are different types of hardware, and each different protocol normally communicates with specific ports.

Q: *For example, port 80 is the port for Hypertext Markup Language, Web pages. That's why you will sometimes see :80 added to a domain name in an URL.*

A: Correct. There are exceptions. You may see :8000 for Web traffic; port 110 is usually where POP (Post Office Protocol) e-mail clients connect. It's just a code used for communicating e-mail purposes. Many ports are possible. Some of these ports are set up to be listened to. If your machine happens to be listening on a certain port, then it may be vulnerable to some type of an attack.

Q: *How does that put a user at risk?*

A: As an example, Windows 95 can be configured to share printers and to share disk drive devices. This is a typical workgroup thing on Windows 95. It was designed to be done on a peer basis, with people on a local group. Problem is, however, Microsoft did not put the right security on there, and if you are not careful, there is a certain port, I forget the number, that can be attached to from the Internet, and someone can gain wide-open access to everything that you have set up to be shared. Keep in mind, too, that the default installation of Windows 95 is to share everything.

Q: *I think that may have been true in the pre-release version of Windows 95, but not in the commercial version everyone has. Anyway, it is simple enough to open the Network dialog in Control Panel, click the File Sharing button, and check to see whether you have sharing set up. If you do, you need to turn it off before connecting to the Net, or password protect the sharing.*

A: That should take care of the problem. I'm pretty sure there are some circumstances, however, where sharing is the default.

Anyway, that is just an example. Another way in which a machine can be attacked is to exploit a bug in a piece of software. For example, you might be able to crack a POP mail server by sending too long a string. If the mail client, for instance, is expecting a string 100 characters long, and you send it one that is 150 characters, and a bug exists in the program that allows the excess to be written to a stack in memory, there is the potential for mischief if the overflow on the stack contains code. It could potentially take over your machine. Now that gets very technical to try and go into exactly how all that happens. The point is that as flaws in programs are discovered and published, you need to patch or upgrade your software. There were some early versions of some commercial client software that contained security holes. Those that have been exposed have all been fixed, and you can make sure that you aren't vulnerable simply by upgrading to the latest versions of your software. If you are using a program used for Internet access that is more than a year old, upgrade.

Q: *OK, assuming I'm running the latest versions of browsers and utilities, and I have sharing turned off, what general risks do I face in connecting to the Web?*

A: Computerwise, practically none, again so long as you aren't doing things you shouldn't be doing, and aren't infamous or outrageous. As a general proposition, however, there are some non-computer related risks.

If you post phone numbers or addresses or other identifying information, then you have the possibility where somebody may call and harass you on the phone or actually try to track you down physically and harass you. There are bad people out there on the Net, just like there are bad people out there on the street. You need to be somewhat judicious in the personal information you choose to post. But that's just common sense, like not giving out credit card information to strange callers on the phone.

There are lots of forms you can fill out on the Web, too. Obviously, there are certain times when it is appropriate to give out information. For example, when ordering something, you have to tell [the store] where to send the product. But if there seems to be no reason for giving out that information, don't do it.

Q: *One of the hottest things these days is personal Web pages. Can they get you into trouble?*

A: Oh, in general, I don't think so. I mean if you put the words "hey hackers, see if you can mess with this page" in big type across the top of your page and send the URL to the alt.2600 newsgroups, you can expect to be messed with. But in general, what could somebody do? They could change your Web page files, substitute inappropriate stuff, or something like that, but it isn't very likely, especially if you have a strong password. Of course, if something like that happens, be sure to inform your system administrator so they can take the appropriate measures.

On the Net, from posting a Web page, the only real vulnerability you've got is that, theoretically, somebody could break into whatever system is listing your Web page and make changes to it, as in the example we gave earlier about the hacker's movie.

Q: *There is also a potential vulnerability when folks keep files stored on their provider's server, and they don't have the topmost home page stored in each directory named INDEX.HTML, which enables someone to leave off the name of the page from the address. This causes the server to slide into an FTP session that lets people inspect all the files in the directory, whether or not the files were intended to be publicly accessible.*

A: You mean like if you publish the URL http://www.xyz.com/~user/mypage.html and someone just links to http://www.xyz.com/~user/ without the page name. Yes, on many UNIX systems, that's true; it will put you into an FTP type session where your public HTML folders can be browsed. Actually, that comes from the Web server software that will generate, on the fly, an INDEX.HTML that lists the documents in the directory. You will find that more and more server administrators are disabling that feature because it is considered to be a little bit of a security hole. Potentially, there are files there that somebody could access and download that you don't want them to have access to.

Q: *I use that "feature" all the time. If you do a search on a subject on one of the popular search engines, quite often you will get an old address, or sometimes you will get an address that has a misspelling or some other problem. You can sometimes take the last bit of the address off the URL to get into that FTP-style interface and crawl through there to find where the document you are actually looking for is.*

A: Right, if there is a document named INDEX.HTML, [someone] cannot generate that view of your account directories. Of course you shouldn't have anything in those directories you don't want seen. If someone knows the name of a file in that directory, they can put that name directly on the URL line and pull up that file, but they do not have a way to find out that file.

Q: *So someone could sit and try to make guesses of names of files that might be in your account directories. The bottom line is it's not a real good idea to try and use secrecy to hide something up there.*

A: Very true. Also a lot of folks like to put "secret" links into their pages. Kids like to do that as a sort of puzzle. Some people forget, however, that almost all of the popular Web browsers have an option on them to view source. That lets anybody who accesses your page see the HTML lines that get rendered into your home page. The source will include the name of the files that you are using for your various graphics, the names of the files that you've set up for your various links, and [anyone who accesses your page] will be able to see that all of that information in text format. If you have set up secret hot spots on your pages, they really aren't secret, since they can be viewed at any time.

Q: *What about some of the other popular Internet utilities like Finger and Ping? What risks do they represent, and what can people find out about you?*

A: Finger was originally designed before the Internet existed. The real purpose was to see who else was online and to find out certain information about them, like what terminal they were connected to, and stuff like that. These days, the Internet includes other information, which varies from provider to provider. Some providers have disabled [Finger], but you can let users have Finger set up so you can see when a user reads their mail or something. As an example, we have a user on our system who advertises his Finger file, and whenever you finger him it brings up the daily weather report so you not only find out who he is, but you get the daily weather as well. A lot of people like to finger him to find out what the weather will be. You have to be aware that the more information that is given out about you, it is easier for a hacker. A hacker will use that information, for instance, to feed into his password cracker to try and help crack your password. In addition, hackers will look for people who do not log in very often, using Finger. Those are the accounts they will put extra effort into trying to break because they figure if you don't come in very often, you are not going to notice they are there and they can have a free ride on your account. Be careful what goes into your Finger plan file.

Q: What about Ping?

A: Ping is mostly a testing tool to make sure that two machines can connect. Ping, unfortunately, can be used to do a denial of service attack. For example, if I'm mad at you, I could try to overwhelm your system. I might set up a routine or script that would ping your server with large packets on a continual basis. Your system would be overloaded, and you would not be able to do anything else.

Q: Are you talking about my personal machine or the server that I am connected to?

A: If I have your IP address, I can [ping] your personal machine simply by specifying that address, even though it's temporary. You are not at risk of damage from this type of attack. [People] can't break into your machine this way, but they could prevent you from working or using your computer on the Internet.

Q: What about the security of e-mail?

A: E-mail is potentially readable by people other than those you intend, and you need to be aware of that, but that's really rare. E-mail is sent across the network in plain text, and it may go through multiple post offices, if you will, before it arrives at the individual it's addressed to. At any point along the way, because it is plain text, theoretically it can be read.

The perception is that there are all kinds of people just scanning, sniffing, and snooping all day long. I think mainly that has to do with inaccurate press coverage. Fact is, messages are broken up into packets, and different packets may arrive at the destination via different routes. The routing of messages is dynamic, so a message can't be predicted to pass through a particular router on its way to the destination.

For someone to target you specifically, they would basically have to do it at the site of your personal mailbox. If they are snooping in general on anything that comes through the lines, the sheer volume of traffic makes it impractical.

Just keep in mind that your administrator always has the ability to read your mail because he or she has the ability to read any file on the system. So if you leave mail in your mailbox — mail that you have received — or mail that you have sent, that could possibly be read by your administrator. If you don't want it exposed to scrutiny, collect it often and delete it quickly. Use a mail reader that stores your e-mail archives on your local system. Most administrators barely have enough time to do their own job, much less look at other people's personal business. So very few administrators actually do. Does it happen? Occasionally you hear of it.

Q: What about someone putting a sniffer (a machine capable of reading transmissions as they go by) on the network at some point and scanning for, say credit card numbers?

A: You know, that's another place where the press has done us dirty. They have people so afraid to use a credit card that electronic commerce is almost dead in the water. That's perception, because the truth is there is less risk of credit card fraud on the Internet than there is when you physically use your card at a store or restaurant. There, the employees take physical control of your card and can make a copy of your number and signature. Or someone might steal the carbons or read your number standing behind you in line. Truth is that there isn't any credit card fraud to speak of on the Internet compared to what goes on in the mall every day.

Things have been blown all out of proportion. Like the pornography issue. If you read some of these news stories, you'd think that is all there is on the Net. Security is the same way. Credit card fraud on the Internet is not real business yet. To date, there has been no credit card fraud perpetrated on the Internet, and yet if you listened to the stories, you'd think it was happening all the time.

The same thing is true of all this talk about sniffing. Is it possible for somebody to use a sniffer to read your e-mail? Yes, it is possible. Will it happen? Very unlikely, unless you do something to merit it.

Q: *But it is possible to set up a sniffer program and monitor e-mail that comes through a particular point on the Internet?*

A: E-mail is passed over the Net unencrypted. Everything on the Internet is broken down into small pieces known as packets in order to be sent around on the Internet. Now these packets all have a header on them that tells who it's from, who it's to, along with a sequence count. Your five page e-mail does not go across the Net as a single big package, it will go as multiple smaller packets and then be assembled in sequence order by the receiving system.

When e-mail is sent from point A to point Z, it doesn't necessarily follow the same route every time it is sent. There is a utility called Traceroute that lets you send a trace message and see all the routers it passes through on its way to the destination address. Come back and do it again in five minutes; you'll probably see a very different route.

In a lot of ways [the way e-mail travels] is similar to your telephone. If you pick up the telephone to call the house across the street, the call doesn't go directly between your house and your friend's house. It's going to go to the nearest substation, to the next substation, and eventually to the telephone central office, then back out through the substations again. And which pair of wires it uses between stations is totally unpredictable.

Then Internet was designed to be fault tolerant. If there is a problem somewhere on the Internet, messages route around it and still get your message through. That makes it really difficult to do any sniffing or snooping other than at the point of origin of your target.

The administrator of your Internet provider has the ability to sniff, to set up sniffers, and to look at what is going on with the network. There are legitimate uses for a sniffer. A sniffer is either hardware or software designed to listen to the packets that pass through your system. In the case of the hardware sniffer, it has to be physically located on the network. That limits a lot of your exposure there. There are more hardware sniffers than there are software sniffers. But in most cases, hackers are using software sniffers because they don't have physical access to the network. It's real network administrators who will use hardware sniffers.

There are absolutely good reasons for putting hardware sniffers on a system to measure bandwidth, determine causes for routing problems, to correct socket problems — those types of issues can best be diagnosed with a sniffer. If you are dealing with a reputable provider, then the likelihood of someone being nosy with a sniffer is very low.

It is relatively difficult for a hacker to set up a sniffer, unless they have physical access to the system. Usually they are looking to find passwords, not read your e-mail. Without the cooperation of the administrator, it is very difficult. It would require two things to happen: the hacker would have to break the security of the provider in order to gain the access to set up, and would have to remove it later undetected. Unless your provider is in collusion against you, you are relatively secure from that type of thing. Either that or security is so lax that you should get your account elsewhere.

Summary

This chapter gave you a quick overview of how the Internet is constructed and designed. You have also been introduced to the views of a system administrator for an independent service provider.

- ✦ In this chapter, you learned how the Internet is an outgrowth of Cold War disaster planning that called for a computer network that would be as robust as possible about sending messages to their proper destination, even if part of the network is down or missing.
- ✦ Also in this chapter, you have seen how the open design of the Internet, and its lack of a single owner, places a premium on self-policing and cooperation between system administrators.
- ✦ You have also heard from a system administrator that there are many types of activities that can happen on a system that can affect your security.
- ✦ There is a gap between what is possible to do and what is practical to do, which keeps the risks you take in joining the Internet community to a minimum.

✦ ✦ ✦

Protecting Yourself from Unwanted Material

CHAPTER 9

In This Chapter

What's on the World Wide Web

Why the government can't — and won't — sweep the Internet clean

Protecting your children from unsuitable materials

Fear of serious injury cannot alone justify suppression of free speech and assembly. Men feared witches and burned women. It is the function of speech to free men from the bondage of irrational fears.
—Justice Louis Brandeis

The World Wide Web has gone from obscurity to the hottest thing on the planet in the space of just a few years. The explosion of the Web, like other pioneering adventures mankind has taken before, has been largely unregulated. After all, how do you police things that don't even exist yet?

In his novel *The Abortion,* the late Richard Braughtigan's protagonist has a job in a library where nobody ever visits the stacks. Instead, visitors come at all hours of the day and night to leave books of their own creation to be archived. In this library there is no thought of literary criticism, only the loving and equal treatment of any submission anyone wants to make, no matter how banal or vile. I'm sure Braughtigan never considered his fictional library to be a metaphor for the real thing, but essentially the World Wide Web is that library. The sole exception — and it is an important one — is that there are many people browsing the stacks.

The World Wide Web reflects the broad range of human interests, both good and bad. Sandwiched in between the collected works of Robert Frost and mountains of scientific research are the occasionally offensive expressions of the puerile and the immature. The Web is a good deal like an unedited encyclopedia, and any reader can add to or annotate the information contained in it.

A Bad Rap

It is a natural human reaction to fear the unknown. The Web is a new frontier, a vast unknown that, for the first time in human history, is a world of our own creation. For folks who don't understand the Internet and the World Wide Web, the fear factor is running high. As usual, when something is hot, media leeches like your humble author have taken up the Web as a favorite topic, which can only mean that sensationalism and distortion are as easily found as the straight answers to legitimate questions.

The Web is so new that it is like the blind leading the blind. For millions of Americans, the Internet is still the Undiscovered Country. Unfortunately, it remains undiscovered even by most of those in the media who would be scout and guide to the masses. All the average person knows about what's on the Web before he sees it for himself is what he hears and reads in the media. The well-known *Time* magazine cyberporn issue and the controversial and flawed Rimm report that sparked it are obvious examples.

Given the current appetite of the American public for yellow journalism that exploits the sensational and magnifies the squalid while ignoring the normal, it is no wonder that some people think surfing the Web is akin to attending the palace orgies of Caesar. The truth is, however, that most Web sites are boring. How many home pages of college students can you stomach before pictures of cats and girlfriends and rants about the genealogy of professors becomes old hat? Yes, there are Web sites where the prurient and disgusting hold court, but these kinds of offerings are not the norm. They account for less than one percent of all home pages I've encountered in my travels around the Web. For every naked female or autopsy photograph, there are hundreds of charming, informative, useful, and, yes, boring home pages to visit.

The Web is no different from any other media. There are things you just wouldn't walk across the street to look at, and there are some fine examples of human ingenuity and artistic presentation. The biggest difference between traditional media and the Web is that there are hundreds of thousands of private programmers, each with his own agenda and moral character. The World Wide Web has been likened to cable TV, with 1,000,000 channels, most of which are programmed by one person, and so reflect only that one person's views, tastes, and standards.

Freedom of Speech in Cyberspace

There is no doubt that you can find all sorts of unsavory content on Web pages. You can find much the same stuff on the magazine racks of your local convenience store. It is simply a given that some people will use their freedom of speech to offend others.

Abigail Van Buren, one of the Founding Mothers of the American Republic, once said, "If you want a place in the sun, prepare to put up with a few blisters." The World Wide Web is for many a place in the sun, and yes, there are definitely some blisters. On balance, however, there is an overwhelming ratio of good to bad by using nearly any measure you want to employ.

In years gone by, when reading was the most common form of entertainment, filtering out materials not in agreement with your own morals and philosophies was much easier. You simply didn't bring those materials into the home. Of course those were different times. One of the popular boy's magazines of the day, *Captain Billy's Whiz Bang,* was banned in many households as unsuitable. Children today would find Captain Billy unbelievably tame, if not downright boring.

Broadcast media and the motion picture changed the landscape of entertainment worldwide. When radio became the hottest thing on the planet, for the first time media content could come into your home without your physically carrying it over the threshold. Television, early television, was just radio with pictures. Broadcasting, from its inception was governmentally regulated and remained squeaky clean. George Carlin's comedy routine about the seven words you can't say on TV was hilarious in part because it was so true. Lucy and Desi were required by the Standards and Practices Office of CBS to have twin beds; and even when she got quite large about the middle one season, the word *pregnant* was forbidden. Ozzie and Harriet, Ward and June, and Rob and Laura Petrie were all similarly sanitized.

Movies in the heyday of the Hayes Office were also squeaky clean for the most part. The rules were that good always triumphed over evil, and no bad deed went unpunished. Movies like *The Blackboard Jungle, Rebel Without a Cause,* and Marlon Brando's classic *The Wild One* changed the way the world went to the movies. The birth of the anti-hero was also the conception of a new level of freedom of expression in Hollywood.

To say that things have loosened up in the entertainment industry is a gross understatement. The rise of spatter-and-slash movies and the exponential increase in sexual content have been controversial. Efforts to return to a more innocent era have run smack dab into the First Amendment rights of freedom of speech and freedom of expression. The genie is out of the bottle, and there are few who are willing, or even eager, to put the genie back in.

Recent years have seen the proliferation of cable television, where all the rules are turned upside down. Subscription channels are free to do just about any kind of programming they wish. If the communications deregulation bill, passed by both House and Senate and in conference at the time of this writing, performs as expected, cable television, your home computer, the Internet, and your telephone may soon merge into a single appliance. The current controversy over content on the Internet goes way beyond the Prurient Home Page or Jeff's Nude of the Month. The way Internet issues are decided now will have long-reaching effects on the entertainment business for decades to come.

Against this backdrop, Senator Robert Dole of Kansas, during his campaign for the Republican nomination for President, lambasted Hollywood for making pictures whose main attractions are gratuitous violence and sexual content. Senator James Exon, in introducing his Communications Decency Act to the Senate, stated that he wanted "to keep the information superhighway from resembling a red-light district."

Cyberspace and the First Amendment

First Amendment issues, as they affect computer generated speech, aren't limited to erotic content. Other issues include hate speech, libel, sedition, and slander, as well as political speech. Speech as it is used in the context of freedom of expression is not limited to the uttering of words or of the writing down of words to be published. Speech in this context extends to the communication of ideas and images in whatever form. That form is likely to be very different in the coming years. Although they won't yet admit it, over-the-air television stations are obsolete. Many television stations now reach a majority of their viewers by dint of their being carried on cable systems. What happens when all those cable systems and the channels they carry are indistinguishable from the rest of the World Wide Web? Ten years from now you will be able to order movies, with a starting time of your choosing, and browse home pages by using the same information appliance.

Despite the fact that the Constitution reads, "Congress shall make no law respecting an establishment of religion, or prohibiting the free exercise thereof; or abridging the freedom of speech, or of the press; or the right of the people peaceably to assemble, and to petition the government for a redress of grievances," the Supreme Court has held that there are certain exceptions. The classic example is that you are not free to scream "Fire!" in a crowded theater.

Other exceptions have been carved out of the *no law* clause of the First Amendment. For example, distributing leaflets and petitions at an elementary school to ask the principal to change an onerous policy or regulation may be protected free speech, but distributing pictures of sexual acts or commercial advertisements for such pictures at an elementary school does not enjoy the same protection. Electioneering in a polling place and libel are also examples of unprotected speech.

In fact, however, almost all First Amendment cases raised to the level of the U.S. Supreme Court deal with indecency and obscenity, and the Court has wrestled mightily over the years with obscenity issues. Court decisions regarding slander, hate speech, and other forms of expression are simple compared to cases involving obscenity.

The Court has held time and time again that obscenity is not protected speech. The problem has always been one of defining obscenity. The current standard was arrived at in the 1973 *Miller v. California* ruling. Here the conviction of the defendant was upheld, relying on "community standards" as one yardstick in determining if something is or isn't obscene.

Avoiding the considerations of the merits of any kind of speech, clearly there are some forms of speech that are legally protected, even though they are offensive to some members of society. Racial supremacists are free, within limits, to peddle their distorted world view; people who hold unpopular political opinions are tolerated; and, again within limits, pornographers are free to porn. You are free to decline to be a consumer. The old cliché about changing the channel if you don't like something is as true of the Internet and the World Wide Web as it ever was about television.

The problem is, as it has always been, that a certain segment of the population finds sexually explicit materials engaging rather than offensive, while another, similarly small, segment of the population is vehement in its opposition to the availability of such material. Time and again the Supreme Court of the United States has held that truly obscene speech is not protected by the Constitution, but that merely indecent, lewd, or filthy speech is. In 1973, in the landmark case *Miller v. California,* the Court established a murky definition of obscenity. This definition separates obscene speech, which is unprotected, from the merely naughty, which is protected by the Constitution.

In part the standard, which has remained unchanged for more than twenty years, reads

> a. Whether the average person, applying contemporary community standards, would find that work, taken as a whole, appeals to prurient interest.
>
> b. Whether the work depicts or describes in a patently offensive way, sexual conduct, which may be specifically defined by applicable state law and which may include but not be limited to:
>
>> 1. Patently offensive representations or descriptions of ultimate sexual acts, normal or perverted, actual or simulated.
>>
>> 2. Patently offensive representations or descriptions of masturbation, excretory functions, and lewd exhibition of the genitals.
>
> c. Whether the work taken as a whole lacks serious artistic, political, literary, or scientific value.

In short, the Supreme Court punted the ball back to the States and localities. From the viewpoint of state and local prosecutors, however, the ruling is so vague that most prosecutors are reluctant to bring obscenity cases to trial, fearing reversal on appeals from the Federal courts. By defining obscenity relative to community standards and by requiring that the work taken as a whole must lack serious value, the Court has left open fertile ground for litigation as to what constitutes obscenity.

One of the major problems of the community standards provision is in defining what constitutes a community. Although nominally unrelated to the Internet, the case of Robert and Carleen Thomas is illustrative of how hard it is to define *community* when dealing with online behavior.

The Thomases operate an enterprise known as the Amateur Action Bulletin Board Service from their Milpitas, California, home, which is to this day still online, despite the fact that they began serving prison sentences in 1995. A members-only operation, users pay $99 a year to subscribe to the service. At the time of their arrest AABBS had 3,500 subscribers.

The new Canadian standard

In 1992 the Canadian Supreme Court altered its definition of obscenity in a case, *Regina v. Butler,* involving the prosecution of a Winnipeg video store owner. Previously the Canadian test of obscenity was similar to that of the U.S. test, but under the Butler decision the test is no longer whether the community will tolerate being exposed to the material. Rather the test is now whether Canadians would tolerate others in their community being exposed to the material on the basis of the degree of harm resulting from that exposure. In other words, it isn't so much what Canadians wouldn't want to see as what they would like to protect others from seeing. In its ruling the Canadian Court also separated the idea of obscenity and morals by allowing materials to be banned "... not because it offends against morals but because it is perceived by public opinion to be harmful to society, particularly to women."

Thus, at least in Canada, the door is opened wider to obscenity prosecutions than before, especially where the materials depict "degrading or dehumanizing" conduct despite the fact that the ruling explicitly confirms a so-called Artistic Defense. Under the Artistic Defense, if the offensive material is "essential to a wider artistic, literary or other similar purpose," courts are mandated to resolve the case in favor of freedom of expression. The Artistic Defense, however, has proven to be less than optimal for defendants, since the burden of proving the material's essential nature falls on the accused, which can prove expensive and arduous.

During the fall of 1993, according to an affidavit for a search warrant filed by U.S. Postal Inspector David H. Dirmeyer, a complaint was received by a resident of Memphis, to the effect that the Thomas' AABBS was distributing obscene materials. Investigating the complaint, Dirmeyer, despite the obvious California address of the BBS, began to check out the Thomas' operation by posing as a customer. Dirmeyer, using the alias Lance White, subscribed to the bulletin board service, downloaded various of the more than 17,000 pictures available, and ordered videotapes.

Although there are many adult-oriented BBS systems across the country with similar offerings, the Amateur Action BBS differed in several respects. The Thomases were both producing original materials and aggressively marketing their materials with the strongest possible descriptions. Categories of their sexually-oriented products included bestiality (sexual conduct with animals), young models (many obviously prepubescent), alleged incest, and scatology (pictures and videos depicting urination and defecation).

In short, AABBS was, in the vernacular, *out there* in terms of the type of materials it was selling. While much of the content that subscribers could download was similar to the files that can be downloaded from bulletin boards in most major cities of the United States, it was the kinky material that attracted attention. Descriptions of videos and pictures were carefully written to accentuate the kinky. The wording of the affidavit submitted by Inspector Dirmeyer would certainly be unsuitable for reproduction here, but you can assess the case for yourself by downloading files available from the Electronic Frontier Foundation at http://www.eff.org/pub/Legal/Cases/AABBS_Thomases_Memphis/aabbs_case.docs.

On January 10, 1994, four days after application for the warrant, the home of Robert and Carleen Thomas was raided, searched, and computer equipment confiscated. Two weeks later, on January 25, 1994, a federal grand jury indicted the Thomases on charges that they were guilty of distributing obscene materials. Robert Thomas was also charged with knowingly receiving child pornography through the mail, a charge that was later dropped.

Ultimately the Thomases were indicted on multiple counts of using a common carrier to transport obscene videotapes from California to Tennessee (USC Title 18, Section 1462) and multiple counts of transporting obscene computer-generated images from California to Tennessee (USC Title 18, Section 1465). Each of the 11 counts could have resulted in a five-year prison sentence and/or a $250,000 fine.

One remarkable twist to the case was that less than two years earlier the Thomas operation had been raided by the local police department. After an investigation of five weeks, the San Jose California Police Department returned the files and equipment it confiscated, determining that no crime had been committed. Thus one could argue that within the geographical community the Thomases lived in, they fell within acceptable community standards.

It is also interesting to note that the charges were filed in Memphis, a bedrock conservative area where the producers and distributors of the movie *Deep Throat* were put on trial in 1976. This occurred not because the movie was playing in Memphis but because a copy of the movie was transported by an airplane that flew over the region. It is doubtful that the choice of venue as a community was a coincidence.

The Thomases were convicted and sentenced to prison terms — he to 37 months and she to 30 months — in federal prison. Robert Thomas is serving his sentence in Dublin, Missouri, and his wife is serving in California. The distance between their incarceration sites has surely contributed difficulties to their appeals, which were denied on January, 29, 1996 by the 6th Circuit Court of Appeals in Cincinnati. The appeals held that each individual community was free to judge obscenity by local standards, negating the argument that cyberspace communities supercede geographical communities. Unless this ruling is overturned by a higher court, it is logical to assume that local geographical community standards will be applied to worldwide network content.

The impact of the Thomas case on the Internet and telecommunications

In 1973 when the Supreme Court ruled in Miller that community standards should apply, there were no computer networks available to the general public. Ward Christensen's CBBS, the first bulletin board software, had yet to be written. Physical distance provided a real boundary between communities. The widespread adoption of personal computers equipped with modems has radically changed that landscape.

Part of the idea behind the Supreme Court's Miller ruling was that the United States is so large and diverse that no two regions of the country can be expected to have exactly the same moral and cultural outlook. Evidence of the diversity of sexual attitudes, in particular, isn't hard to discover. Female revelers in the French Quarter of New Orleans may legally walk the streets bare breasted, while such conduct would not be tolerated in downtown Salt Lake City, Utah. California has a number of public beaches where nudity is not only allowed, but bathers are protected from gawking and harassment by others; however, don't try going naked on Myrtle Beach, South Carolina. There are geographically different community standards.

Cyberspace creates some unique problems for community-based standards tests that simply do not apply to geographical communities. The whole notion of community has come into question. Online services like CompuServe, Prodigy, and America Online serve users worldwide, all of whom can communicate with each other, regardless of distance. I personally have friends I've never met face to face, but I've gotten to know them over the years by corresponding with them in CompuServe forums and via e-mail. They are closer to me in reality than many of the people who live within a few blocks of my home. Which constitutes the stronger community?

Another of the Constitution's First Amendment rights is the right to free assembly for lawful and peaceful purposes. Nowhere does this right get more exercise than it does online. Chat groups, Internet phone connections, Usenet groups, and commercial forums of online services are all examples of digital assembly. It is just as easy to join one of these communities in this day and age as it was for your grandfather to hang with his contemporaries at the general store around the legendary cracker barrel. Increasingly, citizens are gathering in online groups without regard to physical, state, or national borders to discuss the issues of the day, to trade ideas, to conduct commerce, and sometimes to trade dirty pictures.

There are people who feel the Thomases got what they deserved, but there are some issues involved in the case that render previous legal rulings perilously close to obsolescence. Consider for a moment that Inspector Dirmeyer, posing as Lance White, had to contact Robert Thomas, pay a fee, view a disclaimer that the materials available were possibly offensive to some people, and then enter a password in order to download the pictures that were placed into evidence before the jury.

In addition to the community standards yardstick, another important precept was handed down in the 1973 Miller ruling. The majority opinion stated: "The States have a legitimate interest in prohibiting dissemination or exhibition of obscene material when the mode of dissemination carries with it a significant danger of offending the sensibilities of unwilling recipients or of exposure to juveniles."

The Miller ruling is responsible, at least in part, for the fact that *Playboy* and *Penthouse* magazines, when sold in neighborhood stores, are shrink wrapped and sold from racks that display only the title of the magazine or are available by request only. That's why strip bars, in localities that allow them, don't have windows that enable passersby, especially minors, to see exotic dancers performing.

Indecent communications are protected by the First Amendment, unlike obscenity, which is altogether unprotected. *Sable Communications of California v. FCC,* the famous Dial-a-Porn case that was decided in 1989, struck down federal law banning all indecent speech conducted by telephone for commercial purposes. The Court opined: "Sexual expression which is indecent but not obscene is protected by the First Amendment; and the federal parties do not submit that the sale of such materials to adults could be criminalized solely because they are indecent. . . ."

In so finding, the Court did affirm an earlier ruling in 1969, *Ginsberg v. New York,* in which indecent speech was unprotected when it was distributed to minors. In Sable, the Court held that in protecting minors against access to indecent material, barriers to adult access must take the least restrictive form, stating: "It is not enough that the Government's ends are compelling; the means must be carefully tailored to achieve those ends." Thus the Sable court established the "least restrictive means" test.

The ruling in Sable is balanced against a 1957 unanimous ruling in the case of *Butler v. Michigan,* which reversed Butler's conviction and struck down a statute making it a criminal offense to make available to the public at large materials that might be potentially harmful to minors. The Court's ruling stated that such a law violated the free speech rights of adults by limiting them to only those materials suitable for children. Writing for the majority, Justice Frankfurter said that enforcing such a statute "is to burn the house to roast the pig."

Similarly, the Court held in *Carlin Communications v. FCC (Carlin I)*, a 1984 case rising from the playing on the radio of George Carlin's monologue on the seven words you can't say on the radio, that restricting broadcasts of sensitive material to hours when children might reasonably be expected to be asleep in their beds was unconstitutional on the grounds that such regulations denied access to adults as well as children. A second case of *Carlin Communications v. FCC (Carlin II)* was decided in 1986. In this case, the Court held that a requirement that access to indecent services be denied to customers, unless they entered access codes or passwords, and that the passwords be issued only after the customer was verified to be over 18, was unconstitutional as well.

The bottom line

Simply stated, the First Amendment rights of U.S. citizens and foreign nationals visiting or residing in this country have been expanded over the years. In *Redrup v. New York*, the Supreme Court stated "that consenting adults in the United States ought to be constitutionally entitled to read and acquire any publication that they wished — including concededly obscene or pornographic ones — without governmental interference." Again, in *Stanley v. Georgia*, the court held that adults had the right to possess, read, or watch concededly obscene movies and books privately in their own homes.

The liberal Burger Court limited the application of Stanley to the facts of that case and stated that Stanley implied "that people had a constitutional right to exhibit or sell such materials outside the home, or that anyone had a constitutional right to bring them to his home, for example, from abroad." In limiting Stanley to the facts in this fashion, the Burger Court denied the opinion in Stanley from serving as a precedent for other cases or serving as a blanket protection for people to possess whatever they want in their homes, but it did put the nose of the camel under the tent. The more conservative Rehnquist Court later refined Stanley further in the case *Osborne v. Ohio* by stating that the right of Americans to read and watch anything they wanted to did not include child pornography.

Thus, both liberal and conservative Supreme Courts have held that indecent speech is protected by the First Amendment and that most sexually-explicit materials are not obscene on their face. Materials like *Playboy*, *Penthouse*, and *Hustler* pinups have consistently been found not to be obscene, community standards notwithstanding.

In short, you cannot count on the Supreme Court of the United States to keep nude photographs of the Pink Ranger, real or faked, off the Internet or even off your local BBS. You cannot count on the Supreme Court of the United States to keep people from using four-letter words in postings to bulletin boards or Usenet groups. Apparently the Court has been taking heed of Abigail Van Buren's advice about blisters and a place in the sun. Unfortunately, you can't really look to Congress to make much of a change either.

The Communications Decency Act of 1995

Senator James Exon, in the fall of 1995, filed a bill that would have amended Title 18 of the U.S. Code to criminalize certain transmissions of indecent materials via the Internet or other online service. Immediately a howl went up from people concerned with First Amendment issues. The howl grew louder when the Senate, prodded by a scrapbook assembled by Exon depicting the worst of the worst to be found on the Net, passed the Communications Decency Act of 1995. Not until Speaker of the House Newt Gingrich publicly stated that the House would simply not pass the bill did opponents breathe a short-lived sigh of relief.

In a rush to complete work before the end of the year, the amended Exon bill was slipped into the Telecommunications Reform Act, which was passed by both houses and was passed and signed into law February 1996. The Telecommunications Competition and Deregulation Act of 1995 is sure to change all our lives because it is designed to allow the communications business to become a real free-for-all, as your telephone, computer, Internet connection, and cable TV all melt together into a single fiber-optic drop into your home. Essentially, the addition of the Communications Decency Act language to the Telecommunications Competition and Deregulation Act of 1995 revives the whole issue of regulating Internet content.

As you might expect, the Electronic Frontier Foundation, the ACLU, and others are out leading the bandwagon, trying to stir up the members of the electorate into calling and faxing their senators and representatives. It seems to be working because Congressional lines and fax machines are ringing off the hook. According to the opponents of the bill, Congress would unconstitutionally deny adults access to adult material, reducing the Web to the level of children's fare. Proponents argue that, left unregulated, the Internet will quickly degenerate into a cesspool that nobody except the depraved would want to visit.

A close reading of the Communications Decency Act suggests, however, that Congress is intending to take a middle ground and, in fact, is opening new ground by legitimizing adult "sexually explicit" television programming. Language in the bill encourages the development of effective methods of filtering out obscene, indecent, and undesirable Web content to protect both adults who do not wish to encounter such matter and minors who might stumble across indecent content. In this encouragement of filtering mechanisms is the implicit suggestion that adult topics and material can peacefully coexist with the vast majority of the content of the Web.

The Communications Decency Act of 1995 as included in the Telecommunications Competition and Deregulation Act is well worth reading simply because of the controversy surrounding the issues of indecent speech and electronic communications. On February 8, 1996, the day President Clinton signed the bill into law, the American Civil Liberties Union, the Electronic Frontier Foundation, and 18 other groups filed suit in Federal Court seeking to have the law overturned. On February 15, U.S. District Judge Ronald L. Buckwalter issued a temporary restraining order against enforcement of a portion of the law pending legal arguments.

Text of the Communications Decency Act of 1995

S.652

(House Appropriation Bill as Passed by Senate)

TITLE IV— OBSCENE, HARRASSING, AND WRONGFUL UTILIZATION OF TELECOMMUNICATIONS FACILITIES

SEC. 401. SHORT TITLE.

This title may be cited as the 'Communications Decency Act of 1995.

SEC. 402. OBSCENE OR HARASSING USE OF TELECOMMUNICATIONS FACILITIES UNDER THE COMMUNICATIONS ACT OF 1934.

(a) OFFENSES- Section 223 (47 U.S.C. 223) is amended —

(1) by striking subsection (a) and inserting in lieu thereof:

(a) Whoever —

(1) in the District of Columbia or in interstate or foreign communications —

(A) by means of telecommunications device knowingly —

(i) makes, creates, or solicits, and

(ii) initiates the transmission of, any comment, request, suggestion, proposal, image, or other communication which is obscene, lewd, lascivious, filthy, or indecent, with intent to annoy, abuse, threaten, or harass another person;

(B) makes a telephone call or utilizes a telecommunications device, whether or not conversation or communication ensues, without disclosing his identity and with intent to annoy, abuse, threaten, or harass any person at the called number or who receives the communications;

(C) makes or causes the telephone of another repeatedly or continuously to ring, with intent to harass any person at the called number; or

(D) makes repeated telephone calls or repeatedly initiates communication with a telecommunications device, during which conversation or communication ensues, solely to harass any person at the called number or who receives the communication;

(2) knowingly permits any telecommunications facility under his control to be used for any activity prohibited by paragraph (1) with the intent that it be used for such activity,

shall be fined not more than $100,000 or imprisoned not more than two years, or both.'; and

(2) by adding at the end the following new subsections:

(d) Whoever —

(1) knowingly within the United States or in foreign communications with the United States by means of telecommunications device makes or makes available any obscene communication in any form including any comment, request, suggestion, proposal, or

image regardless of whether the maker of such communication placed the call or initiated the communications; or

(2) knowingly permits any telecommunications facility under such person's control to be used for an activity prohibited by subsection (d)(1) with the intent that it be used for such activity;

shall be fined not more than $100,000 or imprisoned not more than two years, or both.

(e) Whoever —

(1) knowingly within the United States or in foreign communications with the United States by means of telecommunications device makes or makes available any indecent communication in any form including any comment, request, suggestion, proposal, image, to any person under 18 years of age regardless of whether the maker of such communication placed the call or initiated the communication; or

(2) knowingly permits any telecommunications facility under such person's control to be used for an activity prohibited by paragraph (1) with the intent that it be used for such activity,

shall be fined not more than $100,000 or imprisoned not more than two years, or both.

(f) Defenses to the subsections (a), (d), and (e), restrictions on access, judicial remedies respecting restrictions for persons providing information services and access to information services-

(1) No person shall be held to have violated subsections (a), (d), or (e) solely for providing access or connection to or from a facility, system, or network over which that person has no control, including related capabilities which are incidental to providing access or connection. This subsection shall not be applicable to a person who is owned or controlled by, or a conspirator with, an entity actively involved in the creation, editing or knowing distribution of communications which violate this section.

(2) No employer shall be held liable under this section for the actions of an employee or agent unless the employee's or agent's conduct is within the scope of his employment or agency and the employer has knowledge of, authorizes, or ratifies the employee's or agent's conduct.

(3) It is a defense to prosecution under subsection (a), (d)(2), or (e) that a person has taken reasonable, effective and appropriate actions in good faith to restrict or prevent the transmission of, or access to a communication specified in such subsections, or complied with procedures as the Commission may prescribe in furtherance of this section. Until such regulations become effective, it is a defense to prosecution that the person has complied with the procedures prescribed by regulation pursuant to subsection (b)(3). Nothing in this subsection shall be construed to treat enhanced information services as common carriage.

(4) No cause of action may be brought in any court or administrative agency against any person on account of any activity which is not in violation of any law punishable by criminal or civil penalty, which activity the person has taken in good faith to implement a defense authorized under this section or otherwise to restrict or prevent the transmission of, or access to, a communication specified in this section.

(continued)

(continued)

(g) No State or local government may impose any liability for commercial activities or actions by commercial entities in connection with an activity or action which constitutes a violation described in subsection (a)(2), (d)(2), or (e)(2) that is inconsistent with the treatment of those activities or actions under this section: Provided, however, That nothing herein shall preclude any State or local government from enacting and enforcing complementary oversight, liability, and regulatory systems, procedures, and requirements, so long as such systems, procedures, and requirements govern only intrastate services and do not result in the imposition of inconsistent rights, duties or obligations on the provision of interstate services. Nothing in this subsection shall preclude any State or local government from governing conduct not covered by this section.

(h) Nothing in subsection (a), (d), (e), or (f) or in the defenses to prosecution under (a), (d), or (e) shall be construed to affect or limit the application or enforcement of any other Federal law.

(i) The use of the term 'telecommunications device' in this section shall not impose new obligations on (one-way) broadcast radio or (one-way) broadcast television operators licensed by the Commission or (one-way) cable service registered with the Federal Communications Commission and covered by obscenity and indecency provisions elsewhere in this Act.

(j) Within two years from the date of enactment and every two years thereafter, the Commission shall report on the effectiveness of this section.

SEC. 403. OBSCENE PROGRAMMING ON CABLE TELEVISION.

Section 639 (47 U.S.C. 559) is amended by striking '$10,000' and inserting '$100,000'.

SEC. 404. BROADCASTING OBSCENE LANGUAGE ON RADIO.

Section 1464 of title 18, United States Code, is amended by striking out '$10,000' and inserting '$100,000'.

SEC. 405. SEPARABILITY.

(a) If any provision of this title, including amendments to this title or the application thereof to any person or circumstance is held invalid, the remainder of this title and the application of such provision to other persons or circumstances shall not be affected thereby.

SEC. 406. ADDITIONAL PROHIBITION ON BILLING FOR TOLL-FREE TELEPHONE CALLS.

Section 228(c)(7) (47 U.S.C. 228(c)(7)) is amended —

(1) by striking 'or' at the end of subparagraph (C);

(2) by striking the period at the end of subparagraph (D) and inserting a semicolon and 'or'; and

(3) by adding at the end thereof the following:

(E) the calling party being assessed, by virtue of being asked to connect or otherwise transfer to a pay-per-call service, a charge for the call.

SEC. 407. SCRAMBLING OF CABLE CHANNELS FOR NONSUBSCRIBERS.

Part IV of title VI (47 U.S. C. 551 et seq.) is amended by adding at the end the following:

SEC. 640. SCRAMBLING OF CABLE CHANNELS FOR NONSUBSCRIBERS.

(a) REQUIREMENT- In providing video programming unsuitable for children to any subscriber through a cable system, a cable operator shall fully scramble or otherwise fully block the video and audio portion of each channel carrying such programming upon subscriber request and without any charge so that one not a subscriber does not receive it.

(b) DEFINITION- As used in this section, the term 'scramble' means to rearrange the content of the signal of the programming so that the programming cannot be received by persons unauthorized to receive the programming.

SEC. 408. SCRAMBLING OF SEXUALLY EXPLICIT ADULT VIDEO SERVICE PROGRAMMING.

(a) REQUIREMENT- Part IV of title VI (47 U.S.C. 551 et seq.), as amended by this Act, is further amended by adding at the end the following:

SEC. 641. SCRAMBLING OF SEXUALLY EXPLICIT ADULT VIDEO SERVICE PROGRAMMING.

(a) REQUIREMENT- In providing sexually explicit adult programming or other programming that is indecent and harmful to children on any channel of its service primarily dedicated to sexually-oriented programming, a multichannel video programming distributor shall fully scramble or otherwise fully block the video and audio portion of such channel so that one not a subscriber to such channel or programming does not receive it.

(b) IMPLEMENTATION- Until a multichannel video programming distributor complies with the requirement set forth in subsection (a), the distributor shall limit the access of children to the programming referred to in that subsection by not providing such programming during the hours of the day (as determined by the Commission) when a significant number of children are likely to view it.

(c) DEFINITION- As used in this section, the term 'scramble' means to rearrange the content of the signal of the programming so that audio and video portions of the programming cannot be received by persons unauthorized to receive the programming.

(b) EFFECTIVE DATE- The amendment made by subsection (a) shall take effect 30 days after the date of the enactment of this Act.

SEC. 409. CABLE OPERATOR REFUSAL TO CARRY CERTAIN PROGRAMS.

(a) PUBLIC, EDUCATIONAL, AND GOVERNMENTAL CHANNELS- Section 611(e) (47 U.S.C. 531(e)) is amended by inserting before the period the following: 'except a cable operator may refuse to transmit any public access program or portion of a public access program which contains obscenity, indecency, or nudity.'

(b) CABLE CHANNELS FOR COMMERCIAL USE- Section 612(c)(2) (47 U.S.C. 532(c)(2)) is amended by striking 'an operator' and inserting 'a cable operator may refuse to transmit any leased access program or portion of a leased access program which contains obscenity, indecency, or nudity.'

SEC. 410. RESTRICTIONS ON ACCESS BY CHILDREN TO OBSCENE AND INDECENT MATERIAL ON ELECTRONIC INFORMATION NETWORKS OPEN TO THE PUBLIC.

(a) AVAILABILITY OF TAG INFORMATION- In order —

(1) to encourage the voluntary use of tags in the names, addresses, or text of electronic files containing obscene, indecent, or mature text or graphics that are made available to the public through public information networks in order to ensure the ready identification of files containing such text or graphics;

(continued)

(continued)

>   (2) to encourage developers of computer software that provides access to or interface with a public information network to develop software that permits users of such software to block access to or interface with text or graphics identified by such tags; and
>
>   (3) to encourage the telecommunications industry and the providers and users of public information networks to take practical actions (including the establishment of a board consisting of appropriate members of such industry, providers, and users) to develop a highly effective means of preventing the access of children through public information networks to electronic files that contain such text or graphics,
>
>   the Secretary of Commerce shall take appropriate steps to make information on the tags established and utilized in voluntary compliance with this subsection available to the public through public information networks.
>
> (b) REPORT- Not later than 1 year after the date of the enactment of this Act, the Comptroller General shall submit to Congress a report on the tags established and utilized in voluntary compliance with this section. The report shall —
>
>   (1) describe the tags so established and utilized;
>
>   (2) assess the effectiveness of such tags in preventing the access of children to electronic files that contain obscene, indecent, or mature text or graphics through public information networks; and
>
>   (3) provide recommendations for additional means of preventing such access.
>
> (c) DEFINITIONS- In this section:
>
>   (1) The term 'public information network' means the Internet, electronic bulletin boards, and other electronic information networks that are open to the public.
>
>   (2) The term 'tag' means a part or segment of the name, address, or text of an electronic file.

Analysis of the Communications Decency Act of 1995

Although the topic under discussion is the Internet and other public networks, there are several provisions of the CDA that bear examination for their possible effect on computer usage. For example, Section 402(a) broadens prohibitions against making obscene and/or harassment phone calls or other communications with the intent to harass another person. The wording of this section would outlaw using a demon dialer to tie up the phone lines of someone who has made you angry, and might also be interpreted to outlaw filling the e-mail boxes of people who send you unwanted e-mail solicitations. Of course, the reverse is true: people who continue to send solicitations after they have been asked to stop would also be considered criminals.

Section 402(d) contains language from the Exon bill that is perhaps the most controversial in the bill, in which obscene communications, regardless of who initiates the contact, would be criminalized. From this it seems that carriers like Internet Service Providers, online services, bulletin board operators, and so on could be held criminally liable for such transmissions. Section 402(e) extends similar criminal penalties for indecent material that fails to rise to obscenity but to which minors can gain access. Again, service providers would seemingly come under the provision.

Section 402(f), however, softens the statute by providing a defense consisting of circumstances that nullify criminal sanctions when "a person has taken reasonable, effective, and appropriate actions in good faith to restrict or prevent the transmission of, or access to, a communication specified in such subsections, or complied with procedures as the Commission may prescribe in furtherance of this section." Elsewhere in the bill, the Federal Communications Commission has been charged with developing regulations for limiting the access of minors to offensive or harmful materials. The defense section specifically says that if you follow the regulations in a reasonable and good faith manner, you are not liable for prosecution.

Also contained in Section 402(f) is language that seemingly lets service providers off the hook by stating that providers do not risk prosecution "solely for providing access or connection to or from a facility, system, or network over which that person has no control, including related capabilities which are incidental to providing access or connection." This means that providers do not have control over what subscribers may do and should therefore not be held liable for the actions of subscribers.

Section 410, an amendment proffered by Senator Chuck Robb of Virginia, anticipates and seemingly sanctions the existence of objectionable material by mandating that a system of tags be developed that can be used to filter out obscene and indecent materials on public networks. The regulations mandated by 402(f) are coupled with the development of these tags. It is reasonable to infer from these sections that the intent of the legislation is not to stamp out free speech or even erotic content on the Web. Rather it is intended to restrict access to such materials by minors, while reserving the right to go after things like child pornography, the one form of expression that almost everyone condemns outright.

One interesting section of the bill that has avoided reportage of any significant scale is Section 641 "SCRAMBLING OF SEXUALLY EXPLICIT ADULT VIDEO SERVICE PROGRAMMING." This section, aimed primarily at cable television operators, states, "In providing sexually explicit adult programming or other programming that is indecent and harmful to children on any channel of its service primarily dedicated to sexually-oriented programming, a multichannel video programming distributor shall fully scramble or otherwise fully block the video and audio portion of such channel so that one not a subscriber to such channel or programming does not receive it."

The effect of Section 641 is to recognize the legitimacy of sexually explicit programming, making it just another color in the spectrum. Within the context of the Telecommunications Competition and Deregulation Act, the bill to which the CDA is attached, this provision is remarkable if the intent of Congress is to stamp out smut of all kinds on the Internet. Given that the deregulation envisioned by the overall act enables and facilitates using the Internet, or similar network, as a vehicle for delivering television programming into American homes, this section seems to enshrine the right of Americans to view explicit programming. For a bill that has been slickly depicted as the flaming left versus the religious right, the CDA, properly applied, has the potential to regulate the worst of the worst, while protecting access to the not so bad of the worst.

Holding providers not liable

When creating an account for a user, Internet Service Providers routinely enable users to create and publish their own Web pages. Legal precedent, set in the case of *Cubby Inc. v. CompuServe,* provides that an online service cannot be held responsible for the content of postings to a public forum. Legal scholars at the time posited that the Cubby ruling may not be applicable to services like Prodigy that prescreen content and police public forums. The World Wide Web is the ultimate public forum, and so Internet Service Providers are reluctant to perform as censors. That doesn't mean they won't do it, but most do so only in the most extreme situations.

Cubby, Inc. v. CompuServe

In 1991, Cubby, Inc. headed by Robert G. Blanchard, filed suit in U.S. District Court against CompuServe Information Services because of allegedly defamatory remarks about Cubby's online service, Skuttlebutt, posted by a user in a competing service's forum. In providing a summary judgment for the defendants, Judge Peter Leisure dismissed the suit before it could come to trial.

In his ruling Judge Leisure likened CompuServe to a bookseller who cannot be held liable for defamation as publishers can. He wrote, "CompuServe has no more editorial control over such a publication than does a public library, bookstore, or newsstand, and it would be no more feasible for CompuServe to examine every publication it carries for potentially defamatory statements than it would be for any other distributor to do so."

According to legal experts, Judge Leisure's ruling, unless reversed by a higher court, establishes an important precedent for upholding freedom of speech by making CompuServe, and other similar online services, on a par with a common carrier like the telephone networks. You may utter libelous statements in a phone conversation for which you may later be sued, but the telephone company cannot be held responsible for your statements, even though they supplied the forum from which you made your libelous statements.

The Dow Jones News Retrieval Service, in analyzing the decision, pointed out that such protections may not be forthcoming to online services, like Prodigy, who prescreen postings, or who have a pattern of enforcing restrictions. Wrapping themselves in the common carrier mantle as a protection against liability, most Internet Service Providers are reluctant to regulate content of subscriber's home pages. For the same reasons, most do not censor or block controversial Usenet groups.

Given the defenses provided to service providers of public network access in the Communications Decency Act, it is likely that the protections derived from *Cubby v. CompuServe* will continue. Thus, providers who do not endeavor to control the content generated by their subscribers will likely enjoy a buffer from prosecution, even when their facilities are used for indecent speech.

For example, nobody contemplated holding the University of Michigan liable for the postings by Jake Baker of short stories containing fictional accounts of the rape, mutilation, and torture of women (one of whom was a real person) in a Usenet group.

The People v. Jake Baker

No case in recent years has stirred up more debate over free speech issues in cyberspace than the story of Abraham Jacob Alkhabaz, a.k.a. Jake Baker. While a student at the University of Michigan, Jake Baker was arrested in 1995 for publishing controversial fiction on the Internet. Subsequent events reveal several interesting aspects concerning the law, cyberspace, and the news media.

During a period of several months, from October 1994 until January of 1995, Jake published several stories in the Usenet group alt.sex.stories. Although you'd never know it from press accounts, Usenet is quite distinct from the World Wide Web. Rather, Usenet is like a gigantic bulletin board system with more than ten thousand individual groups. Groups are generally sorted by subject content, which is usually described by the name of the group. Thus, as you might expect, comp.os.ms-windows.win95.misc contains messages back and forth from people concerning Windows 95.

Many Usenet groups are the modern-day equivalent of the soapbox in the park where people can air their views, debate issues great and small, and generally interact with other Internet users. Most Usenet groups are like public e-mail sites where everybody can read your postings, and you can read everyone else's. Usenet groups are a part of the community-building and bonding that cyberspace is so famous for, and the overwhelming effect of having Usenet access is positive. Reading many of the postings in the alt.sex.stories section of Usenet is a little like reading through an old issue of *Penthouse* Letters. The writing is seldom of professional quality, and the erotic content varies from day to day.

Jake Baker posted several short stories of rape, mutilation, and torture to a Usenet group. Jake's troubles with the law didn't begin, however, until he published a story using a real woman as the victim. As the legend has it, a 16-year-old girl living in Moscow read the story and told her father about it. The father, a University of Michigan alumnus, reported the posting to the university. Members of the Department of Public Safety (the university's police department) interviewed

(continued)

> *(continued)*
>
> Mr. Baker. Baker, after being read his rights, allowed the police to search his computer, where they found archives of the postings as well as transcripts of messages between Baker and various correspondents. One of the correspondents was an Arthur Gonda, allegedly of Ontario, Canada. Gonda later turned out to be an alias, and the account could not be traced to an actual person, so the true identity of Gonda is unknown. Still, the authorities found the fact that Baker's correspondent was in another country to be significant in light of federal statute. In 18 U.S.C. s 875(c) is the language: "transmission in interstate or foreign commerce of a communication containing any threat to kidnap any person or any threat to injure the person of another," makes this activity a federal felony.
>
> Baker was suspended from school, and then he was arrested by FBI agents. Prosecutors argue that Baker exhibits a pattern of escalating behavior, citing messages like the one to Gonda where Baker says, "Just thinking about it anymore doesn't do the trick. I need to DO IT." Baker was deemed a danger to society by two federal judges and the 6th Circuit Court of Appeals, and held without bail until March 9, 1995 when he was released on $10,000 bond. By March 15, charges dealing with posting the story were dropped, but a five-count indictment was filed based on Baker's messages to Gonda.
>
> Ultimately a judge ruled that the prosecution could not show that Baker had intent to do harm to the woman. She was unaware of the incident and Jake Baker until told by reporters. Baker never directly threatened her. On June 21, 1995, Judge Avern Cohn dismissed the indictments against Baker. Prosecutors vowed to appeal and refile the case. As of this writing, the appeal verdict is still unknown and may be in the courts for years to come.

Please keep in mind that cases like the Thomases and Baker represent only two incidents in the development of cyber law. The actions of the defendants were on the outside extreme of the normal usage of public networks. They do not represent the actions of the vast majority of middle-of-the-road folks. It is almost always the most outrageous and most controversial actions that are used to formulate precedent. The danger in studying these types of cases, important though they may be, is that it is easy to come away with the misunderstanding that there is grossness and obscenity lurking just behind every click of the mouse.

The generally healthy and lively exchange of ideas that happens every day on online services, the Internet, and local bulletin boards is largely self-regulating.

Self-Regulation of the Internet

In large measure the content of the World Wide Web is self-regulating. Internet Service Providers are often able to shed unwanted subscribers and their offensive Web pages by switching the issues to economics. By terminating an unwanted user's service on economic grounds, they are able to bypass the inevitable lawsuits that would result from open censorship.

The mechanism for this self-regulation is deceptively simple. Web sites that get little or no traffic seldom become engulfed in controversy. If, however, a user puts up a Web page that contains nude photos of supermodels, Playboy Playmates, and the like, it is a sure bet that many web surfers will visit. Photos, especially high-quality bitmaps, require a great deal of data to be transmitted across the network.

Home pages that offer this type of material become known quickly on the Web, with the result that soon the ISP is seeing a marked increase in traffic and a big jump in the number of megabytes of data the server is being asked to deliver. A Web page that generates large amounts of traffic can require so much of the system's resources that ISPs have been forced to include fine print in their subscriber contract that requires owners of high-traffic Web pages to pay for the increased usage of resources. Most owners of this type of page are young and seldom affluent. Therefore, Web pages that offer significant erotic content come and go with astonishing rapidity because the owners are unwilling or unable to pay the high costs of serving thousands of visitors daily.

Avoiding Offensive Web Content

Justin Hall regularly publishes an Internet E-zine (electronic magazine) named *Links from the Underground*. You can find him at http://www.links.net/. Justin's writings and ramblings can take you almost anywhere, including discussions of sex. In a recent issue he wrote, "Online porn archives are another story. Like the corner porn store, they exemplify the screwed-up sexuality of our culture. I firmly believe that if people were permitted open channels of sexual communication, we wouldn't have 700,000 horny geeks dialing daily into *Playboy* for their bizarre, alienating sense of the erotic."

Without realizing it, perhaps, Justin has framed the whole set of arguments, pro and con, about indecent or sexually explicit Web content. Part of the sexually free culture of the Internet has, no doubt, to do with its academic ancestry where university students, liberated from their parent's homes, first encountered the full flower of independent thought and speech. The fact that there is so much interest in sexual expression is a reflection of our culture. By making any regulation of content controversial, with one side screaming for Ozzie and Harriet purity and the other decrying censorship in any form, adult content on the Web is brought into the spotlight. A spotlight which is far brighter than it deserves to be.

Imbuing anything with the patina of the forbidden fruit nearly always guarantees at least experimental consumption. Eve couldn't bear not eating the apple; David had to have Bathsheba; Napoleon couldn't help coveting Russia; King Edward had to have Mrs. Wallace; and some people can't resist pictures of naked girls. It is the way of the world. If it isn't allowed, a certain portion of the population just has to have it.

That doesn't mean that those people who have no desire for, or find offense in, breaking taboo need to be affronted either. It may be your right to collect explicit photographs, and it may even be your right to exhibit your collection discreetly, but you don't have the right to throw it in my face if that isn't what I want to see, or if I object to seeing the collection. It is also my right to raise my children to have the values I wish to pass along, and thus it is my right and my duty to regulate the things that my children come into contact with.

Any parent will concede, regretfully, that he or she cannot fully control everything a child is exposed to. That too is the way of the world. If your child makes friends with another child, whose values are not a mirror image of your own, there is little you can do. You must balance harming the child by prohibiting contact with a friend against anything that child might bring your child into contact with.

As the father of four children who are all nearer the end of their childhood than the beginning, I can now look back and see that it is probably a good thing that children come into contact with values not your own. It gives them a way of testing and weighing the values you are trying to give them against something else. There is no human adult so unprepared to take up a happy life as the one who has been sheltered against the extremes of the world. In a happy home, your children will nearly always choose the values closest to home and hearth. They are amazing little people, and it doesn't take a leap of faith to believe that a child who has a friend with bizarre or troubled parents will come to appreciate a stable and sedate home all the more.

Regardless of any laws passed and regardless of any sort of shift in the judicial winds, there will always be content on the Web that contains smut, hate speech, radical political ideas, and the like. If you are a person who is easily offended or simply doesn't want to come into contact with offensive materials, or you have a self-imposed duty to protect your child, there are a number of products that you can easily pick up and install on your computer that will limit your computer's access to whatever material you deem inappropriate.

Cyber Patrol

It has long been true that effective self-regulation is the best way to avoid governmentally imposed restrictions. That is why the Communications Decency Act proposes a set of tags and guidelines for keeping adult materials out of the hands of minors. Another approach, which is available today, is to screen Web addresses against a master list of known sites with potentially offensive materials and to analyze page content for profanities and other catchwords and phrases. In this way, parents can help protect their children from adult themes and topics. This methodology is called *filtering*.

Cyber Patrol is one of the best applications that provide Internet filtering capabilities. By installing Cyber Patrol on your system, you can effectively block out a broad range of unwanted material. A free Home Edition, which can be downloaded from http://www.microsys.com/CYBER/, is available to provide a demonstration of the program's features. Cyber Patrol not only blocks Web sites, but also Usenet groups, chats, and other Internet protocols. A more versatile and customizable version of Cyber Patrol can be ordered from the same home page. Cyber Patrol is available for both Macintosh and Windows computers.

Although the policeman metaphor wears a bit thin after a while, the object of Cyber Patrol is not, according to its creators, an attempt to promote censorship on the Internet. Rather, it is an attempt to avoid censorship being imposed. Figure 9-1 shows the installation procedure for Cyber Patrol.

Figure 9-1: Cyber Patrol isn't tamper-proof, but its maximum security setting makes it difficult, especially for kids, to disable Cyber Patrol.

During the installation process, you are prompted to enter a master password. In Cyber Patrol's cop-like jargon, this is called the Headquarters Password. This password is used to control the actions of Cyber Patrol. You can also create a Deputy password that is good until midnight. This enables someone who has the Deputy password to gain unfettered access to the Internet.

After you have the software installed, you can use the Options menu to get to the screen shown in Figure 9-2, which allows you to customize your usage of the program. By visually editing a time line for each day of the week (the screen partially hidden from view), you can establish times of day, maximum daily hours, and maximum weekly hours for accessing the Internet. By restricting times to those times when you are most likely to be available for supervision, you can increase the effectiveness of Cyber Patrol filtering. The top window shown in Figure 9-2 enables you to customize the categories that Web sites are divided into.

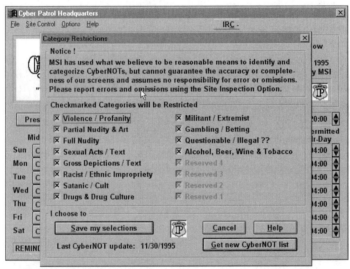

Figure 9-2: You have control over the types of sites that are blocked. Sites are divided into various categories, each of which can be separately addressed.

If your kids find a site that should be blocked, you can use your password to add that site to the CyberNOT list. You can also unblock sites that might be blocked, making them available.

The CyberNOT list is similar to the databases of viruses used by most antiviral software. If anything, however, the way Web sites spring up and disappear, such a list quickly becomes obsolete. The basic CyberNot list is updated weekly and can be downloaded automatically by the Cyber Patrol program.

After Cyber Patrol is installed, Internet connections work exactly as before, except when Cyber Patrol locates an Internet resource that it thinks should be blocked. Figure 9-3 shows the screen that appears when you attempt to access a Usenet group that is blocked. As you can see, two errors occur. First, the news reader Free Agent in this example, is given an error that indicates to it that the resource doesn't actually exist. Cyber Patrol then notifies you that a block is being enforced. In effect, Second Cyber Patrol convinces Free Agent that the requested resource doesn't exist, which is why Free Agent reports an error.

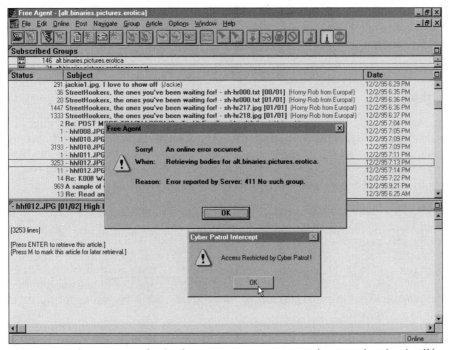

Figure 9-3: When an unauthorized access attempt occurs, Cyber Patrol makes itself known.

If there is no objectionable content detected, an attempt to access Internet resources occurs normally. You may detect a slight slowdown when a scan is made of the resource to see if it should be blocked on the basis of the CyberNOT list, or the blocking criteria, but all other operations continue unhindered.

Tip Remember the password you use in installing Cyber Patrol because you will need it to uninstall the program or to control the features of the program. If you forget the password, you might end up having to reformat the hard disk to get unrestricted access to the Internet.

Other filtering sources

Two other similar programs are worth noting. Both use similar techniques to provide a barrier between you and whatever you want to block out. The first is Net Nanny, which can be viewed and downloaded at http://www.netnanny.com/netnanny/home.html. Another popular site blocker is SurfWatch, which can be found at http://www.interserf.net/surfwatch.html.

Each of the commercial online services such as AOL, CompuServe, Prodigy, and so on, have individual policies concerning adult materials and parental lockouts. There are also ways to track the activity on your online service account so that you can see just what Junior has been up to. For specific information, contact your online service provider or check its member services information online.

SafeSurf

On the other side of the fence from the filtering approach is the SafeSurf approach. Instead of identifying objectionable resources, the SafeSurf ratings system proposal encourages authors of Web sites to place an HTML tag into their documents that certifies the page has no adult themes or objectionable content and to register their site so that it can be inspected and certified as kid friendly.

HTML (hypertext markup language) is the programming language of the World Wide Web. The SafeSurf HTML tag is placed into the <HEAD> portion of Web pages. It is, in reality, just a comment code that reads: <! — SS~~0001 — >.

As of the writing of this book, SafeSurf is not yet fully implemented, but the ideas behind SafeSurf seem to be gaining steam. Both Netscape Communications and Microsoft are looking into supporting the SafeSurf rating system in future versions of their software.

Taking the positive approach to identifying kid-friendly Web sites may provide a secondary benefit. Sites that sport the SafeSurf identification may make it easier for parents to find Web sites specifically designed for and in line with the tastes of their children. You can find out more about the SafeSurf program at http://www.safesurf.com/.

Summary

The variety of information and entertainment available on the Web is astounding. There are hundreds of thousands of sites on the World Wide Web just waiting for you to explore them. The vast majority of these Web sites provide no problems to anyone who might visit them. There are, however, a small minority of potentially objectionable Web sites that might be encountered.

By far the most controversial debates about freedom of speech and freedom of expression on the Internet center around erotic and sexually oriented materials that may be viewed by easily-offended adults or by minors.

- ✦ You have learned about some of the legal wrangling and Supreme Court decisions that regulate what may be placed in view of the public.

- ✦ The conclusion is that there is simply no way to prevent people from putting objectionable materials in places where your kids might gain access to them.

- ✦ You have seen how one software company has tackled the problem by releasing Cyber Patrol, a software program designed to block access to potentially offensive Internet resources.

- ✦ You have also seen how one group is taking an opposite, but complementary approach, by identifying sites that are kid friendly using the SafeSurf ratings system.

✦   ✦   ✦

Security When Working with Others

PART III

In This Part

Chapter 10
Enforcing Your Privacy

Chapter 11
Network Security and You

Chapter 12
Sharing Resources with Windows Networks

Enforcing Your Privacy

In This Chapter

♦ ♦ ♦ ♦

The controversy over consumer-oriented strong encryption

The alphabet soup of encryption

Using PGP (Pretty Good Privacy)

♦ ♦ ♦ ♦

Civilization is the progress toward a society of privacy. The savage's whole existence is public, ruled by the laws of his tribe. Civilization is the process of setting man free from men.
—Ayn Rand

A man is crazy who writes a secret in any other way than one which will conceal it from the vulgar.
—Roger Bacon

In the last chapter I detailed for you some of the societal, legal, and constitutional issues surrounding free speech. Those issues pale in comparison to the current furor over the use by rank and file computer users of strong encryption.

The Art and Science of Encryption

The word *cryptography* comes to us via ancient Greece and literally means secret writing. In his book *The Codebreakers*, published by Macmillan in 1967, author David Kahn speculates that cryptography is as natural to human civilization as language and writing since it appears almost spontaneously in widely diverse cultures whenever civilization reaches a certain point of development.

Cryptography is probably almost as old as mankind, given our seeming instinct for such things as secret handshakes, code words, and the naturalness with which we separate other people into "us and them." According to Kahn, the earliest known written example of cryptography appeared almost two thousand years before the birth of Christ when an Egyptian scribe created an inscription containing unusual and unknown hieroglyphs.

The first known commercial use of cryptography, cited by Kahn, appeared some four hundred years later on a Mesopotamian clay tablet that contains an encrypted formula for making the glaze used to manufacture pottery.

There are many other examples of cryptography throughout history. When writing down the Biblical book of Jeremiah, a substitution cipher (Atbash) was used. The Greeks used a thin length of leather wrapped around a pole called a *skytale* to write messages on, which, when wrapped around another pole of the same diameter, allowed the characters to properly align so the message could be read. Julius Caesar simply substituted one letter for another in sensitive government communications.

In the late 1500s, Blaise de Vigenère published a manuscript that detailed the first autokey ciphers in which the substitution of one letter depends on the previous letter in the text being encrypted. Two hundred years later, no less a personage than Thomas Jefferson, the third President of the United States, applied himself to the invention of a mechanical wheel encryption device that was used in modified form by the Navy in World War II under the name Strip Cipher. Charles Babbage, known as the father of computing for his invention of the analytical engine and the logic it used, invented a device similar to Jefferson's in the mid 1800s. According to Kahn, a research of patents issued by the United States government between 1861 and 1980 lists more than 1,750 patents issued for devices related to cryptography.

Computers and cryptography

Cryptography was perhaps the single most important driving factor behind the race during World War II to invent the electronic computer. The stage was set in 1923 when Arthur Scherbius incorporated his company, Chiffriermaschinen Aktiengesellschaft, to manufacture and sell a device known as the Enigma machine. Enigma uses a series of wheels and gears of different sizes to create encrypted text. The operator, before entering the message, would set the Enigma machine for that day's key. As each letter was typed, the gears would spin, creating pseudo-random transpositions. To decipher text, the same key had to be dialed in on the receiving end, and the encrypted text typed in to print out the original message.

At Bletchley Park, the secret British World War II cryptanalysis center, the Colossus machine was arguably the world's first working computer. The American effort to create electronic calculation devices centered originally around creating complex trajectory tables to compute ballistic tendencies for artillery forces, but cryptanalysis soon followed as a major function of these new devices.

After the war, the National Security Agency was secretly created to provide intelligence-gathering capabilities and to monitor foreign communications. The agency was so secret that the joke among Washington insiders for years was that NSA stood for No Such Agency. The NSA effectively made advanced cryptography its own black art, clamping down on developments in the field by first employing the best and the brightest cryptographers in the country and then by making sure that information about developments in cryptography were classified in the interests of "national security."

The mission of the NSA throughout the Cold War was to establish and maintain superiority (read that *worldwide dominance*) in creating and, more importantly, breaking codes. By all accounts — and there are few regarding this super-secret agency — it has done its job with skill and vigor. Rumors and legends abound concerning the activities of the NSA. Limited by law to spying only on international communications, the NSA is rumored to monitor large percentages of all cables, telephone calls, and online communications between the United States and anywhere else in the world. It has been speculated that the NSA has computers that randomly tap into overseas calls, listening for code words and/or comparing voice prints to identify the speaker. Almost certainly these capabilities are wildly overstated, yet agency spokesmen will only dance around any questions they are asked about monitoring activities, neither confirming nor denying any substantive issue.

What is clear is that the NSA works quietly in the background to serve the interests of the law enforcement branches of the federal government, and privately-held strong encryption software scares the beejeebers out of them. Perhaps for good reason.

The National Security Agency has always worked quietly behind the scenes, but seems lately to be taking a more active role in trying to shape the policy of the American government with regard to private cryptography. One of the ways NSA does this is through its close cooperation with NIST, the National Institute of Standards and Technology, formerly known as the National Bureau of Standards. The NIST served as the mouthpiece of the NSA in the days when NSA officially didn't exist. There has also been evidence that the NSA and the FBI have been working together to place legal limits on the legality of strong encryption software, as evidenced by their joint publications to the National Security Council.

Strong encryption is defined as a cipher that requires incredible expertise and computational bandwidth to crack. Encryption software is unique in the respect that the source code and algorithms (mathematical formulas) used to encrypt data can be published without compromising the security of the encrypted output of the software. If you had the source code (the actual lines of computer instructions that are compiled to create a program you can run on your computer) to Lotus 1-2-3 or to Microsoft Windows, you could easily figure out how everything is done and just what output would result from any particular action. Encryption software, due to its highly mathematical nature, resists giving up its secrets, even to experts, because the output of the program is entirely dependent on a key value given to the program when it runs. Without knowing the key, you cannot predict the output of encryption algorithms. This is the fact that scares agencies like the NSA and the FBI.

John Gilmore takes on the NSA

John Gilmore is an interesting fellow. A lot of people would like to have his problems. As an early employee (employee #5) of Sun Microsystems, Gilmore helped turn Sun into a six billion dollar company. While still in his early thirties, Gilmore took the opportunity to retire, cash in his stock options, and sit back and take a look at his world. Buffered from the slings and arrows of outrageous fortune by a fortune of his own, Gilmore has created several businesses and has spent considerable amounts of time and cash tilting at windmills and working on causes he believes in.

Gilmore is a founding member of the Electronic Frontier Foundation, along with Mitch Kapor, John Perry Barlow, and Steve Wozniak. The aim of the foundation is to help identify and fight the battles to preserve freedom in the electronic age. Some have compared the American Civil Liberties Union to the EFF, not always in the friendliest manner, by referring to EFF as the Digital ACLU. It is probably a comparison its members find complimentary, as they are frequently joined with the ACLU in filing suits and amicus briefs in some of the most controversial cases cyberspace has to offer.

Gilmore is also a founder, along with Eric Hughes and Tim May, of a group called The Cypherpunks, which Gilmore describes in his home page as "an informal group dedicated to public education and dissemination of cryptography (the science and art of secret writing)."

Cryptography is a long-time interest of John Gilmore, going back into his boyhood. Like most boys, he dabbled with secret codes and decoder rings. Unlike most boys, however, Gilmore's fascination for encryption never faded. He is a strong supporter of the notion that strong encryption tools belong in the hands of ordinary people, and that a government monopoly on encryption technology is not a good thing.

Typical of Gilmore's involvement in the fight for cryptographic freedom is the story of how he is at war with the NSA for sharing a library book. But of course there lies a tale to be told.

One fine November day in 1992, the U.S. Justice Department notified one of Gilmore's lawyers, Lee Tien, that he was perilously close to violating the Espionage Act and that he could face a jail term of ten years if he continued. It was a fight that Gilmore had picked with the government in his quest to make cryptography information public, and now the game was afoot.

Over the years, Gilmore has earned a reputation for brashness. At one time he published a paper he had gotten hold of that was written by a Xerox cryptographer. The NSA had previously dissuaded Xerox Corporation from publishing the paper, but Gilmore posted the contents of this paper on the Internet. Thousands of folks downloaded a copy for themselves, effectively distributing the paper's contents far wider than they ever would have been if Xerox had published it to the business and government community. This act effectively threw down the gauntlet, daring the government to respond.

Gilmore then got into a legal tussle with the NSA over a Freedom of Information Act request that he submitted for the text of cryptographic manuals written more than 30 years ago by William F. Friedman, who many call the father of American cryptography. At one point in time the Friedman texts had been declassified, but had mysteriously been reclassified, making them unavailable to anyone without security clearance and the "need to know."

Under the Freedom of Information Act (FOIA), a government agency must respond to the request within a set time frame. When the NSA exceeded that time frame, Gilmore filed suit against the NSA for non-compliance.

During the legal wrangling, someone Gilmore knew found copies of the disputed texts available for distribution. A printed copy was found at the Virginia Military Institute Library, and a copy on microfilm at Boston University. Apparently these institutions were unaware that the materials had been reclassified. Gilmore informed the judge hearing the suit that these materials were already publicly available and that he was in possession of a copy. Matters escalated when the Justice Department informed Gilmore that distribution of the Friedman manuscript would be a violation of the Espionage Act and threatened him with ten years in a federal penitentiary.

Gilmore presented the judge with a sealed copy of the manuscript. He asked whether his First Amendment rights were being violated by the NSA's refusal to respond to his FOIA requests and its threat of a jail term for distributing a manuscript that was freely accessible to the public. Of course, Gilmore also made a press release to let the news media know what was going on. Within days the NSA had just as mysteriously again declassified the Friedman manuscript, and Aegean Park Press subsequently published the manuscript with the title *Military Crypt-analysis, Part III and Part IV*.

Of course, that isn't the end of the story, because Gilmore is still pressing his FOIA suite against the NSA. He hopes to get the federal courts to rule that the NSA is subject to the Freedom of Information Act and that the prior restraint provisions of the Espionage Act are unconstitutional.

In subsequent testimony to Congressional committee hearings, Gilmore stated, "The Government seized control of telegraphy, radio, and television early in their development, and they have never had full First Amendment protection. Private, interactive, electronic media involve Fourth and Fifth Amendment issues as well. The Executive Branch is already advocating broad wiretapping, and banning of privacy technologies, and they don't even own the network. If the government owned the network, there'd be no stopping them.

"The risk of moving society into media where individual rights are regularly abridged is too great. Economics is pushing us into individual electronic communication, regardless. If Congress truly believes in the Bill of Rights, it should get the hell out of the networking business and stay out of it. Privacy and authenticity technologies are key to reliable and trustworthy social and business interactions over networks. Current government policies actively prohibit and inhibit the research, design, manufacturing, sale, and use of these technologies."

There are currently several encryption programs available, such as PGP, which is covered later in this chapter, that produce stronger encryption than the currently government-approved encryption software products such as DES. DES encryption and its history was covered briefly in Chapter 5 and will be touched upon again briefly in this chapter.

U.S. law enforcement agencies, like the FBI and NSA, worry that if strong encryption comes into regular private use, they will not be able to wiretap and intercept communications as easily as before, thus hampering their ability to protect us from hostile and terrorist attacks against targets in this country.

Using the Freedom of Information Act, the Electronic Privacy Information Center (EPIC) forced the government to release a briefing document on encryption called *Encryption: The Threat, Applications and Potential Solutions,* which was prepared jointly by the Federal Bureau of Investigation, the National Security Agency, and the Department of Justice. This document was presented to the National Security Council in early 1993. One chilling remark in this document concluded that no technical solution to the perceived problems resulting from private encryption would suffice unless all encryption products are certified to meet government standards, and that legislation is required to make prior government approval for encryption software mandatory. Government approval, in this case, would require encryption software to have trap doors or escrowed keys to ensure that the government could decrypt any encrypted data. If you've read along this far in this book, the government's position probably scares you as much as you scare it.

The alphabet soup of encryption

In order to understand the furor over private encryption schemes, you need just a little background on the development of cryptography technology. Understand that the world of cryptography revolves around some heavy-duty mathematical computations involving the factoring of large prime numbers. I don't understand the math much better than the average reader, so I'm not going to bore you with details of the algorithms. Just keep in mind that any encryption scheme can be broken by brute force — that is, trying one password key after another until you pick the right one.

For example, you can use brute force on a typical combination padlock by trying every combination of three numbers in succession until, finally, you find the right one. In cryptographic terms, three numbers between 0 and 36 (the typical range on a padlock dial) yields 36^4 possible combinations. In human numbers, that means that you can open any Master padlock as long as you have the time and opportunity to try all 46,656 possible combinations. Physically manipulating the lock that many times would take the average person days before he found the right one.

Now there are tricks to opening combination padlocks, and you can discover those tricks by browsing through Web sites put up by hackers and other members of the so-called Computer Underground (so-called because real undergrounders seldom want to advertise their expertise). Knowing these tricks can radically reduce the amount of time it takes to open the lock. The same is true of encrypted data. There are a number of tricks cryptanalysts use to make breaking ciphers easier. These include plain text attacks and theft of keys. (Those types of attacks were discussed in Chapter 5.)

Still, the only 100 percent, guaranteed way of cracking encrypted data is brute force. The main trick, if you will, to making encryption secure is to use a key that is long enough to make the possible key combinations number in the hundreds of billions. Even with the fastest computers on earth, a long enough key will dictate that, unless the key chosen is weak, the number of computer years needed to crack the encrypted information will number in the billions of years.

Over the years, a number of different encryption algorithms and schemes have been developed by various organizations, agencies, and individuals. Each has a place in the overall encryption scenario. The one thing that all encryption algorithms have in common is the fact that the longer the key, the more theoretically secure the encryption system is.

The pages that follow are distilled from information provided by RSA Laboratories on its Web pages, which can be reached by linking to http://www.rsa.com/. Other sources have also been utilized. What follows are some explanations of cryptographic terms and encryption methods:

> **MD2, MD4, MD5, and SHS.** These designations represent different *hash functions* used in modern cryptography. A hash function is a piece of programming code that reduces information into a string of standard length that represents the information being hashed. In short, a cryptographic hash function provides an identifiable fingerprint of the larger data in such a way that no two documents could have the same value. If the value cannot be used to recover the original data completely, the string value returned by the hash function is known as a message digest. A message digest can be used to create a digital signature that authenticates a document as being genuine. The MD functions were designed by Ron Rivest, the R in RSA. SHS stands for *Secure Hash Standard*, a function promulgated by NIST, which has been adopted as standard by the government for use with the DSS (Digital Signature Standard) proposed as part of *Capstone* (the government's program to propose standardized encryption methods). The MD functions are also used in a wide variety of encryption programs, including Tiny IDEA and PGP.
>
> **IDEA**. The International Data Encryption Algorithm was created by Xuejia Lai and James Massey of the Swiss Federal Institute of Technology, where it has been under review and analysis since 1990. IDEA is proposed as a replacement for DES. IDEA theoretically provides stronger encryption than DES because of its 128-bit key. IDEA is a component in the PGP program, providing the *symmetric cipher* (single key) features of the program.

Kerberos. Kerberos is a secret key encryption method. In a secret key, both the sender and receiver must have a single key that both encrypts and decrypts the data. The primary use for Kerberos is as a network logon authentication scheme. In a Kerberos-protected environment, a single server acts on all requests for authentication in administering access to resources, providing session keys for secure communications among users, and authenticating the identity of users. The weakness of Kerberos is that a successful attack on the server renders the system wide open to attack because all security services reside on the server.

RC2 and RC4. RC2 and RC4 are encryption functions that were designed by Ron Rivest to provide bulk encryption for large amounts of data. Depending on the length of the key, these functions can provide stronger encryption than DES and are intended as alternatives to DES. An agreement between the SPA (Software Publishers Association) and the Department of State, which must approve the export of strong cryptography, allows a streamlined export licensing. This licensing is provided if the key is limited to 40 bits, 56 bits for foreign subsidiaries and out-of-country offices of American companies, plus a 40-bit string called a *salt*. The purpose of the salt, which is included in the encrypted message in unencrypted form, is to prevent hackers from using previously created lists of keys to try to break a message.

PEM. This acronym stands for Privacy Enhanced Mail, once considered for adoption as a standard way of encrypting e-mail, providing digital signatures, and authentication. PEM allows both public key and secret key encryption. Since that time, Netscape Communications has adopted a different encryption methodology in Version 2 of its Netscape browser, so it is likely that PEM will remain a niche market product. However, Trusted Information Systems has released a freeware version of the product that can be downloaded. An enhanced version of PEM has been developed and distributed by Michael Riordan. This version is not totally PEM compliant in terms of digital signatures, but it can be downloaded and used to encrypt e-mail if you are not using Version 2 of Netscape.

PKCS. The Public Key Cryptography Standards are a set of implementation standards for public key cryptography that have been promulgated by RSA Data Security, Inc. and a group of software companies that include Apple, Microsoft, Digital Equipment Company, Lotus Development, Sun, and the Massachusetts Institute of Technology. Public key encryption uses two keys, one of which can be made public. Only the private key can be used to decrypt messages encrypted with the public key. The public key can be used to authenticate documents digitally signed with the private key.

RSAREF. RSA Laboratories has released a library of cryptographic programming routines written in the C programming language and designed to be portable to many different computing platforms. RSAREF enables programmers to create software with encryption features. RSAREF is available free from RSA Laboratories to citizens of the United States and Canada for use in personal, non-commercial applications. Export and commercial use are restricted by the license and by U.S. law.

The U.S. Government vs. Communications Technology

In the hours immediately following the April 19, 1995, bombing of the federal office building in Oklahoma City, Oklahoma, several news reporters indicated that investigators were thinking the bombing was the work of Muslim extremists with Middle Eastern connections. When Timothy McVey was arrested and charged with the crime, the fact that he had no connections whatsoever with Middle East terrorism seemed not to matter, as government officials from President Clinton and Attorney General Janet Reno on down to freshmen congressmen called for a renewed look at terrorism laws in the United States.

The only indication that computer usage was involved in the planning of the Oklahoma City bombing was the information that McVey had an account with America Online. Nevertheless, Louis Freeh, Director of the Federal Bureau of Investigation, testified before Senate Judiciary Committee hearings that the use and availability of cryptographic software must be restricted by new legislation.

Digital telephony

The way a telephone works is simple. Although the telephone has been improved greatly in the last 50 years, the basic design has remained the same. About the only thing different from Alexander Graham Bell's original instrument is that we say "hello," and Bell felt that "ahoy" was the proper greeting. In the basic telephone design, a microphone picks up the speaker's voice and turns it into an analog electrical signal that is amplified and sent down a wire to the phone company's switching office, where it is routed to the wire attached to the phone of the person you are calling. The analog electrical signal is then reversed by making the loudspeaker in the handset vibrate a paper plate to re-create the sound. Each telephone has both a microphone and a speaker, and both operate continuously in both directions (full duplex) so you don't have to signal the person you are talking to that you have finished speaking. (Over.)

What has changed radically over the years is the way the phone company handles the signal once it gets to the switching office. Try calling 202-555-1212 and interacting with the new computer assisted directory assistance that recognizes your speech to look up numbers, and you will see what I mean. Once the signal hits dial central, the phone company can do some pretty amazing things. One of the things it can do is capture your speech into the phone and turn it into digital packets that can be decoded on the other end of the country back into an analog signal.

Once your conversation is digitized, all the phone company has to do is compress it and send it by modem or satellite to another switch office in time for it to be decompressed and decoded into an analog signal before the previous packet is finished playing. Piece of cake.

Now imagine that you are Joe or Jane G-man, and you have a warrant to tap the telephone of someone whom the FBI has reason to believe is planning to shoot a congressman. You go to the telephone company, and the manager of the central office tells you, "With this new equipment, I have no idea how I'm going to help you out unless you tap in right before the wire hits the substation." Great. Now you have to go relatively near the suspect and stake out a telephone pedestal (those little green boxes along the roadsides) somewhere. You need to put an around-the-clock team on the phone tap instead of just setting up a recorder in the central office, or better yet, just routing an echo of the line to your office where you can control the recording equipment more securely.

You can imagine how frustrating it must be for a cop to find that technology is messing up a valuable investigative tool. Now imagine that the suspect is using a cellular phone as well, or that he is using encryption technology to scramble his conversations with co-conspirators. You can find out all the numbers he is calling, and there it ends. You are then stuck with having to put a unit in close proximity and use sophisticated equipment to pick up sounds bouncing off plate glass windows and the like, or having to physically bug the suspect's telephone instrument. A real pain, and expensive, too.

For these reasons, and more, federal law enforcement began lobbying hard for the Digital Telephony Bill (HR 4922/S 2375). Sometimes known as the Wiretap Bill by its opponents, the Digital Telephony Bill contained language that required telephone companies to alter their equipment to make it easier for law enforcement to implement court-ordered wiretaps. Several years passed, and several different versions of the bill were effectively stymied by intense lobbying efforts from folks like the EFF, EPIC, the ACLU, and similar rights-oriented organizations. Then, Senator Patrick Leahy of Vermont, sensing that passage of a Digital Telephony Bill of some sort was inevitable, introduced a rewritten version of the bill drafted in part with the help and cooperation of the Electronic Frontier Foundation.

It is hard for even the most ardent civil libertarian to argue the fact that wiretaps, as they have been used over the last 50 years, are an important tool in law enforcement. Successive Supreme Court decisions over the years have affirmed the constitutionality of court-ordered wiretaps. It only makes sense that the ability to pursue such wiretaps be maintained in some fashion. Earlier versions of the DT Bill were much broader in scope and more Draconian in nature. Senator Leahy was right: some sort of legislation was going to be enacted into law. In the end there were two issues to be settled. How much, if any, extra power was law enforcement going to get, and who would pay the bill for the needed equipment changes.

Despite some of the headlines that called EFF's participation a "cave in," the media also sensed that a bill was going to pass in the 104th Congress. With the President ready to sign the bill into law, the EFF reasoned that any legislation it did not actively participate in drafting would be even worse. The EFF reluctantly crossed the line and helped draft the final bill. In the process, both sides gave a little, and the version that was finally passed on October 7, 1994, contained exemptions for computer networks and Internet providers and made it tougher for government agents to get hold of subscription records to online services.

In a press release the following day, the EFF summarized its role in watering down the provisions of the DT Bill. It noted that while the new law requires telecommunications carriers to make design changes in equipment to allow easier technical access to wiretapping, the final version of the DT Bill does not expand the authority of law enforcement to tap phone lines. One provision of the bill requires that carriers have to provide the link to the tap, meaning law enforcement officials cannot simply tap into systems unknown to the carrier. The EFF noted further that the bill did not require online services, such as bulletin board systems, commercial services like CIS or AOL, or Internet providers, to comply. The EFF press release then went on to say that the bill did, in fact, contain several privacy measures that actually provided more protection from surveillance.

The EFF noted that the bill elevated the requirements for law enforcement access to online subscription records from the issuance of a subpoena to a court order. Law enforcement was effectively prevented from using devices to track locations of suspects via the phone network, and wiretap information could not include phone tones dialed that might reveal bank account numbers, PINs, or other online transaction information.

Because of the heavy logging that commercial services do to accurately bill customers, a subpoena for their subscription information can often reveal as much information as a wiretap, thus the requirement for a warrant. In the case of devices known as *pin registers*, a wiretapping device that records dialing information, the law requires phone companies to avoid recording information that may not be strictly telephone numbers, as happens when you dial into complex phone answering systems, bank transaction lines, and so forth.

The solution to the money question requires the government to reimburse carriers for the costs of modifying equipment required to meet the provisions of the new law. After four years, the government is required to pay only for enhancements that are not "reasonably achievable." The agency charged with carrying out the requirements of the Digital Telephony Bill is the FCC, which will arbitrate who should pay for future costs related to privacy, consumer issues, national security, technological development, as well as public safety. Your phone bill won't be going down.

The Digital Telephony Bill that was eventually signed into law differs significantly in one respect from all previous versions. The new law does not require telecommunications carriers to unencrypt any signals that have been encrypted by the user, unless the carrier is in possession of the key. Also, there are no provisions that prohibit users from employing encryption on their own.

Tip
Although it is outside the province of this book, you may be interested to know that Phil Zimmerman, the developer of the PGP encryption software detailed later in this chapter, is also the developer of PGP Phone, a software product that enables you to encrypt telephone conversations by using your computer.

The NSA crypto monopoly jeopardized

After World War II, the United States mostly avoided the mistakes of previous postwar eras by not retreating into isolationism. The Soviet threat of nuclear war made such a position impossible, even had the country wanted to follow an isolationist policy. The state of present-day world affairs would be unimaginable if the communist model of government had been allowed to spread. Deprived of the invigoration of expansion during the Cold War, the Soviet empire did finally run out of steam and collapse.

During the height of the Cold War, however, anti-communist sentiment ran high, even after the excesses of the McCarthy period. The National Security Agency, along with the CIA and other agencies, was a part of our intelligence-gathering capabilities as a nation. Unlike the other agencies, however, the NSA was so secret that for many years the government even denied that it existed. The mission of the NSA was pretty straightforward: monitor communications coming to this country from overseas, monitor as much overseas traffic as it could, and be the nation's cryptography expert.

The NSA took up cryptography with a vengeance. Armed with legislation that enabled it to shroud cryptographic developments behind national security interests and the document classification system, the NSA over the years built a virtual monopoly on cryptographic development and research. Often the NSA, because it "didn't exist," used the National Bureau of Standards (now the National Institute for Standards and Technology) as the front for conducting business in public. While the NSA held a monopoly on the latest cryptographic technology, major computer corporations also had competent crypto teams that provided security measures for commerce.

In the 1960s, Dr. Horst Feistel headed a research and development team at IBM's Watson Research lab that developed a cryptographic algorithm known as Lucifer. When the NIST put out a request for proposals from business to create a new encryption algorithm in the late 60s, IBM's Lucifer was chosen as the model. A reworked version, which at the insistence of the NSA was intentionally made less secure than the original, was eventually adopted and renamed Defense Encryption Standard, or DES for short. Since its adoption in 1976 as the government standard for encrypting all but classified documents, DES has been a workhorse. Originally intended as a hardware-only encryption scheme, over the years several good software-only implementations of DES have been released to the public. Businesses like banks, brokerage firms, and the like have used DES to encrypt sensitive financial data. In 20 years of usage, it has never been proven that DES has ever been cracked.

There are those people who believe that, in addition to weakening the algorithm for DES, other changes incorporated into the standard for DES provide the NSA with a back door, sometimes also called a trap door. This trap door would enable them to easily break DES encrypted data. While this has never been proven, it is curious to note that the NSA did not become active in any large way with prohibitions on encryption until more robust encryption schemes than DES became technically feasible and known to the public.

Secret key encryption

Until the mid 1970s, almost all strong encryption, like DES, used *secret key technology*. Secret key technology means that the same key or password is used to both encrypt and decrypt the message. The weakest link in secret key technology is the need for both parties to have the same key. That means the key to decryption must somehow be passed on to the person or persons responsible for decrypting messages through a trusted agency. When I was in the Army Signal Corps in the early 1970s, each cryptographic unit received a packet of cards each week that provided them with the crypto keys for the coming week. If the package never arrived or showed evidence of tampering, all of the keys had to be replaced at great expense in couriers, and all the keys for related sites had to be replaced as well.

Secret key encryption is the basis for most software products that use passwords like PKZip, database applications, and so on. Generally, they are secure enough for low security applications like passwords to log into small business applications and to gain access to network resources.

A breakthrough

In the mid 1970s, the NSA's monopoly on cryptography was shattered. Whitfield Diffie, working with Stanford's Martin Hellman, invented a totally new form of encryption that all but erased the weakness of single key technology.

Diffie, like John Gilmore, studied ciphers as a kid and never lost his fascination with them. In the mid 1960s, Diffie ended up at MIT, where he had a part-time job administering a multi-user computer system. His interest in encryption was rekindled when he realized that perhaps the weakest link in the security chain was the system administrator's respect for privacy. He also reasoned that a subpoena or warrant issued to the system administrator put him in the position of having to violate someone's privacy.

During the early 1970s, Diffie transferred to Stanford, where research on computer network security was being conducted on the ARPAnet, which is a close ancestor to the Internet. That is when a copy of David Kahn's book, *The Codebreakers,* came into his hands. Diffie dissected that book meticulously. Inspired, he set out to learn everything he could about cryptography, a difficult quest considering that almost all the advanced work in cryptography was controlled by the NSA, and what it knew was classified. Fortunately, the quest paid off in spades.

Diffie foresaw that one day people would communicate and work in electronic environments, and that secret key encryption would not work in this environment. Secret keys would need to be sent to people via unsecured channels, or key escrow banks would be needed to hand out keys to authorized people. Instead, he had a vision of people being able to encrypt their stuff without having to send keys clandestinely or give them out to anyone else.

Diffie and Hellman distributed advance copies of their work to selected people as early as 1975. The result was a growing group of academic cryptographers who realized the importance of the work Diffie and Hellman were doing. David Kahn once called their algorithm the most revolutionary concept in cryptography since the Renaissance.

In 1976, the bicentennial year of the U.S. Declaration of Independence, Diffie and Hellman published a paper called *New Directions in Cryptography*. The first line of their paper summed up their advance. It read, "We stand today on the brink of a revolution in cryptography." They probably had no idea that their revolution would be nearly as dramatic as the one that forged a new nation 200 years before and would, within a few years, cause the government and civil libertarians to do battle on constitutional ground.

The way public key cryptography works is mathematically complex but fairly simple to grasp. You generate two keys, one public and one private. Anything encrypted with the public key can be decrypted only by using the private key. Anything encrypted with the private key can be authenticated by decrypting it with the public key, which provides the ability to place digital signatures on documents to prove their origin. Public keys can be circulated widely without compromising the security of the private key.

If you want to create a message that only I can read, you encrypt it by using my public key. If I want to respond to you privately, I encrypt my message with your public key. If you want to know that a document comes directly from me and has not been altered, you can use my public key to authenticate my digital signature.

Because public keys do not require secrecy, they can safely be exchanged or published through unsecured channels without compromising the system. Only disclosure of the private key is a compromise, and then only one person's communications are vulnerable, not the entire community. Many people sign their e-mail with their public key or disclose their public key when the Finger program is used to look them up.

Cashing in on public key cryptography

Three MIT scientists with little practical experience in cryptography or business, Ronald L. Rivest, Adi Shamir, and Leonard M. Adleman, began discussing how to use the Diffie-Hellman algorithm in a practical way. Legend has it that in April 1977, Rivest had a horrible headache, and that during the spell the algorithm came to him for making public key technology a viable product. The next day he wrote out the formula and gave it to Shamir and Adleman. Soon after, the three men submitted their algorithm to *Scientific American* magazine, where it was published in September 1977. Included in the article was an offer to mail a full technical report to anyone who sent a self-addressed, stamped envelope.

Thousands of requests from all over the world came in as result of their mail-back offer, and that's when the NSA stepped in with objections that the report should not be given to foreign nationals or mailed overseas. For a time, Rivest, Shamir, and Adleman suspended mailing out the report, pending an inquiry to the NSA about the legality of mailing the document. The NSA failed to respond to their requests for legal information, so eventually they resumed their mailings. Finally in August 1995, regulations were clarified so that publishing such papers is protected by First Amendment rights of free speech. Interestingly, the United States government has two standards, one for written material and one for digital material, even when the digital form is just a copy of the printed material.

Cryptography as a munition of war

Title USC 2778 of the U.S. Code, amended by the Arms Export Control Act, is called "Control of arms exports and imports." This particular section of the Code is the legal backup for a set of regulations called the International Traffic in Arms Regulations (ITAR), 22 CFR 120.1 et seq. of the Code of Federal Regulations. Section 120.1 of ITAR specifically lists software capable of performing strong encryption as a munition. Just as federal drug laws lump marijuana in with narcotics like heroin, ITAR lumps encryption software in with tanks, rocket launchers, mortars, and bombs.

In order to export guns, bombs, or strong encryption, you must register with the U.S. Department of State as a munitions dealer and obtain an export license. In issuing licenses, the State Department relies heavily on the NSA for advice. Some folks would say that State is a stalking horse for NSA in this regard. Fact is, unless NSA says OK, you aren't going to get a license. However, out of some twisted logic, the State Department has ruled repeatedly that printed copies of manuscripts do not fall under ITAR regulations due to First Amendment free speech interpretations.

Enter Phil Karn, whose mission is to point out the inconsistencies and absurdities involved in these regulations. Phil Karn is a mild-mannered fellow who works for Qualcomm, the company that makes the Eudora Internet mail reader software, as well as other products used in communications and telephony. His home page even has a picture of him with no less a subversive character than Mickey Mouse. Phil has another side too, as a fighter and tilter at windmills.

In an effort to challenge export regulations, on February 12, 1994, Phil filed a *Commodity Jurisdiction Request* (CJR) to find out if the Department of State had any objection to the exportation of the 1994 book *Applied Cryptography* by Bruce Schneier. His sole purpose was to test export restrictions of crypto software. Schneier's book includes much information about the inner workings of cryptography and has many code listings, including the source code for DES, IDEA, and other cryptographic algorithms. In a response dated March 2, 1994, from the

(continued)

> *(continued)*
>
> State Department's Bureau of Politico-Military Affairs, Office of Defense Trade Controls, Karn was told that export of the book, since it was in the "public domain," was acceptable, but that exporting the source code disks, available separately from the author, would not be. In this context public domain does not mean copyright free, but instead refers to the fact that the book is in wide public circulation.
>
> Karn followed the ruling a week later with another CJR, dated March 9, requesting a ruling on a single diskette offered by the author, as opposed to the comprehensive two-disk set available from the author. The CJR noted that the information contained on the diskette was a character-for-character duplicate of the information printed in the book. The only difference was that the floppy was written by using magnetic media instead of ink on paper. This request brought a letter from the NSA requesting to see a copy of the floppy.
>
> After a delay of many weeks, Karn was finally informed that in the opinion of the Department of State, after consultation with NSA, the representation of the floppy was not exactly that of the book, since the disk contained files that made the compilation into executable code much easier. The ruling also noted that the purpose of the book was to allow programmers to include encryption in their applications, and that applications created with those algorithms would not be exportable. Therefore, Karn was told, he needed an export license if he was going to send the disk overseas.
>
> Throughout the spring and summer, Karn appealed the decision without success, and at times without response. Finally in September 1995, he filed suit in the U.S. District Court for the District of Columbia before Judge Charles Richey naming both the Department of State and Thomas E. McNamara, Assistant Secretary of State, Bureau of Political-Military Affairs, as defendants.
>
> Since that time, arguments have been heard on the merits of the suit, but the trial itself has not been scheduled. The result of this case will undoubtedly have an impact on the viability of using ITAR as a way of restricting export of encryption software.

As mentioned earlier in this chapter, cryptographic schemes can be patented. U.S. Patent #4,200,770 is held by Diffie, Hellman, and Merkle. Rivest, Shamir, and Adleman, who went on to form RSA Data Security, Inc., made improvements upon the original Diffie-Hellman scheme and patented those improvements. The basic difference between Diffie-Hellman and RSA is that the original public key system was primarily intended to negotiate on a session-by-session basis, whereas the RSA algorithm is intended for public and private keys to persist from use (session) to use. Because the patents are so intertwined — you can hardly use one without the others — licensing of both sets of patents is done by Public Key Partners of Sunnyvale, California, and both sets of patents are usually licensed as a package.

Capstone, the Clipper Chip, and Key Escrow

Federal law enforcement officials have been encouraged by their success in lobbying the Digital Telephony Bill into law, even in a watered down form. Because of that, and aided by the NSA, they have now begun to lobby for bans on private encryption software that is, for all practical purposes, unbreakable.

The effective life of DES, the current government standard for encryption technology, is coming to an end. The DES standard is more than 20 years old. Advances in cryptosystems, including the invention of public key cryptography, have made DES obsolete for all practical purposes. NIST, in cooperation with the NSA, is actively pursuing replacements for DES as a standard. Creating a standard involves many things, including business acceptance of the standard, since the government and any companies that do business with the government would be required to use any new standard.

Just as the government asked for input when DES was under consideration, NIST is working with the NSA and business to create new standard technologies. The name given to this project is Capstone. The Capstone project's goal is to arrive at standards for bulk encryption, digital signatures, key exchange protocols (that is, Diffie-Hellman type algorithms), and a hash function. To this point, the main encryption algorithm under study is called Skipjack. Each of the Capstone components uses 80-bit keys, and eventually the government wants all components to reside on a single chip. One such incarnation is the infamous Clipper chip.

Clipper

In April 1993, the Clinton administration announced its position vis-à-vis encryption by endorsing the Clipper chip as a voluntary standard around which government and business plan their needs for encryption. The idea behind Clipper is to standardize on a single encryption system built into a semiconductor chip that would provide a wide range of encryption services, including scrambling of data and telephone calls. Using the Skipjack algorithm, a classified cryptosystem designed by the NSA, the Clipper chip would deliberately have a trap door built into the chip that would allow government officials to decrypt any Clipper-encrypted communication. In short, the government would have the ability to wiretap any communication generated with the help of a Clipper chip.

Despite the fact that Clipper, as part of the Capstone project, was inherited from the Bush administration, even Vice President Al Gore, normally a savvy technologist, lent his wholehearted support to the Clipper initiative. The immediate response from business and civil libertarian leaders was derision, scorn, and immediate mobilization to sink the Clipper chip before it could get off the ground.

As you might expect, civil libertarians and business leaders went ballistic over the thought of this proposal. The fly in the ointment, as far as they are concerned, is the fact that each Clipper chip would have an individual serial number that serves as a unique key, and those keys would be escrowed (stored) just in case a need arises to decrypt any phone message, computer data, fax, or other similar communication created by the Clipper chip. The administration claimed that the use of Clipper chips would be voluntary, and that other forms of encryption would not be restricted. Even so, FBI Director Louis Freeh answered a question in a 1994 press conference by stating that if the Clipper initiative failed and law enforcement was stymied by cryptography out of the government's control, the government would have little choice but to seek legislative action. Read that "outlawing uncontrolled forms of encryption."

According to an article published in *Investors Business Daily* on January 9, 1996, the Clinton administration is reluctant to ease up on export controls on encryption software partly because pressure is being applied by U.S. law enforcement agencies, including the Internal Revenue Service and the FBI. The article states that the IRS is afraid that strong encryption makes income and sales tax evasion easier and that the FBI is worried about criminal and terrorist activities that make use of computer communications.

The export controls placed on cryptographic software and domestic use of strong encryption are simply two sides of the same coin. The NSA is primarily concerned with encrypted communications to and from the United States, while the FBI has responsibility for controlling terrorism within our borders. In essence, if export controls are relaxed, domestic encryption gains a measure of respectability. By opposing export control relaxation, officials are able to maintain more militant stances against the domestic use of strong encryption products.

In a 1995 article entitled *Jacking in from the Narco-Terrorist Encryption Port,* Brock N. Meeks points out that FBI Director Freeh has begun to be more outspoken about the need for government control of encryption. On May 11, 1995, Meeks reports that Director Freeh testified at an appropriations hearing that the FBI was in favor of strong, robust encryption, so long as law enforcement has a trap door to be able to decrypt encrypted data when a judge issues a warrant. According to Freeh, encryption programs are being used by terrorists and drug traffickers, making private encryption a threat to national security.

On April 27, Freeh testified before the Senate Judiciary Committee that encryption technology endangers "the future usefulness of court authorized wiretaps. This problem must be resolved."

Not everyone agrees with Director Freeh's assessment, however. Speaking on the floor of the House of Representatives on June 15, 1994, Congressman Jack Brooks, who serves on the Intelligence Committee, made a speech on the Clipper chip proposal that flatly contradicts the positions of most law enforcement officials. In his speech, he noted that strong encryption products are already a reality by saying, "The law enforcement and intelligence communities have a legitimate concern that advances in technology will make their jobs more difficult. But the issue here is whether attempts to restrict the development, use, and export of encryption amounts to closing the barn door after the horse has already escaped. The notion that we can limit encryption is just plain fanciful. Encryption technology is available worldwide — and will become more available as time goes on."

Brooks made several further points about the current general availability of software by pointing out:

> "First, generally available software with encryption capabilities is sold within the U.S. at thousands of retail outlets, by mail, even over the phone. These programs may be transferred abroad in minutes by anyone using a public telephone line and a computer modem.
>
> "Second, it is estimated that over 200 programs from some 22 countries — including Great Britain, France, Germany, Russia, Japan, India, and South Africa — use some form of encryption that the government currently prohibits U.S. companies from exporting. And this is just the beginning. According to the May 16, 1994 issue of *Fortune,* not only are U.S. companies willing to purchase foreign encryption devices, American producers of encrypted software are also moving production overseas to escape the current U.S. export controls.
>
> "Third, encryption techniques and technology are well understood throughout the world. Encryption is routinely taught in computer science programs. Text books explain the underlying encryption technology. International organizations have published protocols for implementing high level encryption. Actual implementations of encryption — programs ready to use by even computer novices — are on the Internet."

Congressman Brooks ended his remarks by asserting:

> "The only result of continued U.S. export controls is to threaten the continued preeminence of America's computer software and hardware companies in the world markets. These restrictive policies jeopardize the health of American companies, and the jobs and revenues they generate. I support, therefore, the immediate revision of current export controls over encryption devices to comport with the reality of worldwide encryption availability.
>
> "I believe law enforcement and the intelligence community would be better served by finding real and targeted ways to deal with international terrorists and criminals rather than promoting scattershot policies, which restrict American industries' ability to design, produce, and market technology. Now — more than ever — we cannot afford to harm our economic competitiveness and justify it in the name of National Security."

In 1994 testimony before Congress, Special Agent James Kallstrom stated that between 1982 and 1992, more than 22,000 convictions resulted from court-authorized surveillance. Those figures, however, seem a bit high considering the Administrative Office of the U.S. Courts' 1993 Report on Applications for Orders Authorizing or Approving the Interception of Wire, Oral, or Electronic Communications. This report stated that, of the 2,429 arrests made using evidence gathered by electronic surveillance, only 413 people were convicted. A 20 percent conviction rate hardly bears out law enforcement's declarations that wiretapping provides an effective tool for fighting crime. Still the Clinton administration pushes on.

Clipper redux

Since the hue and cry over the Clipper chip plans, which would have split the keys to each chip between two government agencies, the Clinton administration has backpedaled only a little. This despite strong opposition from civil libertarians and major business interests, including the computer industry, which marches in near total lockstep on this issue.

The latest proposals to come out of Washington involve a *mandatory key escrow* (MKE) that would be administered jointly by government and private interests. Under this proposal, the linkage between export and domestic use of strong encryption is even tighter.

Although still in trial balloon form, the MKE proposals seem to be coalescing around the ability of privately-developed strong encryption software to be exported if the developer registers the software along with any keys that might be needed in the event of a wiretap. In spite of Congressman Brooks' assertions that a government assault on cryptography is counterproductive, the Clinton administration is actively considering outlawing programs like PGP (Pretty Good Privacy), which was created and released as a way of getting strong encryption into people's hands before the government could outlaw such software.

Phil Zimmerman's PGP

When is a software program more than a software program? When it is a political statement as well. Phil Zimmerman has long been a political animal. He is a veteran of the anti-nuke movement and an advisor to political candidates. Like the other folks mentioned in this chapter, he has also always had a soft spot in his heart for cryptography. He has been an active member of the Cypherpunks for years.

When, in 1977, he first heard of the revolutionary work of Diffie and Hellman, Zimmerman began asking himself how he might combine his interests in politics, computers, and privacy. Zimmerman's interest in cryptography stemmed from his days as a boy scout and from his reading of *Codes and Secret Writing* by Herbert S. Zim, where he learned Morse code, braille, and how to make code wheels and invisible ink. Zimmerman had also written away for the 1977 article in *Scientific American* published by Rivest, Shamir, and Adleman.

Somewhere in the mid-1980s, the idea struck him that unless large numbers of people began using cryptographic programs to protect their privacy, cryptography would remain in the control of the government, and the government would move to curtail people's access to strong cryptography. In hindsight, he was absolutely right.

Working under the maxim, "If privacy is outlawed, only outlaws will have privacy," Zimmerman began working on building a strong military-grade cryptosystem. His original effort was called Bass-O-Matic, a reference to Dan Ackroyd's famous *Saturday*

Night Live skit in which a fish was scrambled by using a Waring blender. Along the way Phil added public key routines created by RSA Data Security, and in 1991 he released his creation to the world. Called simply PGP — the letters standing for Pretty Good Privacy — the program was both an immediate hit with computer users and a near-immediate nightmare for Phil.

Space limitations prevent giving you an in-depth reporting of the history of Zimmerman and PGP, but it is a history well worth reading if you are a computer history buff. A good source for detailed information about the interesting history of PGP and how to use the product to its fullest can be found in the book *PGP; Encryption for Everyone* by Simson Garfinkel, published by O'Reilly and Associates.

Under current U.S. law, private citizens have the right to use strong encryption products. However, those products are listed as a munition with respect to ITAR, so they can be sold only for use within the U.S. and Canada, unless an export license is granted by the State Department. The State Department never issues a license without the approval of the NSA.

Although Zimmerman originally thought about selling PGP as shareware, he was afraid that the government might outlaw private cryptography before it could get off the ground, so he instead made PGP freeware. In his zeal to get PGP out the door, he missed five mortgage payments and came within an inch of losing his home to foreclosure. In retrospect, however, it was probably his decision to make the program freely available that kept him from losing his freedom. The program was placed for download on several bulletin boards and on the Internet.

Two issues came tumbling down on top of Zimmerman's head almost immediately. First Jim Bizdos, president of RSA, made himself known to Zimmerman because PGP used RSA's patented algorithms. That dispute was finally settled by Zimmerman's negotiating a license first with ViaCrypt and then later with MIT, who has an interest in the patents. (Remember, Rivest, Shamir and Adleman all have MIT connections.) MIT agreed to distribute a revised edition of PGP that didn't infringe.

The expected reaction from the U.S. government didn't come as Zimmerman had expected. In fact, he worried that the government's silence meant that it had found a way to crack data encrypted with PGP, and so it wasn't worried about his program. In February 1993, however, the government's silence came to an end when Zimmerman was visited by officials of the United States Customs Service. They wanted to know how PGP might have found its way overseas. Subsequently, Zimmerman was notified that he was the subject of a federal grand jury probe into whether he was criminally liable for exporting PGP without a license.

All along, Zimmerman acknowledged that he did not apply for an export license to sell PGP because he never sold PGP. In fact, he warned people that exporting PGP out of the U.S. and Canada was probably a violation of law. It wasn't until the second week of 1996 that Phil finally learned the federal government was dropping its probe, and the case was closed as far as it was concerned.

Encryption politics

Since its first release in 1991, PGP has become the de facto standard for personal and small business encryption software. It is tough and robust and has never been proven to be vulnerable to attack. For this reason, many people and businesses use PGP as their main instrument for preserving the privacy of their communications. PGP is the primary reason U.S. officials want to limit the ability of private citizens to use encryption tools. The ability of PGP to use large keys makes it nearly impossible to crack. Theoretically, it is stronger than DES by several orders of magnitude. No matter which side of the crypto fence you stand on, PGP cannot be ignored.

PGP and similar programs are likely to be the target of legislation in the next few years as the government tries to protect its current position in terms of being able to enforce wiretaps. Whatever legislation comes out of Congress, you can be sure that there will be battles in the federal courts for years afterward. In all likelihood, the matter will have to be settled by the Supreme Court of the United States, and the Court will have to balance the harm to law enforcement against the protections afforded Americans under the First and Fifth Amendments to the Constitution.

Zimmerman is right about one thing, though: the more people who use tools like PGP to protect their privacy, the less likely it is that the government will be able to outlaw private cryptography altogether. The more unfettered access the public has to strong encryption tools, the more likely it is that cryptography will be "grandfathered," that is, accepted as an everyday tool. Even the most ardent supporters of Capstone and Clipper chip cryptosystems agree that Americans and American businesses need strong cryptographic tools to remain competitive in the global market. In these markets, foreign governments are often willing to help their own home industries by spying, not on other governments, but on competitor companies that operate within their home country. This illicitly gained information is then passed on to these native businesses in order to provide them a competitive edge.

One fact is clear: PGP has spread throughout computer communities to the point where it is now available all over the world. If you use anything less strong, you are possibly putting yourself at a disadvantage. In the pages that follow, you will learn where to get your own copy of PGP and how to begin using it to protect your own privacy.

There have recently been rumors circulated that MIT "stole" PGP from Zimmerman. This isn't true. According to a digitally signed statement released to the Cypherpunks mailing list on August 18, 1994, Phil has been cooperating with MIT. In part the statement reads, "MIT did not steal PGP from me. This was a joint venture by MIT and myself to solve PGP's legal problems. It took a lot of maneuvering by me and my lawyers and by my friends at MIT and MIT's lawyers to pull this off. It worked. We should all be glad this came off the way it did. This is a major advance in our efforts to chip away at the formidable legal and political obstacles placed in front of PGP; we will continue to chip away at the remaining obstacles."

Using PGP

As of the writing of this book, the latest version of PGP available from MIT's server was 2.62. The MIT server attempts to screen out folks who might be downloading PGP illegally, that is, from a site outside the U.S. or Canada. For this reason, you must go through a process of answering a few questions on a form before you are given permission to download your copy. The directory where PGP is stored for downloading changes every half hour, so you must fill in the form and download the software within the same 30-minute period. Thus if it is 11:29, wait a few minutes before answering the form. To download PGP 2.62, link to http://web.mit.edu/network/pgp-form.html.

There are a number of ports of PGP, which was originally released for DOS, so that you can run PGP on any machine capable of compiling and running the C code that PGP is written in. Make sure that you get the version appropriate to your hardware. The examples shown in this section all use the DOS version.

If you are outside the United States, there are a number of Web sites around the world where you can find international versions of PGP. There are a number of versions, and some versions use RSAREF for encryption routines, while others don't. Versions before 2.3 are not compatible with more recent versions. Make sure that you download your copy of PGP from a reputable site, and you should, of course, scan the ZIP file and its contents for viruses.

> A commercial version (2.7) of PGP is available from ViaCrypt. The price varies depending on platform and usage requirements. For pricing and availability information, call 1-800-526-2664, 8:30 a.m. until 5:00 p.m. (mountain standard time) weekdays.

Installing PGP

In general, all you have to do to install PGP is to unzip the file you downloaded into a directory. Once the files are written to the disk in whatever directory you have chosen, you are good to go. There are some initialization and customization issues that may need to be addressed, depending on how you use PGP. Several of PGP's settings can be controlled by using DOS environment variables. For explicit instructions for installing PGP on your system, see SETUP.DOC, which details setup procedures for DOS and other operating system platforms like UNIX.

Once installed, PGP is run by entering commands at the DOS prompt. The command line interface always starts with PGP, which is the name of the .EXE file that runs the program. Different actions are specified on the command line by including a switch, sometimes called a parameter. Most of the switches are mnemonic; that is, the letters stand for the name of the operation (for example, in PGP -kg, the kg stands for key generation). To see a list of the things PGP will do, type

PGP -h

When you press Enter, you will be shown a list of the actions PGP can perform. There are some commands that require a third parameter, usually a user ID. This parameter should follow the switch, and a space should be put between the parameters.

Step One: generating keys

The first thing you want to do is generate your own set of public and private keys. These keys will be stored on a *keyring* that you can retrieve at a later time. To begin generating keys, type

PGP -kg

The -kg switch tells PGP to create a key pair. Some input is required from you. The first thing PGP needs is for you to decide the strength of encryption you want. There are three levels, numbered 1–3. The least secure level uses a key of 512 bits, while the most secure level uses 1024 bits. The choice is yours. You must balance the sensitivity of your data against the fact that 1024-bit keys slow down the running of the program. You trade speed for extra security. Figure 10-1 illustrates the levels and their relative security.

```
For a usage summary, type:  pgp -h

D:\pgp>pgp -kg
WARNING: Environmental variable TZ is not defined, so GMT timestamps
may be wrong.  See the PGP User's Guide to properly define TZ
in AUTOEXEC.BAT file.
Pretty Good Privacy(tm) 2.6.2 - Public-key encryption for the masses.
(c) 1990-1994 Philip Zimmermann. [The Rebellious Guerrilla May 21 1995]
Does NOT use the RSAREF(tm) Toolkit!
Export of this software may be restricted by the U.S. government.
Current time: 1996/01/16 07:24 GMT
Pick your RSA key size:
    1)   512 bits- Low commercial grade, fast but less secure
    2)   768 bits- High commercial grade, medium speed, good security
    3)  1024 bits- "Military" grade, slow, highest security
Choose 1, 2, or 3, or enter desired number of bits: 3
Generating an RSA key with a 1024-bit modulus.

You need a user ID for your public key.  The desired form for this
user ID is your name, followed by your E-mail address enclosed in
<angle brackets>, if you have an E-mail address.
For example:  John Q. Smith <12345.6789@compuserve.com>
Enter a user ID for your public key:
John Smith <jsmith@pocahantas.net>_
```

Figure 10-1: You need to enter the strength of encryption that you need and a user ID before you can generate keys.

The next thing PGP needs is a user ID. This ID will be appended to the output of your public key, so you will want to provide meaningful information, unless you are going to use the key with anonymous *re-mailers* (systems that enable e-mail to be sent without revealing your real account ID). As you can see in Figure 10-1, the program recommends that you provide your name followed by your e-mail address. You should enclose the e-mail address inside angle brackets.

The next step is to help PGP to randomly generate the seed for the keys. This is done by typing gibberish at the keyboard and timing the pauses between keystrokes. The best thing you can do at this stage is to type a bunch of random characters and vary the speed at which you type them. Figure 10-2 shows this process.

```
Generating an RSA key with a 1024-bit modulus.

You need a user ID for your public key.  The desired form for this
user ID is your name, followed by your E-mail address enclosed in
<angle brackets>, if you have an E-mail address.
For example:   John Q. Smith <12345.6789@compuserve.com>
Enter a user ID for your public key:
John Smith <jsmith@pocahantas.net>

You need a pass phrase to protect your RSA secret key.
Your pass phrase can be any sentence or phrase and may have many
words, spaces, punctuation, or any other printable characters.

Enter pass phrase:
Enter same pass phrase again:
Error: Pass phrases were different.  Try again.
Enter pass phrase:
Enter same pass phrase again:
Note that key generation is a lengthy process.

We need to generate 664 random bits.  This is done by measuring the
time intervals between your keystrokes.  Please enter some random text
on your keyboard until you hear the beep:
     0 * -Enough, thank you.
....*_
```

Figure 10-2: Type random characters and vary the pauses between keystrokes to generate the keys.

PGP will also ask you to enter a user passphrase. This passphrase is required to work on the private side of PGP keys and operations. Make sure that your passphrase is a good one (see Chapter 4 for more about what makes a good passphrase), and also make sure it is something you will remember. If you let your passphrase become known to anyone else, he or she can use your secret keys to unencrypt data sent to you in confidence.

Generating the key will take a while. Once generated, the keys are placed on the user's keyring. The keyrings used by PGP are stored in encrypted form on the disk. You must extract keys in order to use them.

By default, two keyrings are created for your user account: PUBRING.PGP and SECRING.PGP. A keyring is a file that stores keys you have gathered. You can create other keyrings by creating new key sets using a different user name. As you might guess from their names, PUBRING is for public keys and SECRING is the keyring for secret, or private keys.

To prepare a block of ASCII text that you can use in publishing your public key, all you have to do is issue a command like

PGP -kxa John Smith

The effect of this command is to create a file on the disk that contains John Smith's public key. In the switch setting shown above, -kxa stands for key extract ASCII. When you want to have PGP create output that is capable of being sent over text-only mail systems, add the **a** to the switch to PGP commands to create ASCII output. In the preceeding sample, adding A to the -kx command forces PGP to output the result as ASCII text. The effect of this command is to create a file named SMITH.ASC, which contains the public key in a form that you can append to e-mail messages. You can also give someone a copy of the file on diskette or inside a ZIP file.

```
-----BEGIN PGP PUBLIC KEY BLOCK-----
Version: 2.6.2

mQCNAjDvEZUAAAEEAM/YqbzznIPTnC8urFWndtGLyVjhsk2yg/I8PbRSHXWwr5g8
VI5fq+67niOjQyi/VdvXkoYDD5vUePF8Vh8L13VXrbORMeDsuY88m/zH+QbCtRR5
Oez7a9wyZPy1Ue2jV99hjaxDQp/tbZOTBhkOO5RsSzcWjsXB4n1tBzxciSztAAUR
tCNQYXVsIEouIEx1Y2FzIDxwamxAYmFyZWZvb3R1cnMub3JnPokA1QIFEDDvGRd9
bQc8XIks7QEBUWcD/j1UBMWyMTWeN5/EErq5VsNUwzLf9OtH4Cm3rmkJEd8xa8/6
2BIfr22cX16d9qngVwp1X3P1q/yD/Cuh5k4INOO83ws/r/3LVeJGOXWpYHAelWI7
1kzFcmsq1ccRrtnZoqP673QCkbyBue5yVHCbGZvFn1XxqtJkqDgrdFQVcJNO
=gFkl
-----END PGP PUBLIC KEY BLOCK-----
```

As you can see, the output contains an identifying line at the top of the file, the version of the program that created the file. The part that looks like gibberish is the public key you let people have.

Whenever someone sends you his or her public key, or you obtain his or her public key from an e-mail message or from a key escrow, all you have to do is save the key, or even the entire message, to a file. Then enter the command to add a key to your keyring, as in

PGP -ka paul.pgp

Figure 10-3 shows how PGP notifies you that the person's public key has been added to the ring of public keys. If you want to add the key to a different keyring, you would specify the name of the keyring file as a fourth parameter. PGP is capable of parsing any text file that is looking for the beginning block message. This is a real convenience. Say you receive e-mail from a friend, and he or she has included a public key in his signature at the bottom of the message. You do not have to edit out the text of the message; PGP extracts the key automatically.

Note that the operation ends by asking you whether you want to certify the key. What is meant by certification is proof that the key actually is the key of the person you want to communicate with. In this case, Paul gave me the disk himself, so I don't have to authenticate Paul's key.

```
D:\pgp>PGP -ka paul
WARNING: Environmental variable TZ is not defined, so GMT timestamps
may be wrong.  See the PGP User's Guide to properly define TZ
in AUTOEXEC.BAT file.
Pretty Good Privacy(tm) 2.6.2 - Public-key encryption for the masses.
(c) 1990-1994 Philip Zimmermann. [The Rebellious Guerrilla May 21 1995]
Does NOT use the RSAREF(tm) Toolkit!
Export of this software may be restricted by the U.S. government.
Current time: 1996/01/16 09:15 GMT

Looking for new keys...
pub  1024/5C545CED 1996/01/07   Paul K. Smith <pks@someinet.org>

Checking signatures...
pub  1024/5C545CED 1996/01/07   Paul K. Smith <pks@someinet.org>
sig!      5C545CED 1996/01/07   Paul K. Smith <pks@someinet.org>

Keyfile contains:
   1 new key(s)

One or more of the new keys are not fully certified.
Do you want to certify any of these keys yourself (y/N)?n

D:\pgp>
```

Figure 10-3: Adding a key to the ring is simple; you don't even have to edit the source file.

Step Two: certifying keys

If you want to certify the key, you need to contact the key's owner in a secure fashion. Ask him or her to enter the command PGP -kvc for his keyring, and compare the fingerprints of his output to the fingerprint shown in your display. A fingerprint is derived from using a hash function to create a message digest, as was discussed earlier in this chapter. In this case, security lies in knowing that you are talking to the key's owner. Discussing the fingerprint on the phone, for example, reveals nothing that would compromise the integrity of encryptions, so long as you are not getting the information from an impostor.

Figure 10-4 shows the result of using the -kvc (key view check) switch. As you can see, each key on the ring has a fingerprint. This concrete example of a message digest may help you to better understand how it is extremely unlikely that a fingerprint will be duplicated and how you can use the fingerprint to certify that the key you are checking is genuine.

If you cannot certify the key at the time it is added, you still have a chance to go back and certify it later, so there is no problem with answering **No** to the initial certification question posed by PGP. To certify a key already on the keyring, type a command similar to

PGP -ks paul

In this situation, you are asking PGP to certify Paul in the default public keyring. Figure 10-5 shows how PGP shows you the fingerprint of the key in question and asks you to solemnly certify the key. Despite the heavy sounding words like *solemn,* you do

```
D:\pgp>pgp -kvc
WARNING: Environmental variable TZ is not defined, so GMT timestamps
may be wrong.  See the PGP User's Guide to properly define TZ
in AUTOEXEC.BAT file.
Pretty Good Privacy(tm) 2.6.2 - Public-key encryption for the masses.
(c) 1990-1994 Philip Zimmermann. [The Rebellious Guerrilla May 21 1995]
Does NOT use the RSAREF(tm) Toolkit!
Export of this software may be restricted by the U.S. government.
Current time: 1996/01/16 09:37 GMT

Key ring: 'pubring.pgp'
Type bits/keyID    Date     User ID
pub  1024/5C545CED 1996/01/07 Paul K. Smith <pks@someinet.org>
          Key fingerprint =  FE 2A E9 8E 1F 4B EF ED  B8 68 E4 39 64 95 25 22
pub  1024/CFE37411 1996/01/16 John Smith <jsmith@pocahantas.net>
          Key fingerprint =  8D 8E B8 4B D9 44 F6 CF  EA E9 76 B3 AC 5C B6 E7
2 matching keys found.

D:\pgp>
```

Figure 10-4: Use a key's fingerprint to certify the authenticity of the key.

need to be aware that certifying a forged key can enable *man-in-the-middle attacks* to be successful. In a man-in-the-middle attack, a message is intercepted and saved and then is again encrypted by using the proper key and passed along to the destination. Certification is serious stuff.

```
Pretty Good Privacy(tm) 2.6.2 - Public-key encryption for the masses.
(c) 1990-1994 Philip Zimmermann. [The Rebellious Guerrilla May 21 1995]
Does NOT use the RSAREF(tm) Toolkit!
Export of this software may be restricted by the U.S. government.
Current time: 1996/01/16 09:58 GMT

A secret key is required to make a signature.
You specified no user ID to select your secret key,
so the default user ID and key will be the most recently
added key on your secret keyring.

Looking for key for user 'paul':

Key for user ID: Paul K. Smith <pks@someinet.org>
1024-bit key, Key ID 5C545CED, created 1996/01/07
          Key fingerprint =  FE 2A E9 8E 1F 4B EF ED  B8 68 E4 39 64 95 25 22

READ CAREFULLY:  Based on your own direct first-hand knowledge, are
you absolutely certain that you are prepared to solemnly certify that
the above public key actually belongs to the user specified by the
above user ID (y/N)?

D:\pgp>
```

Figure 10-5: Certification indicates that you have confidence that the key in question is genuine.

Step Three: encrypting messages

Once you have someone's public key certified and on your keyring, you can then send him or her an encrypted message. To encrypt a message, place the text in a file and use the -e switch. For example, type

PGP -e Forjoe.txt

Note in Figure 10-6 how PGP asks that you enter the ID of the person for whom the message is intended. Once you have entered the user's ID, PGP encrypts the message, writes the output to disk, and then tells you the name of the file it has created. The message is now encrypted, and only the user you intend it for can decipher the contents of the message.

```
D:\pgp>copy fig3.txt forjoe.txt
        1 file(s) copied

D:\pgp>PGP -e forjoe.txt
WARNING: Environmental variable TZ is not defined, so GMT timestamps
may be wrong.  See the PGP User's Guide to properly define TZ
in AUTOEXEC.BAT file.
Pretty Good Privacy(tm) 2.6.2 - Public-key encryption for the masses.
(c) 1990-1994 Philip Zimmermann. [The Rebellious Guerrilla May 21 1995]
Does NOT use the RSAREF(tm) Toolkit!
Export of this software may be restricted by the U.S. government.
Current time: 1996/01/16 10:50 GMT


Recipients' public key(s) will be used to encrypt.
A user ID is required to select the recipient's public key.
Enter the recipient's user ID: john smith

Key for user ID: John Smith <jsmith@pocahantas.net>
1024-bit key, Key ID CFE37411, created 1996/01/16
.
Ciphertext file: forjoe.pgp

D:\pgp>
```

Figure 10-6: Encrypting a message using PGP.

Depending on the method of communication, you may also want to add the **a** for ASCII output. This causes PGP to add what is called *transport armor*. Transport armor is a fancy way of saying that the encrypted data is manipulated so that only printable text characters are generated. The command line would be

PGP -ea Forjoe.txt

Caution!

Unless you specify the **w** switch, which causes PGP to wipe the original file out of existence, a plain text copy of your message will remain on the hard disk. Once you are comfortable with encrypting data, get into the habit of throwing the **w** switch so you don't have to remember to come back and clear the original message off your hard disk later. Typing **PGP -eaw Forjoe.txt** has the effect of destroying the original text file at the time the encrypted ASCII file is written.

Figure 10-7 shows the contents of FORJOE.ASC. As you can see, the actual cipher is embedded between two banners. The recipient of this message will have no trouble getting PGP to unencrypt the message, as long as he or she has the proper secret key.

```
D:\pgp>pgp forjoe.asc
WARNING: Environmental variable TZ is not defined, so GMT timestamps
may be wrong.  See the PGP User's Guide to properly define TZ
in AUTOEXEC.BAT file.
Pretty Good Privacy(tm) 2.6.2 - Public-key encryption for the masses.
(c) 1990-1994 Philip Zimmermann. [The Rebellious Guerrilla May 21 1995]
Does NOT use the RSAREF(tm) Toolkit!
Export of this software may be restricted by the U.S. government.
Current time: 1996/01/16 11:11 GMT

File is encrypted.  Secret key is required to read it.
Key for user ID: John Smith <jsmith@pocahantas.net>
1024-bit key, Key ID CFE37411, created 1996/01/16

You need a pass phrase to unlock your RSA secret key.
Enter pass phrase: Pass phrase is good.  Just a moment......
Plaintext filename: forjoe

D:\pgp>
```

Figure 10-7: Encrypted text output by PGP as ASCII so it can be sent on text-only mail systems.

```
-----BEGIN PGP MESSAGE-----
Version: 2.6.2

hIwDgpMi1M/jdBEBBACpUh6AjfBZDCHRpvrbaoUU3zIJfZUcGBMH+vTC30BROYUR
NtqYOXzbZ51m+2Z/LOB4PjEBRQ8q/qEnI+xmE1C++deyU/dYNYLDAO/tx1+F/SGP
5ALpAeilBO/HXhew8mgiXj7L4c51HhYD6YkvqReAk3NYEk4R8UKnpyuj0jVWmqYA
AALdwOm8dOXNXfVz4VMWvU1Qu694ed/tEb16/x5JPeDo10oSFzGpI7YF7ALA7YkL
jOSxuf4kyjrZFQUj55Hm82oVIp/5qZrvZx3Roky9kJ6oKhfqYieTSken+S1NPoV1
gCbyEZw/8PFxiEJL0CUL7LS+S1W+NCaucFF4r2ecz4XmEv99A5cmvp65BzDSS9QI
mZdqBY2fqx3zdMiu2Re442NmPhXnp4ZZFxmxNMrc8ybp1vhvJq7RcpeTXxz8IMfX
F++cCItL/VLTDs6zqUvK6+hpKOkewOWcMDAtwz/kNhO/XQJKtWiRVRZ9K2xsgX1G
eDLRSxgphRcA7PJ9rz/yINMF5ZgCvIpLqFw9eH+JOJy649FbMgK3LK5XwLK65Uxy
ddDZoxtYeXQRdd689t1feOYF21zK8GsfB71UXJtDTLpb77s5X7jaRaB3TFy7MmwN
```

```
bda2akSlBoPcrpm8W40liw08D+1pLtIKkBJYxVL252uz9HmbutjDf/pJcOIw31J6
YtG9KPtSD9WTdmmmOuBWIV23KhrtwT9b9TBVCc4BNy4uRJKQG57wa5KY91G9kbdF
baihUyD4Tl3pg33SdoRj31b8dCICE4uP7Z9922RgRTihUqAjp9MA8cLlUs5SwSft
40t6VMTp8w8Yo9ztSNdUKlIYja9TpKkHXZab9ZXTTosahSqHlMoCPaeuyNscuQHt
Tya2hFj3XCJ56iusb2mz9+OMjziWkZmaOhbA6+VeRu9ycAhtIubU/bAtFj8bahcA
HHzcg6u3cXjPVDt6KFMB3DLwrsAuyz8fsC4ArfybRRFEwZSbmpNso4x7/TWleXpM
vsnQaUSu5na8JymHDAHqdoBRRpP8OURT5CMOGeAFXidbG9PulzrQfKN1OZw6OI1D
x/EAcEEW2COZTOVrvm+wcpNiCfjahtwu+pamvMzw9L72eLlPcsJO7TccXGN3RklL
x2EzrMdrzr6NZH8jfYEfFA==
=Kd5b
—END PGP MESSAGE—
```

Step Four: unencrypting messages

When you receive a message that has been encrypted with your public key, all you have to do is save the encrypted message to disk and use a command like

PGP Forjoe.asc

When encrypting, you do not normally need switches, although you may have to specify the name of a keyring if the key is stored in a file other than SECRING.PGP. In order to unencrypt the file, you need to enter the password you created at the time you generated your private key. If you enter the proper password, PGP gives you a message informing you of the name of the plain text file.

Step Five: signatures

In the event you want to sign a message but not encrypt it, use the -s switch. As always, you can add the **a** switch on the command line to create ASCII output, as in

PGP -sa sometext.txt

The effect of this command will be to create a file that is not readable by humans. It may look like it is encrypted, but it really isn't. Anybody with your public key can read the signed message with the command

PGP sometext.txt

It is also possible to sign an encrypted message. To encrypt and sign a message for ASCII output, use the command line

PGP -sea sometext.txt

The effect of this command is that PGP will ask you for the public key of the recipient and then output encrypted text that only his or her private key will unencrypt. Signing such a message can provide an assurance that the message has not been tampered with.

More PGP

In the limited space available, I have been able to show you only a fraction of the features and functions that PGP can perform. For more complete coverage of the features and functions of PGP, you can either acquire the Garfinkel book, or you can search the Web for tutorial pages. Many home pages contain the text of, or a link to, informational pages that take things a step further than the online help that comes with the product.

Be sure to safeguard your password to the parts of PGP that work with your private key. If your password or private key are compromised, you will need to revoke its certification, which is a pain.

Do not overuse PGP. There is little in this world so annoying as getting an unimportant message in encrypted form, only to go through the steps of unencrypting it to find that the encryption was unnecessary.

Those computer users who have a phobia or an aversion to DOS will be happy to know that there are several decent Windows front ends to PGP. These Windows versions make it easier to take advantage of the power of PGP, without having to memorize all the possible commands.

Summary

This chapter introduced you to some of the issues surrounding the U.S. Government's opposition to unfettered private cryptography, which would hamper its ability to conduct electronic surveillance of persons suspected of committing or planning crimes.

- ✦ You learned how several government sponsored cryptographic schemes have met with stiff resistance from civil libertarians and computer industry leaders.
- ✦ You can use PGP (Pretty Good Privacy) to encrypt your most private and sensitive data.
- ✦ You have the ability to determine how strongly text is encrypted with PGP.
- ✦ You can sign documents so that anyone with your public key can read the message and be certain that you have written it.

✦ ✦ ✦

Network Security and You

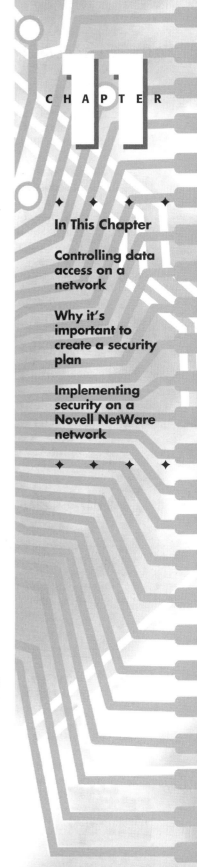

CHAPTER 11

◆ ◆ ◆

In This Chapter

Controlling data access on a network

Why it's important to create a security plan

Implementing security on a Novell NetWare network

◆ ◆ ◆

By John Mueller

But lay up for yourselves treasures in heaven, where neither moth nor rust doth corrupt, and where thieves do not break through nor steal.
  —*Matthew 6:20*

Many of us have spent some time watching those old westerns on television on a lazy Saturday afternoon. One of my favorites is *For a Few Dollars More*. Clint Eastwood plays a bounty hunter turned bank robber confidant. He plays along with the bank robbers just long enough to get the information he needs to hand them over to the law — for a price, of course. The story has a lot of twists and turns, but at the end of the movie, he stacks up his ex-partners like so much cord wood in the back of a cart and heads off to town for the payoff.

I used to wonder why the bank robbers even made the attempt. They were certain to get caught (or at least I thought so when I was younger), so why even take the risk? According to a recent statistic, nearly 70 percent of all bank robbers get convicted. Still, there will probably always be bank robbers. Why? When Willie Sutton was asked why he robbed banks, he replied, "Because that's where the money is."

Money — of sorts — is one of the reasons that computer hackers try to get into your system. Their success rate is much better than a bank robber. A recent statistic from The National Computer Crimes Squad states that anywhere from 85 percent to 97 percent of all computer crime goes undetected, and only 10 percent actually gets reported.

Money today takes many different forms. It's not just the hard currency in your pocket or the funds you can transfer from your bank using an ATM card. When you talk to people about the data stored on their network, you get the feeling that, to them, it's like money in the bank. In reality, it is. If more people considered the true value of the data on their network, we'd have fewer problems with some easily correctable flaws in security systems.

Whether you're a small business owner, the person charged with network administrator duties at your company, or one of the users who must work with that administrator, it's important that you understand what safeguards a network should include.

The bank in *For a Few Dollars More* was supposedly impregnable — even the bank robbers acknowledged that it would take so much dynamite to blow up the safe that there wouldn't be any way to recover the money. However, the bank in this story had a fatal flaw. The bank president had a back door — a small safe that really stored all his cash. The theory was that a bandit would spend so much time looking at the big impregnable safe that he would never notice the small one hidden away in a cabinet.

Like the bank in the movie, there are a lot of computer systems out there with back doors — places a crook with the right knowledge could exploit. The following sections begin a journey through a typical network setup and the types of back doors that you can find there. I'll also take a look at what you can do to close those back doors to keep your computer system safe — not only from hackers, but also anyone who works with you.

Who Can Access Data on a Network Server?

In 1985, Bill Landreth made the news by publishing the book *Out of the Inner Circle*. It's about the exploits of a computer hacker named The Cracker and the ways that he got in and out of computer systems. (Another edition in 1989 expanded on the original by adding information about viruses.) The Cracker was a member of a computer hacking group called the Inner Circle. By the way, Bill and The Cracker were one and the same. He wrote the book as part of his reparation to society for his computer crimes.

I was pretty interested in the techniques that Bill used to get in and out of computer systems. One of the techniques that he used was to walk into an office building under some pretense — say to perform janitorial work, or to visit someone, or even to attend a job interview. Then he would look around. It wouldn't take him very long to find a piece of paper or two next to various computer monitors. What was on the paper? The person's password, of course.

When I read this bit of information, I was surprised that access to a computer system could be gotten so easily; so I went through several of my client sites (with permission from the upper echelon people, of course) and checked for this little back door. To my surprise, nearly half the people I checked had written down their password and stored it in an easily accessible place. Their reason for writing the password down? It was too hard to remember.

Bill Landreth's legacy to the computer world

You may be wondering what Bill did that was so terrible that he got arrested. Bill didn't start out being someone you couldn't trust; he was merely a teenager looking for a bit of fun. Like many of the 14 year olds that he hung out with, he lived for the fun he could have with his computer.

There wasn't anything wrong with trying to learn about the TRS-80 he bought — in fact, learning about the computer was good. That initial experience led to the desire to learn more about how and why computers work. Bill started out as many hackers do, by tinkering with the inner workings of the operating system of his machine.

The dangerous part was when he started hacking computer systems. Some late-night sessions lasted until 3 a.m., despite the fact that he hadn't even started his homework yet. The "glamour" of hacking computer systems soon overshadowed every other part of his life.

Bill still wasn't in much trouble — he'd looked at a few things that he wasn't supposed to, but he hadn't done much more than that. All that changed, however, when he started breaking into larger computers owned by corporations. Once his activities became visible to them, these companies became bent on curbing his activity. While his nightly exploits seemed like the stuff of James Bond to Bill, it was some network administrator's nightmare, and it cost the companies that he broke into money to at least monitor his activities (even if a hacker doesn't break anything, the cost of hiring someone competent to watch him isn't cheap).

One day in 1983 the FBI came knocking at Bill's door after it caught him breaking into the GTE Telemail computer network based in Vienna, Virginia. It took his computer equipment and arrested him. End of story, right? Wrong! There are literally thousands of Bills out there, all looking for a cheap thrill. A computer network administrator can make it real difficult for Bill to get in, but without the help of users on a system, an administrator would find it difficult to keep his type out.

The fact that really surprised me is that administrative assistants and other management helpers often had their boss' password. The reason? The boss was too busy doing his work to respond to an assistant's request, so he gave his password out so the assistant could access the required information.

Never check the security of your own network — you're too familiar with it to do the job right. It may cost a little to have an outside consultant check your security, but you'll find that it's worth it. Always have the consultant check the network, your security procedures, and individual workstations as part of the inspection (use the materials in this book to help you define a list of things to check). Make sure that the consultant you hire is bonded, so that you can recover the cost of any mistakes he might make. Check the consultant's references as well; you don't want a Bill Landreth breaking into your system.

If you're a network administrator on even a small network, you might assume that providing strict passwords and forcing people to change them each month (or even each quarter) is sufficient. The first thing you need to learn is that it's people who maintain security on a system, not passwords. If people don't see the need to eliminate back doors into a secure environment, then it doesn't matter how secure you make it. A hacker can always break in.

System administrator

There are a couple of problems that most companies have when it comes to a network. One of the biggest problems is a lack of understanding about what a network operating system is all about. Unlike a workstation, a network operating system is fairly complex. A network administrator needs better-than-average knowledge of computers — after all, he is the person that everyone else looks to for help.

Tip

A network administrator should have a minimum of three years of computer experience. I'm not talking about using a word processor here; I'm talking about time spent working with other users and really learning the operating system itself. The administrator candidate also needs a good knowledge of the components that make up a computer. For example, the administrator should know how to detect common workstation problems and how to fix them.

The first day I went to CNE (Certified NetWare Engineer) school, there was one pupil there who obviously had no place in the class. He could hardly turn his machine on, much less manage a network. So why did a company waste its money sending this person to school? He owned a Nintendo — the most advanced computer system that any of the employees knew how to use. Unfortunately, there are a lot of people who administer networks out there who really don't have a clue as to what's going on.

The network administrator is the cornerstone of your human control of data. You need to choose someone knowledgeable who works well with other people. It's the network administrator who will convince the other people in an organization to maintain good networking habits.

Supervisor privileges

If you're like me, you're interested in finding out about a variety of things when a client calls you on site for the first time. In fact, one of the first things I ask the client about is his network security — does he have a security plan and does the administrator know who has access to what? Along with passwords, I also check things like directory access and overall network structure.

Imagine my disbelief when I walked into several client sites during my first few years of business and found that everyone on the network was a supervisor. Sure, the company had a single person who maintained the network, but there wasn't anyone in charge of the most valuable network entity, the data it contained. If each user is set up as a supervisor, every user has access to every part of the network. Things like directory structure don't really do much from a security perspective without at least some preliminary password controls in place.

One of the first places I went to work for as a consultant was an accounting firm. It was a small place — only 10 or 11 people worked there, including the accountants. They used a Novell NetWare file server left in open view of everyone working there. According to the person I talked to, the place was a madhouse during tax season, making it an open target to someone who really wanted to do something to the network.

The company called me in to fix a problem it was having with the network — it seems that no one could log in. It didn't take me too long to figure out that someone had sabotaged the network by changing all the passwords. The problem, as I figured it out later, was that the boss had decided on some extra hours of work from his salaried workers. The network damage was a sign of his employee's displeasure with that decision. The problem was that since everyone had supervisor privileges, there wasn't any way to figure out who the culprit was. In fact, because of the placement of the file server, I couldn't even assume that the damage was done by someone within the company. It could have been done by a hacker, like Bill Landreth, looking for a cheap thrill, or even a disgruntled client.

So what are the lessons to learn here?

- ✦ First, you've got to keep the file server out of view — preferably locked away so that no one but the network administrator can even get at it.
- ✦ Second, you have to put someone in charge of the network and give him or her exclusive supervisor rights.

My philosophy of network management is that there can be only one chief. If you have more than one chief, then no one is taking responsibility for the network. Only the network administrator should have supervisor privileges on a network, and that person probably shouldn't be the boss. A network administrator is in a position of trust. He has to have the tools required to get the job done. One of the most valuable tools available to a network administrator is password security.

Obviously, a network administrator on a large network needs helpers. These helpers shouldn't have supervisor privileges; they need only supervisor-equivalent rights for the parts of the network that they administer. Don't allow someone any more access than he or she absolutely needs.

Some organizations feel uncomfortable with my philosophy. The higher echelon people in particular don't like the idea of losing control over some valuable part of the business. I see the trade-off as a simple one. The network administrator has to be the king of his particular hill, or the company will definitely suffer some kind of catastrophic security breach somewhere along the way. Obviously, if there's some kind of security breach and the network administrator has the tools to do the job, then it would be equally easy to figure out who is to blame.

Still, there has to be some kind of a backup. What if the network administrator gets hit by a bus or can't get into work for some reason? There's a simple, but effective, way to handle this situation. Have the supervisor write the administrator's password down on a sheet of paper, place it in a sealed envelope, and then lock the envelope in a safe. The network administrator should check the envelope from time-to-time to make sure it's still sealed. Since the administrator should change his password at least once a month, then checking the envelope halfway through the cycle (every two weeks) would help ensure that no one has stolen the password. Management should feel a little better because it will always have a back door into the system, should the unexpected happen.

Managing Security on a Network

Managing a small office network usually means grabbing a few minutes out of someone's day to take care of details like backing up the data. The problem with this "one person, two job" approach is that some of the needed duties get shoved under the carpet. Often the person in charge of the network has too little time to really do the job right. For example, take a look at security plans.

Just what is a security plan?

It's a written document that all employees should get when they start at the company. The person in charge of the employees' indoctrination should make sure that they fully understand everything in that document. Unfortunately, few, if any, of the places I visit for the first time have a security plan in place.

A good security plan should tell new employees everything that they need to know to help the administrator plug any security leaks. It should be organized in such a way that new employees can read through it once and then refer to it as needed. What do I include in my security plan? The following points tell you the minimum topics you need to cover. Obviously, most companies will also need to add some company-specific policies like login and logout times or areas of the building that are off-limits to anyone but the network administrator.

+ **Password Requirements.** It's pretty obvious that you need to answer the question of how often to change the password. Not as obvious is the need to tell the employee, in writing, not to write his password down or to share it with anyone. There are two reasons to do this. For one thing, a written policy like this makes it easier for you to pursue any breaches in security in court (if need be). Second, some employees just aren't all that bright, and you have to tell them everything. Finally, you should also include things in your written instructions like the length of the password and some password guidelines (like not using SECRET as a password). For more about creating secure passwords, see Chapter 4.

- **Network Administrator Name and Phone Number.** It's amazing to find out that some people don't know who to contact if they have a problem with the network. (It doesn't take very long for them to find out as a general rule, but I still find the occasional user who sits there wondering what to do about a machine that doesn't work right.) There are two situations where this becomes very important. If you use an off-site consultant to manage your network, then people need to know how to contact him or her. Larger companies also need to let people know who the appropriate person is if there is more than one person managing the network.

- **Emergency Procedures.** What happens in the case of an emergency (I'm talking about everything from a bomb threat to a fire here)? Few people know. You need to tell people to, at least, log out of the network in an emergency situation. Since network security often includes building security, you need to refer the employee to your general emergency procedure document as well. Make sure that someone is responsible for checking (in as much as possible) that the security issues are taken care of before he or she leaves the building in an emergency.

- **Standard Operating Procedures.** Did you tell your employee not to leave his desk without logging out of the network? If you didn't, you can be sure that he won't log out of the network until the end of the day. A security breach like this might leave that terminal open for someone to use while the employee goes to lunch or on a break. In essence, you can't assume any knowledge or willingness to comply on the part of the employee. If you want it done, write it down and make your employee responsible for carrying it out.

These are just a few of the more common things I put in a security plan. You'll need to cover specifics for your company as well. For example, a larger company may put some of the responsibility for network security into the hands of workgroup managers. If so, you need to cover that issue in your security plan. Make sure that you add a section for penalties. For example, one of the things that I typically do is charge a penalty for forgetting a password. The money collected goes into a pizza fund. Once a year (more often if you have forgetful employees), your company can have a pizza party courtesy of those who forgot their password.

Why documenting security procedures is important

By now you're probably thinking to yourself that I'm a little paranoid: why go through all this work for a small, or even a large, company? The reason is simple. You can pay a little for security right now, or pay a lot later when someone breaches your network. A recent court case will probably serve as the best example of what can happen if you don't have a written policy.

File servers: the parts of a network you should keep to yourself

I work a lot with small businesses that insist on keeping their file server right out in the open where anyone can see it. My first visit usually convinces them to change that policy. After getting permission, I usually send everyone out of the room and proceed not only to break into the file server, but to lock everyone else out in a matter of minutes. I'm talking no more than five or six minutes. My only tool is a copy of DEBUG (which I show the network administrator).

Now you may think that I've used some deep dark secret to break into that computer. Nothing could be further from the truth. I'm simply using a technique that Novell actually teaches in the CNE courses. It is shown as a means of helping users get back into a system if they accidentally forget their password.

It's important to realize that any file server is a sitting duck to someone who really wants to get into it. A file server is secure only if you keep it physically locked away. Place it in a locked closet, at least.

You can do other things to make life difficult for someone wanting to break in. Ever try to access a computer without a keyboard? You can actually remove the keyboard from most servers once you get them running. In fact, you can place locks over the keyboard hole, making it next to impossible for someone to plug in another keyboard.

The important thing to remember is that physical server security goes hand-in-hand with other parts of your security plan. If you decide to leave your file server exposed, then you have no one but yourself to blame when someone breaks in.

Randal Schwartz was an Intel consultant in 1993. His job was to write application programs. To say that Randal knew his stuff would be an understatement — he not only contributed to the computing community as a whole but also wrote two books on the PERL programming language and added to its design. (PERL is a programming language commonly used by network administrators.) He started his career at Tektronix as a technical writer in 1978 at the age of 16, a time when other kids don't have a clue as to what they plan to do with their lives. Suffice it to say that he wasn't your typical computer user. Randal really knows how to make a computer jump through hoops.

So what did Randal do that he wasn't supposed to do? He got a little over ambitious. Intel originally hired Randal Schwartz as a programmer and a security consultant. A disagreement with an administrator at Intel's Cornell Oaks division over how to handle electronic mail was the beginning of his troubles. Randal quit that contract late in 1993. When Randal quit this job, he effectively gave up his right to do anything about Intel's computer security measures.

Randal still had work to do for Intel writing network management tools for the Intel campus at Hawthorne Farms in Oregon. The contract was running down, and he wanted to do something to get additional work, so he decided to test network security and then tell the administrator about the results he got. During September and October of 1993, Randal ran an application named Crack on the network. A lot of network administrators run that particular program to check for weak passwords and let users know to change them. Randal didn't try to hide the fact that he was running the program — in his mind he was simply trying to help the network administrator sort out some perceived security problems.

Randal did find more than a few problems with network security, but not before the network administrator, Mark Morrissey, had caught him running Crack. In Mark's mind Randal wasn't a hero, he was a hacker trying to steal passwords to the network. Mark had caught Randal in minor security breaches before, like setting up a remote access terminal so that he could work from home, but this time Mark decided that he had to call the police.

In March 1994, Randal was formally indicted on three charges of computer tampering. He was tried and eventually sentenced to 5 years of probation, 90 days in jail, 480 hours of community service, and a $63,000-plus fine. The 90 days in jail might be removed if Randal behaved himself and demonstrated his good conduct to the court. He also has to tell any potential clients about his conviction as a computer felon.

Don't think that Intel got off without a scratch in this case. That $63,000-plus fine that Randal has to pay is the amount of money it cost in employee time to fix the damage caused by Randal's intrusion. Even if Intel makes the money back, it can't recoup the time lost, nor will it ever regain the confidence of the programming community. At least 300 programmers from 22 countries have publically offered support for Randal, according to Kevin Luster, a Silicon Graphics, Inc. programmer. It's pretty obvious from the amount of traffic on the Internet that there's a lot more programmer support that isn't quite so public.

So what went wrong in this situation? According to the network administrator, Randal was simply over anxious and refused to obey the rules. According to Randal, the rules weren't adequately posted. The truth probably lies somewhere in between. The bottom line is that you, as a network administrator, have to make sure that everyone knows the ground rules for working on the network. Otherwise, you open yourself up to this no-win scenario.

Whether you run a small network in a mom-and-pop business or a large network like the one at Intel, the bottom line is that you're responsible for managing a network. You have to spend the time required to educate users about security and put it down in writing so that they can't say they weren't told. Finding ways for the over-zealous user to make a positive contribution probably wouldn't hurt either.

Novell Security

I wanted to spend some time introducing you to the idea of network security in the previous sections of the chapter to let you know that security is important, even if you run a small network. You have to get into the right mind-set before the precautions that Novell makes available on NetWare become more important than things you can do in your spare time.

Most of the administration tools that Novell provides are still character-based. Fortunately, you can run them in a DOS box under Windows. In most cases, you'll find that you need to use these utilities to add new users, delete old ones, or change security measures based on your company's current needs.

The number one security tool for the network administrator is SYSCON (short for system configuration). It allows you to add or delete users and groups from the system — the two basic elements that define security under NetWare. An individual user has a specific set of rights. They're limited to his or her trustee assignments and which groups he or she belongs to.

Each of the following sections takes a look at a different aspect of NetWare security. The important thing to remember is that because of NetWare's design, you really can't use one of these security measures without the other.

Keeping the sales department out of bookkeeping's files

The first step in setting up security for a NetWare network is creating a directory structure. In essence, this structure allows you to build walls to keep people out of certain areas of the network. The rights you assign to a particular directory determine — in part — what kind of access the user will have to it. Novell calls the overall assignment of access to a directory or file the *inherited rights mask* (IRM). These rights are modified using the ALLOW command or the FILER utility.

As a minimum, you'll want to set aside one directory for each application type and another directory for each class of user. A database application will probably require you to keep the data and application in one place. On the other hand, you could have a separate directory for each workgroup in your company when using a word processing application. A user would require one level of access (read-only) to the application directory. He would also have to have read/write access to the data directory associated with his workgroup. A user wouldn't need any access at all to the directories containing data for other workgroups.

You also have to consider a user's trustee and group rights when you think about the rights he has to a particular directory. (The specifics of trustee and group rights are looked at a little later in this section.) For example, if a directory offers every right to a user, but he has only the read-trustee right, the user will be able to read only data in

> ### NetWare Directory Services (NDS) — new tools for a new networking environment
>
> Many large businesses have changed from *bindery emulation* — the method of maintaining information about the network that we explore in this chapter — to NDS, provided with NetWare 4.*x*. This is a new way of storing network configuration information by using objects and a complex database.
>
> An *object* is defined as any network element. For example, a file server and a user are both objects. Each object possesses certain properties. When you look at an apple, you say that it's red or yellow. Color is one of the apple's properties. Using objects allows you to look at the network from a real world perspective.
>
> NDS is better than bindery emulation for a large business for a number of reasons. It provides a very complex set of network administration tools that help the network administrator track a lot of servers and users. These tools work well when you have a lot of users, but they tend to get cumbersome if you have only a few users.
>
> The bindery emulation method stores all information about a server in a database on that server. Using NDS allows you to replicate that data on a number of servers, making it locally available and reducing the chance of damage. Obviously, this capability has limited appeal for someone with a single server.
>
> There are also a few problems in using NDS. For one thing, all these new tools mean that administrator time is increased, not decreased, on a small network. It takes more time to navigate through all the various options that an administrator for a large network would need, and it becomes difficult for him to see the forest for the trees.
>
> You'll also experience problems using NDS in certain environments. For example, you'll need a special patch to make NDS work with Windows 95. It's pretty unstable under Windows 3.*x* as well.

that directory. But say that this user also belongs to a group that has both read and write access to that directory. The user would now have read and write access to the directory as well, because his group rights give it to him.

NetWare doesn't restrict your use of these rights to just directories. You can also use them on individual files. This means that you can create an extremely customized access scheme for a particular network setup. In general, it's easier to group files with like security needs together. A directory access scheme reduces the amount of changes you need to make to reflect new security needs by one level.

Keeping console commands handy

It's pretty likely that an administrator for a small network ends up wearing several hats. Someone who has to work on the network only on an occasional basis might find it easy to forget all those long-winded console commands that Novell provides.

Very few people realize that you can create console batch files — just like the ones you use with DOS on your workstation. The difference is that you use an NCF extension in place of the normal BAT extension.

For example, what if you have a problem remembering the TRACK ON and TRACK OFF command? Just stick them in a batch file and use a name that you will remember. When you need to use TRACK ON, just type the name of your batch file at the console prompt; and voila, you'll see the results on screen.

You can make the batch files as long as needed and even display comments on screen by using the ECHO command. The only requirement for using batch files under NetWare is that you should place them in the SYS:SYSTEM directory to make sure that they're always accessible.

Here are the rights provided by NetWare groups, trustee rights, and directory rights:

- **Supervisory.** This right gives the user all rights to the directory, its files, and its subdirectories. It overrides the IRM. It also allows the user to grant or modify any rights in the IRM when used with a file.

- **Read.** Allows the user to read either an individual file or all the files in a directory.

- **Write.** Allows the user to write to an individual file or any file in the directory. The file must already exist, unless the user also has the create right described in the next paragraph. You can quickly get into trouble with this right. For example, word processing programs typically rename the existing file and then create a new file to store the data a user types. If you don't give users the read, modify, write, and create rights, they won't be able to use their word processor. The read and write rights are pretty obvious, but some newer administrators might not think about the create and modify rights.

- **Create.** NetWare looks at creating files as a different right than simply writing them. For example, if you create a new file, you can write to it as long as it's open. Once you close the file, you need the write right to reopen it and modify the file's contents. There are situations where you wouldn't want to give users both rights. For example, giving someone the create right without adding the write right would allow you to perform a survey where users couldn't change their answers once they exited the survey program.

✦ **Erase.** This right allows you to delete an individual file or any of the files in a directory. You can allow users to erase an individual file by giving them that right at the file level, but revoking the erase right at the directory level.

✦ **Modify.** Use this right to allow users to change any of the file's or directory's attributes. For example, if you add the hidden attribute, then DOS won't display the file when you use the DIR command. NetWare utilities tend to ignore file and directory attributes in favor of the IRM. This right also allows users to change the name of a directory or file. Users will have to have this to use some types of applications, like word processors.

✦ **File Scan.** Users need this right to see the contents of a directory or an individual filename within the directory. The file scan right is like the hidden file attribute — the difference is that it affects both DOS and NetWare utilities.

✦ **Access Control.** This right is just like the supervisory right except that it also allows users to change the trustee assignments for a directory or file. Giving the owner of a directory or file the supervisory right is fine. Giving him or her access control affects your ability to manage the network property. The network administrator has to maintain the right to assign trustee rights.

Now that you have some idea of what rights are available and how they work, it might be nice to know how you can see how rights are assigned. Figure 11-1 shows the results of using NetWare's LISTDIR command on two directories: DATA and APPS.

```
F:\>LISTDIR APPS /A

The subdirectory structure of 312/SYS:APPS
Date      Time    Inherited    Effective    Directory
-------------------------------------------------------------
2-10-94   10:00a  [SRWCEMFA]   [SRWCEMFA]   ->SS
2-10-94   10:00a  [SRWCEMFA]   [SRWCEMFA]   ->DB
2-10-94   10:00a  [SRWCEMFA]   [SRWCEMFA]   ->WP
2-10-94   10:00a  [SRWCEMFA]   [SRWCEMFA]   ->ACCT
4 subdirectories found

F:\>LISTDIR DATA /A

The subdirectory structure of 312/SYS:DATA
Date      Time    Inherited    Effective    Directory
-------------------------------------------------------------
2-10-94   6:59p   [SRWCEMFA]   [SRWCEMFA]   ->WP
2-10-94   6:59p   [SRWCEMFA]   [SRWCEMFA]   ->DB
2-10-94   6:59p   [SRWCEMFA]   [SRWCEMFA]   ->SS
2-10-94   6:59p   [SRWCEMFA]   [SRWCEMFA]   ->ACCT
4 subdirectories found

F:\>
```

Figure 11-1: The NetWare LISTDIR command allows you to see what the IRM is for a specific directory or file.

Assigning security rights

The SYSCON utility is the one that you need to assign specific user rights. However, before you can assign the user any specific rights to the data on the network, you need to perform a couple of other steps. First, you have to create the user. Second, you need to assign some account restrictions.

Account restrictions are an important part of the NetWare security scheme. There are two levels of account restriction that I normally look at for a small network and for very specific reasons. Remember the story about Bill Landreth that I related earlier? What were Bill's four main tools in gaining access to a network? First, the user could log in at any time. That means Bill could log in at, say, 3:00 a.m. when the administrator is at home asleep. Second, the user provided a short or very easy password. You can control the length of a password, but you still can't prevent the user from using something obvious like SECRET as a password. Third, Bill could use a program to search through a list of common passwords. Novell provides the means to stop someone from logging in after a specific number of attempts. Finally, the password didn't change. Once Bill had a password, he could usually depend on it's remaining constant. If Bill had to figure out a password too often, then the "fun" would have been taken out and drudgery added in its place.

Take a look at Figure 11-2. It shows the Default Account Balance/Restrictions dialog box in SYSCON. You access it by choosing the Supervisor Options selection on the SYSCON Available Topics menu and then selecting Default Account Balance/Restrictions option. Notice that this dialog box answers all but one of the needs mentioned in the previous paragraph. You can specify a minimum password length, the number of days between password changes, and the number of *grace logins* (the times that the user

A dangerous guest

Everyone who uses NetWare knows that it provides an account named Guest. This account gets created automatically whenever you install NetWare. Most people don't realize that Guest starts out with some fairly significant rights — rights that a computer hacker could use to get into your system.

Someone with enough knowledge and just the default guest rights to your system can eventually gain access to just about every part of it. The hacker won't get in overnight. It takes time and effort to do it, but it can be done.

My first recommendation to new network administrators is that Guest is too dangerous to have around. It's important to know precisely who's on your network. That means assigning a precise name to everyone who uses it. Even if you only plan to allow someone access to your network for an hour, it's worth it to you to create an account for them. It doesn't really take all that long, and you'll sleep better if you do.

can type the wrong password). You can even force the user to come up with a unique password each time — NetWare will remember the last ten passwords that the user types (more than enough to keep people like Bill off your network). Note that this particular dialog box controls the default account options for the entire system. Each user also has a personal account restrictions dialog box that looks just like the default account dialog box. You access the user options by using the User Information option on the Available Topics (main SYSCON) menu.

```
SYSCON 3.75                          Tuesday March 8, 1994  3:03 am
                    User BOB On File Server 312

              ┌─────── Default Account Balance/Restrictions ───────┐
              │ Account has expiration date:            No         │
              │    Date account expires:                           │
              │ Limit Concurrent Connections:           Yes        │
              │    Maximum Connections:                 1          │ ctions
              │ Create Home Directory for User:         Yes        │
              │ Require Password:                       Yes        │
              │    Minimum Password Length:             5          │
              │ Force Periodic Password Changes:        Yes        │
              │    Days Between Forced Changes:         40         │
              │    Limit Grace Logins:                  Yes        │
              │       Grace Logins Allowed:             6          │
              │ Require Unique Passwords:               Yes        │
              │ Account Balance:                        0          │
              │ Allow Unlimited Credit:                 No         │
              │    Low Balance Limit:                   0          │
              └────────────────────────────────────────────────────┘
```

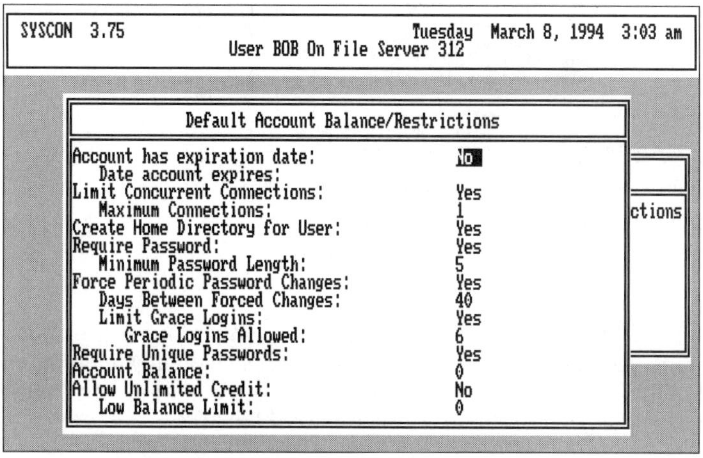

Figure 11-2: The Default Account Balance/Restrictions dialog box allows you to set up a first line of defense against hackers.

There's another important feature in this dialog box, but you probably won't see it right away. Some hackers will actually get on at the same time as the person whose password they stole. That way the network administrator can call that person and verify that he's logged into the network. This tactic might fool the network administrator into thinking that nothing is wrong. You can limit the number of concurrent logins to one. That prevents a hacker from trying to log in to the network at the same time the actual user does.

There's still the problem with controlling the time of user access. Figure 11-3 shows the answer. You use the Default Time Restrictions dialog box to change the hours that a user can log in to the network. You access it by choosing the Supervisor Options selection on the Available Topics menu and then selecting the Default Time Restrictions option. The asterisks show when a user is allowed to access the network. Trying to access the network outside these constraints results in an error message to the user and an entry into NetWare's security logs. Note that this particular dialog box controls the default time restrictions for the entire system. Each user also has a personal time restrictions dialog box that looks just like the default account dialog box. You access the user options by using the User Information option on the Available Topics (main SYSCON) menu.

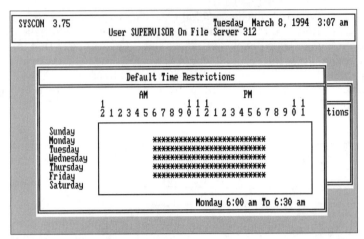

Figure 11-3: The Default Time Restrictions dialog box allows you to define standard login hours and keep hackers at bay at night.

As you can see, just this phase of assigning user rights greatly reduces the chances of someone getting onto your network. The next two sections concentrate on limiting someone's access. Obviously, this keeps an honest user out of harm's way, but it could also reduce the level of damage that a hacker could produce.

Assigning rights to users

NetWare calls the rights that an individual or group has to a file or directory *trustee rights*. If you don't assign any specific rights to a *user*, then he has the rights assigned by the IRM.

Always use individual trustee rights when a user has a special access requirement. For example, you would use an individual trustee assignment to give a user access to his personal data directory on the network. The problem with individual rights is that you have to change them one at a time. That's not such a big deal for a personal directory, since only one person needs access to it. However, if you had to change the rights of 20 or 30 users, security could become a very time-consuming task. (The next section shows you how to get around this problem when you have more than one user accessing a directory or file.)

To get to the Trustee Directory Assignments dialog box shown in Figure 11-4, select User Information from the Available Topics menu. Highlight a particular user and press Enter, then select Trustee Directory Assignments from the User Information menu. Notice that the trustee rights shown to the right of each directory or file entry in the figure match those described in the previous section.

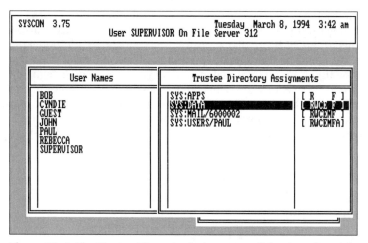

Figure 11-4: The Trustee Directory Assignments dialog box shows the rights that an individual user has to a file or directory.

Adding a new directory to the list is fairly easy. Just press the Insert key on your keyboard and you'll see a dialog box similar to the one shown in Figure 11-5. Type in the name of the directory that you want to assign to this particular user and press Enter. Notice that a directory assignment always has a volume name followed by a colon and then the directory on that volume. NetWare doesn't use drive letters internally; it uses volume names instead.

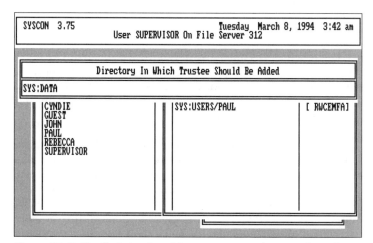

Figure 11-5: The first step in adding a trustee assignment is typing the directory name.

Once you choose a trustee directory, SYSCON displays the dual dialog boxes shown in Figure 11-6. The dialog box on the left shows the rights that the user has to a specific directory. It defaults to the IRM. The dialog box on the right shows additional rights you can assign to the user. The user can do the things shown in the left dialog box. He or she cannot do the things in the right dialog box. All you need to do is highlight the rights you want to add by selecting the right and pressing F5. Pressing Enter moves the selections from one side to the other. You can remove rights by pressing Tab to get to the left dialog box and then following the same procedure you would follow for adding rights. Press Escape to exit back to the Trustee Directory Assignments dialog box.

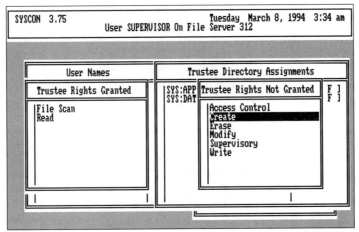

Figure 11-6: Once you choose a trustee directory, choose the rights you want the user to have.

Changing a trustee assignment works much like adding an assignment. The only difference is that you highlight an existing assignment and then press Enter to display the two dialog boxes shown in Figure 11-6. Moving rights from the left dialog box to the right decreases the number of things that the user can do. Moving rights in the opposite direction increases a user's capabilities.

If you ever need to delete a current trustee assignment, simply select the assignment and press Delete. SYSCON removes the user's access to that directory. Unfortunately, SYSCON doesn't provide any kind of an undo feature. If you remove a trustee assignment, it's gone for good. A good carpenter always follows the rule of "measure twice, cut once." It's a good rule to follow with NetWare as well — always think about what you want to do twice, or even three times if need be, and then follow through with an action.

Assigning users to groups

The SYSCON utility allows you to define groups. There are two kinds of groups that I normally define for a NetWare network. The first is a department or other workgroup. You might create an accounting or engineering group, for example. The purpose of this kind of group is to allow people with common goals to access a common set of data. If your company wanted to maintain a private directory of engineering notes, only the engineers would require access to this directory.

The other kind of group is for people who require generalized access to something. The most common one in this category is the group Everyone. NetWare automatically creates this group for you. Everyone may require access to a public notes directory containing company directives. Adding this trustee assignment to the group Everyone will save you a lot of time.

Adding groups to the system is easy. All you need to do is select the Group Information option from the Available Topics menu to display a list of groups. If you want to add a group, just press Insert and type a new group name. Conversely, if you want to remove a group, highlight it and press Delete.

Every group that you create will have members (or users depending on the way you look at it). To add new members to a group, highlight the group name in the Group Information dialog box, press Enter, and select the Member List option from the Group Information menu. SYSCON will display two dialog boxes similar to the one in Figure 11-6. However, instead of a list of rights, you'll see a list of user names. Highlight a list of users by selecting their names and pressing F5. Press Enter when the list is complete. This moves user names from the right dialog box (those that aren't part of the group) to the left dialog box (those who are part of the group). Use the Tab key to move from the right to the left window. This allows you to remove users from the group list. Press Escape to finish the process.

As with users, groups have rights to specific directories and files on the network. The previous section showed you how to add trustee rights to an individual user. Follow the same procedure for a group. The only difference is that you select a group name from the Group Information dialog box in place of a user name.

Summary

This chapter introduced you to the concepts of network management and why managing your network is important. If you don't manage your network, then some hotshot hacker will show up on your doorstep and make life — interesting.

- ✦ It's important to get the users involved in network management; otherwise, you may just as well turn over the keys to your network room to the nearest 16 year old.

- ✦ You should create a security plan. Helping people understand the importance of security is only one reason to create such a plan. You also need to make sure that your company is on firm legal footing when someone does decide to breach security.

- ✦ Finally, we looked at some specifics of security on a Novell network. NetWare currently provides two types of network security database: bindery and NDS. This chapter tells you about the bindery method of securing your network. NDS is designed for large corporate installations where there are at least two file servers.

✦ ✦ ✦

CHAPTER 12

Sharing Resources with Windows Networks

♦ ♦ ♦ ♦

In This Chapter

Looking at the Windows family

Understanding network terminology

Exploring network security issues

Developing internal and network policies

Recognizing security holes

Establishing network resources

Managing users

♦ ♦ ♦ ♦

by Allen L. Wyatt

How little security we have when we trust our happiness in the hands of others.
—William Hazlitt

It goes without saying that Windows is the most popular operating system in use today. There are millions and millions of copies of Windows running on just as many computers. In fact, it is difficult to even buy a PC-compatible these days that does not already have some version of network-ready Windows installed.

This chapter is designed to show you not only how Windows networking works, but what security features it has, and how those features can possibly work against you. When you apply the information in this chapter to your Windows network (whether it is two computers or 200), you will end up with a more secure system.

The Windows Family

Windows is more than a single product. In fact, it can easily be viewed as an entire family of products. The goal Microsoft has been shooting for is a wide range of Windows-based operating systems. Each member of the family is designed to run on different hardware platforms, but they each share the following:

- ✦ Common operating system elements
- ✦ Common user interface
- ✦ Common programming platform

With this in mind, Microsoft currently has three versions of Windows available to the general public. These versions of the operating system are differentiated by the hardware on which they run. There is no firm division on which operating system runs on which hardware. Windows 95 can run on the same hardware as Windows NT (but not necessarily vice versa), and the determining factors are the needs of the users.

The reliance on a common interface has enormous implications for medium to large businesses. Basically, it means that you train your employees only once, and they will know how to use any computer you set them in front of — from the smallest portable to the largest server. Granted, there are nuances based on the version of Windows being used and the tasks to be accomplished, but the user interface is the same, which means that the learning curve is diminished considerably.

Windows for Workgroups

Windows for Workgroups is essentially Windows 3.11 with added networking support. This product was released in late 1993 and early 1994 in response to simple networking products released by Microsoft's competitors. Since the release of Windows 95, the Microsoft emphasis on Windows for Workgroups has understandably died down. You can still get the product by specifically ordering it, but it is expected that it will go away over the next year or so.

Even though Windows for Workgroups is not easily found in stores, it is still used on millions of computer systems. Because of this, it is an integral part of most networking environments in many businesses. This means that when planning your network or network improvements, you need to understand how Windows for Workgroups works in relation to other Microsoft operating systems.

Windows 95

Windows 95, released formally in August 1995, is designed for the average Intel-based desktop or portable system. It is ideally suited for home and small business use. With the changes implemented in the operating system, Windows 95 provides a responsive, stable environment for those users who place moderate demands on their systems.

While Windows 95 works equally well for the single-user and multiple-user environment, the integration of networking capabilities is much better in Windows 95 than in Windows for Workgroups. Unfortunately, Microsoft has not paid as much attention to security as it might have otherwise done. (Later in this chapter you will learn more about the security problems in Windows 95.)

Windows NT Workstation

Windows NT has long been the *high end* operating system in the Windows family. The system requirements for this family member are quite high when compared to older versions of Windows.

Windows NT is a much more stable operating system than Windows 95. (Even with the improvements in Windows 95, this can still be said.) It takes full advantage of the hardware in your computer and works on a wide range of processors — not just Intel systems. It also will take advantage of dual processors within the system.

Windows NT was released between 1992 and 1993, but the latest version of the product — Windows NT 3.5 Workstation — was released in late 1994, and a minor upgrade to Windows NT 3.51 Workstation was released in 1995. This latest product is meant to be used on single-user PCs, on workstations in small peer-to-peer networks, or as a workstation in a larger Windows NT client/server network.

Windows NT Server

Windows NT Server is a *souped up* version of Windows NT Workstation. It is designed to operate on a file server in a client/server network. It provides advanced file and print service features, as well as more extensive security and fault tolerance for data integrity.

As you will learn later in this chapter, Windows NT Server also features centralized management of user accounts and security-related issues. This allows a network administrator to use NT Server to control the configuration and support of a wide range of Windows-based systems from a central location.

Network Terminology

In order to understand how Windows networks work, you need to have a good grasp of the terminology. Many of the terms used in relation to Windows networks may sound the same as those used in other networking environments, but most have a bit of a different slant.

- ✦ **Node.** This is an individual physical connection to the network. A node could be a computer, a printer, or any other device directly connected to the network.
- ✦ **User.** This is a single individual, logged in to a computer network. In many networks, it is possible for a single user to log in to different workstations, so that the same user could actually appear more than once on the network. Don't confuse users with nodes; one is a person, as represented by a network account, and the other is a physical connection to the network.

+ **Workgroup.** A group of users using the same general resources. The same policies can be used to govern all members of a workgroup.

+ **Domain.** A group of users and workgroups which constitute a physical network. In smaller networks, the domain is often the same as the workgroup. For example, all network users at a company's downtown office could be a single domain, while all those at another office would be an entirely different domain.

+ **Peer-to-peer.** A type of network layout in which all the nodes on the network are peers, meaning they are equal in processing power and authority. This does not mean they all have the same CPU or memory capacity. It simply means there is no single computer designated as a center-point for the network. Instead, each node has resources that it makes available to other nodes.

+ **Client/server.** A type of network layout in which there are computers on the network that are designated as servers and all other nodes are classified as clients. The servers are used to consolidate specific resources and then make them available to the clients. For instance, a file server is used to consolidate the files shared over the network. Likewise, a print server is used for printing and a communication server is used for modem or fax operations. The servers are often optimized for their specific use. Under a client/server arrangement, the cost of high-powered resources can effectively be shared among a relatively large number of clients.

Network Security Issues

From a management standpoint, the most critical issues in implementing a network are those related to security. Unfortunately, they are often the issues that are left until last or until a crisis arises. Thoughtfully implementing sound security policies from the beginning can make your networking experience much better. The following sections discuss some of the more pertinent security issues for Windows-based networks.

Developing internal policies

Throughout this book you have learned many different policies that you can adapt and adopt in order to ensure the security of your computer systems. These policies have very little to do with bits and bytes, but instead focus on the human side of computing. For instance, many companies institute backup policies. These policies are internal guidelines that control the type, frequency, and responsibility for making backups. These policies, however, are only as good as the foresight and persistence of the people who implement them. If the policies are not well thought out, or if they are enforced sporadically, they are of little value and do not act as a defense against disaster.

Similar policies should be developed for other security issues, as well. Before you can implement security policies for your Windows network, you need to develop your policies in the following areas:

- **Who will have access to the network?** These individuals become the users who will later have access to your network resources.

- **Can these users be grouped together logically?** For instance, if your company has departments, it may make sense to group the users by department.

- **How should passwords be implemented?** This includes the length of the passwords and how often they should be changed.

- **How will data be organized on common servers?** The organization of data can directly affect your ability to make it available to others over the network.

- **How will data be stored on your servers?** Depending on the version of Windows you are using, you can select from a couple of different file formats for storing information. The format you choose can affect the security of your data.

- **Which users should have access to which data?** After your data is organized, you need to decide who can get to it. You may want to limit use either by individual or by groups of individuals.

- **What hardware will be made accessible over the network?** One of the biggest attractions to implementing networks is that you can share equipment among a large number of people. However, sharing some hardware just doesn't make sense. For example, if the high-powered laser printer is in the boss's office, you might not want to share it on the network.

Windows NT network policies

After you have your internal computer security procedures figured out, you are ready to implement them in the operating system itself. You do this by using the tools provided with your operating system. If you are using Windows NT, you have much more control over who does what, and when, on your system. With Windows 95, you can set up system policies which describe how the user can interact with the network, or how the user can use a particular workstation.

The following sections address the four areas used in implementing security policies: account policies, users rights, access logging, and system policies. The first three sections apply to Windows NT and the final one to Windows 95.

Account policies

Account policies are used to control the default parameters under which the operating system manages individual user accounts. In the Windows NT operating system, you have quite a bit of control over how a person can interact with your system. You manage this by using the User Manager tool, which is located in the Administrative Tools program group. When you open the User Manager, you see the dialog box shown in Figure 12-1.

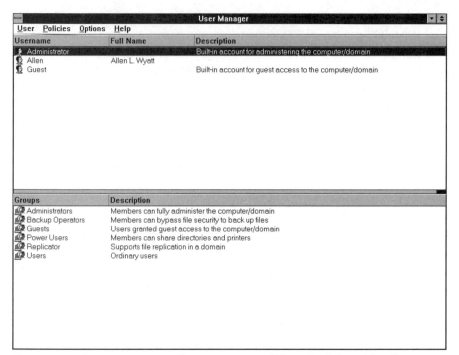

Figure 12-1: The User Manager allows you to set policies to be followed by all user accounts.

The number of users in your system can vary, as can the number of groups you have defined. Later in this chapter, in the section entitled "Managing Users," you will find the information you need to work with individual user accounts, as well as entire groups of users.

In order to set account policies, select the Account option from the Policies menu. This displays the dialog box shown in Figure 12-2.

The top half of the dialog box is used to define the length and persistence characteristics of user passwords. You can set both a minimum and maximum age for passwords. Generally, the more often you force passwords to be changed, the more secure your system is. You can also specify the length of your passwords and whether they can be blank. The final password item allows you to indicate how many previous passwords the system should remember for each user. Setting this option forces users to invent passwords they have not used before.

Tip

The password settings you make in this dialog box are perhaps the most critical to the security of your system.

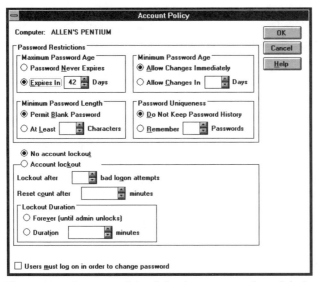

Figure 12-2: Account policies define how passwords and their use are governed on the system.

Password security

I am reminded of a client of mine, whom we will call Janet. She was responsible for network management and hadn't given much thought to setting passwords for her Windows NT network. One day, she was quite agitated. Apparently, she was called on the carpet by some security consultants her boss had hired. They had been able to walk around the office and find enough information to be able to get into the most sensitive areas of the system. It was not long before Janet got the message and began implementing account policies that better protected their network.

In the bottom half of the dialog box in Figure 12-2, you can set account lockout information. This has to do with how the system reacts to failed logon attempts. If someone unauthorized is attempting to get into your system, they may try several passwords that they feel are most likely for a given account. You can instruct Windows NT to lock them out after a few failed attempts.

It is a good idea to turn on the lockout feature. This may depend, however, on the makeup of your users. If you have a bunch of users who can't type very accurately, then locking them out when they mess up may result in unhappy users. A good compromise may be to lock them out after three failed attempts. The lockout duration can then be set to some meaningful value, such as 15 or 20 minutes. It is unlikely that an unauthorized user will sit about waiting for the lockout period to expire. The purpose of the lockout feature, after all, is to simply slow down unauthorized users.

Finally, the check box at the bottom of the dialog box allows you to indicate how users can change their passwords. In a secure system, this check box should be selected. When selected, users must log in to the system successfully in order to change their passwords. If the check box is cleared, then a user can change his or her password during the login procedure if it has already expired. With the check box selected, if a user's password expires before he logs in, then he must contact a network administrator who can change the password for him or her.

If you are serious about security, you should at least consider the following:

- Set the maximum password age to no more than 28 days.
- Set the minimum password age so changes can be made immediately.
- Set the minimum password length to at least six characters.
- Set the password uniqueness so the system remembers the previous three or four passwords.

User rights

User rights control who can do what on your system or network. This is how you indicate what each user (or group of users) should be able to do in relation to the computer or the network as a whole. You set user rights by selecting the User Rights option from the Policies menu in the User Manager. This displays the small dialog box shown in Figure 12-3.

Using this dialog box is very simple. At the top of the dialog box you select a right to be granted to someone. Then you ensure that the appropriate users or groups of users appear at the bottom of the dialog box. You can add or remove users (or groups) by clicking on the appropriate buttons at the right side of the dialog box.

The available rights defined within Windows NT are rather extensive. These rights give you quite a bit of control over your system, and, if applied thoughtfully and properly, can make your system very secure. The rights which you can set are the following:

- **Access this computer from network.** Allows users to access resources on your system from other computers connected to the network.
- **Back up files and directories.** Allows the user to run the backup programs provided with Windows NT. This is a powerful right which should not be granted to everyone.
- **Change the system time.** Allows the user to change the system date and time from the Control Panel.

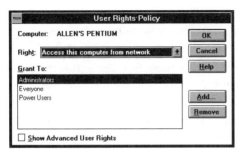

Figure 12-3: User rights define what individuals can do on a system.

- **Force shutdown from a remote system.** Allows the user, if logged on from a remote system, to shut down your computer.
- **Load and unload device drivers.** Allows the user to manage system device drivers.
- **Log on locally.** Allows the user to log on to the computer when he is physically in front of it.
- **Manage auditing and security log.** Allows the user to modify the various access logs generated by Windows NT. These logs are covered, in the section "Access logging."
- **Restore files and directories.** Allows the user to restore files from backups that were previously made. This, again, is a powerful right, since it means the user can overwrite existing files on your system.
- **Shut down the system.** Allows the user to shut down your system.
- **Take ownership of files or other objects.** Allows the user to take ownership, meaning complete control, of Windows NT objects. This means the user can change who has access to your files.

In addition to the rights just listed, Windows NT maintains a group of advanced rights. You can access these rights by clicking on the check box at the bottom of the dialog box shown in Figure 12-3. These rights are typically used by programmers or when setting up user accounts that belong to specific programs. (User accounts are not simply for humans; they also can be used by programs running in the background.) The advanced user rights consist of the following:

- **Act as part of the operating system.** Allows the user to act as a secure, trusted part of the operating system. This is usually granted to secure programs so they can operate with the highest clearance possible. This right should be granted only if you are sure you can trust the program, since improper use can seriously compromise your system.
- **Add workstations to domain.** Allows the user to add new workstation definitions to an existing domain.

- **Bypass traverse checking.** Allows the user to move through directory trees freely. Generally this is granted to everyone, unless you want the user to stay within a particular directory.
- **Create a page file.** Allows the user to create page files. Again, this is primarily used for programs that need page files to do their work. (Page files are similar to swap files; they are used to store part of a program on disk during execution.)
- **Create a token object.** Allows the user to create access tokens, which are used by the security routines of Windows NT. This is another right that should not be granted lightly or freely.
- **Create permanent shared objects.** Allows the user (a program) to create special permanent objects, such as \\Device, which are used elsewhere within Windows NT.
- **Debug programs.** Allows the user to debug low-level objects such as threads. This right is necessary when developing programs for Windows NT.
- **Generate security audits.** Allows the user (a program) to add entries to the security audit log. This log is described in the next section, "Access logging."
- **Increase quotas.** Allows the user to increase object quotas. This right is not currently implemented in Windows NT.
- **Increase scheduling priority.** Allows the user to raise the priority level assigned to a program or process.
- **Lock pages in memory.** Allows the user (a program) to lock memory pages so they can't be paged out to the swap file.
- **Log on as a batch file.** Allows the user to log on to Windows NT using a batch queue facility.
- **Log on as a service.** Allows the user (a program) to log on to Windows NT as a system service, which means it has access to high-level security procedures.
- **Modify firmware environment values.** Allows the user to modify system environment variables which affect all of Windows NT.
- **Profile single process.** Allows the user to use the profiling (performance sampling) capabilities of Windows NT on a program or process.
- **Profile system performance.** Allows the user to use the profiling (performance sampling) capabilities of Windows NT on the entire system.
- **Replace a process level token.** Allows the user (a program) to modify a process's security access token. This effectively gives the program complete run of your system and should not be granted lightly.

As you looked through the list of available rights, you probably noticed that many of them are used for programs. Some programs need access to normally protected files, directories, or other resources. Some programs even need to operate at the same security level as the operating system. These programs cannot set the security rights themselves; you need to do it for them. If such settings are required, you will be instructed on which rights to grant by the documentation for the program. You should follow the instructions precisely; do not grant more (or fewer) rights than required by the program. To do so could present the possibility of a security problem or cause the program not to work at all.

For those rights which are appropriate for human users rather than programs, make sure you grant the minimum rights required for the users to do their authorized work on the system. Again, granting additional rights introduces security risks.

When you are through modifying rights, you can click on the OK button. The rights are saved and are effective immediately.

Access logging

Access logging allows you to track exactly what happens on your system. Every time a qualified event occurs, Windows NT makes an entry in the appropriate log file. You can later review the log files to determine what happened on your system. To enable event logging, you should select the Audit option from the Policies menu of the User Manager. This displays the dialog box shown in Figure 12-4.

Notice that there are several classifications of events you can log, and each has two check boxes to its right. If you select a check box in the Success column, then a log entry is recorded when a successful event in that category is performed. Likewise, if you select a check box in the Failure column, a log entry is generated if an event is attempted in a category and the event does not succeed.

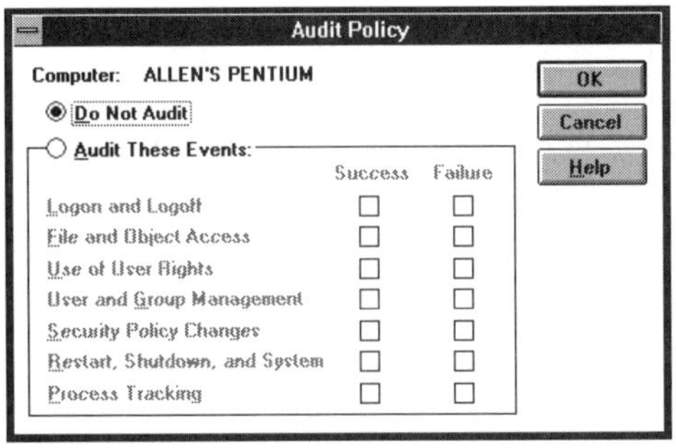

Figure 12-4: Access logging is enabled through the User Manager.

At a very minimum, for security purposes, you should select the following events for logging:

- **Logon and Logoff.** Select both the Success and Failure columns here. That way, you will always be able to tell who has been on — or attempting to get on — your system.
- **Use of User Rights.** Select the Failure column. This will let you know when someone is attempting to use a right to which they have no access.
- **User and Group Management.** Select both the Success and Failure columns. This will keep you informed of what changes have been made to both users and groups.
- **Security Policy Changes.** Select both the Success and Failure columns. Changes to policies affect everything that happens on your system, and you should record such changes.

Events that have been recorded can be viewed using the Event Viewer, which is located in the Administrative Tools program group.

Windows 95 System Policy Editor

In the Windows 95 environment, you do not have the same type of control over accounts as you do under Windows NT. In fact, you don't have the capability to modify policies by default. Instead, you need to use a program called the System Policy Editor. This editor is provided with the Windows 95 Resource Kit, which is included on the Windows 95 CD-ROM. To install the System Policy Editor, follow these steps:

1. Use the Add/Remove Programs option in the Control Panel, choosing the Windows Setup tab.
2. Click on the Have Disk button and specify the directory E:\ADMIN\APPTOOLS\POLEDIT, assuming your CD-ROM is in drive E.
3. Select the System Policy Editor program from the resulting Have Disk dialog box, and then click on the Install button.
4. Click on OK to close the Add/Remove Programs dialog box.

After installation, you can use the System Policy Editor by choosing Programs from the Start menu, then Accessories, then System Tools, and finally clicking on System Policy Editor. Shortly afterward, you will see the System Policy Editor program window, as shown in Figure 12-5.

The System Policy Editor is used to create or modify policy files or to modify the Registry directly. In most instances, you will use the program only to modify policy

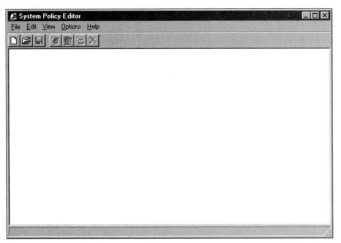

Figure 12-5: Windows 95 allows you to set account policies by using the System Policy Editor.

files. These are much more flexible and can be administered remotely, if you desire. Policy files can either be stored on the local computer (in which case they affect only the local computer) or on a Windows NT server (in which case they affect the Windows 95 systems logging in to the network).

System policy files end with a POL extension. You can name the file anything you want, but in a Windows NT network the policy file is downloaded automatically if you name it CONFIG.POL and store it in the NETLOGON directory of the server. If you don't already have a policy file in effect, you can create one by choosing the New File option from the File menu. At this point, you will see two icons appear in the System Policy Editor window — Default User and Default Computer.

At this point, you can modify any settings you desire for either users or the computer itself. Simply double-click on the icon representing the types of settings you wish to change. For example, if you want to change the user settings, double-click on the Default User icon. This displays a properties dialog box, as shown in Figure 12-6.

Notice that the available policy settings are presented in a tree format, similar to what is used in other Windows 95 tools such as the Registry Editor or the Device Manager. It is not the purpose of this book to provide a complete reference to every policy setting you can make. You will find most policy settings to be intuitively clear if you have worked with networks and Windows 95 for any length of time. There are, however, a few settings you will want to examine carefully in order to increase security on your system.

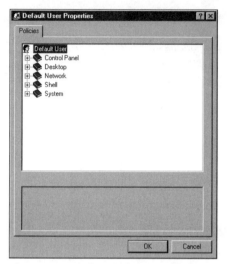

Figure 12-6: Policy settings are displayed in a tree fashion by the System Policy Editor.

In the Default User Properties sheet, expand the tree under System and then under Restrictions (see Figure 12-7). Make sure the Disable Registry editing tools option is selected. This prevents individual users in your network from modifying their Registry. You'll be happy that you made such a choice if you have a curiously clumsy user or one that simply wants to be troublesome.

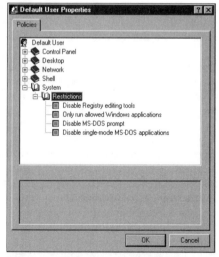

Figure 12-7: You can easily disable a user's ability to edit the Registry.

In the Default Computer properties, there are quite a few settings you may want to use. In the Passwords section, you can disable password caching, which is a good idea for maximum security. (The reason for disabling password caching is discussed at length later in this chapter.) You can also specify other password-related restrictions and requirements that can serve to make your systems more secure.

In addition, under the Dial-Up Networking section, you will probably want to disable dial-in. This prevents a knowledgeable user from setting up a Dial-Up Networking server on his or her computer. If you did allow this, that same user could give whoever called in access to portions of your network. Needless to say, most network administrators find this prospect unpleasant.

When you are finished making changes in your policies, you should save the file. Again, if you want the file to be downloaded automatically from a Windows NT server, store it in the NETLOGON directory on the server, under the name CONFIG.POL. The next time you start the Windows 95 system and log into the server, the policies file is automatically downloaded and used to modify how Windows 95 works.

Server format

If you are using a Windows NT workstation or server, many of the additional security features available to you depend on the use of the NTFS filing system. NTFS is an acronym for NT (as in Windows NT) filing system. This is an enhanced disk filing system that allows the implementation of additional safeguards that cannot be used under the FAT filing system used in other versions of Windows. These safeguards allow you to set access permissions on individual directories and files.

There are two ways you can create an NTFS drive. The first is to create it from scratch, by using the FORMAT command at the DOS command line. For instance, if you wanted to format Drive D using NTFS, you would enter the following command:

```
FORMAT D: /FS:NTFS
```

The other method is to convert an existing FAT drive to an NTFS drive. This is done when you don't want to loose the information already stored on the drive. To do a conversion, you enter the following at the DOS prompt:

```
CONVERT D: /FS:NTFS
```

Notice that the syntax of this command is very similar to that used by the FORMAT command. The effects, however, are completely different. When the CONVERT command is finished, the entire disk you specify is transformed from a FAT volume to an NTFS volume.

Why should you convert to NTFS? Quite simply because of the security features it enables you to implement. Without NTFS, the files on your disk are no more secure than they are under DOS.

Security holes

Despite all the security that is supposedly built into the Windows family, there are still problems. There is an old saying that "anything that can be secured can be unsecured." Computer users (of all types) are proving this every day. This does not mean that Windows (whatever flavor you use) cannot be trusted; indeed, you may not have much of a choice in today's computer world. Instead, if you are deeply concerned about security, you need to be aware of what problems exist. Several of the more common (and therefore dangerous) security holes are discussed in the following sections.

Windows for Workgroups

Windows for Workgroups has been around for a couple of years, so it has had quite a bit of scrutiny by the computing community. There are many bugs in the software, but most of them do not affect the security of your system. The biggest security bug has to do with caching of passwords in memory while you are using the system. This is done so that the operating system can automatically reconnect to resources that require passwords when reconnection is necessary.

The problem is that a Trojan horse program, running on your Windows for Workgroups system, can read this password from memory and then e-mail it somewhere else or save it on disk for later retrieval. This can be done behind the scenes, without your even knowing it is happening. Unfortunately, there is no cure for this problem; it is fundamental to Windows for Workgroups itself. The only way to correct it would be to rewrite the programmer's API for the operating system so that it did not allow a program to fetch the unencrypted password from memory.

Windows for Workgroups also exhibits the same password cache file problems as Windows 95 (described in the next section). The reason that problem is not discussed fully here (under Windows for Workgroups) is that it appears that Microsoft has dropped support for Windows for Workgroups and a fix is no longer readily available.

Windows 95

Perhaps the biggest security problem with Windows 95 is related to passwords. Millions of systems have been installed that use the password capability of the operating systems and are unknowingly at risk. The problem is related to password caching, which is used to store passwords for future use. You have probably chosen to use password caching, without even being aware that you were doing so. When you log on to a Windows network, the login box has a check box at the bottom of it. If the box is checked, your password is saved for future use by the system. For instance, if your name is Mary, and this is the login ID that you use, then your password is saved in the file C:\WINDOWS\MARY.PWL.

The password is written into the cache file using what some view as a weak encryption method. Microsoft claims the encryption method meets U.S. Government DES standards and uses the best encryption method that can legally be used in products designed for export to other countries. The critics counter that the encryption method is only secure if it is implemented correctly, and Microsoft did not do this with the cache files. The first 20 bytes of the file are easily determined, and you can use this as a starting point for decrypting the whole file.

To prove the vulnerability of the encryption method, a program was developed to decode the PWL files; this program was subsequently spread around the Internet. This means that someone with this program could easily access your password if you have used password caching. (If you want to check the vulnerability of your system, you can download the program from http://www.c2.org/hackmsoft/.)

To solve this problem, there are two choices. First, you can change your password and disable password caching. This feature is enabled, by default, and you must take positive steps to disable it by using the System Policy Editor described earlier in the chapter. Understand that if you do disable it, this means you need to enter your password every time you log in to your system.

The other way you can minimize the problem is to download, from Microsoft, operating system patches that make the password caching files harder to decode. The drawback to this is that the patches have not been tested and may not provide total security (the jury is still out on this matter). Regardless, the patch provides a more secure password system than a system without the patch. In addition, the patch cannot be used on systems outside the U.S., since the encryption algorithm is not authorized for export to other countries.

The patch for Windows 95 is available through any of the standard online services on which Microsoft has a presence, or you can download it via the Internet at http://www.microsoft.com/windows/software/mspwlupd.htm.

Windows NT

Microsoft has been touting for some time that Windows NT is a very secure operating system. You need to realize that this is true only as far as the system user (you) applies the safeguards provided by Windows NT. This is true with any operating system, however. You need to be familiar with the security tools available, and then apply them as appropriate for your needs.

One of the biggest safety concerns with Windows NT is related to physical security of the computer itself. If someone can get physical access to your system, he or she can generally get access to your data — even if you have logged off your computer.

If you can touch it, you can break it

The sad reality of this was driven home to John, who works at the headquarters of an up-scale New York retailer. John is responsible for the company's information systems, and all employees are connected using a Windows NT network and Windows NT workstations.

One day, the company management decided to fire one of the marketing people, whom we will call Bob. While the "exit interview" was being conducted, John was instructed to change Bob's passwords so that competitive information could not be taken from his PC. When Bob returned to his office (unfortunately, unescorted) and found that he was locked out of the computer, he simply pulled out a DOS boot disk and rebooted his computer. The files he wanted were then available to be copied to a floppy disk. Since the operating system never started, the security measures of the operating system also never started. Had Bob had access to the main servers used by the company, the damage could have been much greater.

There are two ways to get around this problem. The first is to make sure that you utilize the NTFS filing system on all drives in the NT computer. Even if someone then boots to a DOS floppy (which uses the FAT filing system), he cannot get at the information on the NTFS drives because the two filing systems are incompatible.

The second way is potentially more secure, but may not be available on all computer systems. Most PCs sold today allow you to control which disks are used for booting a system. Normally, the booting sequence uses drive A and then drive C. If the CMOS setup on your system allows it, you can bypass drive A and boot directly to drive C. Had this been done on Bob's system as described in the accompanying Horror Story, he would not have been able to boot to his DOS disk.

Establishing Network Resources

One of the primary uses of networks is to share resources among the users of the network. Windows networks allow you to quickly and easily share resources. The trick is to make sure that you share the resources without compromising the security of either the individual resources or the network as a whole.

There are two types of resources you can share: directories (and their files) and printers. The following sections detail the specifics of how you can share both directories and printers over the network.

Windows 95 specifics

Windows NT automatically allows you to share these resources across your network, and gives you a great deal of control over how those resources are shared. Windows 95, on the other hand, takes a few more steps to enable the type of sharing you desire. In fact, there are two considerations you need to make when working with Windows 95. The first deals with making printer and file sharing available, and the second deals with how you actually do your sharing.

Enabling sharing

Under Windows 95 you need to add this capability; it is not enabled automatically. To add printer and file sharing to Windows 95, follow these steps:

1. Choose the Settings option from the Start menu. This displays the Settings menu.
2. Choose Control Panel from the Settings menu. Shortly, you will see the Control Panel appear.
3. Double-click on the Network icon. This displays the Network dialog box.
4. Click on the File and Print Sharing button. This displays the File and Print Sharing dialog box, as shown in Figure 12-8.

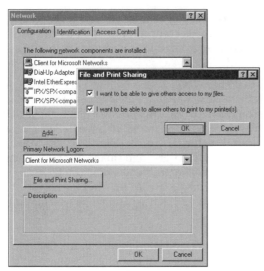

Figure 12-8: Windows 95 requires you to enable file and printer sharing.

5. Make sure the two check boxes in the dialog box are selected.

6. Click on OK to close the File and Print Sharing dialog box.

7. Click on OK to close the Network dialog box.

8. Restart Windows 95 when prompted.

If you do not take these steps, you will not be able to share resources using the Windows 95 system, regardless of whether you can access the network from the system.

Access control

Windows 95 allows you to perform two types of access control to resources you make available. By default, Windows 95 uses what is called share-level access control. This means that you can assign passwords for each resource you share. Users on the network can then access the resource based on their knowledge of the password. The other type of control is called user-level access control. This means that you can specify individual users or groups of users whom you want to have access to a resource, and then only those users or groups of users can utilize the resource.

Determining which type of access control to use may be tricky, depending on your network configuration.

+ First, if you are in a peer-to-peer network, you cannot use user-level access control. This is because this type of access control relies upon a centralized source for information about users and groups. That information is only available in a client/server environment.

+ Next, you should understand that share-level access is inherently less secure than user-level access. This is because under share-level access you need to provide a password to others on the network. This password may be used by any number of people, even by some you don't intend to have it. Perhaps an example is in order. If you share a directory using share-level access, you can set a password for it. You give the password to Carla and Duane, both of whom need access to the files in the directory. The problem is that you have no control over who Carla or Duane gives the password to. After a while, it is possible that the password is so widespread that you might as well have no password at all.

Of course, if you don't care who has access to the resources you share, then picking an access control method is no big deal. In this case, you simply pick share-level access and then don't specify a password. Your resources are then open to *anyone* using the network.

If you decide you want a more secure system, and you want to use user-level access control, then follow these steps:

1. Choose the Settings option from the Control Panel. This displays the Settings menu.
2. Choose Control Panel from the Settings menu. The Control Panel appears.
3. Double-click on the Network icon. This displays the Network dialog box.
4. Click on the Access Control tab. The Network dialog box now appears as shown in Figure 12-9.
5. Select the radio button next to User-level access control.
6. In the field at the bottom of the dialog box, specify the domain or workstation from which the user and group lists should be retrieved.
7. Click on OK to close the Network dialog box.
8. Restart Windows 95 when prompted.

After you have enabled sharing and determined which access method you want to use, you are ready to start sharing resources in Windows 95. (Remember that Windows NT has sharing enabled automatically.) As you work through the next couple of sections, you will notice that your choice of an access control method affects the dialog boxes you see when sharing resources.

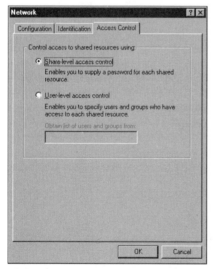

Figure 12-9: The Access Control tab of the Network dialog box allows you to specify how you want Windows 95 to manage access to your resources.

Sharing directories

Sharing a directory means making it available to other network users. The directories you share are entirely up to you, as is the security you may place on those directories. Sharing a directory is simple, but varies depending on whether you are using the new Windows 95 interface or the older Windows NT interface.

Windows 95

To share a directory under Windows 95, you simply right-click on the disk drive or folder you want to share. This displays a context menu, from which you can pick the Sharing option. This displays the Properties dialog box for the folder or directory, with the Sharing tab already selected. An example of this dialog box is shown in Figure 12-10.

To share the folder, click on the Shared As radio button. This makes all the options on the dialog box available. You can then specify how you want the folder shared. Most of the dialog box is self explanatory, but from a security perspective, the Access Type area is the most critical. Here you can specify how people have access to the contents of the folder. On a very small network, or for a totally public directory, you may want to select Read-Only or Full. In all other instances, you will probably want to select Depends on Password, which requires a password on the part of the person attempting to connect to the shared folder. If you select this option, you may specify two passwords for the two different types of access supported under Windows 95.

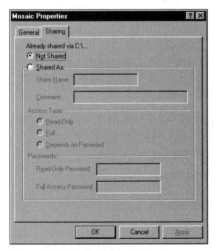

Figure 12-10: Sharing a folder is easy under Windows 95.

If you set a password for access to a shared folder, you should be extremely careful that you use passwords that are not the same as (or even close to) the password you use to log on your system. By its very nature, the password for a shared directory is distributed to a wide number of people and, therefore, is quite insecure. You never know who may ultimately get the password, and you don't want that person to try the same password to get full access to your system.

If you are using user-level access control for your system, then the sharing tab looks like the one shown in Figure 12-11. Notice that it is just a bit more complex than the dialog box used in share-level access control.

Again, to enable sharing, you simply click on the Shared As button and then supply a name for the resource. At the bottom of the dialog box, you may add, remove, or edit users who should have access to the folder. If you click on the Add button, you see a list of available users and groups, as shown in Figure 12-12.

Pick from the list of users and groups, assigning them to the different permissions categories. Only the users or groups you specify will have access; all others will have no access. When you click on OK, the users or groups are shown in the Properties dialog box for the folder.

When you no longer want to share a folder, you simply display the Sharing tab on the Properties dialog box again, and then click on the Not Shared radio button.

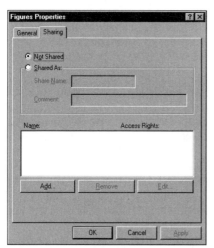

Figure 12-11: The dialog box for sharing a folder when using user-level access allows you to indicate users or groups who should have access to your folder.

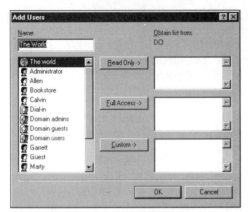

Figure 12-12: Using user-level access, you can pick which users or groups should have access to your folder.

One of the big drawbacks of Windows (not just Windows 95) is that if you share a directory, it is broadcast to all the world to see. It isn't until the remote user attempts to access the directory that the security kicks into effect and stops them. For many purposes, it would be much better to have security checked before the shared directories are displayed. That way, you could completely hide shared directories from everyone except those you intend to have access.

Unfortunately, there is no way around this problem. If you share a directory, the existence of the directory is available for all the world to see. The contents of the directory, however, are not visible unless the viewer has the proper security clearance.

Windows NT

To share a directory under Windows NT, use the File Manager. Simply highlight the directory you want to share and then click on the share icon. (This is the one that looks like a hand holding a solid folder.) You will then see the dialog box shown in Figure 12-13.

You can change the name under which the directory is shared and indicate the number of users who can access the directory at the same time. When you are finished, click on the OK button to make the directory immediately available to others on the network.

Windows NT also allows you to specify security options for files and directories on disks using the NTFS filing system. Again, this is done using the File Manager. For instance, if you wanted to modify who could access a particular directory, you simply highlight the directory name and then choose Permissions from the Security menu. This displays the dialog box shown in Figure 12-14.

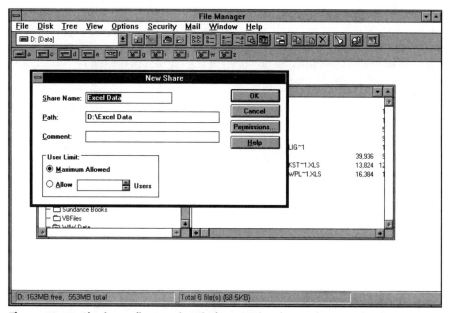

Figure 12-13: Sharing a directory in Windows NT involves only a couple of steps.

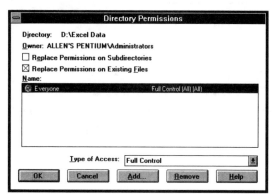

Figure 12-14: You can set permissions for any directory or file on an NTFS volume.

Notice that the default permissions for a directory allow anyone (all members of the Everyone group) to do anything they want with the directory or any files and directories it contains. This is no big deal as long as there are not multiple people who have access to your system and as long as you have not shared the directory on the network. In these instances, you will definitely want to change who has permission to modify the directory or file.

To modify who can do what to your resource, simply click on the Add button. This displays the dialog box shown in Figure 12-15. From here, you can select the users or groups you want to have access to the directory or file, and then pick the type of access you wish to grant (from the pull-down list at the bottom of the dialog box). Clicking on the Add button grants the group or user the permission you have specified.

When you are finished granting permissions, click on the OK button to save your changes.

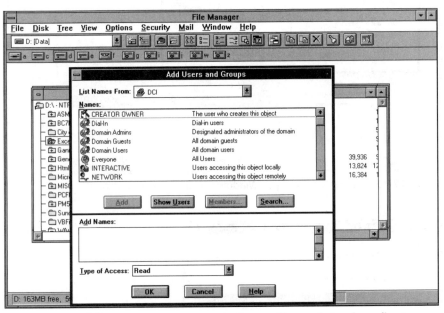

Figure 12-15: Adding new groups or users to those with permission for a directory or file is easy to do.

Sharing printers

Although by historical standards computer hardware is rather inexpensive, it can still be a very expensive proposition to provide each computer user in a company with his or her own specialized resources that may get used only part of the time. The most common example is a high-quality printer. A Windows network allows you to easily share printers so that you don't need to get one for everybody.

With Windows 95, printers are shared in much the same way as directories — you simply make them available to the network. To do this, you display the Printers folder and then right-click on the printer you want shared. This displays a context menu, from which you should choose the Sharing option. You will then see the Properties dialog box for the printer with the Sharing tab already selected, as shown in Figure 12-16.

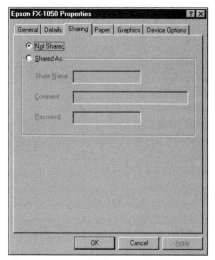

Figure 12-16: Sharing a printer under Windows 95 is similar to sharing folders.

Notice that the dialog box looks very much like the one you used for sharing folders. Simply click on the Shared As button and then supply a name. If you desire, you may also supply a password that effectively restricts who can use the printer. When you are satisfied, click on the OK button. Immediately, others on the network will be able to access your printer.

If you are using user-level access control with Windows 95, the dialog box shown in Figure 12-17 appears. Here, again, you specify that you want the printer shared and the name to use, but you can also specify the individual or groups who can use the printer. You do this using the same techniques you used when sharing folders.

With Windows NT, your sharing options are a bit more sophisticated. Printer sharing is controlled using the Print Manager. To share a printer, open the Print Manager and select the printer you want to share. Then choose the Properties option from the Printer menu. This displays a dialog box, similar to what is shown in Figure 12-18.

To share the printer, select the check box near the bottom of the dialog box. You then specify a name to be used when sharing this printer. When you finish, click on the OK button and the printer becomes available on the network.

Notice that Windows NT did not give you an opportunity to set a password when you shared the printer. Instead, if you want to somehow limit the access to your printer, you need to select the printer in the Print Manager and then choose the Permissions option from the Security menu. This displays a whole new dialog box, similar to the ones you used to limit access using the File Manager. A typical Printer Permissions dialog box is shown in Figure 12-19.

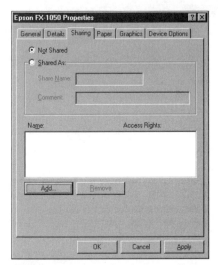

Figure 12-17: User-level access allows you to specify who can have access to your printer.

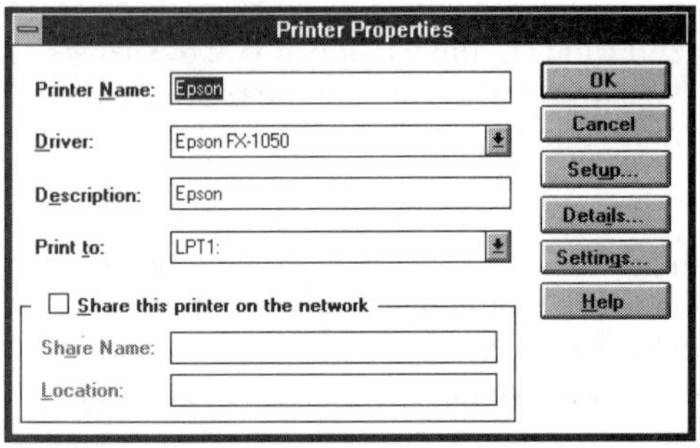

Figure 12-18: Under Windows NT, sharing a printer is handled from the Print Manager.

Using this dialog box, you can add, remove, or modify the things that a user (or group of users) can do with your printer. To do any of these tasks, simply follow the same steps as when you set security permissions for your directories. There are four levels of access you can grant to your printers: no access, print, manage documents, and full control. *No access* is straightforward; it means the user or group cannot use the printer. Exactly what can be done under the other three access levels may not be immediately clear. Table 12-1 details exactly what can be done for each level. When you are finished setting permissions, click on the OK button to save the information.

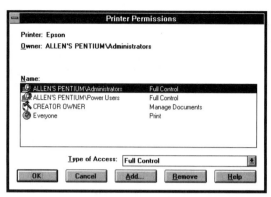

Figure 12-19: Windows NT gives you complete control over who can access your printer.

Table 12-1
Printer Access Levels

Action	Print	Manage Documents	Full Control
Printing documents	x		x
Changing print job settings		x	x
Pause print jobs		x	x
Resume print jobs		x	x
Delete print jobs		x	x
Restarting print jobs		x	x
Changing print job order			x
Pause the printer			x
Resume the printer			x
Purge the printer			x
Changing printer properties			x
Changing printer permissions			x
Deleting the printer			x

Managing Users

It makes sense that a network is not really a network without users. Thus, there must be some way for you to manage the users who have access to the network. Both Windows NT and Windows 95 allow you to set up individual users and groups of users, as discussed in the following sections.

Local groups

You might wonder why we would examine groups before examining users. While it may seem a top-down approach, it generally makes more sense from an organizational standpoint to develop your groups before you start adding users.

In a company that is already organized into groups, you may be tempted to use those groups for your network groups. For instance, if you have accounting, production, and administration departments, you may want to start with these as the basis for your network groups. In other companies, it might not make sense to do this. You may want to organize your network groups by their data clearance level instead. For example, maybe your entry-level people (regardless of which department they are in) have the lowest clearance for sensitive data. They could be organized into a single network group.

When you have devised the network groups you want to use, you are ready to add them to your operating system. The way you do this depends on whether you are using Windows 95 or Windows NT. Local groups can be supported under Windows 95 only if you install the proper client software. This software is part of the Windows 95 Resource Kit and can be installed if you have the Windows 95 CD-ROM. To install it, follow these steps:

1. Use the Add/Remove Programs option in the Control Panel, choosing the Windows Setup tab.
2. Click on the Have Disk button and specify the directory E:\ADMIN\APPTOOLS\POLEDIT, assuming your CD-ROM is in drive E.
3. Select the Group policies option from the resulting Have Disk dialog box and then click on the Install button.
4. Click on OK to close the Add/Remove Programs dialog box.

Remember that you need to install the software on every Windows 95 node on the network. After this is done, you can manage your groups by using the System Policy Editor, as described earlier in this chapter. If you look back at Figure 12-6, you will remember that the System Policy Editor normally shows icons for the Default User and the Default Computer. You can add a group to the mix by clicking on the Add Group icon, which is the fifth from the left on the toolbar. You are then asked for the name of the group you want created. (You should type the name of the group and press Enter.) An icon for the new group is then added, as shown in Figure 12-20.

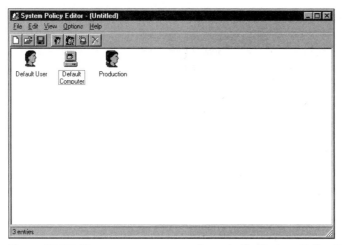

Figure 12-20: New groups appear as icons in the System Policy Editor.

At this point, you can edit policies for the group the same way you did for users earlier in the chapter. You should only need to change the policies that are different from those you set up for the default user, however. These defaults are used as a starting point when creating the new group.

If you are using Windows NT, you have much simpler control over groups. Groups are managed in the User Manager, which is located in the Administrative Tools program group. When you start User Manager, you will see a listing of both the users and groups defined for your system (refer back to Figure 12-1). To add a new group, simply choose New Local Group from the User menu. This displays the dialog box shown in Figure 12-21.

In this dialog box, you supply the name of the new group and (if desired) provide a description of the group. You can add users to a new group by simply clicking on the Add button and then selecting the users you want added. (If you had a username selected when you created the new group, it is automatically added to the group.) When you are satisfied with the composition of the group, click on the OK button.

After a group is created, it appears in the window at the bottom of the User Manager window. You can then change the constitution of the group by double-clicking on the group in the list. This displays the same dialog box you used to set up the group (Figure 12-21), and you are free to make changes.

To grant rights to groups you create under Windows NT, you would use the User Rights option from the Policies menu, as described earlier in this chapter.

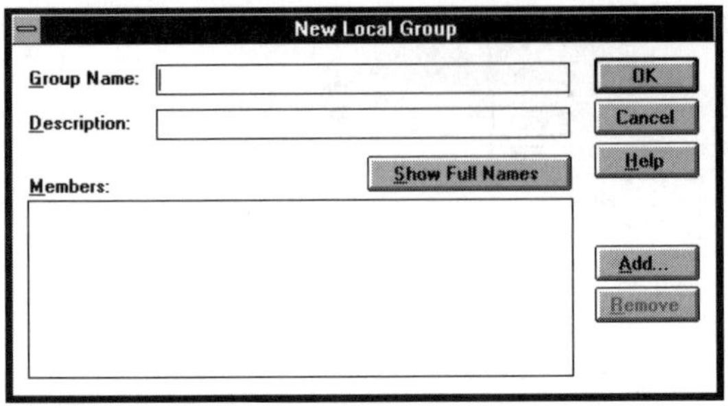

Figure 12-21: New groups and their members can be designated quickly under Windows NT.

User accounts

Users are the heart of a network, and you will need to set up a user account for each person using your network on a regular basis. In some instances, you may even need to set up special user accounts for software that is running on your server. (The documentation for your software describes when such an action is necessary.) To set up a user under Windows 95, you use the System Policy Editor, which is described earlier in this chapter. Click on the New User button and provide a name for the new user. The default policies which you set up under the Default User icon are copied to the new user, and you can then make any changes you desire.

Under Windows NT, all you need is the User Manager. To add a user, simply choose New User from the User menu. The dialog box shown in Figure 12-22 is then displayed.

In this dialog box, you provide the name of the user and a password. The user's name (user ID) is placed in the Username field, and his or her full name can be placed in the Full Name field. The password is placed in both the Password and Confirm Password fields. The username, along with the password, is subsequently supplied by the user to log on to the network or computer system.

At the bottom of the dialog box are some account parameters you can set. These settings override the policies you set up in Account Policies. From a security standpoint, the only check box you might want to consider checking is User Must Change Password at Next Logon. This forces the user to create his own password once he logs on the system.

If you click on the Groups button at the bottom of the dialog box, you can specify the groups to which this user should belong. When you are finished setting up the account, you can click on the OK button. The user then appears in the User Manager window. If you later want to change anything for the user, simply double-click on the username.

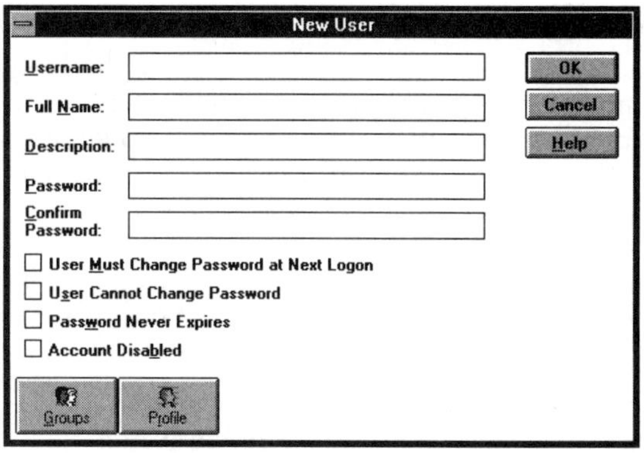

Figure 12-22: Adding a new user under Windows NT involves assigning a username and password.

Summary

This chapter provides the information you need to make your Windows network secure. There are many versions of Windows, and many ways you can put your Windows network together. This chapter has introduced you to the various Windows flavors and then discussed the networking and security issues related to those flavors. Specifically, you have learned the following:

- There are many different members of the Windows family, but only three or four of them are applicable to Windows networks.

- Developing effective Windows network policies starts by developing written internal policies that can easily be managed by the operating system.

- There are bugs and fundamental flaws within the various versions of Windows that can affect the security of your network.

- Windows allows you to share both printers and files over the network. Exactly how you do the sharing depends on the version of Windows you use.

- Windows includes various tools that allow you to manage both individual users and entire groups of users.

✦ ✦ ✦

Index

✦ Numbers ✦

32-bit programming, 101
  Eudora Pro version, 130
  WinZip version, 105

✦ A ✦

AABBS (Amateur Action Bulletin Board Service), 190–192
abortion, 118, 158, 185
Abortion, The (Braughtigan), 185
ACLU (American Civil Liberties Union), 192, 195, 218, 224
A.C. Nielson Company, 141, 142
acts of God, 13, 14–15
actuaries, 15, 18. *See also* insurance coverage
Adleman, Leonard M., 228–229, 230, 234
Adobe, 56
adult materials. *See* indecent materials
advertising, unwanted, 175
Advisory Council on the National Information Infrastructure, 124
Aegean Park Press, 219
algorithms
  DEA (Data Encryption Algorithm), 107
  Diffie-Hellman type algorithms, 153, 227–228, 230–231, 234
  IDEA (International Data Encryption Algorithm), 221, 229
  Lucifer algorithm, 226
aliases, for hackers, 45

Allen, George, 159
allocation units, 60
ALLOW command, 256
alt.sex.stories, 203–204
AMD, 85
American Banker, 159
American Civil Liberties Union (ACLU), 192, 195, 218, 224
American Express, 144
Ameritech, 164
analog signals, 223
Andreessen, Marc, 161, 170
anon.penet.fi, 128
anonymous remailers, 125–128, 238
antivirus software. *See also* viruses
  basic description of, 71–75
  checksums and, 68
  creating virus recovery disks with, 74
  how it works, 71
  identifying virus infections with, 73–74
  using, 71–75
AOL (America Online), 47, 71, 77, 170
  community-based standards and, 192–193
  Digital Telephony Bill and, 225
  e-mail, 116
  financial transactions and, 139
  indecent materials and, 192–193, 210
  subscribers, number of, vs. other online services, 142
Apple Computer, 222
Applied Cryptography (Schneier), 229

ARC files, 72, 105
archive files. *See also* backup systems; Zip archive files
  archive attributes, 25, 31, 92
  creating password-protected, with WinZip, 105–107
  for e-mail, 117
  viruses and, 72
Arms Export Control Act, 229
Armstrong v. Executive Office of the President, 117
Army Signal Corps, 227
ARPAnet, 167–168, 227
Articles of the Confederation, 136
Artistic Defense, 190
ASCII (American Standard Code for Information Interchange)
  encrypted messages based in, 131
  Nuke and, 100
  PGP and, 239–240, 243–245
  text encrypted in, 110
  viruses and, 58
ASM, 61
AT&T (American Telephone & Telegraph), 43–44, 78, 143, 168
  breakup of, 170
  Wireless Services, 161
ATMs (automatic teller machines), 77–78, 145, 151, 163, 248
ATTRIB, 74, 93
attributes, file, 92–94
  archive attribute, 25, 31, 92
  hidden attribute, 93
  system attribute, 92
AUTOEXEC.BAT, 71, 74
autosave features, 15
AVI files, 105

Babbage, Charles, 216
Baby Bell companies, 170
Bacard, Andre, 120

backup systems. *See also* archive files; tape backup
  the age of your equipment and, 27
  alternative strategies for, 30–31
  archive attributes and, 25
  automatic, 34, 35
  choosing tools for, 20–23
  creating good routines for, 23–24
  disaster planning and, 15, 16
  filtering out file types from, 32–34
  full, 20, 24–27, 31
  full vs. partial, 24–27
  importance of, 10–12
  networking and, 274
  password protection and, 88
  protection against hackers and, 50, 80
  restoring files after, example of, 31–35
  sample routine for, 31–35
  schedules, 15, 16, 22–24, 26–27, 34–35
  testing, 28–30
  viruses and, 61, 65
Bacon, Roger, 215
bacterium viruses, 61
Baker, Jake, 203–204
banking online, 1–2. *See also* financial transactions
  E-cash and, 150–161
  electronic checking, 145–150, 153, 154
  the Electronic Commerce Project and, 149–150
  overview of, 143–154
Bank of America, 144, 163
Bank of Montreal, 144
Bank One, 144
Barksdale, Jim, 161
Barlow, John Perry, 218
Barnett Bank, 144
Bass-O-Matic, 234
Bausewein, Hans, 130
BBSs (bulletin board systems), 44–45, 47
  AABBS (Amateur Action Bulletin Board Service), 190–192
  Communications Decency Act and, 200–202
  copyright infringements and, 55

e-mail and, 115, 116
filtering access to, 205–210
freedom of speech and, 190–192, 194, 200–202
indecent materials and, 190–192, 194, 200–202, 205–210
introduction of, 139
shareware and, 56
viruses and, 55–56, 59–60, 67, 71
Bell, Alexander Graham, 42, 223
Bell Labs, 42, 44, 64
Bell Telephone, 43–44
Berkeley Software, 80
Berners-Lee, Tim, 140, 162, 170
Bernoulli drives, 30
Bessemer Venture Partners, 164
Biham, Eli, 104
Bill of Rights, 2, 118, 158, 219
BIN extensions, 57
bindery emulation, 257
BIOS (Basic Input/Output System), 85–88
BIX, 139
Bizdos, Jim, 235
Blanchard, Robert G., 202
Bland, Stewart, 38
bookkeeping departments, 256–259
booting
  boot sector viruses, 67, 69
  boot sectors, 13, 14, 67, 69
  boot time passwords, 87
  DOS, 59
  from floppy disks, 59, 74
Boston Computer Exchange, 18
Boston Herald, 63
Boston University, 219
bottlenecks, 120
Brandeis, Louis, 185
Braughtigan, Richard, 185
Breasts virus, 70
Brooks, Jack, 233–234
browsers. *See also* Netscape Navigator browser
  accessing Web pages with, information provided when, 175
basic description of, 140
history of, 161–162
Internet Explorer, 67
Lynx browser, 170
Mosaic browser, 161–162, 170
text-only browsers, 170
Brunner, John, 62
brute force (cracking method), 78, 84, 221
bugs, 13, 61, 282. *See also* debugging

C (programming language), 13, 43, 104, 222
  PGP and, 237
  viruses and, 61
Caesar, Julius, 216
CAFE (Conditional Access for Europe), 155
Caltech, 41
Canada
  export laws and, 133, 222, 235
  obscenity standards in, 190
Capstone standard, 221, 231–234, 236
Captain Billy@sps Whiz Bang, 187
Carlin, George, 2, 194
Carlin Communications v. FCC, 194
CBS Network, 138, 140–141, 187, 223
CBS News, 140–141, 223
CBBS, 139, 192
cc:mail, 117
CD-ROMs, 16, 21
  floptical drives and, comparison of, 30
  Windows 95, 278, 296
CDs (compact discs), 30
cellular telephones, 224
censorship. *See* freedom of speech; indecent materials
Center for Mathematics and Computer Science, 157
CERN (European Particle Physics Laboratory), 140, 161–162, 170
Chaum, David, 154, 157
check objects, 145, 147
checksums, 68

Chemical Bank, 144
Chiffriermaschinen Aktiengesellschaft, 216
children, filtering Internet access for, 2, 205–210
ChinaTalk viruses, 66
Chinese language, version of Windows, 55
Christensen, Ward, 139, 192
Church of Scientology, 128
CIA (Central Intelligence Agency), 226
CitiBank, 144
CJRs (Commodity Jurisdiction Requests), 229, 230
Clark, James H., 161
client/server layouts, definition of, 270
Clinton, Bill, 124, 223, 224
  administration, 2, 47, 231–232, 234–235
Clipboard, 108–110
Clipper chip, 2, 47, 123, 231–234, 236
CMED104.ZIP, 93
CMOS (complimentary metal oxide semi-conductor) chip, 85–87
CNE (Certified NetWare Engineer), 250
CODE-1 virus, 70
Codebreakers, The (Kahn), 215, 227
Code of Academic Integrity, 63
Cohen, Fred, 62
Cohn, Avern, 204
Cold War, 40–41, 111, 139–140, 167, 217, 226
Colonial America, 136
Colorado Backup, 31–35
Colossus machine, 216
Comerwell Software Web page, 130
COM files, 57–59, 66, 68–69, 73
COMMAND.COM, 68
command line switches, 98–99
CommerceNet, 141, 142
commerce online. *See also* credit cards
  AOL and, 139
  ATMs (automatic teller machines) and, 77–78, 145, 151, 163, 248
  CompuServe and, 139, 142, 159–160
  E-cash (electronic cash), 150–161
  electronic checking and, 145–150, 153, 154
  history of, 136–142
  home shopping and, 137–138
  Netscape and, 161–163
  overview of, 135–165
  PINs (Personal Identification Numbers) and, 77–79, 160, 225
  Prodigy and, 139
  protocols and, 150, 162–164
  the World Wide Web and, 139–142
Commerce Server (Netscape), 161–162, 165
Commodore 64, 20
Common Ground: Fundamental Principles for the National Information Infrastructure, 124
Communications Decency Act of 1995 (CDA), 188, 203, 206
  analysis of, 195, 200–202
  text for, 195–200
compression, data, 60. *See also* ZIP archive files
  backup systems and, 20, 30
  PKZIP and, 30, 62, 65, 104–106, 227
  viruses and, 74
  WinZip and, 30, 56, 72–73, 105–107
CompuServe (CIS), 71, 116, 170
  community-based standards and, 192–193
  Digital Telephony Bill and, 225
  financial transactions and, 139, 142, 159–160
  indecent materials and, 192–193, 202–203, 210
  password protection and, 77
  subscribers, number of, vs. other online services, 142
computer(s)
  prices of, 10, 18–19
  replacing, recovery plans for, 17–19
  systems, cost of, vs. the cost of data, 10
Computer Fraud and Abuse Act, 63–64
Computer Privacy Handbook (Bacard), 120
Computer Systems Research Group, 63
"computer underground," 44–48, 220–221
CONFIG.POL, 279
CONFIG.SYS, 74

Congress, 64, 123, 143, 168, 219
  Arms Export Control Act, 229
  Computer Fraud and Abuse Act, 63–64
  Digital Telephony Bill, 122, 224–225, 231
  Electronic Communications Privacy Act, 118, 121, 134
  Espionage Act, 218, 219
  Federal Records Act, 117
  Freedom of Information Act (FOIA), 219, 220
  Telecommunications Competition and Deregulation Act of 1995, 195, 201
  Telecommunications Reform Act of 1996, 170, 195
console commands, 258
Constitution, 2, 45–46, 118, 122, 134, 158, 236
  Bill of Rights, 2, 118, 158, 219
  First Amendment, 187–195, 219, 229, 236
  Fourth Amendment, 2, 45–46, 158, 219
  Ninth Amendment, 2, 158
Constitutional Convention of 1787, 136
Control Panel, 274, 278, 287, 296
CONVERT command, 281
Cookies virus, 66
COPY command, 94
copyright protection, 54–55, 128, 230
Corel, 56
Core War, 64
Cornell University, 63, 64
court cases
  Armstrong v. Executive Office of the President, 117
  Carlin Communications v. FCC, 194
  Cubby, Inc. v. CompuServe, 202–203
  Ginsberg v. New York, 193
  Miller v. California, 189
  Osborne v. Ohio, 194
  People v. Jake Baker, 203–204
  Roe v. Wade, 118, 158
  Sable Communications of California v. FCC, 192
  Stanley v. Georgia, 194
CP/M, 139

CP-V systems, 40–41
CPUs (central processing units), 62, 74
Crack (application), 255
crackers, 2, 12, 165. *See also* hackers
  basic description of, 38, 41–42
  the computer underground and, 44–48
crashes, loss of e-mail due to, 117, 120. *See* hardware failures
create rights, 258
credit bureaus, 47
credit card(s), 47, 77–78, 182. *See also* financial transactions
  E-cash and, 154–155
  history of, 135, 151
  Netscape and, 164
  numbers, scanning for, with sniffers, 181–182
  privacy rights and, 46
  smart cards and, 153
  transactions, level of trust in, 143, 145, 163
  transactions with CompuServe, 159
cryptography. *See also* encryption
  e-mail and, 130–133
  history of, 215–222
  as a munition of war, 229–230
Ctrl+Alt+Del, 14
Ctrl+Alt+Esc, 86
Cubby v. CompuServe, 202–203
Cuckoo's Egg, The (Stoll), 41
Cyberbucks, 159
Cyber Patrol, 207–210
Cyber Patrol Web page, 207

daemons, definition of, 40
DAT (digital audio tape), 20–21
data, high cost of recreating, 1, 10, 15, 19
data compression, 60. *See also* ZIP archive files
  backup systems and, 20, 30
  PKZIP and, 30, 62, 65, 104–106, 227

(continued)

data compression *(continued)*
   viruses and, 74
   WinZip and, 30, 56, 72–73, 105–107
date, system, 274
DD.EXE, 94
DEA (Data Encryption Algorithm), 107
debit cards, 151
DEBUG, 65, 254
debugging, 65, 254, 276
Declaration of Independence, 228
Defense Department (United States), 167–168
DEL command, 97, 98
deleted files. *See also* deleting files
   entries for, in the FAT, 97
   which are overwritten, recovering, 98–99
deleting files. *See also* deleted files
   networking and, 259
   Nuke and, 98–101
Deluxe, 144
demographic information, for Internet users, 140–142
demonstration versions (demos), 14
Department of Defense (United States), 167–168
Department of Justice (United States), 63, 218–220
Department of State (United States), 222, 229, 230, 235
DES (Data Encryption Standard) encryption, 220, 222, 229, 231, 236, 283
   basic description of, 107–111
   DES for Windows, 108–109
   development of, 226–227
   Single DES mode, 109
   Triple DES mode, 109
DETLOG.OLD, 100
Dial-a-Porn case, 193
Dial-up Networking, 80–81, 281
DialAccess() function, 78–79
Diffie, Whitfield, 153, 227–228, 230–231, 234
Diffie-Hellman type algorithms, 153, 227–228, 230–231, 234
DigiCash, 154–156, 159

DigiCash Web Page, 155
Digital Equipment, 222
digital signatures, 131, 228
   basic description of, 153
   blind, 153, 157–159
   DSS (Digital Signature Standard) for, 221
   E-cash and, 156–157
   electronic checking and, 147, 148, 153
   Netscape and, 164–165
   PGP and, 245
   smart cards and, 153, 159
   VeriSign and, 164–165
Digital Telephony Bill (Wiretap Bill), 122, 224–225, 231
Diller, Barry, 138
Diners Club, 151
DIR command, 93–94
directories
   directory rights and, 258–259
   root, 14
   sharing, 284, 288–292
Dirmeyer, David H., 190
disaster recovery plans, 15–19
   creating, 16–19
   five simple questions for, 16–19
disks, floppy
   backup systems and, 20, 30, 88
   booting from, 59, 74
   capacity of, 20, 21
   copying, intellectual property issues and, 54–55
   cracking programs on, 104–105
   failure of, 13
   floppy disk controllers, 22
   high-density, 30
   viruses and, 53–56, 59, 66, 69, 74
   write-protecting, 74
DLLs (Dynamic Link Libraries), 32, 33
   file trick for, 94–95
   viruses and, 57, 68
DOC files, 96
Dole, Robert, 188
domain, definition of, 270

DOS (Disk Operating System), 86, 258
  640K barrier, 57
  backup systems and, 20, 21, 25, 31
  basic description of, 43
  booting, 59
  COPY command, 94
  DEBUG command, 65
  DEL command, 97, 98
  ERASE command, 98
  error messages, 59
  file attributes and, 93–94
  FORMAT command, 100, 281
  hidden files and, 92
  Internet access and, 170
  PGP and, 130–132, 237, 246
  trick involving deleted files, 97
  UNIX daemons and, 40
  viruses and, 55, 57–59, 67–68, 73–74
Dow Jones News Retrieval Service, 202
downloading files
  downloading versions of PGP, 237
  viruses and, 50, 57, 59–60, 64
driver's license numbers, 145, 158, 164
DriveSpace, 60
DSS (Digital Signature Standard), 221
Dynamic Link Libraries (DLLs), 32, 33
  file trick for, 94–95
  viruses and, 57, 68

◆ E ◆

E-cash (electronic cash), 150–161. *See also*
   financial transactions
Ecclesiastes, 135
ECHO command, 258
EDS (Electronic Data Systems), 160
Edwards, Dan, 62
EFF (Electronic Frontier Foundation), 124,
   191–192, 195, 218
  Digital Telephony Bill and, 224–225
  Web Page, 191
electrodes, 42

electronic checking, 145–150
  bad checks and, 146
  digital signatures and, 147, 148, 153
  the Electronic Check Project and, 145–149
  security of, vs. other forms of transactions, 145
  smart cards and, 154
Electronic Commerce Project (FSTC),
   149–150
Electronic Communications Privacy Act,
   118, 121, 134
Electronic Privacy Information Center
   (EPIC), 220, 224
e-mail, 29, 47, 117–119
  anonymous remailers and, 125–128, 238
  deleting, 120
  DES for Windows and, 110–111
  division of, into packets, 181, 182
  fakemail, 125–127, 175
  passwords and, 172
  privacy rights and, 3, 122–125
  reading of, with a sniffer, 182
  removing, from servers, 120
  security of, vs. other kinds of mail,
    116–121, 181
  steps for securing, 128–133
  types of, 115–116
  viruses and, 58
  what to include and exclude from, 125, 133
emergency procedures, 253
EMV (Europay, MasterCard, VISA) standard, 154
encryption
  cracking, with brute force, 78, 84, 221
  DES (Data Encryption Standard) encryption,
    107–111, 220, 222, 226–227, 229, 231,
    236, 283
  E-cash and, 151–161
  electronic checking and, 147, 149, 150
  EPIC briefing report on, 220
  file formats and, 96
  IDEA (International Data Encryption
    Algorithm), 221, 229
  methods, overview of, 103–107, 215–246

encryption *(continued)*
  PGP (Pretty Good Privacy) encryption, 130–133, 162, 221, 234–246
  public key encryption, 130, 147, 155–157, 162–164, 222, 228–230
  RSA (Rivest-Shamir-Adleman) encryption, 155, 162–164
  strong, government regulations regarding, 131, 133, 222, 229–230, 235
English common law, 123
English Learning Center, 127
Enigma machine, 216
EPIC (Electronic Privacy Information Center), 220, 224
Equifax, 144
ERASE command, 98
error messages, 59
Espionage Act, 218, 219
Eudora, 229
Eudora Lite, 130–131
Eudora Pro for 32-bit Windows, 130
Europay, 154
European Particle Physics Laboratory (CERN), 140, 161–162, 170
EXE files
  PGP and, 237
  viruses and, 57–59, 66, 68–69, 73, 94
Executive Order 12864, 124
Exon, James, 47, 188, 195, 200
Explorer (Windows 95), 32, 106
export law, 133, 222, 229–230, 235

fakemail, 125–127, 175
FAQs (Frequently Asked Questions), 120
FAT (File Allocation Table)
  corrupt, 13
  C programming and, 13
  entries in, for deleted files, 97
  Nuke and, 100
  security holes and, 284
  viruses and, 68

FDISK, 74
Federal Bureau of Investigation (FBI), 41, 47, 122–123, 130, 204, 217, 220, 223–224, 232, 249
Federal Communications Commission (FCC), 168–169, 192, 194
  Carlin Communications v. FCC, 194
  Communications Decency Act and, 201
  Digital Telephony Bill and, 225
  Sable Communications of California v. FCC, 192
Federal Express, 161
Federal Records Act, 117
Federal Reserve, 107, 135, 150
FedWire, 150
Feistel, Horst, 226
fiber-optic cable, 170
FidoNet, 115
Fifth Amendment, 158, 219, 236
file(s). *See also* file attributes; file extensions; file types
  formats, 96
  hidden, 25, 49, 92–94
  individual, password protection for, 88
  names, long, 22
  overwriting, 98–101
  page, creating, 276
  read-only, 25, 32, 49, 93
  sharing, 178, 284–286
  shredding, 98–103, 108
  size changes, viruses and, 73
file attributes, 92–94
  archive attribute, 25, 31, 92
  hidden attribute, 93
  system attribute, 92
file extensions
  BAT, 258
  DLL, 57
  TWL, 81
file infectors, 68, 73. *See also* viruses
filing systems
  NTFS filing system, 281–282, 284, 290–291
  Windows NT filing system, 281
File Manager, 103, 106, 290

File⇨Open, 32
FILER, 256
File⇨Save, 32
File⇨Save As, 32
file types. *See also* archive files
  ARC files, 72, 105
  ASC files, 244
  AVI files, 105
  COM files, 57–59, 66, 68–69, 73
  DOC files, 96
  EXE files, 57–59, 66, 68–69, 73, 94, 237
  filtering out, from backup systems, 32–34
  FST files, 32
  LHZ files, 72
  OVL files, 57
  OVR files, 57
  PWL files, 283
filtering programs, 205–210
financial transactions. *See also* credit cards
  AOL and, 139
  ATMs (automatic teller machines) and, 77–78, 145, 151, 163, 248
  CompuServe and, 139, 142, 159–160
  E-cash (electronic cash), 150–161
  electronic checking and, 145–150, 153, 154
  history of, 136–142
  home shopping and, 137–138
  Netscape and, 161–163
  overview of, 135–165
  PINs (Personal Identification Numbers) and, 77–79, 160, 225
  Prodigy and, 139
  protocols and, 150, 162–164
  World Wide Web and, 139–142
Finger, 180
Finland, 128
firewalls, 177
First Amendment, 187–195, 219, 229, 236
First Data Corporation, 163
First USA, 160
First Virtual, 144, 159–161
First Virtual Web page, 161
Fischer International, 164
Flame virus, 69

floppy disk(s)
  backup systems and, 20, 30, 88
  booting from, 59, 74
  capacity of, 20, 21
  controllers, 22
  copying, intellectual property issues and, 54–55
  cracking programs on, 104–105
  failure of, 13
  high-density, 30
  viruses and, 53–56, 59, 66, 69, 74
  write-protecting, 74
floptical drives, 30
FIOA (Freedom of Information Act), 219, 220
FontFinder viruses, 66
FOR command, 78
FORJOE.ASC, 244
FORMAT, 65, 74, 281
Fortune, 233
Fourth Amendment, 2, 45–46, 158, 219
Fox Network, 138
France Telecom, 152
Franklin, Benjamin, 115
fraud, electronic, 63–64, 143–144, 149, 182. *See also* hackers
Free Agent newsreader, 209
free assembly, right to, 192
Freedom of Information Act (FOIA), 219, 220
freedom of speech, 124, 187–188. *See also* indecent materials
  distribution of encryption information and, 229
  First Amendment and, 187–195, 219, 229, 236
Freeh, Louis, 223, 232
freeware, 56
Friar Tuck, 40–41
Friedman, William F., 219
FSTC (Financial Services Technology Consortium), 144, 145, 147–150
FST files, 32
FTP (File Transfer Protocol), 98, 163, 177
  activity, logs of, 176
  personal Web pages and, 179
  search engines and, 180

✦ G ✦

games, 50, 55, 59
Garfinkel, Simson, 235, 246
Gates, Bill, 116, 127, 128
General Motors, 160
GEnie, 139
Gilmore, John, 218–219, 227
Gimon, Charles A., 127
Gingrich, Newt, 195
Ginsberg v. New York, 193
God, acts of, 13–15
Golden Isle Vacation Property Management program, 24–25
Good Times virus, 58
Gore, Albert, 231
grace logins, 260–261
Greek civilization, 53
grids, telephone technology and, 42
GTE Telemail network, 249
Guest accounts, 260
Guidoboni, Thomas, 64

✦ H ✦

hacker(s), 87, 165. *See also* crackers; phreaks
  aliases for, 45
  basic description of, 37–52
  commercial, 45–47
  computer underground and, 44–48, 220–221
  curious, with high technical competence, 50
  determined, with high technical competence, 50–51
  e-mail and, 119–122
  Finger and, 180
  government, 45–47
  merely curious, with low technical experience, 49–50
  networking and, 261
  system administrators and, 172–175
  thieves, 49
  vs. users who are their own worst enemies, 10
Hacker Crackdown, The (Sterling), 37–38
Hackers (movie), 174
Hall, Justin, 205
handshaking routines, 164
Hannum, Charles M. II, 98
hard disk(s)
  boot sectors, 13, 14, 67, 69
  dead spaces on, 60
  defragmenting, 60
  failures, 13, 16–19, 27
  full backups for, 20, 24–25, 31
  heads, 99
  magnetized surface of, 99
  MTBF (Mean Time Between Failures) ratings for, 13, 27
  prices of, drop in, 18
  root directories, 14
  sectors, 13, 14, 60, 67–69, 87, 97, 100
  space taken up by program code on, 32–33
  storage capacity of, 20
  technical specifications, 13, 27
  tracks, 60
  viruses and, 60–61, 65, 70, 73–74
hardware
  failures, 1, 10, 13, 16–19, 27
  operating systems and, relationship of, 43
hash functions, 221
Hazlitt, William, 267
HBO (Home Box Office), 170
Hellman, Martin, 227, 228, 230, 234
Helsingius, Johan, 128
Hercules graphics cards, 51
hidden files, 25, 49, 92–94
hieroglyphics, 216
Hill, R. J., 101
Hoffman, Abie, 38
home pages (listed by name). *See also* Web pages
  Comerwell Software Web page, 130
  Cyber Patrol Web page, 207

DigiCash Web page, 155
Electronic Frontier Foundation Web page, 191
First Virtual Web page, 161
Lawrence Livermore Labs Web page, 144
Microsoft Web page, 58
Massachusetts Institute of Technology Web page, 237
Net Nanny Web page, 210
SafeSurf Web page, 210
Surf Watch Web page, 210
Homer, 53
Hooper, Grace, 62
HSN (Home Shopping Network), 138
HTML (HyperText Markup Language), 210
HTTP (HyperText Transfer Protocol), 162–164, 177
humor, hacker stories and, 40–41
Hustler, 194

IBM (International Business Machines), 107, 163
  Lucifer algorithm, 226
  PC Monochrome Monitor, 51
IBMIO.SYS, 57
IDEA (International Data Encryption Algorithm), 221, 229
IDE tape drives, 22
Illiad (Homer), 53
indecent materials, 171, 185–212
  AOL and, 192–193, 210
  BBSs and, 190–192, 194, 200–202, 205–210
  Communications Decency Act of 1995 and, 188, 195–203, 206
  CompuServe and, 192–193, 202–203, 210
  filtering access to, 205–210
  ISPs and, 200–203
  legal issues regarding, overview of, 185–202
  online services and, 192–203

Prodigy and, 192–193, 202, 210
  self-regulation of the Internet, 205
INDEX.HTML, 179
installation
  backup systems and, 16, 32, 34
  of PGP, 131, 237–246
  of Windows 95, 178
insurance coverage, 10, 14–15, 17–18
Intel, 254, 255, 269
intellectual property rights, 54–55. *See also* copyright protection
interest rates, 151
International Association of Cryptologic Research, 154
International Data Encryption Algorithm (IDEA), 221, 229
International Traffic in Arms Regulation (ITAR), 229–230, 235
Internet. *See also* ISPs (Internet Service Providers); online services; World Wide Web
  basic description of, 167–170
  demographics, 140–142
  filtering access to, 205–210
  financial transactions and, 135–165
  history of, 139–140, 167–170
  messaging routes on, 120, 167–168, 177, 181, 182
  ownership of, 168–169
  security, overview of, 167–184
  unwanted material on, 185–212
Internet Architecture Board, 169
Internet Explorer (Microsoft), 67
Internet Society, 169
Internet Standards Committee, 169
Internet Worm, 63, 80
Interpol, 128
interrupt
  use of the term, 73
  vector mapping, 73–74
Investors Business Daily, 232
Iomega, 30
IO.SYS, 57, 68

IP (Internet Protocol) addresses, 175, 176–177, 181
Iran-Contra scandal, 120
IRMs (inherited rights masks), 256, 259, 262, 264
IRS (Internal Revenue Service), 19, 47, 157, 232
IS (Information Services) managers, 16
isolationism, 226
ISPs (Internet Service Providers)
  basic description of, 140
  electronic commerce and, 143
  e-mail and, 117, 118, 121
  evaluating the quality of, 173
  indecent materials and, 200–203
  information recorded by, 175–176
ITAR (International Traffic in Arms Regulation), 229–230, 235

◆ J ◆

Jabberwocky, 67
Jargon File, The, 38
Jefferson, Thomas, 216
Jerusalem virus, 69
JPG format, 96
Justice Department (United States), 63, 218–220

◆ K ◆

Kahil Gibran, 37
Kahn, David, 215–216, 227, 228
Kapor, Mitch, 218
Karn, Phil, 229, 230
Katz, Phil, 65
Kerberos, 222
key escrow, 231–234
keyrings, 238, 241–242
KGB, 41
Kocher, Paul C., 104

◆ L ◆

Lai, Xuejia, 221
Landreth, Bill, 248–251, 260
LANs (local area networks), 116
Lantastic, 26
Latin, 62
Lawrence Berkeley Labs, 41
Lawrence Livermore Labs Web page, 144
Leahy, Patrick, 224
legal cases
  Armstrong v. Executive Office of the President, 117
  Carlin Communications v. FCC, 194
  Cubby v. CompuServe, 202–203
  Ginsberg v. New York, 193
  Miller v. California, 189
  Osborne v. Ohio, 194
  People v. Jake Baker, 203–204
  Roe v. Wade, 118, 158
  Sable Communications of California v. FCC, 192
  Stanley v. Georgia, 194
legislation
  Arms Export Control Act, 229
  Computer Fraud and Abuse Act, 63–64
  Digital Telephony Bill, 122, 224–225, 231
  Electronic Communications Privacy Act, 118, 121, 134
  Espionage Act, 218, 219
  Federal Records Act, 117
  Freedom of Information Act (FOIA), 219, 220
  Telecommunications Competition and Deregulation Act of 1995, 195, 201
  Telecommunications Reform Act of 1996, 170, 195
Letterman, David, 92
Leven, Vladimir, 144
LHA, 30
LHZ files, 72
libraries. *See* Dynamic Link Libraries (DLLs)
Links from the Underground, 205

LISTDIR command, 259
Lotus 1-2-3, 217
Lotus Development, 217, 222
Lucifer algorithm, 226
Luster, Kevin, 255
Lynx browser, 170
LZH format, 105

✦ M ✦

MacinTalk, 66, 70
Macintosh
　backup systems and, 31
　Internet access and, 170
　operating system, 43
　viruses and, 62, 66, 70, 71
macro code, 58
MacWorld, 123
mail order companies, 18
Mak, Nico, 56, 105
Malden, Karl, 16
man-in-the-middle attacks, 242
Mark Twain Bank of Saint Louis, 159
Massey, James, 221
MasterCard International, 154, 163
master mode, 40
McCarthy, Joseph, 226
McCaw Cellular, 161
MCI, 78, 116, 139, 163, 168
MCI Mail, 116, 139
McNamara, Thomas E., 230
McVey, Timothy, 223
McWethy, John, 223
MD2 hash function, 221
MD4 hash function, 221
MD5 hash function, 221
Meeks, Brock N., 232
Member utility, 74
memory
　available, unexplained changes in, 74
　locking pages in, 276
　RAM (random-access memory), 74, 85
　smart cards and, 152, 153

Mencken, H. L., 91
MENSA, 88
Mesopotamia, 216
Message⇨Run PGP, 131
Michelangelo virus, 58, 59, 66, 70
Microsoft. *See also* specific software
　Microsoft Access, 65
　Microsoft Mail, 117
　Microsoft Network (MSN), 29, 67, 71
　Microsoft Plus!, 72
　PKCS (Public Key Cryptography Standards) and, 222
　SafeSurf ratings and, 210
　SSL protocol and, 163
　Web page, URL for, 58
MIDS (Matrix Information and Directory Services), 141–142
Miller v. California, 189
MIME (Multipurpose Internet Mail Extensions), 164
misdirection schemes, 94–96
mission-critical data, 26, 27
MIT (Massachusetts Institute of Technology), 62, 64, 155, 222, 227–228, 235–237
MIT Web page, 237
Mitsubishi Corporation, 164
MKE (mandatory key escrow), 234
mockingbird viruses, 61
modems, 4, 47, 115
money. *See* financial transactions
Morris, Robert (father), 80
Morris, Robert Tappan, Jr. (son), 63–64, 80
Morrissey, Mark, 255
Morse code, 234
Mosaic browser, 161–162, 170
motion detectors, 47
Motorola, 40–41
MSBACKUP, 22
MSDOS.SYS, 57
MSN (Microsoft Network), 29, 67, 71
Mueller, John, 247
Munson, Howard G., 64
Murphy's Law, 9

✦ N ✦

Natas virus, 58, 70
National Bureau of Standards, 217, 226
National Center for Superconducting Applications (NCSA), 161–162, 170
National Computer Crimes Squad, 247
National Computer Security Center, 64
National Information Infrastructure (NII), 124
National Institute of Standards and Technology (NIST), 217, 226, 231
National Public Radio, 137
National Science Foundation (NSF), 168
National Security Agency (NSA), 62, 64, 107, 123, 130, 217–220, 226–231, 235
National Security Council, 217
NationsBank, 144
natural disasters, 14–15.
    See also acts of God
Navy (United States), 62, 216
NDS (NetWare Directory Services), 257
NETLOGON, 279
Net Nanny Web page, 210
Netscape Communications Corporation, 161–163. *See also* Netscape Navigator browser
Netscape Navigator browser, 222
    Commerce Server, 161–162, 165
    e-mail and, 119, 129
    financial transactions and, 161–163
    history of, 161–162, 170
    newsgroup access, 176
    SafeSurf ratings and, 210
    SSL (Secure Sockets Layer) protocol, 129, 162–164
NetWare, 251, 256–265
networking, 4, 50, 80–81, 89
    account policies, 271–274
    assigning rights for, 260–265
    backup systems and, 22, 26, 27, 29
    developing internal policies for, 270–271
    documenting security procedures for, 253–255
    local groups and, 296–298
    managing users and, 296–299
    network administrators and, 253, 254, 256
    overview of, 247–260
    resources, establishing, 284–295
    security holes and, 282–284
    sharing directories, 284, 288–292
    sharing files, 178, 284–286
    sharing printers, 178, 284–286, 292–295
    terminology, 269–270
    user accounts for, setting up, 298–299
    viruses and, 59–60, 62–64
    with Windows, sharing resources and, 267–300
New Look, 66
newsgroups, 47. *See also* newsreaders
    anonymous remailers and, 127, 128
    basic description of, 127
    e-mail and, 127–129
    filtering access to, 205–210
    freedom of speech and, 194, 202, 203–204
    ROT-13 and, 129
    spamming and, 174
    subscription information for, documentation of, 176–177
newsreaders
    Free Agent newsreader, 209
    TRN newsreader, 176
    NN newsreader, 176
New Zealand virus, 69
NEXT command, 78
NII (National Information Infrastructure), 124
Ninth Amendment, 2, 158
NIST (National Institute of Standards and Technology), 217, 226, 231
NLM (Netware Loadable Module), 26
NN newsreader, 176
node, definition of, 269
NORMAL.DOT, 58
North, Oliver, 120
North Star Systems, 26
Norton Utilities, 95, 100, 103
NovaBack, 26
Novell, 26, 43, 50, 251, 256–265

NSA (National Security Agency), 62, 64, 107, 123, 130, 217–220, 226–231, 235
NSFNET, 168
NTFS filing system, 281–282, 284, 290–291
Nuke for DOS, 98–101
nVir viruses, 70
NVP viruses, 66

objects
　check objects, 145, 147
　definition of, as network elements, 257
　shared objects, 276
　token objects, 276
obscenity. *See* indecent material
Odyssey (Homer), 53
Oklahoma City bombing, 223
online commerce. *See also* credit cards
　AOL and, 139
　ATMs (automatic teller machines) and, 77–78, 145, 151, 163, 248
　CompuServe and, 139, 142, 159–160
　E-cash (electronic cash), 150–161
　electronic checking and, 145–150, 153, 154
　history of, 136–142
　home shopping and, 137–138
　Netscape and, 161–163
　overview of, 135–165
　PINs (Personal Identification Numbers) and, 77–79, 160, 225
　Prodigy and, 139
　protocols and, 150, 162–164
　World Wide Web and, 139–142
online services. *See also* AOL (America Online); CompuServe (CIS); MSN (Microsoft Network); Prodigy
　backup systems and, 29, 30
　the Communications Decency Act and, 200–202
　community-based standards and, 192–193
　Digital Telephony Bill and, 225
　e-mail and, 115, 116, 125
　financial transactions and, 139, 142, 159–160
　history of, 139, 170
　indecent materials and, 192–193, 202–203, 210
　password protection and, 77
　shareware and, 56
　subscribers, number of, vs. other online services, 142
　user demographics, 141, 142
　viruses and, 58–60, 71
OOP (object-oriented programming), 147
operating systems, definition of, 43
OS/2, 22
Osborne v. Ohio, 194
Out of the Inner Circle (Landreth), 248
overwriting files, 98–101
OVL files, 57
OVR files, 57

page files, creating, 276
Paint (Microsoft), 16
Paint Shop Pro, 56
parallel ports, 22
parameters, 59
Paramount Pictures, 138
paranoia, 48
parental control, of Internet access, 2, 205–210
passphrases, 239
password(s)
　basic description of, 77–90
　BIOS level, 85–86
　boot time, 87
　caching, 283
　choosing, rules of thumb for, 82–85
　cracking, 42, 50, 78–82
　derivative, 84
　DES for Windows and, 107–110
　E-cash and, 155, 156

password(s) *(continued)*
  effectiveness of, 79–82
  e-mail and, 116, 172
  erasing, 87
  for individual files, 88
  mathematics of, 78–79
  networking and, 248–253, 255, 271–274, 281–283, 286–292, 298–299
  personal Web pages and, 179
  secret key encryption and, 227
  security holes and, 282–283
  security plans and, 252–253
  SLL protocols and, 164
  spoofing and, 88–89
  two-step method for, 84
  weak, problem of, 172, 174
  WinZip and, 105–107
patents, 230, 235
PATH statements, 98
Paxson, Lowell W., 138
payloads, 54, 60, 66, 70, 73–74
PBX switchboards, 45
peer-to-peer layouts, definition of, 270
PEM (Privacy Enhanced Mail), 222
pen registers, 118
Pentagon, 139
Penthouse, 193, 194, 203
People v. Jake Baker, 203–204
PERL, 254
Perot, H. Ross, 160
personal Web pages, 179
PGP (Pretty Good Privacy) encryption, 130–133, 162
  available versions of, 237
  basic description of, 234–246
  certifying keys for, 241–242
  digital signatures and, 245
  encrypting messages with, 243–244
  generating keys with, 238–240
  IDEA and, 221
  installing, 237–246
  politics surrounding, overview of, 234–236
  unencrypting messages with, 245

PGP-Eudora, 130–131
PGP Phone, 225
Phoenix Technologies, 85
PhotoPaint, 56
PhotoShop, 56
phreaks, 2, 42–48. *See also* hackers
  basic description of, 42–44
  vs. users who are their own worst enemies, 12
pin registers, 225
Ping, 180–181
PINs (Personal Identification Numbers), 77–79, 160, 225
pirate software, 54–55
PKCS (Public Key Cryptography Standards), 222
PKWare, 65, 104, 106
PKZIP, 30, 104–106, 227
  password protection and, 106
  viruses and, 62, 65
plans
  recovery plans, 17–19
  security plans, 252–253
Playboy, 193, 194, 205
POP (Post Office Protocol), 117, 178
Popular Electronics, 37–38
pornography, 47, 182, 189. *See also* indecent materials
POST (power on self-test), 85
Postal Service (United States), 116, 122, 137
power on self-test (POST), 85
power supplies, CMOS, 87
Prank macro virus, 58
printers, sharing, 178, 284–286, 292–295
Print Manager, 293–294
privacy rights, 2–3, 45–46
  E-cash and, 157–159
  e-mail and, 118–119, 122–125
  in the workplace, 123–124
processors. *See* CPUs (central processing units)
Prodigy, 71, 77
  community-based standards and, 192–193
  development of the Internet and, 170

e-mail, 116
financial transactions and, 139
indecent materials and, 192–193, 202, 210
subscribers, number of, vs. other online services, 142
Program Manager, 103
property rights, 123, 124
PROTECT.ZIP, 105
protocols. *See also* protocols (listed by name)
　electronic checking and, 150
　fakemail and, 126
　financial transactions and, 162–164, 150
protocols (listed by name). *See also* protocols
　FTP (File Transfer Protocol), 98, 163, 176–177, 179–180
　HTTP (HyperText Transfer Protocol), 162–164, 177
　IP (Internet Protocol) addresses, 175–177, 181
　POP (Post Office Protocol), 117, 178
　SMTP (Simple Mail Transfer Protocol), 117
　SSL (Secure Sockets Layer) protocol, 129, 162–164
　TCP/IP (Transmission Control Protocol/Internet Protocol), 163, 168
psychology, of hackers, 44
public key encryption, 228–230
　E-cash and, 155–157
　electronic checking and, 147
　e-mail and, 130
　RSA (Rivest-Shamir-Adleman) encryption, 155, 162–164
　standards, 222
Public Key Partners, 230
PUBRING.PGP, 239
pull payments, 149
Purdue University, 63
push payments, 149
PWL files, 283

QEMM, 74
QIC (Quarter-inch cartridge) tapes, 20–21
Qualicomm, 130
Quick View, 95–96
quotas, increasing, 276
QVC Network, 137, 140

rabbit viruses, 62
radio, 138–139, 142, 169
RAM (random-access memory)
　chips, testing, 85
　unexplained changes in, viruses and, 74
Rand, Ayn, 215
RC2 encryption function, 222
RC4 encryption function, 222
read-only files, 25, 32, 49, 93
read-only rights, 258
recovery
　of overwritten files, 98–99
　plans, 15–19
Recycle Bin (Windows 95), 97
Registry, 22, 31, 80, 279–280
Registry Editor, 279
Renaissance, 228
Reno, Janet, 223
Richey, Charles, 230
Riordan, Michael, 222
Rivest, Ronald L., 221, 228–229, 230, 234
Robb, Chuck, 201
Robin Hood, 40–41
Roccanti, Richard, 11, 115
Roe v. Wade, 118, 158
Rose Bowl, 39
ROT-13 (Netscape), 129
routers, 177
RSA Data Security, 164, 222, 230, 235
RSA (Rivest-Shamir-Adleman) encryption, 155, 162–164. *See also* public key encryption

RSA Laboratories, 221–222
RSAREF, 222–223, 237
RTF (Rich Text Format), 67

Sable Communications of California v. FCC, 192
safe-deposit boxes, 29–30
safe hex, 71–75
SafeSurf ratings system, 210
SafeSurf Web Page, 210
sales departments, 256–259
Saltzman, Jeff, 108–109
Scheduler (Windows 95), 34–35
schedules, backup system, 15–16, 22–24, 26–27, 34–35
Scherbius, Arthur, 216
Schliemann, Heinrich, 53
Schneier, Bruce, 229
Schwartz, Randal, 254–255
Scientific American, 157, 228–229, 234
SCO (Santa Cruz Operation), 43
Scott, Ryan, 126–127
SCSI (Small Computer System Interface), 74
SEARCH.COM, 14
search engines, 180
Sears and Roebuck, 137
secret key encryption, 156, 222, 227
SECRET.TXT, 109
SECRING.PGP, 239, 245
secure HTTP, 164. *See also* HTTP (HyperText Transfer Protocol)
Security Dynamics, 164
Settings⇨File Filter, 32
SETUP.DOC, 237
shadow files, 80
Shamir, Adi, 228–229, 234
shared key cards, 152
shared objects, 276
shareware
  DLL files and, 94
  viruses and, 56

sharing. *See also* networking
  directories, 284, 288–292
  files, 178, 284–286
  printers, 178, 284–286, 292–295
Shehas virus, 70
Shockwave Riders, The (Brunner), 62
shredding files, 98–103, 108
SHS (Secure Hash Standard), 221
shut down, system, 275
Sidekick, 40
signatures, digital, 131, 228
  basic description of, 153
  blind, 153, 157–159
  E-cash and, 156–157
  electronic checking and, 147–148, 153
  Netscape and, 164–165
  PGP and, 245
  smart cards and, 153, 159
  VeriSign and, 164–165
Silicon Graphics, 161, 255
Skipjack, 231
skytales, 216
smart cards
  access to data stored on, types of, 153
  basic description of, 148, 152–154
  digital signatures and, 159
  E-cash and, 155–156
  four types of, 152–154
SMITH.ASC, 240
SMTP (Simple Mail Transport Protocol), 117
snail mail, 116. *See also* Postal Service (United States)
sniffers, 119, 181–183
snoops, 119–122, 164, 177
Social Security Administration (SSA), 158
social security numbers, 145, 158
Socrates, 37
software failures, 13–15. *See also* bugs
Sommer, George, 17
Source, The, 139
SPA (Software Publishers Association), 222
spamming, 174-175
speech synthesizers, 66

spoofing, 88–89, 126, 164
spreadsheets
  importance of securing, 1–2
  password protection and, 88
  proprietary file formats for, 96
Sprint, 78, 152
SSL (Secure Sockets Layer) protocol, 129, 162–164
SSN (Social Security Administration), 158
Stacker, 60
standard(s)
  Capstone standard, 221, 231–234, 236
  community-based standards and, 192–193
  DES (Data Encryption Standard), 107–111, 220, 222, 226–227, 229, 231, 236, 283
  DSS (Digital Signature Standard) for, 221
  EMV (Europay, MasterCard, VISA) standard, 154
  PKCS (Public Key Cryptography Standards), 222
  SHS (Secure Hash Standard), 221
standard operating procedures, 253
Stanford University, 153, 227
Stanley v. Georgia, 194
Star Trek IV: The Voyage Home (movie), 150
State Department (United States), 222, 229–230, 235
STDIO.H, 104
Stein, Lee, 160
Sterling, Bruce, 37–38
Stewart, Jim, 223
Stoll, Clifford, 41
Stoned virus, 59, 69
Strip Cipher, 216
Sun Microsystems, 218, 222
Sunday virus, 69
supervisor
  privileges, 250–252
  rights, 258
Supreme Court, 2, 118, 158, 188–194, 236. *See also* legal cases
Surf Watch, 210
Surf Watch Web Page, 210

Suriv virus, 69
Sweden Post, 159
Swiss Federal Institute of Technology, 221
switches
  /Cn switch, 98–99
  /C switch, 98–99
  /G switch, 98–99
  -kg switch, 238–240
  -kvc switch, 241
  -s switch, 245
  w switch, 244
switching systems, 42
Symantec, 70
symmetric cipher features, 221
SyQuest, 30
SYS, 74
SYSCON, 256, 260–261, 264
system administrator(s)
  basic description of, 250
  interview with, 171–183
system attribute, 92
system date/time, 274
System file, 70
system operators (sysops), 122
System Policy Editor, 278–281
system shut down, 275

T

tape backup
  basic description of, 20–23
  capacity of, 21
  cycling tapes for, 28, 34
  for e-mail systems, 120
  filtering out file types from, 32–34
  full backups with, vs. partial backups, 24–25
  hacker stories involving, 40–41
  internal vs. external, 21
  problems with bad tapes, 28, 34
  sample backup and restore with, 31–35
  storing tapes from, 29–30
  testing, 28–30

tape backup *(continued)*
  viruses and, 61
TAR, 30, 105
tax information, 1–2, 19, 47, 157, 232. *See also* IRS (Internal Revenue Service)
TCP/IP (Transmission Control Protocol/Internet Protocol), 163, 168
Tektronix, 254
Telecommunications Competition and Deregulation Act of 1995, 195, 201
Telecommunications Reform Act of 1996, 170, 195
telegraph, introduction of, 138
telephone, 42–43. *See also* Clipper chip; wiretapping
  calling cards, 152, 163
  calls, routing patterns for, 182, 223
  digital telephony and, 223–225
  historical development of, 42, 138, 142–143, 170, 223
  lines, toll-free, 137
  numbers, posting, 179
  pay telephones, 152
  PINs and, 78–79
television
  cable, 142, 186, 188
  freedom of speech and, 186–188
  introduction of, 139
  ratings, 141
TERM20.zip, 101–103
Terminator 2.0 for Windows, 101–103
testing
  backup systems, 28–30
  power on self-test (POST), 85
Thomas, Carleen, 190–194, 204
Thomas, Robert, 190–194, 204
Thompson, Ken, 80
time
  -sharing systems, 40
  stamping, 81
  system, 81, 274

Time, 38, 128, 186
Tiny IDEA, 221
Titz virus, 70
token objects, 276
toll-free phone lines, 137
Traceroute, 182
TRACK OFF command, 258
TRACK ON command, 258
transactions online. *See also* credit cards
  AOL and, 139
  ATMs (automatic teller machines) and, 77–78, 145, 151, 163, 248
  CompuServe and, 139, 142, 159–160
  E-cash (electronic cash), 150–161
  electronic checking and, 145–150, 153, 154
  history of, 136–142
  home shopping and, 137–138
  Netscape and, 161–163
  overview of, 135–165
  PINs (Personal Identification Numbers) and, 77–79, 160, 225
  Prodigy and, 139
  protocols and, 162–164, 150
  World Wide Web and, 139–142
transistors, 42, 44
transport armor, 243
traverse checking, 276
TRN newsreader, 176
Trojan horses, 2, 51, 91. *See also* viruses
  basic description of, 53–62, 65–66
  basic truths and myths about, 57–61
  downloading files and, 57
  mockingbird viruses and, 61
  MSN and, 67
  security holes and, 282
  types of, 65–66
trustee rights, 258–259, 262–264
TS.EXE, 95
TSR (Terminate and Stay Resident) software, 73–74
TXT format, 96

◆ U ◆

undelete utilities, 97
University of California, 64, 154
University of Illinois, 161
University of Michigan, 203–204
University of Southern California, 62
UNIX, 31, 237
　basic description of, 43, 44
　daemons and, 40
　e-mail and, 126
　hackers and, 40, 43–44
　hidden files and, 92
　history of the Internet and, 168, 170
　password protection and, 80, 82, 86, 88
　personal Web pages and, 179
　viruses and, 63
unwanted materials, 171, 185–212
　AOL and, 192–193, 210
　BBSs and, 190–192, 194, 200–202, 205–210
　Communications Decency Act of 1995 and, 188, 195–203, 206
　CompuServe and, 192–193, 202–203, 210
　filtering access to, 205–210
　ISPs and, 200–203
　legal issues regarding, overview of, 185–202
　online services and, 192–203
　Prodigy and, 192–193, 202, 210
　self-regulation of the Internet, 205
U.S. Code, 229
U.S. Customs Service, 235
U.S. Department of Defense, 167–168
U.S. Department of Justice, 63, 218–220
U.S. Department of State, 222, 229–230, 235
U.S. Postal Service, 116, 122, 137
USA Today, 163
Usenet newsgroups, 47
　anonymous remailers and, 127–128
　basic description of, 127
　e-mail and, 127–129
　filtering access to, 205–210
　freedom of speech and, 194, 202–204
　ROT-13 and, 129
　spamming and, 174
　subscription information for, documentation of, 176–177
user, definition of, 269
User Manager, 271–272, 274, 277, 296, 298–299

◆ V ◆

vacuum tubes, 42
Van Buren, Abigail, 187, 194
vector, use of the term, 73
VeriSign, 164–165
ViaCrypt, 235, 237
Vigenère, Blaise de, 216
Virginia Military Institute Library, 219
viruses, 1. *See also* viruses (listed by type)
　basic description of, 53–76
　basic truths and myths about, 57–61
　classification of, 67–68
　COM files and, 57–59
　computer, overview of, 66–70
　EXE files and, 57–59
　file size changes and, 73
　hackers and, 50–51
　hidden in data files, 60
　interrupt vector mapping and, 73–74
　major sources of, 54–57
　simple security measures and, 91
　types of, 61–70
　unexplained changes in available RAM and, 74
　in unused areas of disks, 60
　use of the term, 62
　vs. users who are their own worst enemies, 13
viruses (listed by type). *See also* viruses
　bacterium viruses, 61
　boot sector viruses, 67, 69
　Breasts virus, 70
　ChinaTalk virus, 66
　CODE-1 viruses, 70

viruses *(continued)*
  Cookies virus, 66
  Flame viruses, 69
  FontFinder viruses, 66
  Good Times virus, 58
  Jerusalem virus, 69
  Michelangelo virus, 58, 59, 66, 70
  mockingbird viruses, 61
  multipartite viruses, 55, 68
  Natas virus, 58, 70
  New Zealand virus, 69
  nVir virus, 70
  NVP viruses, 66
  polymorphic viruses, 68
  Prank macro virus, 58
  rabbit viruses, 62
  Shehas virus, 70
  stealth viruses, 68
  systemic viruses, 68
  Stoned virus, 59, 69
  Sunday virus, 69
  Suriv virus, 69
  Titz virus, 70
  Trojan horse viruses, 2, 51, 53–62, 65–67, 91, 282
  Word Prank virus, 58
  worm viruses, 2, 62–64, 80
VirusScan, 72
VISA International, 154, 156, 163–164
VisiCalc, 69

✦ W ✦

WAN (wide area networks), 116
Web browsers. *See also* Netscape Navigator browser
  accessing Web pages with, information provided when, 175
  basic description of, 140
  history of, 161–162
  Internet Explorer, 67
  Lynx browser, 170
  Mosaic browser, 161–162, 170
  text-only browsers, 170
Web page(s). *See also* Web pages (listed by name)
  that allow visitors to send fakemail, 126–127
  with information about anonymous remailers, 127
  personal, 179–180
  SafeSurf ratings system and, 210
  secret links in, 180
Web pages (listed by name). *See also* Web pages
  Comerwell Software Web page, 130
  Cyber Patrol Web page, 207
  DigiCash Web page, 155
  Electronic Frontier Foundation Web page, 191
  First Virtual Web page, 161
  Lawrence Livermore Labs Web page, 144
  Microsoft Web page, 58
  Massachusetts Institute of Technology Web page, 237
  Net Nanny Web page, 210
  SafeSurf Web page, 210
  Surf Watch Web page, 210
Wells Fargo Bank, 144, 163
Windows (Microsoft). *See also* specific versions
  Chinese language version of, 55
  Clipboard, 108–110
  Control Panel, 274, 278, 287, 296
  family of programs, overview of, 267–268
  file attributes and, 93
  networks, sharing resources with, 267–300
  password protection and, 80, 86–87
  Program Manager, 103
  strong encryption and, 217
  versions of PGP, 246
  viruses and, 67–68
Windows 3.*x* (Microsoft)
  DES for Windows and, 108
  hidden files and, 94
  NDS and, 257

shredder applications and, 101, 103
Windows 95 (Microsoft), 43, 80–81, 89, 178, 268
  access control, 286–287, 293
  backup systems and, 22–23, 25, 27, 31–35
  deleting files in, 97
  DES for Windows and, 108
  Device Manager, 279
  Dial-up Networking, 80–81, 281
  establishing network resources with, 285–287
  Explorer, 32, 106
  file/printer sharing with, 285–286
  Find utility, 72, 95
  hidden files and, 94
  managing users and, 296–299
  MSBACKUP, 22
  Nuke and, 100
  Paint, 16
  Recycle Bin, 97
  Registry, 22, 31, 80, 279–280
  Registry Editor, 279
  Scheduler, 34–35
  security holes and, 282–283
  sharing directories with, 288–290
  shredder applications and, 101
  System Agent, 72
  System Policy Editor, 278–281, 296–297
  viruses and, 72
Windows for Workgroups, 27, 50, 80, 100, 268, 282
Windows NT, 22, 268–269, 296–299
  filing system, 281
  network policies, 271–278
  Nuke and, 100
  security holes and, 283–284
  Server, 269
  setting up user accounts for, 298–299
  sharing directories and, 290–292
  sharing printers and, 292–294
  viruses and, 69
  Workstation, 269
WinZip, 30, 56, 72–73, 105–107
wiretapping
  Clipper chip and, 2, 47, 123, 231–234, 236
  Digital Telephony Bill and, 122, 224–225, 231
Wolf, Hans de, 38
Word Basic, 58
Word for Windows, 88
  DOC format, 96
  Setup routine, 14
wordprocessing software
  backup features and, 15
  networking and, 258
  proprietary file formats for, 96
  Word for Windows, 14, 88, 96
  WordPerfect, 25
Word Prank viruses, 58
workgroups, definition of, 270. *See also* networking; Windows for Workgroups
World War II, 42, 139, 216, 226
World Wide Web, 27, 44, 47. *See also* Web browsers; Web pages
  copyright infringements and, 55
  filtering access to, 205–210
  financial transactions and, 139–142
  history of, 139–140, 170
  security and, overview of, 171–173
  unwanted materials on, 185–212
  user demographics, 140–142
  viruses and, 62, 64, 71
World Wide Web Worm, 62
worm viruses, 2, 62–64, 80
Wozniak, Steve, 218
WYSIWYG (What You See Is What You Get), 84

Xerox Corporation, 40–41, 218
Xtree Gold, 94
X-Windows, 170

✦ Y ✦

Youth International Party, 37–38

✦ Z ✦

Zen, 23–24
Zim, Herbert S., 234
Zimmerman, Phil, 130, 133, 225, 234–246
ZIP archive files, 29, 50
  cracking, 104–105
  encryption for, 103–107
  hidden attribute for, 93
  password protection and, 80, 85, 105
  viruses and, 56–57, 65, 67, 72–73
ZIPCRACK.EXE, 104
ZIP drives, 30

Notes

Notes

DUMMIES PRESS

The Fun & Easy Way™ to learn about computers and more!

10/31/95

Windows® 3.11 For Dummies,® 3rd Edition
by Andy Rathbone
ISBN: 1-56884-370-4
$16.95 USA/
$22.95 Canada

Mutual Funds For Dummies™
by Eric Tyson
ISBN: 1-56884-226-0
$16.99 USA/
$22.99 Canada

DOS For Dummies,® 2nd Edition
by Dan Gookin
ISBN: 1-878058-75-4
$16.95 USA/
$22.95 Canada

The Internet For Dummies,® 2nd Edition
by John Levine & Carol Baroudi
ISBN: 1-56884-222-8
$19.99 USA/
$26.99 Canada

Personal Finance For Dummies™
by Eric Tyson
ISBN: 1-56884-150-7
$16.95 USA/
$22.95 Canada

PCs For Dummies,® 3rd Edition
by Dan Gookin & Andy Rathbone
ISBN: 1-56884-904-4
$16.95 USA/
$22.99 Canada

Macs® For Dummies,® 3rd Edition
by David Pogue
ISBN: 1-56884-239-2
$19.99 USA/
$26.99 Canada

The SAT® I For Dummies™
by Suzee Vlk
ISBN: 1-56884-213-9
$14.99 USA/
$20.99 Canada

Here's a complete listing of IDG Books' ...For Dummies® titles

Title	Author	ISBN	Price
DATABASE			
Access 2 For Dummies®	by Scott Palmer	ISBN: 1-56884-090-X	$19.95 USA/$26.95 Canada
Access Programming For Dummies®	by Rob Krumm	ISBN: 1-56884-091-8	$19.95 USA/$26.95 Canada
Approach 3 For Windows® For Dummies®	by Doug Lowe	ISBN: 1-56884-233-3	$19.99 USA/$26.99 Canada
dBASE For DOS For Dummies®	by Scott Palmer & Michael Stabler	ISBN: 1-56884-188-4	$19.95 USA/$26.95 Canada
dBASE For Windows® For Dummies®	by Scott Palmer	ISBN: 1-56884-179-5	$19.95 USA/$26.95 Canada
dBASE 5 For Windows® Programming For Dummies®	by Ted Coombs & Jason Coombs	ISBN: 1-56884-215-5	$19.99 USA/$26.99 Canada
FoxPro 2.6 For Windows® For Dummies®	by John Kaufeld	ISBN: 1-56884-187-6	$19.95 USA/$26.95 Canada
Paradox 5 For Windows® For Dummies®	by John Kaufeld	ISBN: 1-56884-185-X	$19.95 USA/$26.95 Canada
DESKTOP PUBLISHING/ILLUSTRATION/GRAPHICS			
CorelDRAW! 5 For Dummies®	by Deke McClelland	ISBN: 1-56884-157-4	$19.95 USA/$26.95 Canada
CorelDRAW! For Dummies®	by Deke McClelland	ISBN: 1-56884-042-X	$19.95 USA/$26.95 Canada
Desktop Publishing & Design For Dummies®	by Roger C. Parker	ISBN: 1-56884-234-1	$19.99 USA/$26.99 Canada
Harvard Graphics 2 For Windows® For Dummies®	by Roger C. Parker	ISBN: 1-56884-092-6	$19.95 USA/$26.95 Canada
PageMaker 5 For Macs® For Dummies®	by Galen Gruman & Deke McClelland	ISBN: 1-56884-178-7	$19.95 USA/$26.95 Canada
PageMaker 5 For Windows® For Dummies®	by Deke McClelland & Galen Gruman	ISBN: 1-56884-160-4	$19.95 USA/$26.95 Canada
Photoshop 3 For Macs® For Dummies®	by Deke McClelland	ISBN: 1-56884-208-2	$19.99 USA/$26.99 Canada
QuarkXPress 3.3 For Dummies®	by Galen Gruman & Barbara Assadi	ISBN: 1-56884-217-1	$19.99 USA/$26.99 Canada
FINANCE/PERSONAL FINANCE/TEST TAKING REFERENCE			
Everyday Math For Dummies™	by Charles Seiter	ISBN: 1-56884-248-1	$14.99 USA/$22.99 Canada
Personal Finance For Dummies™ For Canadians	by Eric Tyson & Tony Martin	ISBN: 1-56884-378-X	$18.99 USA/$24.99 Canada
QuickBooks 3 For Dummies®	by Stephen L. Nelson	ISBN: 1-56884-227-9	$19.99 USA/$26.99 Canada
Quicken 8 For DOS For Dummies,® 2nd Edition	by Stephen L. Nelson	ISBN: 1-56884-210-4	$19.95 USA/$26.95 Canada
Quicken 5 For Macs® For Dummies®	by Stephen L. Nelson	ISBN: 1-56884-211-2	$19.95 USA/$26.95 Canada
Quicken 4 For Windows® For Dummies,® 2nd Edition	by Stephen L. Nelson	ISBN: 1-56884-209-0	$19.95 USA/$26.95 Canada
Taxes For Dummies,™ 1995 Edition	by Eric Tyson & David J. Silverman	ISBN: 1-56884-220-1	$14.99 USA/$20.99 Canada
The GMAT® For Dummies™	by Suzee Vlk, Series Editor	ISBN: 1-56884-376-3	$14.99 USA/$20.99 Canada
The GRE® For Dummies™	by Suzee Vlk, Series Editor	ISBN: 1-56884-375-5	$14.99 USA/$20.99 Canada
Time Management For Dummies™	by Jeffrey J. Mayer	ISBN: 1-56884-360-7	$16.99 USA/$22.99 Canada
TurboTax For Windows® For Dummies®	by Gail A. Helsel, CPA	ISBN: 1-56884-228-7	$19.99 USA/$26.99 Canada
GROUPWARE/INTEGRATED			
ClarisWorks For Macs® For Dummies®	by Frank Higgins	ISBN: 1-56884-363-1	$19.99 USA/$26.99 Canada
Lotus Notes For Dummies®	by Pat Freeland & Stephen Londergan	ISBN: 1-56884-212-0	$19.95 USA/$26.95 Canada
Microsoft® Office 4 For Windows® For Dummies®	by Roger C. Parker	ISBN: 1-56884-183-3	$19.95 USA/$26.95 Canada
Microsoft® Works 3 For Windows® For Dummies®	by David C. Kay	ISBN: 1-56884-214-7	$19.95 USA/$26.95 Canada
SmartSuite 3 For Dummies®	by Jan Weingarten & John Weingarten	ISBN: 1-56884-367-4	$19.99 USA/$26.99 Canada
INTERNET/COMMUNICATIONS/NETWORKING			
America Online® For Dummies,® 2nd Edition	by John Kaufeld	ISBN: 1-56884-933-8	$19.99 USA/$26.99 Canada
CompuServe For Dummies,® 2nd Edition	by Wallace Wang	ISBN: 1-56884-937-0	$19.99 USA/$26.99 Canada
Modems For Dummies,® 2nd Edition	by Tina Rathbone	ISBN: 1-56884-223-6	$19.99 USA/$26.99 Canada
MORE Internet For Dummies®	by John R. Levine & Margaret Levine Young	ISBN: 1-56884-164-7	$19.95 USA/$26.95 Canada
MORE Modems & On-line Services For Dummies®	by Tina Rathbone	ISBN: 1-56884-365-8	$19.99 USA/$26.99 Canada
Mosaic For Dummies,® Windows Edition	by David Angell & Brent Heslop	ISBN: 1-56884-242-2	$19.99 USA/$26.99 Canada
NetWare For Dummies,® 2nd Edition	by Ed Tittel, Deni Connor & Earl Follis	ISBN: 1-56884-369-0	$19.99 USA/$26.99 Canada
Networking For Dummies®	by Doug Lowe	ISBN: 1-56884-079-9	$19.95 USA/$26.95 Canada
PROCOMM PLUS 2 For Windows® For Dummies®	by Wallace Wang	ISBN: 1-56884-219-8	$19.99 USA/$26.99 Canada
TCP/IP For Dummies®	by Marshall Wilensky & Candace Leiden	ISBN: 1-56884-241-4	$19.99 USA/$26.99 Canada

Microsoft and Windows are registered trademarks of Microsoft Corporation. Mac is a registered trademark of Apple Computer. SAT is a registered trademark of the College Entrance Examination Board. GMAT is a registered trademark of the Graduate Management Admission Council. GRE is a registered trademark of the Educational Testing Service. America Online is a registered trademark of America Online, Inc. The "...For Dummies Book Series" logo, the IDG Books Worldwide logos, Dummies Press, and The Fun & Easy Way are trademarks, and ---- For Dummies and ...For Dummies are registered trademarks under exclusive license to IDG Books Worldwide, Inc., from International Data Group, Inc.

For scholastic requests & educational orders please call Educational Sales at 1. 800. 434. 2086

FOR MORE INFO OR TO ORDER, PLEASE CALL ▶ 800. 762. 2974

For volume discounts & special orders please call Tony Real, Special Sales, at 415. 655. 3048

DUMMIES PRESS™

Title	Author	ISBN	Price
The Internet For Macs® For Dummies®, 2nd Edition	by Charles Seiter	ISBN: 1-56884-371-2	$19.99 USA/$26.99 Canada
The Internet For Macs® For Dummies® Starter Kit	by Charles Seiter	ISBN: 1-56884-244-9	$29.99 USA/$39.99 Canada
The Internet For Macs® For Dummies® Starter Kit Bestseller Edition	by Charles Seiter	ISBN: 1-56884-245-7	$39.99 USA/$54.99 Canada
The Internet For Windows® For Dummies® Starter Kit	by John R. Levine & Margaret Levine Young	ISBN: 1-56884-237-6	$34.99 USA/$44.99 Canada
The Internet For Windows® For Dummies® Starter Kit, Bestseller Edition	by John R. Levine & Margaret Levine Young	ISBN: 1-56884-246-5	$39.99 USA/$54.99 Canada

MACINTOSH

Title	Author	ISBN	Price
Mac® Programming For Dummies®	by Dan Parks Sydow	ISBN: 1-56884-173-6	$19.95 USA/$26.95 Canada
Macintosh® System 7.5 For Dummies®	by Bob LeVitus	ISBN: 1-56884-197-3	$19.95 USA/$26.95 Canada
MORE Macs® For Dummies®	by David Pogue	ISBN: 1-56884-087-X	$19.95 USA/$26.95 Canada
PageMaker 5 For Macs® For Dummies®	by Galen Gruman & Deke McClelland	ISBN: 1-56884-178-7	$19.95 USA/$26.95 Canada
QuarkXPress 3.3 For Dummies®	by Galen Gruman & Barbara Assadi	ISBN: 1-56884-217-1	$19.99 USA/$26.99 Canada
Upgrading and Fixing Macs® For Dummies®	by Kearney Rietmann & Frank Higgins	ISBN: 1-56884-189-2	$19.95 USA/$26.95 Canada

MULTIMEDIA

Title	Author	ISBN	Price
Multimedia & CD-ROMs For Dummies®, 2nd Edition	by Andy Rathbone	ISBN: 1-56884-907-9	$19.99 USA/$26.99 Canada
Multimedia & CD-ROMs For Dummies®, Interactive Multimedia Value Pack, 2nd Edition	by Andy Rathbone	ISBN: 1-56884-909-5	$29.99 USA/$39.99 Canada

OPERATING SYSTEMS:

DOS

Title	Author	ISBN	Price
MORE DOS For Dummies®	by Dan Gookin	ISBN: 1-56884-046-2	$19.95 USA/$26.95 Canada
OS/2® Warp For Dummies®, 2nd Edition	by Andy Rathbone	ISBN: 1-56884-205-8	$19.99 USA/$26.99 Canada

UNIX

Title	Author	ISBN	Price
MORE UNIX® For Dummies®	by John R. Levine & Margaret Levine Young	ISBN: 1-56884-361-5	$19.99 USA/$26.99 Canada
UNIX® For Dummies®	by John R. Levine & Margaret Levine Young	ISBN: 1-878058-58-4	$19.95 USA/$26.95 Canada

WINDOWS

Title	Author	ISBN	Price
MORE Windows® For Dummies®, 2nd Edition	by Andy Rathbone	ISBN: 1-56884-048-9	$19.95 USA/$26.95 Canada
Windows® 95 For Dummies®	by Andy Rathbone	ISBN: 1-56884-240-6	$19.99 USA/$26.99 Canada

PCS/HARDWARE

Title	Author	ISBN	Price
Illustrated Computer Dictionary For Dummies®, 2nd Edition	by Dan Gookin & Wallace Wang	ISBN: 1-56884-218-X	$12.95 USA/$16.95 Canada
Upgrading and Fixing PCs For Dummies®, 2nd Edition	by Andy Rathbone	ISBN: 1-56884-903-6	$19.99 USA/$26.99 Canada

PRESENTATION/AUTOCAD

Title	Author	ISBN	Price
AutoCAD For Dummies®	by Bud Smith	ISBN: 1-56884-191-4	$19.95 USA/$26.95 Canada
PowerPoint 4 For Windows® For Dummies®	by Doug Lowe	ISBN: 1-56884-161-2	$16.99 USA/$22.99 Canada

PROGRAMMING

Title	Author	ISBN	Price
Borland C++ For Dummies®	by Michael Hyman	ISBN: 1-56884-162-0	$19.95 USA/$26.95 Canada
C For Dummies®, Volume 1	by Dan Gookin	ISBN: 1-878058-78-9	$19.95 USA/$26.95 Canada
C++ For Dummies®	by Stephen R. Davis	ISBN: 1-56884-163-9	$19.95 USA/$26.95 Canada
Delphi Programming For Dummies®	by Neil Rubenking	ISBN: 1-56884-200-7	$19.99 USA/$26.99 Canada
Mac® Programming For Dummies®	by Dan Parks Sydow	ISBN: 1-56884-173-6	$19.95 USA/$26.95 Canada
PowerBuilder 4 Programming For Dummies®	by Ted Coombs & Jason Coombs	ISBN: 1-56884-325-9	$19.99 USA/$26.99 Canada
QBasic Programming For Dummies®	by Douglas Hergert	ISBN: 1-56884-093-4	$19.99 USA/$26.99 Canada
Visual Basic 3 For Dummies®	by Wallace Wang	ISBN: 1-56884-076-4	$19.95 USA/$26.95 Canada
Visual Basic "X" For Dummies®	by Wallace Wang	ISBN: 1-56884-230-9	$19.99 USA/$26.99 Canada
Visual C++ 2 For Dummies®	by Michael Hyman & Bob Arnson	ISBN: 1-56884-328-3	$19.99 USA/$26.99 Canada
Windows® 95 Programming For Dummies®	by S. Randy Davis	ISBN: 1-56884-327-5	$19.99 USA/$26.99 Canada

SPREADSHEET

Title	Author	ISBN	Price
1-2-3 For Dummies®	by Greg Harvey	ISBN: 1-878058-60-6	$16.95 USA/$22.95 Canada
1-2-3 For Windows® 5 For Dummies®, 2nd Edition	by John Walkenbach	ISBN: 1-56884-216-3	$16.95 USA/$22.95 Canada
Excel 5 For Macs® For Dummies®	by Greg Harvey	ISBN: 1-56884-186-8	$19.95 USA/$26.95 Canada
Excel For Dummies®, 2nd Edition	by Greg Harvey	ISBN: 1-56884-050-0	$16.95 USA/$22.95 Canada
MORE 1-2-3 For DOS For Dummies®	by John Weingarten	ISBN: 1-56884-224-4	$19.99 USA/$26.99 Canada
MORE Excel 5 For Windows® For Dummies®	by Greg Harvey	ISBN: 1-56884-207-4	$19.95 USA/$26.95 Canada
Quattro Pro 6 For Windows® For Dummies®	by John Walkenbach	ISBN: 1-56884-174-4	$19.95 USA/$26.95 Canada
Quattro Pro For DOS For Dummies®	by John Walkenbach	ISBN: 1-56884-023-3	$16.95 USA/$22.95 Canada

UTILITIES

Title	Author	ISBN	Price
Norton Utilities 8 For Dummies®	by Beth Slick	ISBN: 1-56884-166-3	$19.95 USA/$26.95 Canada

VCRS/CAMCORDERS

Title	Author	ISBN	Price
VCRs & Camcorders For Dummies™	by Gordon McComb & Andy Rathbone	ISBN: 1-56884-229-5	$14.99 USA/$20.99 Canada

WORD PROCESSING

Title	Author	ISBN	Price
Ami Pro For Dummies®	by Jim Meade	ISBN: 1-56884-049-7	$19.95 USA/$26.95 Canada
MORE Word For Windows® 6 For Dummies®	by Doug Lowe	ISBN: 1-56884-165-5	$19.95 USA/$26.95 Canada
MORE WordPerfect® 6 For Windows® For Dummies®	by Margaret Levine Young & David C. Kay	ISBN: 1-56884-206-6	$19.95 USA/$26.95 Canada
MORE WordPerfect® 6 For DOS For Dummies®	by Wallace Wang, edited by Dan Gookin	ISBN: 1-56884-047-0	$19.95 USA/$26.95 Canada
Word 6 For Macs® For Dummies®	by Dan Gookin	ISBN: 1-56884-190-6	$19.95 USA/$26.95 Canada
Word For Windows® 6 For Dummies®	by Dan Gookin	ISBN: 1-56884-075-6	$16.95 USA/$22.95 Canada
Word For Windows® For Dummies®	by Dan Gookin & Ray Werner	ISBN: 1-878058-86-X	$16.95 USA/$22.95 Canada
WordPerfect® 6 For DOS For Dummies®	by Dan Gookin	ISBN: 1-878058-77-0	$16.95 USA/$22.95 Canada
WordPerfect® 6.1 For Windows® For Dummies®, 2nd Edition	by Margaret Levine Young & David Kay	ISBN: 1-56884-243-0	$16.95 USA/$22.95 Canada
WordPerfect® For Dummies®	by Dan Gookin	ISBN: 1-878058-52-5	$16.95 USA/$22.95 Canada

Windows is a registered trademark of Microsoft Corporation. Mac is a registered trademark of Apple Computer. OS/2 is a registered trademark of IBM. UNIX is a registered trademark of AT&T. WordPerfect is a registered trademark of Novell. The "...For Dummies Book Series" logo, the IDG Books Worldwide logos, Dummies Press, and The Fun & Easy Way are trademarks, and ---- For Dummies and ... For Dummies are registered trademarks under exclusive license to IDG Books Worldwide, Inc., from International Data Group, Inc.

For scholastic requests & educational orders please call Educational Sales at 1. 800. 434. 2086

FOR MORE INFO OR TO ORDER, PLEASE CALL ▶ 800. 762. 2974

For volume discounts & special orders please call Tony Real, Special Sales, at 415. 655. 3048

DUMMIES PRESS™ QUICK REFERENCES

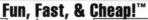

 **NEW!**

 **NEW!**

 **SUPER STAR**

 **SUPER STAR**

The Internet For Macs® For Dummies® Quick Reference
by Charles Seiter
ISBN: 1-56884-967-2
$9.99 USA/$12.99 Canada

Windows® 95 For Dummies® Quick Reference
by Greg Harvey
ISBN: 1-56884-964-8
$9.99 USA/$12.99 Canada

Photoshop 3 For Macs For Dummies® Quick Reference
by Deke McClelland
ISBN: 1-56884-968-0
$9.99 USA/$12.99 Canada

WordPerfect® For DOS For Dummies® Quick Reference
by Greg Harvey
ISBN: 1-56884-009-8
$8.95 USA/$12.95 Canada

Title	Author	ISBN	Price
DATABASE			
Access 2 For Dummies® Quick Reference	by Stuart J. Stuple	ISBN: 1-56884-167-1	$8.95 USA/$11.95 Canada
dBASE 5 For DOS For Dummies® Quick Reference	by Barrie Sosinsky	ISBN: 1-56884-954-0	$9.99 USA/$12.99 Canada
dBASE 5 For Windows® For Dummies® Quick Reference	by Stuart J. Stuple	ISBN: 1-56884-953-2	$9.99 USA/$12.99 Canada
Paradox 5 For Windows® For Dummies® Quick Reference	by Scott Palmer	ISBN: 1-56884-960-5	$9.99 USA/$12.99 Canada
DESKTOP PUBLISHING/ILLUSTRATION/GRAPHICS			
CorelDRAW! 5 For Dummies® Quick Reference	by Raymond E. Werner	ISBN: 1-56884-952-4	$9.99 USA/$12.99 Canada
Harvard Graphics For Windows® For Dummies® Quick Reference	by Raymond E. Werner	ISBN: 1-56884-962-1	$9.99 USA/$12.99 Canada
Photoshop 3 For Macs® For Dummies® Quick Reference	by Deke McClelland	ISBN: 1-56884-968-0	$9.99 USA/$12.99 Canada
FINANCE/PERSONAL FINANCE			
Quicken 4 For Windows® For Dummies® Quick Reference	by Stephen L. Nelson	ISBN: 1-56884-950-8	$9.95 USA/$12.95 Canada
GROUPWARE/INTEGRATED			
Microsoft® Office 4 For Windows® For Dummies® Quick Reference	by Doug Lowe	ISBN: 1-56884-958-3	$9.99 USA/$12.99 Canada
Microsoft® Works 3 For Windows® For Dummies® Quick Reference	by Michael Partington	ISBN: 1-56884-959-1	$9.99 USA/$12.99 Canada
INTERNET/COMMUNICATIONS/NETWORKING			
The Internet For Dummies® Quick Reference	by John R. Levine & Margaret Levine Young	ISBN: 1-56884-168-X	$8.95 USA/$11.95 Canada
MACINTOSH			
Macintosh® System 7.5 For Dummies® Quick Reference	by Stuart J. Stuple	ISBN: 1-56884-956-7	$9.99 USA/$12.99 Canada
OPERATING SYSTEMS:			
DOS			
DOS For Dummies® Quick Reference	by Greg Harvey	ISBN: 1-56884-007-1	$8.95 USA/$11.95 Canada
UNIX			
UNIX® For Dummies® Quick Reference	by John R. Levine & Margaret Levine Young	ISBN: 1-56884-094-2	$8.95 USA/$11.95 Canada
WINDOWS			
Windows® 3.1 For Dummies® Quick Reference, 2nd Edition	by Greg Harvey	ISBN: 1-56884-951-6	$8.95 USA/$11.95 Canada
PCs/HARDWARE			
Memory Management For Dummies® Quick Reference	by Doug Lowe	ISBN: 1-56884-362-3	$9.99 USA/$12.99 Canada
PRESENTATION/AUTOCAD			
AutoCAD For Dummies® Quick Reference	by Ellen Finkelstein	ISBN: 1-56884-198-1	$9.95 USA/$12.95 Canada
SPREADSHEET			
1-2-3 For Dummies® Quick Reference	by John Walkenbach	ISBN: 1-56884-027-6	$8.95 USA/$11.95 Canada
1-2-3 For Windows® 5 For Dummies® Quick Reference	by John Walkenbach	ISBN: 1-56884-957-5	$9.95 USA/$12.95 Canada
Excel For Windows® For Dummies® Quick Reference, 2nd Edition	by John Walkenbach	ISBN: 1-56884-096-9	$8.95 USA/$11.95 Canada
Quattro Pro 6 For Windows® For Dummies® Quick Reference	by Stuart J. Stuple	ISBN: 1-56884-172-8	$9.95 USA/$12.95 Canada
WORD PROCESSING			
Word For Windows® 6 For Dummies® Quick Reference	by George Lynch	ISBN: 1-56884-095-0	$8.95 USA/$11.95 Canada
Word For Windows® For Dummies® Quick Reference	by George Lynch	ISBN: 1-56884-029-2	$8.95 USA/$11.95 Canada
WordPerfect® 6.1 For Windows® For Dummies® Quick Reference, 2nd Edition	by Greg Harvey	ISBN: 1-56884-966-4	$9.99 USA/$12.99/Canada

Microsoft and Windows are registered trademarks of Microsoft Corporation. Mac and Macintosh are registered trademarks of Apple Computer. UNIX is a registered trademark of AT&T. WordPerfect is a registered trademark of Novell. The "...For Dummies Book Series" logo, the IDG Books Worldwide logos, Dummies Press, The Fun & Easy Way, and Fun, Fast, & Cheap! are trademarks, and ---- For Dummies and ... For Dummies are registered trademarks under exclusive license to IDG Books Worldwide, Inc., from International Data Group, Inc.

For scholastic requests & educational orders please call Educational Sales at 1. 800. 434. 2086

FOR MORE INFO OR TO ORDER, PLEASE CALL ▶ 800. 762. 2974

For volume discounts & special orders please call Tony Real, Special Sales, at 415. 655. 3048

PC PRESS

Windows® 3.1 SECRETS™
by Brian Livingston
ISBN: 1-878058-43-6
$39.95 USA/$52.95 Canada
Includes software.

MORE Windows® 3.1 SECRETS™
by Brian Livingston
ISBN: 1-56884-019-5
$39.95 USA/$52.95 Canada
Includes software.

Windows® GIZMOS™
by Brian Livingston
& Margie Livingston
ISBN: 1-878058-66-5
$39.95 USA/$52.95 Canada
Includes software.

Windows® 3.1 Connectivity SECRETS™
by Runnoe Connally,
David Rorabaugh,
& Sheldon Hall
ISBN: 1-56884-030-6
$49.95 USA/$64.95 Canada
Includes software.

Windows® 3.1 Configuration SECRETS™
by Valda Hilley
& James Blakely
ISBN: 1-56884-026-8
$49.95 USA/$64.95 Canada
Includes software.

Internet SECRETS™
by John Levine
& Carol Baroudi
ISBN: 1-56884-452-2
$39.99 USA/$54.99 Canada
Includes software.

Internet GIZMOS™ For Windows®
by Joel Diamond,
Howard Sobel,
& Valda Hilley
ISBN: 1-56884-451-4
$39.99 USA/$54.99 Canada
Includes software.

Network Security SECRETS™
by David Stang
& Sylvia Moon
ISBN: 1-56884-021-7
Int'l. ISBN: 1-56884-151-5
$49.95 USA/$64.95 Canada
Includes software.

PC SECRETS™
by Caroline M. Halliday
ISBN: 1-878058-49-5
$39.95 USA/$52.95 Canada
Includes software.

WordPerfect® 6 SECRETS™
by Roger C. Parker
& David A. Holzgang
ISBN: 1-56884-040-3
$39.95 USA/$52.95 Canada
Includes software.

DOS 6 SECRETS™
by Robert D. Ainsbury
ISBN: 1-878058-70-3
$39.95 USA/$52.95 Canada
Includes software.

Paradox 4 Power Programming SECRETS,™ 2nd Edition
by Gregory B. Salcedo
& Martin W. Rudy
ISBN: 1-878058-54-1
$44.95 USA/$59.95 Canada
Includes software.

Paradox 5 For Windows® Power Programming SECRETS™
by Gregory B. Salcedo
& Martin W. Rudy
ISBN: 1-56884-085-3
$44.95 USA/$59.95 Canada
Includes software.

Hard Disk SECRETS™
by John M. Goodman, Ph.D.
ISBN: 1-878058-64-9
$39.95 USA/$52.95 Canada
Includes software.

WordPerfect® 6 For Windows® Tips & Techniques Revealed
by David A. Holzgang
& Roger C. Parker
ISBN: 1-56884-202-3
$39.95 USA/$52.95 Canada
Includes software.

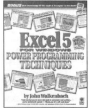
Excel 5 For Windows® Power Programming Techniques
by John Walkenbach
ISBN: 1-56884-303-8
$39.95 USA/$52.95 Canada
Includes software.

...SECRETS®

Windows is a registered trademark of Microsoft Corporation. WordPerfect is a registered trademark of Novell. ----SECRETS, ----GIZMOS, and the IDG Books Worldwide logos are trademarks, and ...SECRETS is a registered trademark under exclusive license to IDG Books Worldwide, Inc., from International Data Group, Inc.

For scholastic requests & educational orders please call Educational Sales, at 1. 800. 434. 2086

FOR MORE INFO OR TO ORDER, PLEASE CALL ▶ 800. 762. 2974

For volume discounts & special orders please call Tony Real, Special Sales, at 415. 655. 3048

PC PRESS

"A lot easier to use than the book Excel gives you!"
Lisa Schmeckpeper, New Berlin, WI, on PC World Excel 5 For Windows Handbook

Official Hayes Modem Communications Companion
by Caroline M. Halliday
ISBN: 1-56884-072-1
$29.95 USA/$39.95 Canada
Includes software.

1,001 Komputer Answers from Kim Komando
by Kim Komando
ISBN: 1-56884-460-3
$29.99 USA/$39.99 Canada
Includes software.

PC World DOS 6 Handbook, 2nd Edition
by John Socha, Clint Hicks, & Devra Hall
ISBN: 1-878058-79-7
$34.95 USA/$44.95 Canada
Includes software.

PC World Word For Windows 6 Handbook
by Brent Heslop & David Angell
ISBN: 1-56884-054-3
$34.95 USA/$44.95 Canada
Includes software.

PC World Microsoft Access 2 Bible, 2nd Edition
by Cary N. Prague & Michael R. Irwin
ISBN: 1-56884-086-1
$39.95 USA/$52.95 Canada
Includes software.

PC World Excel 5 For Windows Handbook, 2nd Edition
by John Walkenbach & Dave Maguiness
ISBN: 1-56884-056-X
$34.95 USA/$44.95 Canada
Includes software.

PC World WordPerfect 6 Handbook
by Greg Harvey
ISBN: 1-878058-80-0
$34.95 USA/$44.95 Canada
Includes software.

QuarkXPress For Windows Designer Handbook
by Barbara Assadi & Galen Gruman
ISBN: 1-878058-45-2
$29.95 USA/$39.95 Canada

Official XTree Companion, 3rd Edition
by Beth Slick
ISBN: 1-878058-57-6
$19.95 USA/$26.95 Canada

PC World DOS 6 Command Reference and Problem Solver
by John Socha & Devra Hall
ISBN: 1-56884-055-1
$24.95 USA/$32.95 Canada

Client/Server Strategies™: A Survival Guide for Corporate Reengineers
by David Vaskevitch
ISBN: 1-56884-064-0
$29.95 USA/$39.95 Canada

"PC World Word For Windows 6 Handbook is very easy to follow with lots of 'hands on' examples. The 'Task at a Glance' is very helpful!"
Jacqueline Martens, Tacoma, WA

"Thanks for publishing this book! It's the best money I've spent this year!"
Robert D. Templeton, Ft. Worth, TX, on MORE Windows 3.1 SECRETS

FOR MORE INFO OR TO ORDER, PLEASE CALL ▶ 800.762.2974

MACWORLD® PRESS

Macworld® Mac® & Power Mac SECRETS,™ 2nd Edition
by David Pogue & Joseph Schorr

This is the definitive Mac reference for those who want to become power users! Includes three disks with 9MB of software!

ISBN: 1-56884-175-2
$39.95 USA/$54.95 Canada

Includes 3 disks chock full of software.

Macworld® Mac® FAQs™
by David Pogue

Written by the hottest Macintosh author around, David Pogue, *Macworld Mac FAQs* gives users the ultimate Mac reference. Hundreds of Mac questions and answers side-by-side, right at your fingertips, and organized into six easy-to-reference sections with lots of sidebars and diagrams.

ISBN: 1-56884-480-8
$19.99 USA/$26.99 Canada

Macworld® System 7.5 Bible, 3rd Edition
by Lon Poole

ISBN: 1-56884-098-5
$29.95 USA/$39.95 Canada

Macworld® ClarisWorks 3.0 Companion, 3rd Edition
by Steven A. Schwartz

ISBN: 1-56884-481-6
$24.99 USA/$34.99 Canada

Macworld® Complete Mac Handbook Plus Interactive CD, 3rd Edition
by Jim Heid

ISBN: 1-56884-192-2
$39.95 USA/$54.95 Canada

Includes an interactive CD-ROM.

Macworld® Ultimate Mac CD-ROM
by Jim Heid

ISBN: 1-56884-477-8
$19.95 USA/$26.99 Canada

CD-ROM includes version 2.0 of QuickTime, and over 65 MB of the best shareware, freeware, fonts, sounds, and more!

Macworld® Networking Bible, 2nd Edition
by Dave Kosiur & Joel M. Snyder

ISBN: 1-56884-194-9
$29.95 USA/$39.95 Canada

Macworld® Photoshop 3 Bible, 2nd Edition
by Deke McClelland

ISBN: 1-56884-158-2
$39.95 USA/$54.95 Canada

Includes stunning CD-ROM with add-ons, digitized photos and more.

Macworld® Photoshop 2.5 Bible
by Deke McClelland

ISBN: 1-56884-022-5
$29.95 USA/$39.95 Canada

Macworld® FreeHand 4 Bible
by Deke McClelland

ISBN: 1-56884-170-1
$29.95 USA/$39.95 Canada

Macworld® Illustrator 5.0/5.5 Bible
by Ted Alspach

ISBN: 1-56884-097-7
$39.95 USA/$54.95 Canada

Includes CD-ROM with QuickTime tutorials.

Mac is a registered trademark of Apple Computer. Macworld is a registered trademark of International Data Group, Inc. ----SECRETS, and ----FAQs are trademarks under exclusive license to IDG Books Worldwide, Inc., from International Data Group, Inc.

For scholastic requests & educational orders please call Educational Sales, at 1. 800. 434. 2086

FOR MORE INFO OR TO ORDER, PLEASE CALL ▶ 800 762 2974

For volume discounts & special orders please ca Tony Real, Special Sales, at 415. 655. 3048

MACWORLD® PRESS

10/31/95

"Macworld Complete Mac Handbook Plus CD covered everything I could think of and more!"

Peter Tsakiris, New York, NY

"Very useful for PageMaker beginners and veterans alike— contains a wealth of tips and tricks to make you a faster, more powerful PageMaker user."

Paul Brainerd, President and founder, Aldus Corporation

"Thanks for the best computer book I've ever read—Photoshop 2.5 Bible. Best $30 I ever spent. I love the detailed index....Yours blows them all out of the water. This is a great book. We must enlighten the masses!"

Kevin Lisankie, Chicago, Illinois

"Macworld Guide to ClarisWorks 2 is the easiest computer book to read that I have ever found!"

Steven Hanson, Lutz, FL

"...thanks to the Macworld Excel 5 Companion, 2nd Edition occupying a permanent position next to my computer, I'll be able to tap more of Excel's power."

Lauren Black, Lab Director, Macworld Magazine

Macworld® QuarkXPress 3.2/3.3 Bible
by Barbara Assadi & Galen Gruman
ISBN: 1-878058-85-1
$39.95 USA/$52.95 Canada
Includes disk with QuarkXPress XTensions and scripts.

Macworld® PageMaker 5 Bible
by Craig Danuloff
ISBN: 1-878058-84-3
$39.95 USA/$52.95 Canada
Includes 2 disks with PageMaker utilities, clip art, and more.

Macworld® FileMaker Pro 2.0/2.1 Bible
by Steven A. Schwartz
ISBN: 1-56884-201-5
$34.95 USA/$46.95 Canada
Includes disk with ready-to-run data bases.

Macworld® Word 6 Companion, 2nd Edition
by Jim Heid
ISBN: 1-56884-082-9
$24.95 USA/$34.95 Canada
NEWBRIDGE BOOK CLUB SELECTION

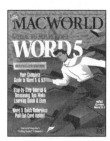

Macworld® Guide To Microsoft® Word 5/5.1
by Jim Heid
ISBN: 1-878058-39-8
$22.95 USA/$29.95 Canada

Macworld® ClarisWorks 2.0/2.1 Companion, 2nd Edition
by Steven A. Schwartz
ISBN: 1-56884-180-9
$24.95 USA/$34.95 Canada

Macworld® Guide To Microsoft® Works 3
by Barrie Sosinsky
ISBN: 1-878058-42-8
$22.95 USA/$29.95 Canada

Macworld® Excel 5 Companion, 2nd Edition
by Chris Van Buren & David Maguiness
ISBN: 1-56884-081-0
$24.95 USA/$34.95 Canada
NEWBRIDGE BOOK CLUB SELECTION

Macworld® Guide To Microsoft® Excel 4
by David Maguiness
ISBN: 1-878058-40-1
$22.95 USA/$29.95 Canada

Microsoft is a registered trademark of Microsoft Corporation. Macworld is a registered trademark of International Data Group, Inc.

For scholastic requests & educational orders please call Educational Sales, at 1. 800. 434. 2086

FOR MORE INFO OR TO ORDER, PLEASE CALL ▶ **800. 762. 2974**

For volume discounts & special orders please call Tony Real, Special Sales, at 415. 655. 3048

PROFESSIONAL PUBLISHING GROUP

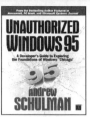

Unauthorized Windows® 95: A Developer's Guide to Exploring the Foundations of Windows "Chicago"
by Andrew Schulman

ISBN: 1-56884-169-8
$29.99 USA/$39.99 Canada

Unauthorized Windows® 95 Developer's Resource Kit
by Andrew Schulman

ISBN: 1-56884-305-4
$39.99 USA/$54.99 Canada

Best of the Net
by Seth Godin

ISBN: 1-56884-313-5
$22.99 USA/$32.99 Canada

Detour: The Truth About the Information Superhighway
by Michael Sullivan-Trainor

ISBN: 1-56884-307-0
$22.99 USA/$32.99 Canada

PowerPC Programming For Intel Programmers
by Kip McClanahan

ISBN: 1-56884-306-2
$49.99 USA/$64.99 Canada

Foundations™ of Visual C++ Programming For Windows® 95
by Paul Yao & Joseph Yao

ISBN: 1-56884-321-6
$39.99 USA/$54.99 Canada

Heavy Metal™ Visual C++ Programming
by Steve Holzner

ISBN: 1-56884-196-5
$39.95 USA/$54.95 Canada

Heavy Metal™ OLE 2.0 Programming
by Steve Holzner

ISBN: 1-56884-301-1
$39.95 USA/$54.95 Canada

Lotus Notes Application Development Handbook
by Erica Kerwien

ISBN: 1-56884-308-9
$39.99 USA/$54.99 Canada

The Internet Direct Connect Kit
by Peter John Harrison

ISBN: 1-56884-135-3
$29.95 USA/$39.95 Canada

Macworld® Ultimate Mac® Programming
by Dave Mark

ISBN: 1-56884-195-7
$39.95 USA/$54.95 Canada

The UNIX®-Haters Handbook
by Simson Garfinkel, Daniel Weise, & Steven Strassmann

ISBN: 1-56884-203-1
$16.95 USA/$22.95 Canada

Learn C++ Today!
by Martin Rinehart

ISBN: 1-56884-310-0
34.99 USA/$44.99 Canada

Type & Learn™ C
by Tom Swan

ISBN: 1-56884-073-X
34.95 USA/$44.95 Canada

Type & Learn™ Windows® Programming
by Tom Swan

ISBN: 1-56884-071-3
34.95 USA/$44.95 Canada

Windows is a registered trademark of Microsoft Corporation. Mac is a registered trademark of Apple Computer. UNIX is a registered trademark of AT&T. Macworld is a registered trademark of International Data Group, Inc. Foundations of ----, Heavy Metal, Type & Learn, and the IDG Books Worldwide logos are trademarks under exclusive license to IDG Books Worldwide, Inc., from International Data Group, Inc.

For scholastic requests & educational orders please call Educational Sales, at 1. 800. 434. 2086

FOR MORE INFO OR TO ORDER, PLEASE CALL ▶ 800 762 2974

For volume discounts & special orders please ca Tony Real, Special Sales, at 415. 655. 3048

DUMMIES PRESS™ PROGRAMMING BOOKS

COMPUTER BOOK SERIES FROM IDG

For Dummies who want to program...

Delphi Programming For Dummies®
by Neil Rubenking
ISBN: 1-56884-200-7
$19.99 USA/$26.99 Canada

Access Programming For Dummies®
by Rob Krumm
ISBN: 1-56884-091-8
$19.95 USA/$26.95 Canada

TCP/IP For Dummies®
by Marshall Wilensky & Candace Leiden
ISBN: 1-56884-241-4
$19.99 USA/$26.99 Canada

HTML For Dummies®
by Ed Tittel & Carl de Cordova
ISBN: 1-56884-330-5
$29.99 USA/$39.99 Canada

Windows® 95 Programming For Dummies®
by S. Randy Davis
ISBN: 1-56884-327-5
$19.99 USA/$26.99 Canada

Mac® Programming For Dummies®
by Dan Parks Sydow
ISBN: 1-56884-173-6
$19.95 USA/$26.95 Canada

PowerBuilder 4 Programming For Dummies®
by Ted Coombs & Jason Coombs
ISBN: 1-56884-325-9
$19.99 USA/$26.99 Canada

Visual Basic 3 For Dummies®
by Wallace Wang
ISBN: 1-56884-076-4
$19.95 USA/$26.95 Canada
Covers version 3.

ISDN For Dummies®
by David Angell
ISBN: 1-56884-331-3
$19.99 USA/$26.99 Canada

Visual C++ "2" For Dummies®
by Michael Hyman & Bob Arnson
ISBN: 1-56884-328-3
$19.99 USA/$26.99 Canada

Borland C++ For Dummies®
by Michael Hyman
ISBN: 1-56884-162-0
$19.95 USA/$26.95 Canada

C For Dummies,® Volume I
by Dan Gookin
ISBN: 1-878058-78-9
$19.95 USA/$26.95 Canada

C++ For Dummies®
by Stephen R. Davis
ISBN: 1-56884-163-9
$19.95 USA/$26.95 Canada

QBasic Programming For Dummies®
by Douglas Hergert
ISBN: 1-56884-093-4
$19.95 USA/$26.95 Canada

dBase 5 For Windows® Programming For Dummies®
by Ted Coombs & Jason Coombs
ISBN: 1-56884-215-5
$19.99 USA/$26.99 Canada

Windows is a registered trademark of Microsoft Corporation. Mac is a registered trademark of Apple Computer. Dummies Press, the "...For Dummies Book Series" logo and the IDG Books Worldwide logos are trademarks, and ----For Dummies, ...For Dummies and the "...For Dummies Computer Book Series" logo are registered trademarks under exclusive license to IDG Books Worldwide, Inc., from International Data Group, Inc.

For scholastic requests & educational orders please call Educational Sales, at 1. 800. 434. 2086

FOR MORE INFO OR TO ORDER, PLEASE CALL ▶ 800. 762. 2974

For volume discounts & special orders please call Tony Real, Special Sales, at 415. 655. 3048

ORDER FORM

Order Center: **(800) 762-2974** (8 a.m.–6 p.m., EST, weekdays)

Quantity	ISBN	Title	Price	Total

Shipping & Handling Charges

	Description	First book	Each additional book	Total
Domestic	Normal	$4.50	$1.50	$
	Two Day Air	$8.50	$2.50	$
	Overnight	$18.00	$3.00	$
International	Surface	$8.00	$8.00	$
	Airmail	$16.00	$16.00	$
	DHL Air	$17.00	$17.00	$

*For large quantities call for shipping & handling charges.
**Prices are subject to change without notice.

Ship to:
Name _____
Company _____
Address _____
City/State/Zip _____
Daytime Phone _____

Payment: ☐ Check to IDG Books Worldwide (US Funds Only)
☐ VISA ☐ MasterCard ☐ American Express
Card # _____ Expires _____
Signature _____

Subtotal _____
CA residents add
applicable sales tax _____
IN, MA, and MD
residents add
5% sales tax _____
IL residents add
6.25% sales tax _____
RI residents add
7% sales tax _____
TX residents add
8.25% sales tax _____

Shipping _____

Total _____

Please send this order form to:
IDG Books Worldwide, Inc.
7260 Shadeland Station, Suite 100
Indianapolis, IN 46256

*Allow up to 3 weeks for delivery.
Thank you!*

IDG BOOKS WORLDWIDE REGISTRATION CARD

RETURN THIS REGISTRATION CARD FOR FREE CATALOG

Title of this book: **Personal Computer Security**

My overall rating of this book: ❏ Very good [1] ❏ Good [2] ❏ Satisfactory [3] ❏ Fair [4] ❏ Poor [5]

How I first heard about this book:

❏ Found in bookstore; name: [6] ❏ Book review: [7]
❏ Advertisement: [8] ❏ Catalog: [9]
❏ Word of mouth; heard about book from friend, co-worker, etc.: [10] ❏ Other: [11]

What I liked most about this book:

What I would change, add, delete, etc., in future editions of this book:

Other comments:

Number of computer books I purchase in a year: ❏ 1 [12] ❏ 2-5 [13] ❏ 6-10 [14] ❏ More than 10 [15]

I would characterize my computer skills as: ❏ Beginner [16] ❏ Intermediate [17] ❏ Advanced [18] ❏ Professional [19]

I use ❏ DOS [20] ❏ Windows [21] ❏ OS/2 [22] ❏ Unix [23] ❏ Macintosh [24] ❏ Other: [25] _____
(please specify)

I would be interested in new books on the following subjects:
(please check all that apply, and use the spaces provided to identify specific software)

❏ Word processing: [26] ❏ Spreadsheets: [27]
❏ Data bases: [28] ❏ Desktop publishing: [29]
❏ File Utilities: [30] ❏ Money management: [31]
❏ Networking: [32] ❏ Programming languages: [33]
❏ Other: [34]

I use a PC at (please check all that apply): ❏ home [35] ❏ work [36] ❏ school [37] ❏ other: [38] _____

The disks I prefer to use are ❏ 5.25 [39] ❏ 3.5 [40] ❏ other: [41] _____

I have a CD ROM: ❏ yes [42] ❏ no [43]

I plan to buy or upgrade computer hardware this year: ❏ yes [44] ❏ no [45]

I plan to buy or upgrade computer software this year: ❏ yes [46] ❏ no [47]

Name: _____ **Business title:** [48] _____ **Type of Business:** [49] _____

Address (❏ home [50] ❏ work [51] **/Company name:** _____ **)**

Street/Suite# _____

City [52] **/State** [53] **/Zipcode** [54]: _____ **Country** [55] _____

❏ **I liked this book!** You may quote me by name in future IDG Books Worldwide promotional materials.

My daytime phone number is _____

IDG BOOKS
THE WORLD OF COMPUTER KNOWLEDGE

❏ **YES!**
Please keep me informed about IDG's World of Computer Knowledge. Send me the latest IDG Books catalog.

NO POSTAGE
NECESSARY
IF MAILED
IN THE
UNITED STATES

BUSINESS REPLY MAIL
FIRST CLASS MAIL   PERMIT NO. 2605   FOSTER CITY, CALIFORNIA

IDG Books Worldwide
919 E Hillsdale Blvd, STE 400
Foster City, CA 94404-9691